TRANSLATED BY   *Alexandra Büchler*

PHOTOGRAPHS BY   *Jan Malý*

FOREWORD BY   *Kenneth Frampton*

ESSAY BY   *Eric Dluhosch*

THE ARCHITECTURE OF NEW PRAGUE 1895-1945

Rostislav Švácha

THE MIT PRESS   CAMBRIDGE, MASSACHUSETTS   LONDON, ENGLAND

© 1995 Massachusetts Institute of Technology.
Photographs © 1994 by Jan Malý.
This work originally appeared in Czech under the title
Od moderny k funkcionalismu
© 1985 by Odeon

Published with the assistance of the Getty Grant
Program.

This book was set in Cochin by Asco Trade
Typesetting Ltd., Hong Kong and was printed and
bound in the United States of America.

Library of Congress Cataloging-in-Publication Data

Švácha, Rostislav.
  [Od moderny k funkcionalismu. English]
  The architecture of new Prague, 1895–1945 /
Rostislav Švácha; translated by Alexandra Büchler;
photographs by Jan Malý; foreword by Kenneth
Frampton; essay by Eric Dluhosch.
     p.   cm.
  Includes bibliographical references and index.
  ISBN 0-262-19358-2
  1. Architecture, Modern—20th century—
Czechoslovakia—Prague. 2. Architecture—
Czechoslovakia—Prague. 3. Prague
(Czechoslovakia)—Buildings, structures, etc.
I. Malý, Jan. II. Title.
NA1033.P7S8313 1995
720′.94371′209041—dc20   94-46230
                          CIP

CONTENTS

There were three periods in the history of Bohemian architecture when architects working in the Czech lands, and especially in Prague, made a significant contribution to the architectural culture of Europe. The first such period was in the late Middle Ages, during the reign of the Luxemburgs and the Jagellons, when thanks to the royal architects Peter Parler and Benedikt Ried Prague flourished as an important center of the late Gothic style, exerting a far-reaching influence on Central European architecture of the fifteenth and sixteenth centuries. The second great era of Bohemian architecture began in the first half of the eighteenth century with the period of high baroque. Architects Christoph Dientzenhofer, Jan Santini, and Kilian Ignaz Dientzenhofer continued to develop the radical baroque style of Borromini and Guarini, preparing the ground for the bold designs of the German architect Balthasar Neumann.[1] The third period during which Bohemian architecture rose above the European standard were the first four decades of the twentieth century with the succession of the modern style, cubism, purism, and functionalism. The first signs of these creative developments appeared in Prague, which in 1918 became the capital of the newly established Czechoslovak Republic. Innovative buildings were being designed and built in other Bohemian and Moravian towns as well, particularly in Brno where the functionalist architecture created in the interwar period compared favorably with that of Prague, Frankfurt, or Rotterdam, and in Hradec Králové and Zlín, where Le Corbusier came to work on commissions in the thirties.

This book focuses on architecture built in Prague between 1895 and 1945, and in this respect it does not have many predecessors. Historians of architecture have so far concentrated mainly on earlier buildings of architectural interest in the famous historical center of Prague. My aim was to cover as many interesting buildings from the given period as possible. This meant that I had to carry out a careful survey of all the streets within the boundaries of the so-called Greater Prague of 1920, identify all buildings of interest, and subsequently examine the archives of the town-planning authorities, estates of the architects, and reference literature of the period to find the relevant information. The outcome of this research is concentrated in the Directory of Buildings at the end of the book. I was greatly assisted in this task by Zdeněk Lukeš from the Architecture Department of the National Technical Museum in Prague, who has contributed to the compilation of this directory with nearly a third of the entries.

At the same time, I have tried to interpret the collected material from an art historian's point of view. In doing so, I selected major personalities from among the dozens of architects active during the given period, examined in greater detail the work they produced at the peak of their careers, and tried to reconstruct their artistic aims and ideals. I noted how these aims and ideals clashed with hard reality, how they were often at odds with the requirements of clients and planning officials, with the opinion of the public, and with the aims and ideals of other architects.

I am grateful to all whose comments and assistance have been invaluable in preparing the text and visual documentation. In particular, I thank Roger L. Conover, editor at The MIT Press, the photographer Jan Malý, art and architecture historians Eric Dluhosch, Robert Benson, Wanda Bubriski, Ákos Morávanszky, Petr Wittlich, the late Emanuel Poche, Zdeněk Lukeš, and Jan Svoboda. Finally, my appreciation goes to Alexandra Büchler for her accurate and sensitive translation of this book into English.

Preface

In the course of translating Rostislav Švácha's *The Architecture of New Prague*, I became aware of how the inevitable profusion of Czech names and words interferes with the flow of the English text, making the reading somewhat difficult for anyone who is not familiar with the Czech language. To help the reader, I have opted for solutions that may not always appear consistent but were guided by the need to convey meaning as clearly as possible.

I have chosen to translate into English words indicating a type of urban space or architectural structure and in some cases to anglicize the names altogether. The names of streets, squares, embankments, bridges, buildings, and suburbs are therefore followed or preceded by the appropriate English word (e.g., Na poříčí Street, Národní Street, Vinohradská Avenue, Jiřího z Poděbrad Square, Ludvíka Svobody Embankment, Adrie Building, and the suburb of Dejvice). These solutions sometimes go against the grain of Czech syntax implied in the grammatical form of the name or in the presence of a preposition, but I believe they are justified by the need to incorporate these names into an English language context. The same names, however, have been left in their original form in the captions where they are part of an address and, of course, in the Directory of Buildings, which should be used in conjunction with a street map. The relevant Czech words and their English equivalents are *ulice* (street), *třída* (avenue), *náměstí* (square), *nábřeží* (embankment), *most* (bridge), and *zahrada* (garden).

Locations named after well-known personalities or families (e.g., Masaryk Embankment, Winston Churchill Square, and Kinsky Garden) and those derived from other place names, as in the case of the Letná Plain, are presented in their nominative form in the English version and correspond to the Czech forms *Masarykovo nábřeží*, *náměstí Winstona Churchilla*, *Kinského zahrada*, and *Letenská pláň*. All the street names, however, have been left in their original possessive form (e.g., Wilsonova, Jungmanova, Mickiewiczova, Chopinova, Milady Horákové, and Petra Rezka).

Several commonly known place names (e.g., Wenceslas Square (*Václavské náměstí*), Charles Bridge (*Karlův most*), the New and Old Town (*Staré a Nové Město*) and the Prague Castle (*Pražský hrad*)) appear in their English form throughout the text as do their derivatives like the Old Town Square (*Staroměstské náměstí*), but the part of the old center of Prague that is sometimes referred to in English as the Lesser Quarter has been left in the Czech form as Malá Strana. Names such as Republic Square and Revolution Square have been anglicized along with all the names of churches and cathedrals (e.g., Saint Vitus Cathedral or Church of the Sacred Heart). Likewise, all the names of educational institutions (e.g., Academy of Fine Arts (*Akademie výtvarných umění*), the School of Applied

Arts (*Uměleckoprůmyslová škola*), Charles University (*Karlova univerzita*), and the Czech Polytechnic (*České vysoké učení technické*) have been translated into English.

Recurrent names of architectural magazines and artists' groups and associations are followed by an English translation in parentheses on their first mention; from then on they appear in Czech only. In some instances, however, the use of the English version seemed more appropriate as in the case of the *Skupina výtvarných umělců*, the cubist Group of Visual Artists, which is sometimes referred to simply as "the Group." Artists' associations such as *Mánes* and groups such as *Devětsil*, whose name has been made known by several recent exhibitions and publications, appear only in the Czech form.

Finally, there are several terms that probably need some clarification. One is the Czech architectural term *trakt* used with reference to apartment floor plans and layouts to describe an area delimited by load-bearing walls and defined by its function. In an apartment the distinction usually corresponds to the servicing area (kitchen and bathroom), the serviced area (the living room, study, and sometimes bedrooms), and finally the communication area (the hall and corridors). There appears to be no exact equivalent in English, and I have therefore adopted the term "bay," kindly suggested by Professor Dluhosch, as "accomodation of a functional space within the positional and dimensional parameters or confines of a structural span."

Two terms that have to do with trying to convey the nature and ambience of a European city in a language that does not always share the appropriate meaning are "suburb" and "villa." The Czech notion of a city quarter or district is identical to the French *quartier*, but as the text often refers to smaller entities such as garden cities that have a certain suburban feel, I have opted for the word "suburb" in all cases, even where the district in question consists largely of apartment buildings as in Vinohrady or Dejvice.

Most of the family houses referred to in the book are described as "villas," that is, large detached or semidetached residences with at least two stories, surrounded by a garden. Most villas located in the garden suburbs of Prague, and especially those of architectural interest, certainly fit this description, and they usually bear the name of the original owner (e.g., Villa Trmal). In the Directory of Buildings, which lists a variety of family residence types, I have preferred to use the generic term "family house" as it was not always possible to make a clear distinction between the two.

Alexandra Büchler

The evolution of Czech architecture over the period 1895 to 1945 reminds us once again of the cultural vitality of the first half of this century or more precisely of that moment that begins with the flowering of the art nouveau in the 1890s and ends with the Spanish Civil War of 1936 and the apocalypse of the Second World War. To all intents and purposes this period coincides, as we know, with the rise and fall of the avant-garde in the Western world, although our understanding of this period has altered considerably over the years, as the avant-gardist production of Central and Eastern Europe has come increasingly to the fore. This reorientation began in the early sixties when we first became aware of the rich contribution of the Russian avant-grade in every conceivable field, particularly during the years 1890 to 1932. Now, as other barriers have fallen — not only that of the Iron Curtain but also of our presumptuous ignorance — we have come to see that alongside the achievements of the Russian avant-garde we must now set those of Czechoslovakia, not only because its activity was likewise distributed over the widest possible cultural spectrum, but also because the country as a whole was able to evolve into a modern, industrialized nation-state in less than twenty years — an achievement that, for reasons that are as obscure as they are tragic, has eluded and, now still, continues to elude the vast continent lying to the east.

To a greater degree than the Russians, both before and after the Revolution, the emerging Bohemian state was able to find a fertile balance between the technocratic challenge of the West and its own more autarchic and ludic roots, and in this particular regard the cultural *parti pris* for Prague after the turn of the century was to be more readily found in Vienna and Paris than in Berlin. This not only accounts for the strong hold that the Viennese *Wagnerschule* exercised over Czech architecture throughout the years 1890 to 1918 (an era dominated by Jan Kotěra who was the ultimate pioneer of Czech modernism in the field) but also for the rapidity with which the Parisian cubist breakthrough in modern painting was instantly reinterpreted in Prague, through the works of Emil Filla, Otto Gutfreund, Václav Špála, and others, a Slavic transcription that had little to do with the Italian futurist divagations from the same source. In this sense, as Jaroslav Anděl has remarked, the Czech contribution to the European avant-garde was always somewhat maverick.

This was certainly true in the case with Czech cubist architecture, which came quite out of the blue with Josef Gočár's Black Mother of God department store of 1911–1912 and the unprecedented spa building he designed in Bohdaneč in the beginning of 1912. Like Josef Chochol's equally original cubist villa built in Vyšehrad at the same time, these works could hardly have been derived from Raymond Duchamp-Villon's *la maison cubiste* that first appeared in 1912. Just as inexplicable, except as some kind of spontaneous nationalism hankering after the lost glories of the Bohemian baroque, was the virtual flood of Czech cubist applied art that followed in the wake of these canonical buildings, until the wave finally spent itself in the short-lived concatenations of rondocubism as these appeared say in Gočár's Legiobank or in Pavel Janák's Adria Insurance Building, both completed in Prague in 1923.

Rondocubism was followed by a short-lived excursus into so-called Czech purism, particularly at the hands of Evžen Linhart and Vít Obrtel, and then almost at once by the full flowering of the Czech constructivist avant-garde as this manifested itself from 1925 to 1940 in the work of such architects as Adolf Benš, Bohuslav Fuchs, Jaroslav Fragner, Jan Gillar, Josef Havlíček, Karel Honzík, Josef Kranz, Ludvík Kysela, Oldřich Starý, Oldřich Tyl, Arnošt Wiesner, and Ladislav Žák. We must include Vladimír Karfík, who was the house architect for the Baťa cartel, Bedřich Feuerstein, who achieved his most brilliant work in Japan for Antonin Raymond, the committed socialist Jiří Kroha, and of course the quite exceptional Jaromír Krejcar, whose Machnáč Sanatorium at Trenčianské Teplice (1932) and the Czech Pavilion for the Paris World Exhibition of 1937 are surely to be regarded as the apotheosis of the Czech movement at the height of its powers.

Rostislav Švácha's meticulous account of the evolution of this movement as it evolved in Prague in conjunction with the expansion of the city beyond its historic core, is, in effect, a translation of his *Od moderny k funkcionalismu*, first published by Odeon in 1985. It comes to us now almost as a culmination of a series of forays into a lost history, beginning with Dostál, Pechar, and Procházka's *Modern Architecture in Czechoslovakia* published in 1970 and continuing with the various contributions made over the years by the ubiquitous Vladimir Šlapeta and now, more recently, the quickening pace of the research being made available by such historians Alena Adlerová, Antonín Dufek, Alena Kubová, Karel Srp, and Jindřich Toman. Within this pantheon of scholars Švácha opens up totally new ground for us by emphasizing how the modernization and expansion of Prague was inextricably bound up with the ideology and syntax of its modern architecture. Švácha makes us aware of the richness and complexity of the ideological debate that attended these developments throughout the twenties and thirties, as the architectural avant-garde oscillated between such nuanced positions as "scientific" versus "emotional" functionalism, and also of the subtly different yet distinct alignments that were evoked during this process. While reminding us of the crucial mutual influence of both Le Corbusier and the Russian constructivists — a hybrid synthesis that was overlaid with the hard-line functionalism of the German *Neue Sachlichkeit* — Švácha tends to side in his account with Obrtel's antimaterialist attack on Karel Teige, who was without doubt the most militantly political Czech architectural critic of the period. And yet it is the Marxist Teige who is prompt to acknowledge the absolutely seminal importance of Krejcar's Villa Vančura, designed for the leader of the Devětsil in 1924. Krejcar followed this triumph with his equally radical Olympic Building projected for Prague in the following year, which as Švácha points out was a celebration of the metropolis in festive garb; sky signs, striped awnings, the cafés and ubiquitous terraces — all these elements were seen as being integral to the poesis of modern urban life.

And it is this rather unique fusion of constructivism, purism, and a certain Baudelairean *mondanité* that colors everything that the Czech avant-garde attempted from architecture to painting, poetry, typography, photography, and film. There was perhaps no other twentieth-century avant-garde that so readily transgressed the boundaries between the different arts, so that a figure like Teige was at once a painter, a poet, a typographer, a polemicist, and a critic of exceptional stature. As Švácha and others have revealed, the polemical discourse that accompanied all this creative activity was equally boundless as one "little magazine" succeeded another or merged with its successor: *Devětsil, Život, Stavba, Stavitel,*

Disk, Plán, ReD, MSA, Fronta, Pásmo, among others; the mere list of titles boggles the mind, and among various international avant-gardes of the interwar era one would be hard pressed to find its equal.

In its creative heyday the production of the Czech avant-garde was distinguishable from similar movements in either the East or the West by virtue of its playful poetism. In this respect the Czechs set great store by the polemical picture/poem or poetic collage, and hence they felt that buildings should be legible in a similar way; that is to say, they should be capable of being experienced as an animation of the lifeworld in the widest possible sense.

Kenneth Frampton
Ware Professor of Architecture
Columbia University

COMING OF AGE IN THE NEW PRAGUE

When Rostislav Švácha asked me to write an introductory essay for the English translation of his book, I hesitated to accept. Having read the Czech original, I realized that Švácha knows all there is to know about the subject, and it would be presumptuous on my part to add another academic commentary.

Instead, I have decided to reach back into my personal memories of the years I lived in this magic city to try to evoke the atmosphere that prevailed in Prague during the thirties and early forties. My intent is to complement Švácha's scholarly oeuvre by acquainting the reader with the perceptions of my own coming of age in the city, before I became an architect myself, and before I had the capacity to understand with my head what my heart already knew: that Prague is the most beautiful city on earth.

There is much controversy among architectural critics and historians about the successes and failures of modernism. Often the same methods used by the modern avant-grade to justify their utopias by using out-of-context illustrations of carefully selected examples of only the best of their designs are frequently applied by their detractors, who choose equally selective examples to make their case and condemn the failures of the modern movement.

Ordinary citizens seldom employ such selective methods. Their city is, by and large, taken in by all the senses as a seamless perceptual as well as temporal continuum, which has more the quality of looking through a kaleidoscope than observing through a microscope. Aside from such methodological distinctions, judgments as to the relative beauty of one's city are by their very nature always highly subjective and seldom expressed in crass either/or categories of unconditionally good or bad. Just as no mother will categorically consider her child — even one who turns out to be a criminal — as incorrigible, loyal citizens will never admit that their city is without redemption. Ask anyone from Liverpool, or Detroit. And, even though the ordinary man or woman on the street vaguely recognizes various styles, he or she readily integrates this stylistic awareness into a broader picture of the city as an experiential whole. This includes the valuation of the modern style, which by now has gathered sufficient decades of patina to have become a permanent part of the general landscape of the architecture of any city, including Prague.

Thus, much of the modern in the architecture of Prague has been accepted by its denizens as part of the general landscape of all buildings, old and new, and has become familiar, even loved.

Such familiarity can develop only by living in a city many years. Only time allows impressions to collect in the mind's eye as the stuff of individual dreams or nightmares, causing one to stay, feel imprisoned, or — in extremis — flee. In my case, Prague survives in the attic of my cluttered memories as a distant but vivid dream. The nightmares came later, when the storms of war tore up the Europe of old, to cause many of Prague's citizens to feel indeed imprisoned and, eventually, caused many to flee. Still, Prague has survived these calamities physically intact. The city stands upon its hills, like Rome, eternal and mute, without taking sides, and continues to offer home and shelter to those who love it. A line inscribed on the monument to Jan Hus on Staroměstské náměstí reads: *Opustíš-li mě, nezahynu; opustíš-li mě zahyneš.* (If you abandon me, I will not perish. If you abandon me, you will perish.) Of course, the line means abandonment of God, and, cryptically, Prague as well.

I have no proof, but I am convinced that the Czechs would not have survived the last half century with their sanity reasonably intact without the sheltering function of their *zlatá Praha* (golden Prague) to tide them over the horrors and provide the citizens with a chance to be free, civilized, and worldly again. But enough about nightmares. All I wish to offer the patient reader is the memory of my dream and a personal testimony that Švácha's narrative is but a rational and scholarly interpretation of that dream.

Our family moved to Prague in 1933 from the provincial town of Jindřichův Hradec in the South of Bohemia. My father, a young professor of history and geography, had just achieved the dream of every academic stuck in a picturesque but provincial town by being promoted and transferred to the capital, Prague.

As mentioned by Švácha, the thirties were a difficult time not only for architects and professors of history and geography but for the nation as a whole. The country was slowly recovering from the worst years of the Great

Depression. A transfer to Prague meant both an improvement in status and an increased salary, not to mention immersion into the intellectual and professional climate of the Czech metropolis.

We moved into one of the courtyard apartments built around the turn of the century in the center of Prague, in a district called Malá Strana. Around the corner, and at the end of Karmelitská ulice, stands the magnificent Saint Nicholas Church, with the quaint Malostranské náměstí just beyond. At the other end of our street, and beyond the blind riperian inlet called Čertovka, one would enter the serene atmosphere of the island Kampa, often called the Venice of Prague.

The street facade of our apartment house, or rather apartment block, was rendered in the heavy faux stucco rustication à la late Renaissance, with its obligatory classical pediments and friezes around the deeply set oblong windows looking out into a narrow crooked street. Behind that prestigious facade, and shedding bourgeois pretensions to Renaissance splendor, we were provided by the developer with a less imposing courtyard whose wrought iron balustrades offered the only ornamental relief against the bare stucco walls of this balcony-tiered opening to the sky. Our apartment was situated on one of the "better" floors, meaning anything above the second, with one of the typical *pavlače* (open balconies) providing access to the apartments on all four sides of the courtyard quadrangle.

The courtyard itself was accessible to tenants by means of a small door cut into the left leaf of a much larger, heavy, iron-hinged wood portal. The janitor, a rotund woman, guarded this gate day and night, charged big tips if one forgot the key after midnight, and in general kept an eagle's eye on everything and everybody, especially at night. She was also the only person authorized to open this creaking monster to admit horse-driven carriages and small trucks to make their daily deliveries inside. This gave her full control not only over our daily philanderings but equally over the flow of all vital supplies, edible and otherwise.

From the open gallery, a tenant would enter the apartment through the kitchen/living area, with its cast iron coal stove in the far corner, and then proceed through a narrow hall with the bathroom on one side to the bedrooms, which were heated by enormous ceramic stoves, called *kachláky*. These were located in the inner corner of the room, back to back and corner to corner with the kitchen stove, with the chimney in between. In the winter, these stoves had to be fed great quantities of soft brown coal all day to heat their enormous earthen bulk, which stored up enough heat during the day to remain reasonably warm throughout the night. The acrid smell of soft coal pollution pervades the air of Prague even today. There was no real view from the bedroom windows in the back; thus, it was the courtyard that provided the stage for daily activities and excitement, as it functioned both as community meeting place and strategic supply base for the whole building. From the balconies, just like in the theater, everybody had a choice view of the operatic events that took place on this stage, featuring the daily life of the *petite bourgeoisie* of Prague.

The sounds, sights, and smells of this window to the sky will never fade from my memory, for they were intimately connected to the activities that filled the courtyard from early morning to late afternoon every day from 1932 to 1934.

Monday announced itself without fail by a cacophony of sounds accompanied by the beat produced by the rhythmical flogging of assorted carpets, which were slung over sturdy round beams supported by even sturdier wood poles in one corner of the courtyard. Maid and housewife alike would attack their precious Orientals and lesser breeds with astonishing amounts of energy, producing in this orgy of flagellation five-story-high billowing clouds of dust, carried upward into the sky by the chimney effect of the open courtyard, to join similar pillars of dust from the other courtyards in the neighborhood. No calendar was needed. When the carpet beaters sounded, it had to be Monday. The effect of this pounding on the lungs of these Amazons was considered at that time to be entirely beneficial, and any pollution inhaled was assumed to be offset by the increased blood circulation caused by the vigorous exercise.

On Tuesday the potato and coal wagons would be admitted with much shouting and cussing by the fortissimo voices of the omnipresent janitor and the coachmen trying to maneuver their wagons into the courtyard. The purpose of this commotion was to deliver the soft coal to feed the *kachláky* and tasty potatoes to feed everybody else. In my mind's eye I can still see the glistening muscles of the workers lugging the fifty-kilo rough jute sacks up into the coal bins of each apartment and down into the dark potato bins in the cellar. Their cussing and swearing certainly did not belong to the language of our gentle philosopher-president Masaryk. It was the language of Švejk and the country; rich, expressive, and funny in its inimitable ability to release anger and frustration.[1] It did not occur to me that repetition of these mellifluous expletives during dinner would cause my father to use the same tool used by the maid to vent her frustrations on innocent Orientals on my equally innocent backside. *Quod licet iovi, non licet bovi* (What is allowed to the gods, is not allowed to cattle).

On Wednesday, an even more melodic event would cause the windows to open on all balconies: it was the arrival of the exotic figure of the gypsy knife sharpener. Only later, when visiting the French Quarter in New Orleans, did I suddenly recall the gypsy sing-song of Prague: *páni, dámy, pěkně prosím, nože, nůžky, krásně brousím* (Ladies, gents, at a good price, knives and scissors I grind real nice). This musical prelude was soon followed by a spectacle of fiery sparks produced by the grinding of assorted cutlery on the rim of the spinning stone grinding wheel. It was coaxed to dizzying speeds by the mighty pumping of a large wooden pedal by the gypsy's dust-caked bare foot. Finished with sharpening a knife or a pair of scissors, the gypsy would allow himself to be begged and bribed (but more bribed than begged) to give us a multilingual account of German-Czech-Slovak-Hungarian-Romanian gypsy pidgin Esperanto of his adventures in such exotic places as Vienna, Budapest, and Uzgorod, and, if in the mood — yes — even of New York, where he claimed to have spent a couple of years during the twenties and from where he was eventually deported for a deed that he swore on his noble gypsy honor he never committed. Did we believe him? Yes and no, depending on our capacity to dream such adventures. But, to us children listening to him, he was a prince, nevertheless.

The next day it was time for the appearance of another magic character, the lucky chimney sweep; black from tip to toe, with only the whites of his eyes and the pink of his mouth betraying his human Moravian origin. He was then and is still today considered the bearer of good fortune. But, luck could only be obtained by the eager fortune seeker by touching a sooty part of his charcoal body with a finger. And not just any finger. For example, index finger touch meant wealth and ring finger touch meant love and/or marriage. It was the *milostivá paní* (gracious lady) who touched with the index and the maids who darkened their ring finger, but not always.

Merchants selling poultry, rabbits, down feathers, and other items arrived on the other days, adding to the constant hustle bustle of this otherwise bare and forbidding hole in the middle of a pile of dark masonry. But it worked, at least at that time.

Outside our palazzo-fortress, the sight and smells of the city were equally exciting. There were no supermarkets then, only small, privately owned specialty stores. Each had its own characteristic aroma, and each of its owners knew all of his or her customers not only by name but, most importantly, by title. To enter such a store meant an experience similar to entering the reception hall of a royal duke, with the owner of the store acting as master of ceremonies. The arrival of each customer was ceremoniously announced by the customary *dobrý den* (good day), followed by the customer's name, husband's rank, questions about the family and everyone's health, a recapitulation of the day's weather outlook, and, of course, the ascertainment of the shopping desires of the day. Departures were treated with less ceremony in consideration of the loads to be carried in full baskets and satchels, on foot, often several blocks away. Fortunately, milk and bread were still delivered from the bakery and the dairy store every morning by rosy-cheeked apprentices on bicycles with large baskets mounted on the mudguard of the rear wheel. The fresh milk and oven-warm *rohlíky* (crescent-shaped buns) were carefully placed into freshly starched napkins nestled inside the baskets by the lady of the house the evening before.

But, there was one event that topped all others. It arrived every spring in the form of the annual melting of the ice on the Vltava and announced itself in the city by huge ice floats piling up against the abutments of ancient Charles Bridge. Full of terror and with a strange tinge of excitement creeping up my spine, I would find my way to the center of Charles Bridge, lean over the stone balustrade, and pretend to be the captain on the bridge of a lost ocean liner advancing slowly but steadily against the churning maelstrom of heaving mountains of ice. As the ice was inexorably climbing inside the ancient arches toward the keystones, the illusion of a sinking ship was perfect. So was the feeling of terror. Occasionally, the angry river would leap over its banks and lap at the very threshold of our fortress. This was the only calamity capable of silencing our otherwise voluble janitor, who could be seen kneeling before the picture of her patron saint, praying with anguished whispers for the restoration of her own authority over that of the evil spirits of the angry Vltava.

Popular superstition had it that it was only the intercession of the saints, lined up along the opposite balustrades of this venerable Gothic relic, that had saved the bridge from being swept away by the floods. A more scientific explanation, but equally mythical, ascribed the saving of the bridge to the fact that the mortar that held the ancient stones together was mixed with egg white by the master masons, thus producing piers of homogenous rocklike strength. The mortar was believed to be harder than the stones themselves. To my knowledge, the first theory is beyond scientific proof, and the second has never been officially refuted.

Objective proof notwithstanding, the point has been rendered moot by the construction of dams and sluices up river during the forties and fifties, thus banishing the rites of nature by the acts of clever engineers for the foreseeable future and leaving the saints who had guarded the bridge so successfully during the past centuries utterly unemployed. Hence their present demotion to the status of unpaid extras acting as quaint historical backdrop to assorted tourist photo opportunities.

Of the frightening spring floods threatening old Prague, only the flood markers on the buildings of the Kampa remain. It is the one marked with the year 1934 that records the memory of my own flood. The floods that followed were of a different kind, and it took more than engineering skill to dam them, for the moment at least.

My initiation to the marvels of the old city center came to an abrupt end in 1934, when my father was promoted to director of a community college in Trutnov. While his will to succeed was made of iron, his heart was more fragile. He died of overwork, a victim of heart arrest in 1936.

With no family around, Mama moved us back to Prague where her brother, who was at that time chief of the foreign exchange section of the National Bank, found us an apartment on the outskirts of Prague in a new garden suburb, called Petřiny. Instead of a dark courtyard and a deep, dark, tripartite floor plan, the designer of these new two-story villa-apartment houses supplied all the requisite elements of the modern functionalist credo: light, air, good plumbing and heating, and the obligatory green backyards with cozy little sheds to raise chickens and to play naughty games in. The fresh exteriors were painted in pleasant pastel colors, without a trace of ornament, with window and door frames rendered in crisp clean lines and lots of glass to admit the sun. Clearly the avant-garde was on the march in Petřiny, and I must say that the improvement over the Renaissance was definitively positive, even though it lacked the operatic qualities of the courtyard scene.

No more smoky coal stoves and heavy ceramic *kachláky*. Instead, gleaming white enameled gas ranges and central steam heat in each room. The noisy agony of expanding steam pipes going clank, clank, clank sounded communal reveille in each apartment on winter mornings, when the engineers of the district steam plant turned up the heat after its nightly rest in a lukewarm state. Today this would be called energy management. Then it was called common sense.

Gone too was the ponderous furniture with its ornamented legs and carved friezes, gone the heavy velvet drapes with their sartorial tussles, and gone the stuffy sofa with its embroidered throw pillows. In came sleek pieces of modern furniture with round plywood corners and cabinets with sliding panes of tempered glass to display the ground crystal glass and Meissen porcelain of Mama's dowry. And, to complete this move into our new functional paradise, I will never forget the day when she told me to dress up in my best and, with great pretensions to secrecy, took me to the new department store *Bílá labuť* to pick up our first radio, with its brand name Empo embossed on a shiny chrome plate that adorned an elegant art deco wood cabinet with beautiful round corners, like the new furniture. Its warm and faintly glowing tubes inside were capable of catching not only Prague, Plzeň, Brno, and Moravská Ostrava but even Berlin and Munich. It was from the latter station that the rasping sounds of the rabble in beer halls disturbed our suburban idyll, and it was from the same Empo that Chamberlain told us that he had achieved peace for his generation. But I was too young to realize that the next generation was me, and that Mr. Chamberlain's peace was bought at my expense, after all. My worries were actually more local, but geopolitical nevertheless. They concerned the defense of the territorial integrity of "my" Petřiny from the Liboc enemy below: "them."

While ferocious intellectual and ideological skirmishes were fought in *Devětsil* and various other factions of the architectural associations of the right and the left, for me personally matters were infinitely simpler, for my battleground was defined by the territorial claims of the gangs of upper Petřiny and lower Liboc for the possession of a mile or so of railroad tracks separating the two empires. But, instead of exchanging theses and manifestos, we hurled taunts and mocked our adversaries in the language learned from the muscular coal and potato carriers in the old courtyard of Malá Strana. And we fought — every weekend, rain or shine, until graduation put a stop to all such nonsense, and the real war started.

To explain the strategic situation of this miniwar, it is necessary to know that the new colony where we lived occupied the rim of an elevated plateau that also included the park and nature reserve called Hvězda. Petřiny was considered without shame to be solidly middle class. Below lay the district of lower Liboc, which was as unabashedly and proudly working class. The two were separated from the plateau by the railroad tracks of the Ruzyně railroad line, considered by the warriors on each side to be part of their territory. Since the adults had no feelings about the strategic importance of these railroad tracks, and since the National Railways did not see fit to post guards to prevent their capture by the warring factions of either upper Petřiny or lower Liboc, it became a free-fire zone long before this term entered the vocabulary of general staffs and shuttle diplomacy.

It was this no-man's land along the Ruzýně line that was contested and fought over in pitched battles by gangs from both sides of the tracks. In many ways it was a civilized war, since action took place only on weekends, after mass, with both sides praying for victory after confession and communion, just as real soldiers do.

Unlike today, the only weapons used by the warriors on both sides were fists throughout the year and snowballs in the winter. Rock throwing was tolerated only during the siege of the hotly contested old railroad shacks — more to enjoy the sound of shattered glass than to maim. Today, after the experiences of the real battles fought on behalf of much loftier causes, it is clear to me that I was already then taking part in a junior edition of the gigantic struggle gathering its forces in the larger theater of war, not only in Europe but throughout the entire world. Soon enough it would be fought with real weapons, by real warriors, breaking more than a few windows in old railroad shacks and cracking more than a few heads, forever. And not only on weekends.

This then was the new Prague of the thirties, so dispassionately described in Švácha's book as the battleground between the modernists and the traditionalists, between left and right, between the past and the future. For me and my pals from lower Liboc, the real oppressors were not this or that ideology but real persons — namely, our professors, who had no regard for status or class and who mercilessly enforced iron discipline in their territorial concentration of raw power: the classroom. Miraculously, it was the results of their oppressive regime that assured our future, not the fights along the railroad line.

Petřiny was one of the new suburbs of Greater Prague, and its relation to the old center was of more than academic interest to us because we had to commute to the old town almost daily for various reasons, some serious, others frivolous, but who can tell today which was which.

Švácha mentions the difficulties of the various planning commissions that tried to tie together the outlying districts with the historical core of the city by public and private transport. My recollection is one of a well-serviced city with a system of noisy but punctual electrical streetcars, a superbly managed municipal cleaning system, and first-class cultural and recreational facilities for all citizens. What city, even today, sprinkles its parched and dusty streets with cool water during the hot summer months? On a hot August day, we would position ourselves near the curb to catch the cool mist of the passing municipal tank truck with its perforated horizontal sprinkler pipe washing down the steaming cobblestones. After the truck's passing, the granite orbs of the cobblestones would glisten like so many twinkling diamond tips in the bright summer sun. A little later, a cool breeze would rise from the relieved stones and offer a breath of moist relief to pedestrians and tram riders alike.

In the thirties, private cars were still the luxury of the prosperous few; most of us got around on foot or by electrical tramway. These brightly painted, clean, white and red trains with rather narrow cars, hitched together in tandem, were not only the only means of public transportation but they also provided a true sporting challenge. It was called tramway jumping. Leaping off the moving car required not only stamina but also style. First, it was necessary to grab the vertical brass handle with both hands, not unlike a paratrooper preparing for the jump. Subsequently, velocity and angle of anticipated impact between body and pavement required the participant to cantilever one's feet outward at an approximately forty-five-degree angle with respect to gravity, crank one's head to check for traffic from behind, and then — let go — with feet hitting the cobblestones in imitation of a ballet dancer's *grand jeté*, landing the jumper either on his sprinting feet or in the hospital. Jumping onto a moving car was considered less of a challenge since all that was required was to jog up to the speed of the moving tram, catch one of the brass handles, and hop onto the low wooden step of the open car platform, while keeping an eagle eye on the conductor to make sure that he was not looking, or pretending not to see. It should be pointed out that the trains seldom went very fast, especially in the old center, considering the irregular, medieval layout of its narrow streets. After World War II, increased automobile traffic on the streets of Prague and new trams with self-closing doors stopped this sport, since the Czechs are adventurous by temperament but not suicidal by nature.

XXII

In general, moving about the city was pleasant and unhurried during those years. It took no more than twenty minutes by streetcar to travel from our house to the old town and an equal time to enjoy a lazy Sunday in the wild nature reserve called Šárka. Beyond was the lovely countryside of Central Bohemia. Even today, these reliable workhorses perform the same duty, but they have been supplemented by a modern and equally efficient subway system, which is one of the few useful public amenities built by the communist regime during the seventies and eighties.

My suburban idyll was shattered by two momentous events: the remarriage of my mother to the director of one of the large machine tool companies of Czechoslovakia and the Munich betrayal of Czechoslovakia by the Western democracies in autumn 1938. The first had an immediate personal impact, as our new papa moved us back into the center of the city. The second event changed my life and that of all of Europe forever. It also caused our next move — not only out of Prague, but out of the country, and finally to the New World, to America. But that came later.

Papa did not move us to another suburb but back into the old center, and indeed close to the very seat of power within the ancient walls of the royal castle, Hradčany. The house that we moved into belonged to the Archdiocese of Prague and was part of a row of houses built against the steep crenelated defense wall surrounding the cathedral and central squares of the castle. This was much better than upper Petřiny. There was no uncontested territory, just the steep old castle defense wall, leaning against our house, and the city below. Owing to its position against the wall, the house could be considered both a cottage and a high rise. Seen from the castle square, it appeared as a mere two-story-high townhouse, but its back dropped almost vertically some thirty to forty feet into a broad ravine that had formerly served as the royal hunting garden, called Jelení příkop (Deer Park). Looking across this deep ravine from the backyard of the house through one of the crenelations of the wall, I would daydream about chivalrous knights courting beautiful princesses in the hauntingly beautiful Royal Belvedere peeking through the greenery across the ravine, with the sinuous curve of its green copper roof enclosing an enfilade of slender, elegant columns and graceful arches surrounding the terrace of this baroque masterpiece.

Facing the house on the street side, barely half a dozen meters away, the flying buttresses of the apse of Saint Vitus's Cathedral loomed high above the low roof of our house. From my bed, on a moonlit night, they looked like inverted troglodytes defying gravity as they pointed like knurled fingers toward heaven, silently reminding me of the fact that my nightly prayers were indeed conveyed to someone, somewhere, up there in heaven.

From the front parlor, and across the little square opposite the towering apse of Saint Vitus's Cathedral, I could glimpse the basilica of Saint George with its frugally bare twin towers, one slightly thinner than the other. Eventually I noticed this anomaly and decided to find out the reason for it. My new papa could not explain, even though he was an engineer. Neither could Mama, but being devout, she referred me to the deacon. He knew. Shocked by my abysmal knowledge of the finer points of theology, he condescended to give me an exclusive private tutorial. It lasted for the better part of an afternoon but boiled down to the simple fact that the builders of the church were certainly more versed in the good book than my useless generation, since every child knew already in the twelfth century that pure symmetry is a symbol of God's perfection and thus the exclusive prerogative of the divine. For this reason, and others too complicated to explain to a barbaric heathen like me, I was sternly told that such a fallen creature as man should never attempt to feign perfection but instead should aspire in his imperfect works only to praise that of the Lord. Thus the perfect geometrical symmetry of the twin towers as intention and their imperfectly realized built form.

Passing through the eastern castle gate on my way to school every morning, my awakening interest in all things architectural became intrigued by the ever-changing landscape and the many hues of the ocher tile roofs of Malá Strana. Like a city on top of a city, this magic world of roofs, skylights, balusters, cornices, saints, crosses, chimneys, terraces, ogives, and a myriad of other forms and details spread out before my eyes on the open side of the castle stairs until they reached the broad band of the winding Vltava. And always, at exactly the right congregational distance, a church tower rose above the waves of tiles like a battery of celestial rockets aimed at heaven, fueled by the faith of generations long gone, and silently measuring the distance between earth and sky not in profane nautical miles but in sacred celestial millennia.

Few cities in the world can boast of a roofscape as spectacular as that of old Prague. It cannot be captured in a photograph, where both observer and observed are frozen in place and time, or on film, where movement is simulated on the screen and the viewer sits immobile. Only by walking the diagonal distance from the top of the castle stairs down into the architectural marvel of what lies below these roofs can one really appreciate the incredible beauty of this city. Never from a tourist bus. It was during those rapid flights down and the slow crawls up that I decided to become an architect, not to imitate what seemed inimitable but to pursue the only thing I found to be existing outside the narrow categories of the here and now: beauty.

It was also during those years of my royal residency inside the castle that I began to explore the modern charms of Prague. Adolescence always favors the new, the contrarian, the rebellious—in short, the modern. We were no different. And, to be really modern, we adored all things coming from the troubadours of all things modern and exotic: The make-believe magicians of Hollywood. The stone wheel and the guttural singsong of the gypsy knife grinder was replaced by mechanical wheels rolling celluloid and electrically amplified sound tracks filling the screens of the new movie houses springing up all over Prague with new magic, just as exotic and exciting as that of the gypsy prince. Instead of going down to the courtyard storyteller, we flocked like Čapek's robots[3] to the local *kino* to be enchanted by the thrilling adventures of Errol Flynn, the modern incarnation of Robin Hood, Zorro, the fantasies of Disney's *Snow White and the Seven Dwarfs* in Czech, the antics of Charlie Chaplin and the Keystone Cops, and, above all, the appearance of my first serious romantic idol, Shirley Temple. Little did I know that my ardent prayers to bring Shirley to Prague in person were duly conveyed to their celestial address by the ever alert gargoyles. Unfortunately, it took the heavenly bureaucracy more than fifty years to grant my wish, when Shirley Temple arrived in Prague as the first U.S. ambassador after the velvet revolution, and after I had left the city some forty-five years before. Well, as the Czech proverb goes: *Boží mlýny melou pomalu, ale jistě* (God's mills grind slowly but surely).

As puberty began to manifest itself by my abandonment of cinematic passions and an increasing interest in the real thing, Mama tried to divert these new energies into respectable channels by prescribing Mr. Valenta's dancing lessons in the Lucerna. As Švácha mentions in the text, this multifunction commercial complex in the center of Wenceslas Square, which included the dancing school in question, was built by the grandfather of President Vaclav Havel. Never has a young man learned to waltz and tango in a more dignified setting as that of the ballroom of this remarkable building. After the formal exercises of strictly supervised and therefore utterly boring ballroom dancing, we would occasionally sneak out before the obligatory folklore group dance, called *beseda*, and go for unsupervised romantic adventure up and down the *korzo* of Wenceslas Square. To avoid uncivilized behavior, but to provide at the same time an outlet for legitimate mutual attraction, there was an unwritten convention concerning courting on the square: if a pair of boys encountered a couple of girls walking on the Lucerna side of the square, it was "legal" to flirt in our hapless but innocent and awkward adolescent ways. If lucky, the reward was usually the permission to invite the young ladies for a *zmrzlina* (ice cream). With real luck and a good deal of faked bravado, helped by presumably irresistible wit, the willing parties might end up over a cup of hot chocolate at one of the numerous buffets or small cafés that lined both sides of the square. These glittering internal streets connected the various blocks of the square with their side and back streets and provided a more intimate setting not only for budding romance in the evenings but also food and shopping opportunities for everybody else throughout the day.

In this connection, it should be pointed out that Wenceslas Square is actually more of a broad boulevard than a real square. It was originally the town's horse market. It inclines slightly to its urban closure by the ponderous pile of neo-Renaissance masonry, the National Museum, at one end and is crossed by another boulevard, the Na příkopě, on the lower end. Compared to its grand cousins in Paris or Rome, it is actually too short for a boulevard and too long for a square. Perhaps this is the reason it has been recently converted into a pedestrian zone, which I consider unfortunate. By removing the contrast between fast-moving cars, the stop-go boogie woogie of the red and white streetcars, and the slow rhythms of pedestrian movement, the planners have also removed the essence of the life of any truly urban boulevard—namely, its contrasts of speed, color, life, and movement. As is, the square has been subjected to pedestrian entropy by homogenizing its opposite streams of movement into a stagnating pond of direction-less foot meanderings. It would be hard to imagine the Champs-Elysees as a pedestrian mall; why Václavské náměsti?

But, back to the Prague of modernity. Švácha mentions the *Bat'a* (House of Shoes) Building as one of the more stunning examples of modernism in Prague. It symbolized not only the essence of all that was new and thus modern but also the place where Mama would buy me a gleaming pair of new tennis shoes for five crowns, which is the equivalent of buying a pair of Reeboks today for five dollars. It is little known that *Bat'a* was the first shoe manufacturer in Europe to mass-produce good quality shoes at an affordable price for all, and that he built a whole new city for his enterprises, based on the principles of modernism, called Zlín.

The Bat'a Building was popular not only for its cheap shoes but even more for its "American" design. It was all gleaming glass, brilliantly lit at night, with its internal *pasáž* from Wenceslas Square to Jungman Square like the inside of a hall of mirrors—not to mention the tempting display of shoes behind the huge plate glass windows. Building and function merged without a false note into the busy pulse of life of Wenceslas Square. It fits into the architecture of a largely commercial boulevard precisely because it is canonical and unique at the same time, as are its neighbors, both old and new. Canonical in the sense of its scale and proportions paying respect to those of its older neighbors, unique in its use of modern materials and methods of construction with the conviction and self-assurance of artistic maturity. It also tells us something about the confidence of the

Czech avant-garde of modernism and their courage to confront and challenge the awesome authority of history.

As for the battle of styles fought between the modernists and the traditionalists, we could not care less. We went to school in an old pseudo-Renaissance palace, but thought nothing of it to go and pay our electrical bills in the functionalist palace of the power company. In the summer we did our gymnastics in the functional facilities of the Strahov Sports Complex and boarded the train to visit Grandma in the country in the nineteenth-century glass and iron halls of Masaryk or Wilson Station. Only the architects seemed to quarrel about what was appropriate for what and when.

Looking back, I have tried to understand why Prague has acquired its reputation as a mysterious city: Kafkaesque, dark, gloomy, and imponderable. The fact is that Prague is actually a very luminous city. Its dark courtyards are always set off by squares full of light on a sunny day. The narrow streets of the historical town are complemented by broad boulevards at its fringes, and its medieval density is relieved along the contours of its green hills by magnificent parks and the broad aquarelle hues of its winding river, the Vltava. It is this transcendent luminosity and the architectural variety of thousands of years of additions, subtractions, and corrections that have congealed into a city with many faces, some gay, others dark, but never Kafkaesque or triste as a whole.

Rather than being a mystery, Prague is like a jigsaw puzzle. Each piece may look strange and even bizarre when examined individually, but when the whole has been carefully fitted together, the result is a miraculously beautiful tableau of both harmonies as well as contrasts, fitted together by the contours of good taste. No piece is too big or too small to look out of place. For, at above all, Prague has what is called human scale. Perhaps this is the real secret of the success of modernism in Prague: the secret of having avoided things too grand, too overbearing, too pretentious. And how could it be otherwise? What could possibly compete with the grandeur of Hradčany (the Castle), or the magnificence of the baroque palaces that have effectively preempted any future attempt to impose even more monumental edifices on the skyline of the city? Prague could hardly be expected to digest anything more colossal than the Insurance Complex, or the Paris boulevard, which is about the maximum surgical intervention that the city can tolerate given its modest core and the geography of the proximate hills surrounding the old center.

The reader is well advised to keep these topographical realities in mind when reading Švácha's narrative on the difficulties encountered by the planners who tried to expand the historical center of Prague and who had to accommodate the voracious appetite for space of the ever-mounting number of automobiles in the city. It is fortunate that Prague escaped the highway-building mania that gripped other cities in recent decades and which tore apart their historical fabric. My current home, Boston, is correcting such a past mistake — putting its elevated expressway, built in the fifties and sixties, underground in the nineties — at the cost of almost 8 billion dollars. This Herculean task will take years longer to accomplish than it took to build the original elevated artery, apart from disrupting the life of the city well into the next century and leaving a scar that will take generations to heal, if it ever can.

Seen from the perspective of the size of the country and its resources, the moderns had no choice but to adapt to the realities of its geography and the economic limitations of both public and private clients. There were no Rockefellers, Vanderbilts, or Fords in Czechoslovakia. Unlike the situation of their German, French, or Russian counterparts, their field of operations was almost by necessity local and not global. That is not to say that the Czech modernists were not internationally connected, or that they did not contribute to the accomplishments of the modern in architecture. It indicates instead that their radius of influence was extending inward rather than outward. It is true that various impulses tended to come first from Vienna and later from Dessau, Frankfurt, Paris, and Moscow. But, inevitably and inexorably, these had to be digested and adapted to the modest scale of a small central European country, where it is possible to go by bicycle from Prague to the borders of the republic in a couple of days if you are young and pedal real hard. The limitations imposed by these conditions put a natural brake on the urge for pompousness and gigantism and certainly did wonders for concentration and focus on essentials.

Prague was remarkably tolerant politically as well as culturally during its brief independence from 1918 to 1938. Just like the old Prague, the new Prague was not afraid to borrow from foreign sources and transform ideas and influences to its own needs and unique national character. And just as Gothic Prague had transformed itself into a baroque city, without losing the presence of either, so did modernism impose its credo without obliterating history — in spite of its verbal pretensions to do so. Even though the casual tourist may see only the ancient marvels of this city, the experience of its permanent residents is one of a functioning city in the modern sense, not a museum.

It is the remarkable accomplishment of Rostislav Švácha to have chronicled, with much clarity and in great detail, this latest transformation of the Prague of the late baroque into a new, modern Prague. Švácha neither condemns modernism nor does he hide its mistakes. Unlike many contemporary critics of architecture, who can see salvation only in the resurrection of some nonexistent ideal architectural past, or escape into the future by some new distopia of deconstruction, Svacha presents us with the story of the architecture and planning of this modern Prague as a fact of a positive effort and without regrets as to its results, a story that bodes well for the future of architecture in the Czech lands. He describes an architecture cognizant of its links to the rest of Europe but also modest enough to eschew the errors of the twin blights of this noble art: fashion and false monumentality. In fact, long before the current return to a new preoccupation with simplicity and modesty, the Czech avant-garde practiced tolerance and restraint in its productions already in the twenties and thirties, notwithstanding the occasional lapses into grand posturing and "poster radicalism." Indeed, the results are much less strident than the force of their rhetoric — fortunately.

My reasons for offering a personal account, rather than an academic commentary on Švácha's book, are simple and were touched upon earlier: I experienced Prague by living in that golden city for most of my formative years with a clear sense that this was not an ordinary place. It took reading Švácha's

xxx

book, however, to translate emotional feeling into intellectual certitude. It was Švácha who provided me with the other part of my memories and who convinced me that my recollections are not merely the fantasies of a sentimental old man but have an intellectual and rational justification in historical fact after all.

I now understand not only with my heart but with my head as well why I never considered this lovely city as a kind of museum of ancient architecture, and I therefore grew up to embrace without regret the spirit of all things modern as part of my development later, as an architect and teacher in my new home, America. I would suggest to the reader to reverse my experience: read Švácha's story, then go and spend some time exploring Prague, using the book as an indispensable guide, to discover all of Prague, old and new, magical and profane, mysterious and transparent, but above all, alive and livable.

NOTES

1. The adventures of *The Good Soldier Švejk* by Karel Hašek is a classic of Czech humor. The book, written in popular Czech slang, is difficult to translate. Even so, it is a must for anyone trying to understand the Czech mentality, and a delight to read.

2. *Hvězda* means "star" in English. This early example of *architecture parlante* was conceived as a summer pavilion by the son of the emperor Ferdinand I. The park and its summer pavilion are worth visiting.

3. Karel Čapek wrote the remarkably prescient play, *R.U.R.*, in which he coined the word *robot* and predicted the mindless mass societies of the late twentieth century with uncanny accuracy. He also wrote another story, "Krakatit," that predicted the coming of the atomic age.

Eric Jan Antonin Dluhosch
Professor Emeritus
Department of Architecture
Massachusetts Institute of Technology

THE ARCHITECTURE OF NEW PRAGUE 1895-1945

1 THE MODERN STYLE IN THE STREETS OF PRAGUE

The city of Prague is situated in a valley in the Central Bohemian Plateau hollowed millions of years ago by the Vltava River. Today the river winds it way through this valley in the shape of a hook, with the hills and outcrops of the plateau rising on both sides. On the left bank of the Vltava, this elevated formation begins in the south with the hill of Barrandov and continues with Děvín, Paví vrch, and Petřín, a hilltop park crowned with a small version of the Eiffel Tower dating from 1891. Further west rises the bulk of Strahov, and north of Petřín towers the hill of Opyš, site of the Prague Castle. In the east, the left bank is dominated by the flat mass of the Letná Plain, which slopes steeply above the river, becoming more gradual toward the north.

Along the right bank of the Vltava, the range of hills begins with Bráník in the south and runs on into Kavčí hory and the rocky outcrop of Vyšehrad, which is divided from the historical center of Prague by the deep gorge of the Nusle Valley with the Botič stream rushing along its bottom. Beyond Vyšehrad, the range retreats from the river, and the only points standing out on the gentle slope where the other half of the historical city center is situated are the rocky base of the Gothic Emmaus Monastery, the hillock of Větrov with its Gothic Church of Saint Apollinaris, Karlov with the Gothic Church of the Virgin Mary and Charlemagne, and finally the highest of all, Vítkov, also called Žižkov, where a liberation memorial was erected between 1926 and 1932.

Around 500 AD, this impressive land formation was settled by the Slavic tribe of the Czechs who, according to legend, founded Prague to fulfill a prophesy made by Princess Libuše, the mother of the first Bohemian dynasty of princes and later kings, the Přemyslids. The real historical Prague began developing in the ninth century from three focal points. The first of these was the bare hill of Opyš where the first documented Přemyslid prince, Bořivoj, (d. approx. 889) founded the Prague Castle, having surrounded the site with walls. Inside the castle, Bořivoj's grandson Václav the Holy built the church of Saint Vitus, and in 973 a bishopric was established at the same time as a Benedictine monastery with a church dedicated to Saint George. The second point from which early Prague developed was a large marketplace on the right bank of the Vltava, today's Old Town

Square, which grew at the crossroads of long-distance trade routes, not far from a ford across the river. The third historical focus was the fortified settlement of Vyšehrad, towering on a rugged rock above the right bank of the river, about three kilometers south of the Prague Castle and the Old Town marketplace.

During the tenth century, an extensive agglomeration of market-places, settlements, and noblemen's estates with several parish churches developed between the Prague Castle and Vyšehrad. The area surrounding Old Town Square was the most densely built-up, and it was there and along the adjacent communications that the characteristic tower-shaped Romanesque houses with vaulted ground-floor spaces were built from the twelfth century onward. At that time, the Jewish ghetto, today's Josefov, developed north of Old Town Square, and a settlement of German merchants grew in the east, around today's Na poříčí Street. The Prague Castle, which was rebuilt from 1135 in the manner of German imperial fortresses, was from 1172 connected to the commercial center of Prague by way of the stone Judita's Bridge, which was later destroyed by floods and rebuilt as the Gothic Charles Bridge. In the 1230s, the Přemyslid King Václav I created Prague's Old Town by erecting walls with towers and gates around the compact nucleus of the Old Town Square area. The course of these fortifications is traced by today's streets Národní, 28. října, Na příkopě, and Revoluční. The predominantly German patrician administration of Prague's Old Town resided from 1338 in Velflin House in Old Town Square, to which it gradually added the surrounding houses through purchase. In 1257, King Přemysl Otakar II built fortifications around Malá Strana along the left bank of the Vltava below the Prague Castle and granted this settlement the status of a town. In the 1320s, the ridge of Opyš west of the Prague Castle was enclosed within walls, forming the third Prague town center, Hradčany. The marketplaces and the picturesque winding streets of these three towns were bordered with Gothic houses built on characteristically narrow and deep lots behind vaulted arcades.

In mid-fourteenth century, the face of Prague was radically changed by the son of John of Luxemburg and the Přemyslid princess Eliška, Charles IV (d. 1378), German Emperor and King of Bohemia. His ambition was to

5

Prague panorama viewed from the Vyšehrad Citadel. In the forefront is the 1901 railway bridge across the Vltava from 1901, above, the suburb of Smíchov and the hill of Petřín; Prague Castle with the Cathedral of Saint Vitus on the horizon; Letná Plain park on the right.

Prague panorama viewed from the Letná Plain. Svatopluk Čech Bridge by Jan Koula and Jiří Soukup, 1905–1908, extending from Pařížská Avenue which was built in 1895 through the quarters of Josefov and Staré Město; right, on the opposite bank of the Vltava is the law school by Jan Kotěra, 1921–1931; left on the horizon the quarter of Vinohrady, right above the Vltava the Děvín Hill.

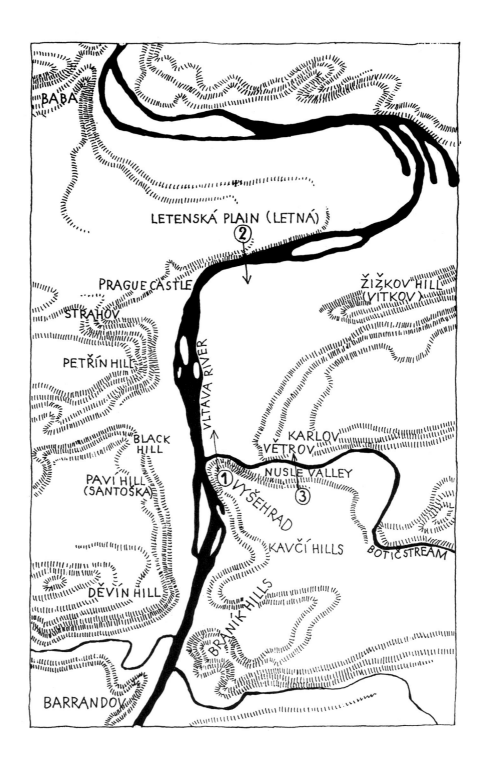

BABA

LETENSKÁ PLAIN (LETNÁ)
②

PRAGUE CASTLE

STRAHOV

ŽIŽKOV HILL
(VITKOV)

PETŘÍN HILL

VLTAVA RIVER

BLACK
HILL

KARLOV

VĚTROV

PAVI HILL
(SANTOŠKA)

① VYŠEHRAD
③

NUSLE VALLEY

KAVČÍ HILLS

BOTIČ STREAM

DĚVÍN HILL

BRANÍK HILLS

BARRANDOV

10

turn Prague into a "second Rome" and a dignified seat of the Holy Roman Empire. During his reign the city gained the name "Golden Prague," which was complemented by the title *Caput Regni* in the sixteenth century. In 1344, Charles achieved the promotion of the Prague bishopric to archbishopric and subsequently embarked on the building of a Gothic cathedral at the Prague Castle. Its first architect, the Frenchman Matthias of Arras, died in 1352, and his plans were changed in the late Gothic style by his successor Peter Parler, a builder from the Swabian town of Gmünd. Between 1344 and 1419, the chancel, the chapel of Saint Wenceslas, and the great tower were built; thereafter the work continued only sporadically over several centuries. In 1348, Charles established the first Central European university in the Old Town area. The Prague Castle was connected with the Old Town by way of the new Charles Bridge, fortified on the right bank of the Vltava with a tower gate designed by Peter Parler. The hill of Petřín was then incorporated within the walls of Malá Strana and Hradčany.

Among King Charles's most significant town-planning achievements was the establishment, in 1348, of Prague's New Town on the right bank of the river, along the east and south boundaries of the Old Town.[1] The walls of this fourth Prague town ran three and a half kilometers from Vyšehrad to Karlov, where they continued north, along the route of today's streets Sokolská, Mezibranská, Washingtonova, Na Florenci, and Těšnov. The rational urban grid of the New Town was designed around three large marketplaces situated on routes fanning out from the Old Town: Dobytčí trh (the Cattle Market, today's Charles Square), Koňský trh (the Horse Market, today's Wenceslas Square), and Senný trh (the Haymarket, today's Maxim Gorky Square). The built-up area in the middle was organized into extensive, mostly rectangular blocks. Within the New Town, Charles established a number of monasteries and churches whose unusual architectural diversity can be explained by his passion for collecting artifacts. Thanks to his efforts, Prague at that time ranked among the largest European cities, with approximately 40,000 inhabitants, and its newly gained capacity remained sufficient until the early nineteenth century.

11

Elevated points in the Prague area. Numbers indicate the photographer's position when taking pictures nos. 1, 2, and 3. Drawing by Rostislav Švácha.

Nové Město panorama viewed from the head of the Nusle Bridge. Nusle Valley below, Petřín Hill and the Prague Castle left on the horizon; Saint Apollinaris Church on the hill of Větrov in the center, Virgin Mary and Charlemagne on the hill of Karlov on the right.

During the reign of Charles's eldest son, Wenceslas IV of Luxemburg (d. 1419), a strong movement for religious reform began in Prague. The burning at the stake in 1415 of its leader, the university rector and priest John Hus, was followed in 1419 by the Hussite revolution, which started in Prague and was considered by Martin Luther as the beginning of the European Reformation. In 1420, the Hussite commander Jan Žižka defeated the crusader army of Sigismund of Luxemburg in the battle of Vítkov in front of the city walls. The Hussite iconoclasts then swept through Prague, burning down the majority of its monasteries and driving the German Catholic patrician class out of town.

It was not until the reign of King Vladislav of Jagellon (d. 1516) that peace prevailed again. Vladislav's architect Benedikt Ried refortified the Prague Castle and rebuilt the Royal Palace in Gothic-Renaissance style, creating the magnificent Vladislav Hall from 1487 to 1502. The largest of contemporary Prague parks, the Stromovka with its Late Gothic pavilion, was then established as King's Park on the left bank of the Vltava, north of Prague. The first Hapsburg kings who ruled Bohemia from 1526 added further landscaped areas to the Stromovka: the extensive gardens of the Prague Castle with the Renaissance pavilion Belvedere, 1536–1563, and the remote park Hvězda, situated near the peak of the White Mountain. In 1583, the Hapsburg Emperor Rudolf II (d. 1612) took up permanent residence in Prague, and his court attracted outstanding European artists and scientists such as Arcimboldo, Giordano Bruno, and Johann Kepler. Rudolfine Prague is also associated with the legend of Golem, the artificial man created by Rabbi Loew. The city became a renowned center of religious tolerance, codified in 1609 by Rudolf's Letter of Majesty, which granted equal rights to all churches in the Bohemian kingdom and made it possible for the subjects to adhere to a faith different from that of their rulers.

Yet, the practice of religious tolerance was brought to an end after the defeat of an anti-Hapsburg rebellion of Czech Protestants in the battle of the White Mountain, which took place in 1620. The Hapsburg army occupied Prague, and the Czechs were faced with the choice of accepting the Catholic faith or emigrating. Prague lost its position as seat of the imperial residence, which was relocated to Vienna. From 1654, a new belt of fortifications was erected around the earlier Gothic walls, with the citadel of Vyšehrad as the strongest point. Prague University fell into the hands of the Jesuits, who from 1654 began to build the extensive early baroque educational complex of Klementinum, near Charles Bridge. Dozens of old burgher houses were demolished to make way for the monumental blocks of the Jesuit colleges and for palaces belonging to the aristocracy who had remained loyal to the Hapsburgs. It was not until 1700 that this brutal early baroque practice was replaced by a new town-planning concept whose proponents Christoph Dientzenhofer, Jan Santini, and Kilian Ignaz Dientzenhofer showed a more sensitive approach to the urban space by creating buildings that added a masterly finishing touch to the various historical areas of Prague. It was then, for instance, that one of the centerpieces of the Prague panorama, Dientzenhofer's famous Church of Saint Nicholas, 1737–1751, was placed in the amphitheater of Malá Strana. Beyond the walls of the city, aristocrats and wealthy burghers laid out estates with mansions and pavilions nestling in the midst of gardens, orchards, and vineyards. The best known of these is perhaps Bertramka, where Mozart completed *Don Giovanni* in 1787.

In 1784, the four Prague towns were brought together in a single administrative entity by the enlightened Emperor Josef II (d. 1790) but were still denied self-government. German, which had long been used in Prague by the upper strata of society, was established as the official language throughout the Hapsburg Empire. The centralization of the state administration and the ensuing Germanization of social life precipitated a reaction on the part of patriotic Czech aristocracy and educated classes, leading to a process of emancipation of the modern Czech nation, called the National Revival, which began in Prague at the end of the eighteenth century. Among other factors contributing to the growth of Czech nationalism was the incipient economic competition between the rich Germans and the economically weaker Czech entrepreneurs.

In 1783, Emperor Josef abolished the institution of serfdom and so enabled free movement of people within the empire. Most of them headed for Prague, which in 1800 had around 80,000 inhabitants and where large manufactures and factories had been growing within the city walls and beyond, spawning a number of spontaneously developed industrial suburbs. One of them was, for example, the quarter of Smíchov, situated on the left bank of the Vltava south of Malá Strana, which was connected with the right bank by means of a chain bridge built along the axis of Národní Street between 1839 and 1841. The suburb of Karlín, planned on a simple grid and filled with factories and large tenement buildings from 1817 onward, was established on the right bank between the river and the hill of Vítkov, according to plans of Jiří Fischer, professor at the Prague Polytechnic. The Karlín example was later followed in the urban developments of Žižkov, Holešovice, and Libeň. On the other hand, the plan for the development of another large Prague suburb, Vinohrady, which in the second half of the nineteenth century became the home of the upper middle class, was based on a street network framed by an extensive public park, the Wimmer Gardens, which had been laid out between Wenceslas Square and today's Peace Square at the turn of the nineteenth century.

In 1845, a railway was built between Prague and the Moravian town of Olomouc, immediately followed by a rail link with Dresden. The bridge that took the railway across the Vltava near Karlín was built in 1845 to 1851 by Alois Negrelli, the future engineer of the Suez Canal.

The sharp contrast between the monotonous and dull character of the new suburbs and the rare beauty of the historical center of the city awakened admiration for old Prague in residents and visitors alike. It was then, during the industrial nineteenth century, that Prague received its best-known epithets "The City of a Hundred Spires" and "Magical Prague."

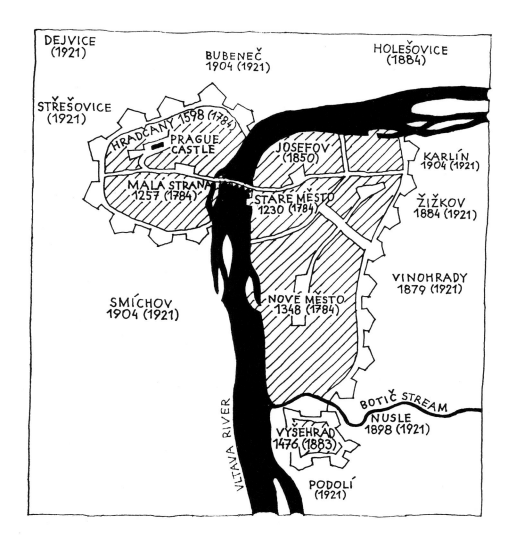

DEJVICE
(1921)

BUBENEČ
1904 (1921)

HOLEŠOVICE
(1884)

STŘEŠOVICE
(1921)

HRADČANY 1598 (1784)

PRAGUE
CASTLE

JOSEFOV
(1850)

KARLÍN
1904 (1921)

MALÁ STRANA
1257 (1784)

STARÉ MĚSTO
1230 (1784)

ŽIŽKOV
1884 (1921)

VINOHRADY
1879 (1921)

SMÍCHOV
1904 (1921)

NOVÉ MĚSTO
1348 (1784)

BOTIČ STREAM

NUSLE
1898 (1921)

VLTAVA RIVER

VYŠEHRAD
1476 (1883)

PODOLÍ
(1921)

Development of the historical center of Prague and adjacent quarters (around 1784). The date indicates the year when the area was granted the status of royal town; the date in brackets indicates the year when the area was integrated into the Prague municipality. Drawing by Rostislav Švácha.

The Modern Style in the Streets of Prague

The Modernization of Prague

In mid-nineteenth century, the Prague agglomeration included approximately 150,000 inhabitants. The majority were Czechs—artisans, small merchants, and manufacturing workers. A slight German majority still prevailed in the historical center of Prague, but even there it was on the decrease. In 1848, the people of Prague joined the revolutionary movement aiming to change the Hapsburg Empire into a constitutional monarchy. Their uprising was a failure, but together with other cities of the Austrian Empire Prague achieved self-government, albeit still dominated by Germans in the first election period of 1850 to 1861.

In the second election for the Prague City Council, which took place in 1861, following the fall of the Vienna-based police regime of Alexander Bach, the representatives of Czech political groups defeated their German opponents and subsequently maintained a majority until the breakdown of the Austrian Empire. This meant that Czech patriots could pursue their emancipatory ambitions at least within the limited space of the Bohemian capital. Their representatives were now given the opportunity to develop Prague into a modern European metropolis without unnecessary political and administrative wrangles.

Czech politicians seized this opportunity, and from the 1860s onward the patriotism of Czech society found its expression in public edifices and important cultural venues that are today considered gems of nineteenth-century architecture: the National Theatre, 1868–1883, the Czech Polytechnic, 1872–1873, the new part of the archiepiscopal Cathedral of Saint Vitus, 1873–1929, the Rudolfinum Palace housing a concert hall and art gallery, 1876–1884, and the National Museum, 1885–1890. Memorials celebrating important personalities of Czech history began appearing in parks and at key intersections. New theaters, museums, churches, schools, and municipal buildings, as well as gymnasiums and stadiums, symbolized the cultural triumph of the newly awakened nation, while the new road networks, industrial and commercial buildings, factories, gasworks, power stations, hotels, market halls, exchanges, office buildings, and banks manifested its economic triumph. Entire blocks of tenement buildings were erected to accommodate the influx of hundreds of thousands of new inhabitants. And finally at the beginning of the twentieth century, the time came for the reconstruction of the political and administrative center of the new activity, the Gothic Old Town City Hall, for which the Prague municipality announced three competitions, each time without conclusive results.

On the whole, the attempts of Prague's municipal authorities to exercise controlled planning of the new urban development were only partially successful. The Municipal Construction Authority, which at the beginning of the twentieth century proved to be the focus of rational urbanistic thinking, tried to regulate construction in the city, while solutions to essential town-planning problems were invited in open competitions. From 1873, the municipality started demolishing Prague's baroque fortifications, an area incorporating a wide esplanade that had to be purchased for a large sum of money from the Viennese military administration. For this reason it was decided to subdivide the land and sell individual lots to land developers and building contractors, instead of establishing a tree-lined circular avenue as was created in Vienna, Brno, or Olomouc, whose German-controlled municipalities bought their fortifications cheaply or received them for free. The lack of sympathy on the part of the Viennese administration, which stemmed from the rivalry of two national representative bodies in Bohemia, threatened to cause serious town-planning problems, and successive attempts to bring the extensive Prague agglomeration under a single administration failed until the fall of the Hapsburg monarchy in 1918. The historical center, comprising the Old and New Towns, Hradčany and Malá Strana, gradually incorporated the adjacent quarters under a single municipal administration: Josefov in 1850, Vyšehrad in 1883, Holešovice in 1884, and Libeň in 1901. However, the remaining densely populated Prague suburbs — for example, Vinohrady, Žižkov, Smíchov, and Karlín — retained their own administrations, often holding the status of royal towns. The administrative fragmentation of this conurbation substantially hindered the development of transport facilities, which had been gradually electrified from 1891, and stood in the way of rational planning of services, leading to an uneven development in various parts of the city and making organic unification of old and new Prague very difficult. The relationship between the old center of Prague and its surrounds, complicated moreover in terms of communications by the wide Vltava

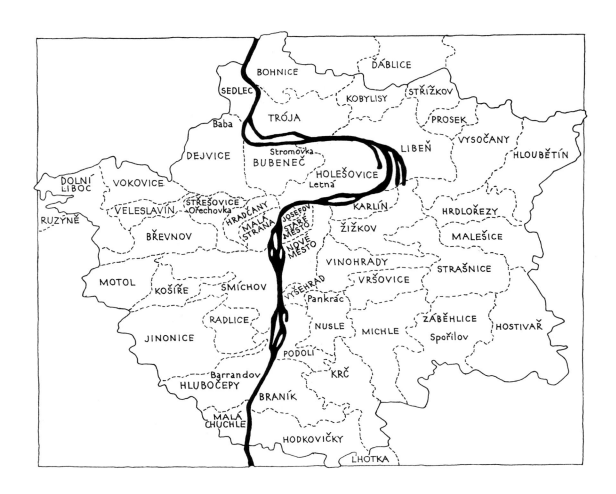

Greater Prague between 1921–1938. Municipal areas in capitals, important local names in lower case. The Directory at the end of the book also lists buildings situated beyond the boundaries of Greater Prague: Ruzyně with the Prague Airport from 1932–1937, Ďáblice, and Lhotka. Drawing by Rostislav Švácha.

River and by the hills of Petřín, Strahov, Prague Castle, and Letná, therefore remained a major town-planning problem long into the twentieth century.

Wherever terrain allowed, new buildings were organized into closed rectangular blocks determined by the grid system of the streets. But in the last decade of the nineteenth century, many Prague architects realized the restrictiveness of this pattern. They began to acknowledge the necessity to make the urban areas more distinctive and scenic, to structure them and brighten them up by means of ending the city's boulevards with conspicuous *points-de-vue*, and by establishing curved streets next to ones running in straight lines. In his commentary on the competition for the redevelopment of Malá Strana, published in the journal *Zprávy SIA* (SIA Bulletin) in 1901, the architect Jan Koula praised the "exquisite sense" with which the winning proposals "formulated and developed new areas creating a harmonious whole with the old parts of the city." According to Koula, new buildings should "if possible, be picturesque, and variation should be achieved by the use of pitched roofs, gables, projections, bay windows etc. but under no circumstances should there be the straight, rigid lines of ledges and roofs."[2] Koula's views were based on theories of the Austrian urbanist Camillo Sitte (1843–1903) and those of the German art historian Cornelius Gurlitt (1850–1938). Such town-planning approaches, however, found little practical application in Prague at the turn of the century, and Koula, the champion of the "picturesque and distinctive," had few opportunities to modify larger urban areas. One project where his directives were subsequently executed was the reconstruction of Maxim Gorky Square,[3] carried out in 1902 according to Koula's plan. There he focused on the reshaping of a block situated at the center of an elongated, triangular square. With the use of an ingenuous ground plan accentuating the corners of this architectural formation with polygonal towers and oriels, Koula divided the space of the square so that "the shape of the newly created body of buildings was more harmonious, more appropriate to a public space."[4] His plan was realized from 1912 to 1915 by the architect Josef Zasche.

Picturesque, irregular arrangements of winding streets also appear in some sections of the largest urban project of the time, the modernization of

Old Town and Josefov. Here, however, this type of layout can be partly explained by the need to respect the medieval street network. Prague authorities justified the project by the urgent need to improve the disastrous hygienic conditions in the area. Yet, it was particularly welcomed by developers eager to build lucrative apartment blocks in the very center of the city, and they are to blame for the ruthless destruction of architecturally valuable buildings in the modernized area. The modernization project was based on the winning plan of the engineers Alfred Hurtig, Jan Heide, and Matěj Strunc that had been entered in the competition of 1887. The aesthetic aspects of the modernization that began in 1893 were to be subsequently resolved by means of another competition announced by the municipality in 1902. The winner, architect Josef Sakař, used the given conditions to apply the principles of distinctiveness and picturesqueness posited by Sitte and Gurlitt. Only the straight-running streets of Kaprova and Pařížská, radiating from Staroměstské Square, point to another urbanistic conception of that time, the rebuilding of the center of Paris, directed in the 1850s and 1860s by the Prefect of the Seine Department, Georges Haussmann (1809–1891).

Pařížská Avenue became the focus of redevelopment activity in the modernized center. In 1893, the architect Jan Zeyer proposed connecting the historical center with the Letná Plain by a bridge that would extend along the axis of the avenue across the river, where it would wind up to Letná along a mild serpentine. Jan Koula rejected the notion of the serpentine in 1897 and decided to take the new avenue up to Letná through a direct, wide pass that would be bridged in front of the slope by a monumental triumphal gate.

The purpose of this communication was to connect the Prague center with a garden suburb planned for the area of Bubeneč, while the Dejvice Gate to Letná, conceived along the lines of classical propylaea, signified an allegorical celebration of the new Prague, a "visible symbol of the giant step in the development of Prague on the right bank of the Vltava."[5]

At first the Prague municipality received Koula's project favorably and began to buy land in Letná to make space for its realization. Between 1905 and 1908, it had a new bridge built from Pařížská across the Vltava, which

Alfred Hurtig, Jan Heide, Matěj Strunc. Modernization of Staré Město and Josefov. 1887, 1902.

Jan Koula. Study for the pass between Svatopluk Čech Bridge and Letná Plain. 1897.

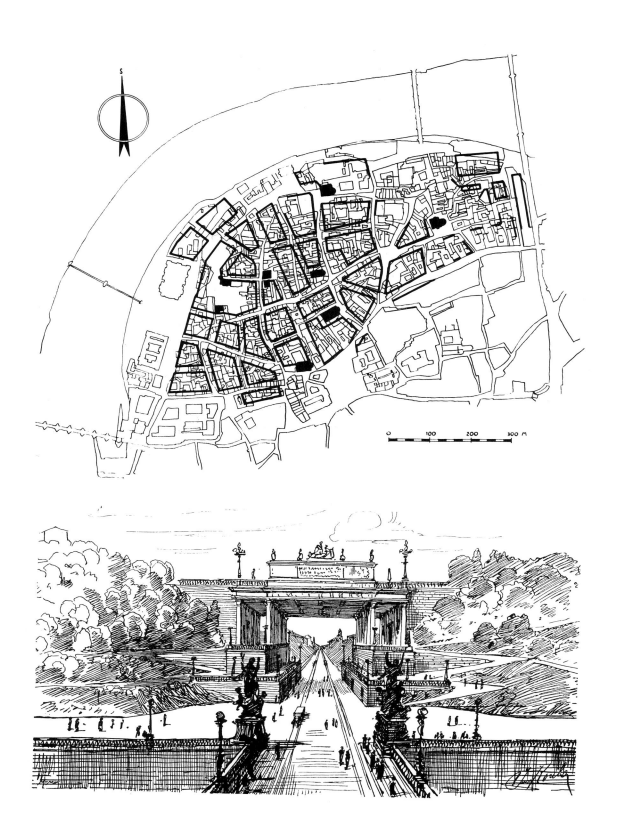

had been designed by Koula in collaboration with the construction engineer Jiří Soukup. To find the most suitable way of linking up Letná, a problem that could have been resolved by means of a pass or a tunnel or even a combination of the two, the municipality announced two competitions, in 1902 and 1909, both of which were accompanied by passionate debates among architects and members of the selection committee. These efforts, however, were obstructed by the Vienna-based government granting autonomy to the town of Bubeneč, which Prague had intended to incorporate with the help of the new communication. Prague authorities began to lose interest in the project and around 1913 asked the Municipal Construction Authority to examine the possibility of connecting the center with Letná from a different point, today's Šverma Bridge. The issues raised in the discussions around the alternatives of pass or tunnel—that is, the question of connecting the Prague center with the higher left bank of the Vltava, as well as the possibility of establishing a modern satellite town in the area of Bubeneč and Dejvice—were to preoccupy Prague urbanists for a long time to come.

Except for several public buildings, the modernized area was filled with apartment blocks. A turning point in the development of the internal arrangement of tenement housing came in 1885, when the water plant in Podolí began to supply water to higher floors. This technological reform made it possible for the more luxurious buildings to shift the sanitary facilities from the balcony to the interior of the building, and as a consequence, a well-planned, three-bay apartment layout evolved as early as the 1880s: the kitchen was oriented toward the courtyard, the corridor was placed centrally with the adjacent hallway, bathroom, and toilet, and the individual rooms of the living section looked toward the street. The shortcoming of this arrangement was the inadequate supply of light and fresh air in the central bay, where it was necessary to use glass doors and skylights, or to make openings into the stairwell or the kitchen.

In the first decade of the twentieth century, the three-bay layout was used by nearly all building contractors and architects, regardless of their artistic views, and it was not until 1910 that attempts were made to revise this type of layout. At that time, however, university-educated architects had minimal

24

influence on the development of tenement layout. The interior of the building was usually designed by the building firm, while the architect was left with the rather undignified role of mere decorator. The architect Josef Fanta ironically commented on this situation in the review *Volné směry* (Free Directions) in 1899: "In Prague it is still accepted that the architect's task is, at best, to design the facade, and that if the building contractor or developer requires collaboration with an architect, it is most often because of the facade. At the most the architect's work extends as far as the passageway."[6]

The floor plans of villas changed much more radically from the beginning of the century. Family homes or villas began to be built in Prague in the 1870s by the most affluent members of the entrepreneurial elite. The focal point of these villas was a grand reception hall surrounded by various drawing rooms and reception rooms, libraries, studies, and bedrooms, the windows of which overlooked extensive gardens. By the end of the century a growing number of the entrepreneurial and professional middle class could afford to build family villas. The means of this class were, however, much more limited, and this was reflected in the smaller size of the buildings and of surrounding land. To leave space for at least a small garden, the house had to be moved to one side of the plot, usually closer to the street. Together with the requirement for a more rational orientation in relation to the cardinal points, this shift led to the regrouping of individual apartments, so that the "servicing" areas (kitchen, staircase, bathroom, and toilet) faced north toward the street, while the "serviced" areas (the living room and the bedrooms) faced south toward the garden. Some architects reached this solution rapidly and fairly early; others worked toward it slowly and with digressions, their artistic convictions playing a surprisingly minor role. The modern, "regrouped" plan was used by Jan Koula as early as 1895 in the design of his own Bubeneč villa, in spite of the fact that he was considered conservative by the modern architects. On the other hand, one of the modernists, Dušan Jurkovič, built in the same suburb a rather old-fashioned villa with a central reception hall as late as 1907–1908. The villas designed at that time by Jan Kotěra, the leader of the modern movement and the most radical of Prague architects, appear in this context as transitional hybrids standing somewhere between the two types of layouts.

25

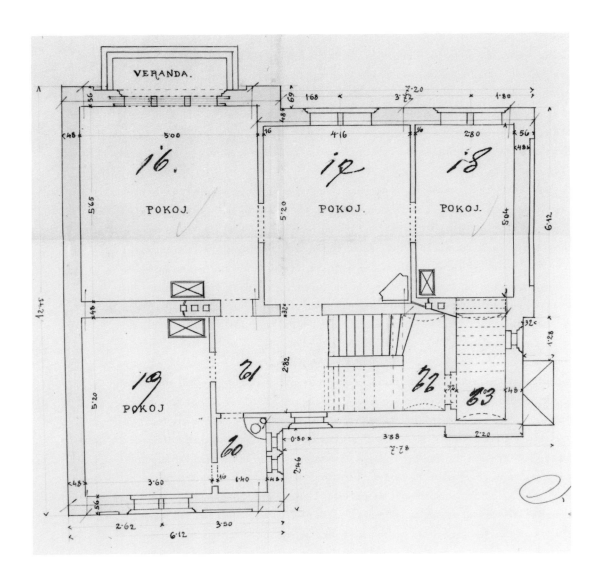

Jan Koula. Architect's own villa, floor plan, Bubeneč, Slavíčk-
ova 17. 1895–1896.

Jan Koula. Project for architect's own villa. Bubeneč, Slavíčkova 17. 1895–1896.

The Modern Style in the Streets of Prague

Prague architecture of the second half of the nineteenth century shared certain characteristics with that of other major European cities. It was a time that favored monumental neo-Gothic, neo-Romanesque, and neo-Renaissance buildings, but in the 1880s Prague architects began to discuss the possibility of creating a specifically national architectural style. Bohemian neo-Renaissance, adopted by the Prague architect Antonín Wiehl (1846–1910), appeared to suggest the most promising direction. It was a style derived from Bohemian buildings of the sixteenth century, with characteristically ornate gables, lunette cornices, and facades decorated with figurative sgraffiti. Wiehl's style found many supporters among other architects as well as among politicians of the nationalist Young Czech Party, which reigned supreme in Czech political life at the turn of the century. The Bohemian neo-Renaissance style can be seen as a local architectural language similar to that which in countries such as Belgium or the Netherlands formed the first step toward the modern style. Yet, none of the Prague architects of that period, including Wiehl and his most talented successor, Friedrich Ohmann, became a Czech Horta or Berlage. Unfortunately, Prague architects of the time were not very interested in questions related to the construction of buildings, a field of research that probably spawned most of the architectural variants of the European modern style.[7]

In their search for a new style, Prague architects were not ready to absorb the impulses offered by new construction possibilities. The industrial exhibition site built in 1891 according to Wiehl's regulation plan for the Regional Jubilee Exhibition on the edge of the Stromovka Park in Bubeneč best illustrates this lack of readiness. Bedřich Münzberger (1846–1928), architect of the Industrial Palace situated in the center of the exhibition site, had at his disposal a magnificent steel construction designed by the engineer František Prášil and the First Bohemian Steelworks. He decided to leave it partly uncovered, but in adding his neobaroque features, he failed to achieve a harmonious blend of two styles, and the whole building gives the impression of an eclectic, incongruous architectural mixture. Several minor buildings standing close to Münzberger's palace, for instance the pavilion of the steelworks Bolzano, Tedesco and Co., whose author was probably Jiří Stibral, present an even more curious example of the ways in which modern structures were combined with traditional, historicizing features.

*Dušan Jurkovič. Villa, floor plan. Bubeneč, Suchardova 4.
1907–1908.*

*Jaroslav Vondrák. Apartment building, floor plan, Bubeneč,
Československé armády 4. 1911.*

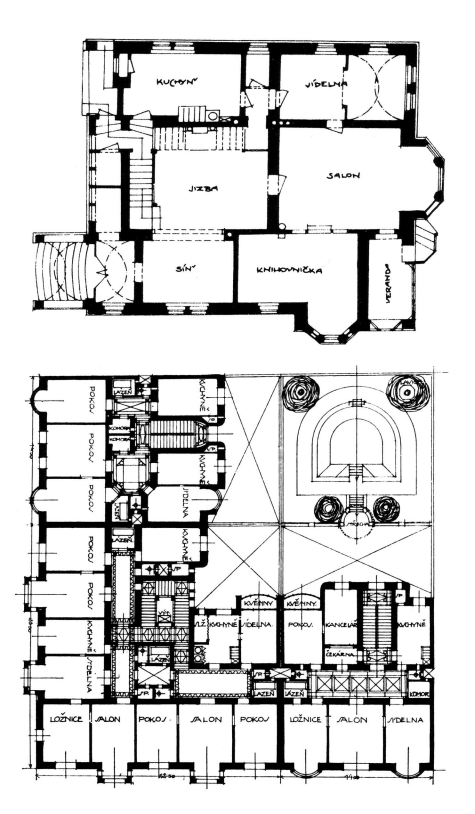

A concentrated development of the possibilities offered by the Bohemian neo-Renaissance style was also hindered by parallel efforts to create similar local versions of neobaroque and neo-Gothic architecture. In the 1890s, these styles, inspired by the work of the great architect of the Prague baroque, Kilian Ignaz Dientzenhofer, and by the so-called Vladislavian Gothic of the turn of the fifteenth and sixteenth centuries, were in serious competition with the national style. As a consequence, at the beginning of the twentieth century, most Czech architects were still unable to free themselves from the limitations of the question What style should we build in?

The wide variety of styles used by architects around 1900 can be seen in Pařížská Avenue and surrounding streets in the redeveloped zone of the Old Town and Josefov. Between 1895 and 1910, architects Rudolf Kříženecký, Jan Vejrych, Richard Klenka, František Weyr, Antonín Makovec, Jiří Justich, Karel

Bedřich Münzberger. Industrial Palace at the exhibition grounds in Stromovka Park. Bubeneč, U výstaviště. 1890–1891.

Jiří Stibral(?). Project for the pavilion of Bolzano, Tedesco & Co. for exhibition grounds in Stromovka Park. 1891.

Vítězslav Mašek, and Matěj Blecha designed several dozen apartment buildings for this area, not only in styles ranging from neo-Gothic to neo-Renaissance and neo-baroque but also in the new Viennese modern style, which many of them viewed unfavorably but learned to use with the same ease as the historical styles.

One of the neobaroque apartment buildings at the lower end of Pařížská Avenue, near Dientzenhofer's church of Saint Nicholas, was designed by Jan Koula (1855–1919), mentioned earlier as town planner and theoretician of urbanism. Koula studied under Theofil von Hansen at the Vienna Academy of Fine Arts and later became professor of architecture at the Czech Polytechnic. He was also an outstanding museum curator and edited the magazines *Zprávy SIA* (SIA Bulletin) and *Architektonický obzor* (Architectural Horizon), where he published polemical articles aimed against the modern movement after 1900. In the 1880s, Koula widely promoted Wiehl's Bohemian neo-Renaissance style and employed its features even in the design for his own villa on Slavíčkova Street in Bubeneč, 1895–1896, which was otherwise dominated by the folkloric elements of the so-called Swiss style. As for the gate planned for the pass leading to Letná, Koula intended to design it in the style of classicizing Italian Renaissance, whereas his apartment building on Pařížská Avenue imitated Dientzenhofer's baroque. The most interesting of Koula's works was probably Svatopluk Čech Bridge, 1905–1908, connecting Pařížská Avenue with the proposed Letná pass. Koula's bronze and gold-plated ornaments, columns with Victoria figures, and pillars in the shape of a ship's prow were combined with the elegant steel structure designed by the engineer Jan Soukup.

Close to Koula's artistic sensibility was another professor at the Czech Polytechnic, Josef Fanta (1856–1954), who had studied architecture under Josef Zítek, the most talented Czech architect of the nineteenth century and author of Prague's National Theater. In comparison with Koula, Fanta's stylistic repertoire was more focused and closer to the modern style.[8] The most significant of Fanta's works was the main hall of the Central Station in Wilsonova Street, 1900–1909. Its gothicizing facade slices through the front of the cylindrical body of the hall shaped on the inside as a spherical sector. It has a triangular gable and is

Pařížská Avenue on the border of Staré Město and Josefov.
1895–circa 1910.

split in the middle by an enormous thermal window underlined by a metal awning suspended above the wide entrance. The central section of the facade is flanked by two monumental towers whose rectangular shapes turn cylindrical at the top where they are crowned with symbolic glass globes. Few Czech architects of the time would have been able to impose the required discipline and order on a building so richly decorated, with such a flamboyant outline, and bearing such a variety of stylistic features, and Fanta certainly succeeded in his task.

On the other hand, the work of Osvald Polívka (1859–1931), which perhaps best exemplifies Prague architecture of the turn of the century, always suffered from a lack of artistic discipline. Polívka, another former student of Josef Zítek, was a prominent architect who designed major Czech banks and insurance company buildings, as well as several large buildings for the Prague municipality. His Zemská Bank, situated at Na příkopě, 1894–1896, was designed in the Bohemian neo-Renaissance style. The building is generously decorated with colorful mosaics and sculptures by prominent contemporary artists. The Prague Insurance Building, erected on the redeveloped north side of Old Town Square, was inspired by Dientzenhofer's baroque style, whereas in the Novák department store in Vodičkova Street, 1901–1904, Polívka arrived at a picturesque and chromatic version of the modern style. Polívka's trademark, however, was his idiosyncratic mixture of neo-Renaissance, neobaroque, and modern elements, the best examples of which are the New City Hall in Mariánské Square, 1906–1911, and above all, the Municipal House in Republic Square, 1903–1912, designed by Polívka in collaboration with Antonín Balšánek (1865–1921), his colleague from the Czech Polytechnic.

In designing the Municipal House, the two architects had to resolve problems created by the difficult, irregular site as well as by the demanding building program reflecting the multiple purpose of the building that was supposed to house restaurants, concert halls, exhibition spaces, lecture theaters, offices, and a casino. Among other things this meant that the number of floors in different sections of the building varied. Equally difficult was their work as a whole from the point of view of the motifs and styles they used. The impressive projecting en-

Antonín Wiehl, Josef Fanta. Wiehl's apartment building. Nové Město, Vodičkova 40. 1894–1896.

Josef Fanta. Central Station. Vinohrady, Wilsonova. 1900–1909.

Osvald Polívka. New City Hall. Staré Město, Mariánské náměstí 2. 1906–1911.

The Modern Style in the Streets of Prague

CHAPTER 1

trance, reminiscent of the Parisian Grand Palais, is sheltered by a monumental glass and metal awning supported by two triumphal columns and culminates in a glass cupola, which was meant to indicate that, among its other functions, the building was to serve as a "Temple of Art." The color mosaic adorning the arch under the cupola, the ornamental and folkloric decorations, and, above all, the art nouveau awning combine to create a modern impression. Nonetheless, elements of late Renaissance and baroque predominate in the total appearance of the building to the extent that, in 1910, one of the staunch supporters of orthodox modern style, Antonín Engel, described the building as the most characteristic example of the contemporary "decadence in artistic attitudes."[9] Theatrical and ostentatious, full of dramatic architectural gestures, Polívka's and Balšánek's design declared its affinity with the work of the hero of all Czech architects of the nineteenth century, Charles Garnier. Aesthetically, Polívka appealed to the views of the German art historian Richard Muther: beauty consists in individuality, and if the artist breaks stylistic rules and "produces something bizarre or wild, the result is more interesting than whatever could have been achieved using the best school recipes."[10]

Similar combinations of historical motifs and modern elements appeared around 1900 in the work of the architects Václav Roštlapil, Alois Čenský, Josef Sakař, Josef Podhajský, Jiří Stibral, František Velich, and František Sander. Included in this group is the architect and developer Matěj Blecha (1861–1919), who owed the modern character of his many buildings to his collaboration with the skillful sculptor-decorator Celda Klouček and with the graduate of the School of Applied Arts in Darmstadt, the architect Emil Králíček. The work of these architects was often cultivated, but unlike Osvald Polívka, they never overstepped the boundaries of stylistic rules in search of a new style, or at least in pursuit of a new personal expression, as had been Polívka's ambition. In spite of such shortcomings, we can still find among the last generation of Prague architectural historicists several exceptional personalities whose names were not forgotten after the era of historicizing architecture came to an end.

One such remarkable architect was Kamil Hilbert (1869–1933), who in 1899 took over from Josef Mocker as the second architect to work on the

Antonín Balšánek, Osvald Polívka. Municipal House, Staré Město, náměstí Republiky 5. 1903–1912.

completion of Saint Vitus Cathedral. Hilbert had little time for "scientific" reconstruction methods of his predecessor, and although he was a most sensitive connoisseur and restorer of medieval buildings, he clearly did not like to spend time consulting sample books of Romanesque and Gothic stylistic forms. He wanted to work creatively even in his role of restorer, and he sought collaboration with modern sculptors and painters, while in the shaping of details he relied on his own inventiveness. Rather than in his work on Saint Vitus Cathedral, where, after all, he was still bound by Mocker's original conception, Hilbert's approach to restoration was more apparent in the small church of Saint Martin on Martinská Street, which he renovated in 1905–1906. His apartment block on Masaryk Embankment, 1904–1905, imitated the Vladislavian Gothic, which was then seen by many of his colleagues as a potential basis for the development of a new national architectural style. The entrance passage and the staircase, however, suggest that Hilbert had already adopted the modern style. The question whether the naturalistic branches above the entrance of Hilbert's building derive from Vladislavian Gothic or from Olbrich's and Wagner's *Sezessionstil* could probably not be answered even by the architect himself.

The work of Friedrich Ohmann (1858–1927), professor of decorative architecture at the Prague School of Applied Arts between 1889 and 1898, bears signs of an even more creative approach to historical styles. Although Ohmann came to Prague from Galicia and concluded his career in Vienna, he was more sensitive to the local stylistic peculiarities of old Prague architecture than most Prague-born or -bred architects. In the Valtera Palace in Voršilská Street, 1890–1891, Ohmann showed his contemporaries the true magic of Dientzenhoferian baroque. Even more interesting were his designs based on Wiehl's Bohemian neo-Renaissance and Vladislavian Gothic, whose elements he combined with a masterly touch. A good example of this is his Bohemian Eagle Building in Ovocný trh, built between 1896 and 1897, where Ohmann combined the late Gothic and Renaissance gables, bays, and windows into a single impressive whole in an essentially baroque manner. Another example was the later demolished Café Corso on Na příkopě, 1897–1898, which was the first building in Prague to display true

Kamil Hilbert. Apartment building. Nové Město, Masarykovo nábřeží 26. 1904–1905.

art nouveau elements as part of its stylistic spectrum, such as the fan-shaped glass awning under the Renaissance-styled attic. Another new element common to both Ohmann's works from the years 1896 to 1898 was his conception of the facade as an empty surface that could be freely decorated with sgraffito, mosaic, or figurative relief, regardless of traditional stylistic conventions. Ohmann's Hotel Central in Hybernská Street, 1898–1901, the details of which Ohmann left in the hands of his modernist pupils, Alois Dryák and Bedřich Bendelmayer, shows how close his playful stylistic collages could get to the modern style, or at least to its decorative external semblance.

The promise of the characteristically local Prague modern style, contained in the work of Friedrich Ohmann and his circle, was, however, suddenly suppressed by the more advanced Viennese *Sezession*, brought to Prague from Otto Wagner's school around 1900.

The demand for each new building erected in Prague around 1900 was that it should adorn the city, but at the same time it had to be dignified, a requirement that for the last five decades of the nineteenth century forced architects to disguise various civic buildings as old Gothic, Renaissance, or baroque palaces, chateaux, or temples. The last Prague historicists, however, did not see their orientation toward the past as the copying of old forms but as a respectful awareness of the local tradition that "refines the architect's imagination and provides the basis for his further development," as Jan Koula put it in 1900.[11] Gothic, Renaissance, and baroque columns, pilasters, cornices, bays, turrets, gables, attics, sgraffito decorations, and other historicizing elements were used to ensure a picturesque and individual character. As the theorist Antonín Bráf wrote in 1902, the architect must approach these elements as if they were an alphabet or the essential "conditions of architectural beauty,"[12] and only when he had mastered them could he proceed to give free reign to his inventiveness and imagination. Modern architecture, which gradually severed its ties with the past, was seen by the representatives of historicism as a style lacking in national color, forced upon the Czechs by the Viennese government. Historicists criticized it for its alleged poverty of thought and lack of artistic ambition. Beside beauty, dignity, picturesqueness,

43

Kamil Hilbert. Staircase of an apartment building. Nové Město, Masarykovo nábřeží 26. 1904–1905.

and a typically Czech character, the historically oriented aesthetic demanded that the building should "speak" to the viewer as much as possible — by its choice of style, by means of the iconography of the paintings and sculptures selected to decorate it, and by means of its architectural symbolism, which around 1900 often implied the motif of triumph. However, if it is possible to identify a key term in the unwritten aesthetic of the late historical revival, it would certainly be the term *effect* or *impression* — words that appear in the Czech architectural thought from the late 1870s and which were more frequently used around 1900. Texts written by the last of Prague historicists brim with expressions like "impression of the color scheme," "exquisite impression," "overall impression," "horrible, empty impression," while the leading spokesman of the historical revival, Antonín Bráf, gave low marks to modern architecture because it did not evoke the "slightest measure of satisfactory impression."[13] It was also the attempt to achieve the most effective impression that led many architects to the use of some formal signs of the otherwise condemned modern style on the facades of their buildings.

At first, the word *impression* may have helped architects express the notion that the building as a whole should hold priority over and above its constituent parts. The importance of impression in the aesthetic of the late historicists, something that became almost a cult, makes us think back to its historical roots and remember the fact that the historicists and their affluent clients liked to cloak their buildings in an unwarranted mantle of significance and glory, that they liked to see their prosaic houses as palaces and temples, that they preferred illusion to reality, impression to actuality. Historicists such as Koula, Polívka, and Ohmann designed buildings for the old liberal bourgeoisie of the nineteenth century: those who relished the heroic gestures of historical paintings and theatrical poses of old portrait photographs, who lived in illusions and would have liked to remain that way.

45

Friedrich Ohmann. Bohemian Eagle Building. Staré Město,
Ovocný trh 15. 1896–1897.

In the 1890s, several prominent personalities in Czech cultural and political life became aware of the need to cast away illusions and to adopt a more realistic attitude toward contemporary life. Among them were the poet Josef Svatopluk Machar, the literary and art critic František Xaver Šalda, and the philosopher and sociologist Tomáš Garrigue Masaryk, who was to become the first Czechoslovak president. In the political sphere, these men shared a dislike for the nationalistic demagogy of the Young Czech Party, which had a tendency to gloss over the conflicts running deep within Czech society instead of trying to resolve them and ignored the urgent need for far-reaching reforms that would improve the living and working conditions of the working class and prevent the upheavals of class struggle. The cultural demands of this new movement were expressed in the "Manifest české moderny" (Manifesto of the Czech Modern) published in 1895 and signed by Machar and Šalda and many other young Czech poets and writers. The manifesto set out a program of artistic and critical freedom: the task of the artist was to express one's inner truth in an original way. The ideals of literary modernism were also supported by young artists from the *Mánes* Artists' Association, particularly by the painter Jan Preisler and sculptor Stanislav Sucharda, who in 1897 founded a new art review *Volné směry* (Free Directions). In its first years, the review hosted a discussion on contemporary architecture with a self-explanatory title "Moderna či směr národní?" (The Modern style or the National Direction?). Here, the influential art critic Karel B. Mádl expressed the view that the historical approach offered contemporary architecture no perspective and declared his hope that Prague architecture would soon find its Messiah — whom he had in the meantime chosen himself from among the disciples of the pioneer of Viennese modern style, Otto Wagner (1841–1918).

This architect was Jan Kotěra (1871–1923), and he became instrumental in the revitalization of Czech architecture. Kotěra, who emerged as the new leader and custodian of the Czech modern style, had studied under Wagner at the Viennese Academy of Fine Arts and succeeded Ohmann as professor of decorative architecture at the Prague School of Applied Art in 1898. He was a man of outstanding qualities, whose behavior, as described by his pupil

Friedrich Ohmann. Café Corso. Staré Město, Na příkopě 31.
1897–1898, demolished 1936.

Otakar Novotný, was "at all times characteristically selfless, noble and gentle-manly." Kotěra brought from Vienna the advanced syntax of the *Wagnerschule*, which he treated as a given language, coming to terms with each of its subsequent developmental changes. His older colleagues from the historical camp and some later art historians—particularly the Austrian Otto A. Graf—accused him of excessive dependence on Wagner.[14] The advocates of Kotěra's work, on the other hand, recognized his originality in qualities that were sometimes difficult to define: in comparison with Wagner, or with Wagner's most significant student Josef Hoffmann (1870–1956), they found Kotěra's work to possess a "Czech sweetness" or, on the contrary, "something firm and healthy."[15] Today we can say that Kotěra surpassed the majority of Wagner's students in his wide knowledge of world architecture. By 1900, he became interested in the work of the Americans Louis Sullivan and Frank Lloyd Wright, and after 1905 he made several trips to study the work of the Dutch architect Hendrik Petrus Berlage (1856–1934). He also displayed exceptional interest in the social aspects of architecture, and in particular in workers' housing reforms. In a letter written to his Viennese friend Richard Gombrich in 1910, he said about such reforms: "...they are now my most cherished idea."[16] The most important aspect of Kotěra's contribution was probably his application of the austere moralistic vocabulary, which came to dominate the *Wagnerschule* after 1905, to the monumental public buildings in Prague and around the country.

Jan Kotěra set out his new program in his article "O novém umění" (On New Art), published in 1900 in the review *Volné směry*. Against the "aesthetic of impression" he posed the demand for truthfulness—which could be traced back through Wagner's ideas to Ruskin's statement that "a building must be truthful." Against excessive respect for tradition and mere combining of historical features he posed the demand for creativity, a characteristically modern argument, as the modernists did not recognize the return to tradition as a creative act. Finally, against the primary interest in the facade and its decoration, he articulated the need to start with the purpose of the building, with the space and its constructive expression. The last requirement in particular, aimed, as it was, against the traditional division of labor between the building contractor and the architect-decorator, must have met with persistent opposition in traditionalist Prague. In his analysis, Kotěra described architects' work primarily as "creation of space," then "construction of space" based on "the eternal natural theme of support and weight," and, finally, he mentioned "decoration, adornment," the function of which was to articulate and enhance "mass defined in clearly constructive terms."[17]

In his early buildings, Kotěra's program of artistic truthfulness was present as a latent tendency rather than being clearly manifest. Nonetheless, even these early works stand out from the run-of-the-mill architectural production of the time by virtue of their obvious artistic quality, purity of their stylistic elements, and the logic applied in combining these into a compositional whole. The facade of the Peterka Building in Wenceslas Square, 1899–1900, designed by Kotěra for the author of the construction and ground plan, Vilém Thierhier, is divided into three parts by means of two taller side pylons. Between them, as if blown up by the arch below, is suspended a softly billowing *avant-corps* whose upper part is decorated with a figurative relief. The whole composition is Wagnerian, but the details of the projecting central section clearly imitate Horta's Hôtel Tassel in Brussels. With its baroque curves, S-shaped lines of the gables, delicate plant ornaments, and sensitively integrated sculptures, the whole facade makes a dreamy, lyrical impression, a word that even Kotěra still used in his theoretical writings. Another of Kotěra's Prague buildings, the temporary Mánes Pavilion at the foot of the Petřín Hill built for August Rodin's exhibition in 1902, had a similar character and was described by the critic F. X. Šalda as a "citadel of pride and dreams." The building was dominated by a gateway in the form of a triumphal arch, asymmetrically placed in the plain, almost undecorated frontal wall, which concealed an octagonal entrance hall, top-lit through a low glass cupola. The gateway, clasped between two towering pylons, was a reference to the front of Harrison Townsend's Whitechapel Gallery in London, 1898, a gesture that was probably meant to symbolize the international impact of the modern movement and its triumphant arrival on the Czech architectural scene. The tops of the robust pylons were decorated with naturalistic wreaths, the timber structure of the front gable was evocative of timber-frame vernacular architecture.

49

Jan Kotěra, Vilém Thierhier. Peterka Building. Nové Město,
Václavské náměstí 12. 1899–1900.

Jan Kotěra. Mánes exhibition pavilion. Smíchov, Kinského
zahrada. 1902, demolished 1917.

The Modern Style in the Streets of Prague

Jan Kotěra. Villa Trmal. Strašnice, Vilová 11. 1902–1903.

Jan Kotěra. Sucharda's villa. Bubeneč, Slavíčkova 6. 1905–
1907.

CHAPTER 1

The Modern Style in the Streets of Prague

Folk architecture of the Czech countryside also provided inspiration for Kotěra's Villa Trmal on Vilová Street, 1902–1903. The overall form evokes a Czech village house, complemented by the vernacular character of the carpentry work and the painted decorations. However, the system of chimneys and other parts, picturesquely jutting out from the main body of the building, and the relatively complicated floor plan with a double-height staircase hall point clearly to the English arts and crafts movement exemplified in the cottages of Charles Annesley Voysey and to Charles Rennie Mackintosh's version of art nouveau. An even stronger English influence can be identified in the last of Kotěra's Prague buildings, the family villa and studio of the sculptor Stanislav Sucharda in Slavíčkova Street, 1905–1907, a building with almost no decorations apart from the characteristic timber-frame walls and strikingly shaped pitched roofs, bays, and chimneys. The layout of the living quarters was again designed around a staircase hall. Here, Kotěra made a clear attempt to organize the individual rooms with reference to the garden, which meant, however, that the drawing room and the large living room on the ground floor had to face north.

What the interiors of these villas tell us about the program of "creation of space" is that Kotěra aimed to give the rooms a strongly defined floor plan and overall form, and that he tried to express the mutual spatial relations between these rooms. One of such spatial "types" integrated into the plans of his buildings was the English double-height staircase hall with a gallery, another was an oblong or square room with a semicircular apse. To allow these spaces to influence one another and so to create a more complex and interesting whole, Kotěra would open up the walls between them by means of a wide arch. In the pamphlet *Dělnické kolonie* (Workers' Housing Colonies) written in 1921, he called this space-creating feature "opening with a vista."[18]

The modern style, which was soon called *secese* after the Viennese example, was adopted by several older architects of the historicist generation, in particular by Osvald Polívka and Josef Fanta, whose building designed for the *Hlahol* association on Masaryk Embankment, 1903–1906, remains one of the most impressive examples of the new style in Prague. But the modern movement would

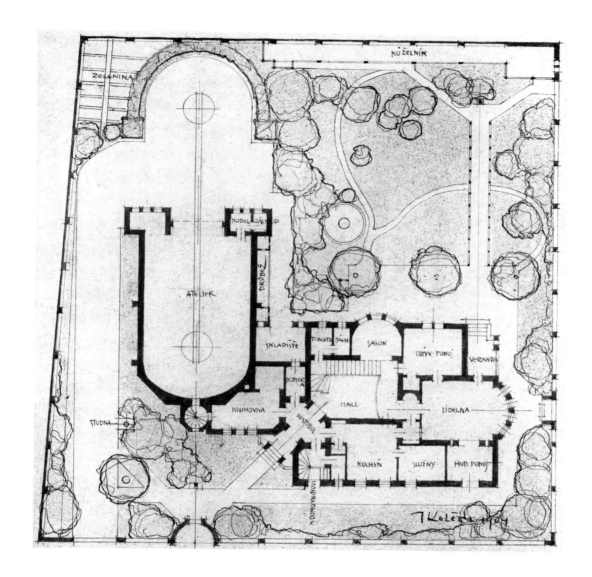

Jan Kotěra. Sucharda's villa, floor plan. Bubeneč, Slavíčkova
6. 1905–1907.

The Modern Style in the Streets of Prague

Jan Kotěra. Sucharda's villa, hall, and living room. Bubeneč,
Slavíčkova 6. 1905–1907.

Josef Fanta, Čeněk Gregor. Hlahol apartment building. Nové
Město, Masarykovo nábřeží 16. 1903–1906.

CHAPTER 1

not have triumphed without the support of powerful developers such as Matěj Blecha and Quido Bělský. Bělský's office also employed Ohmann's pupils Alois Dryák and Bedřich Bendelmayer, authors of the remarkable Hotel Evropa in Wenceslas Square, 1903–1905. Bendelmayer then independently designed the apartment building on U Prašné brány Street, 1903–1904. This building provoked one of the fiercest attacks against the modern movement, which was voiced by the conservative art critic František Xaver Harlas in his article "Moderna v pražských ulicích" (The Modern Style in the Streets of Prague), published in the magazine *Architektonický obzor* (Architectural Horizon) in 1904. Harlas found the smooth white walls, the "flat frames, latticing, and the glasshouse look" of Bendelmayer's building ugly enough, but what angered him most was that with these features the house became an "arrogantly repulsive neighbor" to the late Gothic Gunpowder Tower dating from the end of the fifteenth century.[19]

What most irritated architectural historicists about the modern style were probably the extensive, naked wall surfaces. "Note here," goes the ironic comment made in 1902 by the historicist Antonín Bráf on the modern approach: "how carefully I have managed to avoid all architectural tradition: to me, *avant-corps*, cornices, surrounds, and gables are symbols of antiquated, outdated attitudes. I shall simply surround the windows and doors with masonry and leave the 'calm' wall surfaces to be decorated with naturalistic motifs by the plasterer or painter."[20] In addition to painted decorations or figurative reliefs, modern architects adorned the bare walls with other features characteristic of the early modern style: metal awnings with glass inserts and metal railings whose elegant curves often followed the example of the art nouveau of Brussels and Paris. The most unique characteristic of the modern decorative repertoire was the ornamental plant motif with its "natural lines, shapes, and colors" as it was, a little clumsily, described by Kotěra in the review *Volné směry* in 1900. In the period between 1898 and 1906, these motifs, which were then used by prominent Prague architects, went through a noticeable transformation: from a more or less faithful imitation of plants they turned into strongly geometric patterns.

58

Quido Bělský, Bedřich Bendelmayer, Bohumil Hypšman, Jan Letzel. Hotel Evropa, staircase. Nové Město, Václavské náměstí 25. 1903–1905.

The interest of the modern movement in the world of plants and nature in general had, without doubt, a deeper symbolic meaning. It appears that this was an expression of the romanticism of the time, a visual representation of the myth of nature as a paradise,[21] which was seen as a place of refuge by the same people who only a few years earlier dreamt about the bygone world of the Prague Gothic, Renaissance, and baroque. The vision of spring, of nature in full bloom, symbolizing renewal, found its way to Prague from the circle around the Viennese modern review *Ver sacrum*. But the wider contemporary concept of nature as "life" and "reality," including the reality of physical laws to which nature is subject and which modern architecture — albeit timidly at first — tried to express, suggests also a different interpretation of naturalism in the modern movement. Already in 1899, the critic K. B. Mádl considered modern architecture to be a "realistic architecture" that sought a precise form for "the support and weight, their differences, transitions, and dimensions," and whose decorative aspect, sparse, precise and atmospheric, "found its point of departure in the real world."[22] It appears that the early modern attitude toward nature, or rather toward reality, was characterized by a certain duality: in it, romanticism mingled with realism, dreams with actuality.

At the same time, plant motifs helped modern architecture free itself from the decorative stereotypes of late historicism. The painter and architect Karel Vítězslav Mašek had the following explanation for the modern attitude: "Only the study of nature provides the opportunity for individual development."[23] Motifs adopted from folk architecture played a similar role at the beginning of the modern era. The most sought after expert in the use of these motifs was the Slovak architect Dušan Jurkovič (1868–1947), the author of the spa complex in Luhačovice in Eastern Moravia, who designed and built one of his typical family houses on Suchardova Street, 1907–1908. Elements adopted from folk timber architecture had, of course, been already used by some of the historicists. Jan Koula, for instance, allegedly used them for patriotic reasons, because "the log cabin style of building . . . is typical mainly for the Slavic nations."[24] At the same time, Koula welcomed folk motifs also as an idiosyncratic addition to his rich repertoire of styles. On the other hand, for the modernist Jan Kotěra who considered the works

61

Bedřich Bendelmayer. Apartment building. Staré Město,
U Prašné brány 1,3. 1903–1904.

of the late historicists as nothing but "false pseudoforms," folk architecture was the embodiment of natural qualities, of creativity that "has its origins in the blood."[25]

The early modern style incorporated the individual architectural elements into an open, inconclusive compositional framework often accentuated by the two characteristic Wagnerian pylons projecting above the line of the roof. The distinctive curved lines were applied everywhere: in the outlines of the buildings, in the shapes of the cornices, arches, railings of balconies and staircases, awnings and, above all, in the ornaments decorating the facade. To some extent, the modern style inherited these curves from the neobaroque style, but it is also possible to trace their origin to the art of the Far East, which strongly attracted artists like Toulouse-Lautrec, Beardsley, and Mucha. The Czech art historian Petr Wittlich offered a remarkable interpretation of this phenomenon in 1978.[26] In the S-shaped, curved lines of the modern style, he saw the expression of a "psychic current," of the "line of life," which, according to the painters, sculptors, and poets of the Czech modern movement, passed through people and things, linking them in an endless wave with a mythical past as well as with the future.

THE GEOMETRICAL MODERN STYLE

Following in the footsteps of its older Viennese sister, Prague's modern style went through considerable transformations in the period between 1906 and 1911. It was as if Kotěra's principles of truthfulness, constructiveness, and functionality, postulated already in 1900, had only now received full acceptance. Nature, which had so far been reflected on the facades of buildings in its sensuous, ornamental aspect, now appeared to offer architects its "physical" side. The intuitive world of natural myths gave way to a world of rationally abstracted tectonic forces, and the softly shaped silhouette was replaced with a solid, geometrically defined body. It is also in the context of this process of "geometrization" that we have to consider the first flat — or seemingly flat — roofs of new Prague buildings. The concept of a building as a "tectonic organism" — as it had been formulated by Wagner's disciple Antonín Engel[27] — led to an emphasis on its constructive elements and, in particular, on the physical supports and weights: pilasters, pillars, cornices, and pilaster-strips, which were often the only features retained from the inventory of traditional architectural devices. According to another of Wagner's pupils, Pavel Janák, even these few architectural elements were to be used so that they would "perform their function" as a "confirmation of necessity."[28] In place of the smooth, white planes of the early modern style, decorated with delicate ornamental motifs, appeared a rough brick surface, which was made popular by Berlage and Wright. Where architects did not dare to dispense entirely with ornament, they at least tried to make it as geometrical as possible by employing rectangular shapes. "The visual treatment of the facade is limited to the accentuation of certain constructive elements or even just to surface decoration which, however, always strictly follows the tectonic nature of the materials being used," was how Antonín Engel set down the principles of modern architectural decoration in 1911.[29]

Sculptural decoration of monumental buildings went through a similar process of geometrization. Allegory, which required an academically or naturalistically rendered human figure, no longer suited the constructive style and was therefore replaced with a strongly, almost architectonically stylized plastic symbol formally inspired by Egyptian, Assyrian, and Archaic Greek sculpture. The artistic significance of the transition from allegory to symbol was explained by the architect Otakar Novotný in *Volné směry* in 1915. According to Novotný, allegory "presupposes literary knowledge on the part of the viewer, which is vested in him, not in the allegory itself," whereas symbol has the capacity to make an impact by virtue of "its abstract power, on its own." The aesthetic experience of allegory is never "pure" or "entirely artistic"; each legend, explanation, or label—all indispensable to allegory—"obscures the artistic values."[30] The most original work of architecture designed in Prague in the spirit of modern symbolism was probably the villa in Mickiewiczova Street, built between 1910 and 1912 by its owner, the sculptor František Bílek (1872–1941), according to his own design. The elongated, flat-roofed body of the villa, elevated on a segment floor plan and rhythmically punctuated with swathes of slender columns resembling those of ancient Egyptian temples, symbolizes, according to Bílek's explanation in the review *Styl* (1911–1912), "a field of wheat . . . providing daily sustenance for our brothers."[31]

63

The leading figure in the development of Prague's geometrical style in modern architecture was again Jan Kotěra, who held the chair of architecture at the Prague Academy of Fine Arts from 1910 when he was appointed thanks to T. G. Masaryk's support.[32] Between 1906 and 1907, Kotěra's early "dreamy" expression gave way to the "masculine" style characteristic of the peak period in his creative career when his artistic program embraced the celebration of moral values: the pathos of naked truth was reflected in the uncovered tectonics and unrendered bricks of the building. The design of Kotěra's waterworks on Baarova Street, under construction from 1906, with its chalice-shaped silhouette and accentuated constructive elements of the brick tower, followed the Wagnerian principle of true expression of function. The building bears witness to Kotěra's interest in the contemporary vocabulary of industrial architecture and, of course, also in what had already been derived from it by Berlage. The inconspicuous Villa Kraus in Sibiřské Square, 1907, rediscovered only recently by the historian of architecture Zdeněk Lukeš, points to yet another source of Kotěra's new architectural language: the work of Josef Hoffmann and in particular his Viennese Hochstätter House, built in 1906, which held a special significance for Kotěra.

The key year in Kotěra's architectural career was probably 1908. It was then that he designed the museum buildings for the East Bohemian town of Hradec Králové, which became his most significant realized project.[33] In the same year, he built his own family villa on Hradešínská Street in Prague. The visual language of this building was limited to the perfect equilibrium achieved in its asymmetrical composition, in the precise and strictly functional placement of the small windows, and in the subtle color transition from the brick base to the rough rendering of the walls above. In Hoffmann's hands even such a laconic vocabulary would have been turned into a decorative device: the more austere, the more sophisticated. Kotěra, on the other hand, consistently tried to imbue his ascetic style with monumentality.

This intention is evident in the house Kotěra built in 1908 for the publisher Jan Laichter on Chopinova Street, which combined living quarters with office space for a small publishing venture. Laichter was at that time among the

65

František Bílek. Artist's own villa. Hradčany, Mickiewiczova 1.
1910–1911.

Following pages:

Jan Kotěra. Laichter's apartment and office building. Vinohrady, Chopinova 4. 1908–1909.

Jan Kotěra. Villa Kraus. Bubeneč, Sibiřské náměstí 5. 1907.

Jan Kotěra. Architect's own family villa. Vinohrady, Hradešínská 6. 1908–1909.

Jan Kotěra. Laichter's apartment and office building, living quarters, staircase hall. Vinohrady, Chopinova 4. 1908–1909.

The Modern Style in the Streets of Prague

closest friends of T. G. Masaryk and specialized in the publishing of philosophical, social reformist, and, above all, moralist writing, an interest suggested even by the austere look of his residence. The building seems to address the viewer directly through the forthright tectonics of its vertical and horizontal lines. Bare bricks, only at a closer look forming simple decorative patterns, a suspended block jutting forward from the body of the building, rough, unadorned walls and a flat roof: such were the puritanical and—in view of future developments—prophetic gestures Kotěra made in the same year that saw the construction of Polívka's and Balšánek's Municipal House.

The vocabulary employed in the design for the Laichter House reappeared in a somewhat diminutive and softer form in the semidetached house on Mickiewiczova Street, 1910–1911, the left half of which was built for another of Masaryk's friends, the government official Josef Groh. Between 1912 and 1913, this period of Kotěra's work reached its peak in the design for the monumental commercial building Mozarteum on Jungmannova Street, commissioned by the musical publisher Mojmír Urbánek. Standing ostentatiously apart from its neighbors, this was another austere building in which Kotěra achieved an expression of tectonic poetry. The frontal section of the Mozarteum is inserted into a monumental frame of reinforced concrete that supports a simply shaped pitched roof. On the flat roof of the lower back wing of the building, Kotěra intended to establish a small roof garden to serve as a terrace for Urbánek's apartment. The commercial section of the building, decorated with reliefs by the sculptor Jan Štursa, opens into the street through glass walls. The four brick-clad residential floors recede deeper and deeper into the reinforced concrete frame, with the result that the swaths of concrete pilaster-strips articulating this part of the facade widen accordingly.

Less revolutionary but still interesting were Kotěra's floor plans and spatial solutions of this period. Kotěra discarded the English staircase hall of his earlier designs (with the exception of the Laichter House), but retained his "opening with a vista." In his commentary on the pavilion designed for the 1904 Saint Louis World Exposition, Kotěra described a spatial type particularly char-

70

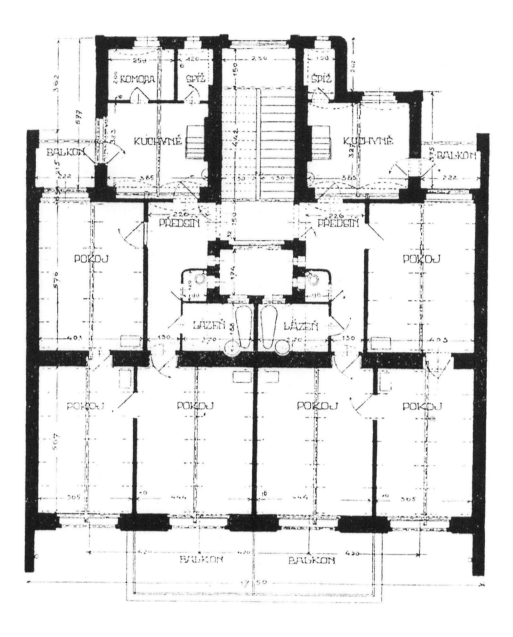

KOMORA SPÍŽ ŠPÍŽ

KUCHYNĚ KUCHYNĚ

BALKON BALKON

PŘEDSIŇ PŘEDSIŇ

POKOJ POKOJ

LÁZEŇ LÁZEŇ

POKOJ POKOJ POKOJ POKOJ

BALKON BALKON

71

Jan Kotěra. Laichter's apartment and office building, living
quarters, floor plan. Vinohrady, Chopinova 4. 1908–1909.

The Modern Style in the Streets of Prague

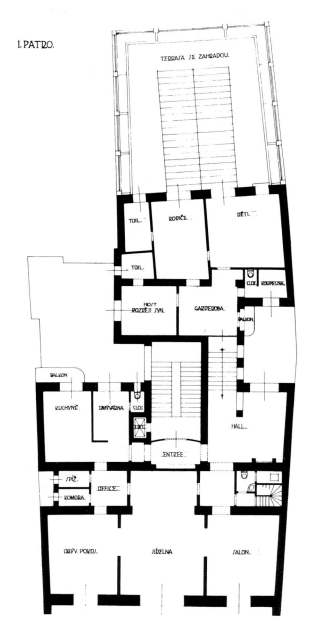

I. PATRO.

TERRASA SE ZAHRADOU.

TOIL.　RODIČE.　DĚTI.

TOIL.

CLOS. KOUPELNA.

HOST POZDĚJI SYN.　GARDEROBA.

BALKON.

BALKON

KUCHYNĚ.　UMÝVÁRNA.　CLOS.

LIFT

HALL.

ENTRÉE.

SPÍŽ.

OFFICE.

KOMORA.

OBÝV. POKOJ.　JÍDELNA.　SALON.

73

Jan Kotěra. Urbánek's Mozarteum Building. Nové Město,
Jungmannova 30. 1912–1913.

Jan Kotěra. Urbánek's Mozarteum Building, living quarters,
floor plan. Nové Město, Jungmannova 30. 1912–1913.

acteristic not only for his own designs but for the whole modern style, as a "central hall . . . situated in the middle of the villa and top-lit from an overhead source."[34] The models for this spatial type were most probably art galleries and artists' studios with the same overhead lighting arrangement. The intention was to provide the best illumination for the *Gesamtkunstwerk* of modern art and craft, and it was with this vision in mind that Kotěra's contemporaries, artists, and intellectuals, designed their apartments. Judging from archival photographs, the drawing room in Kotěra's own family house provided the best example of such intimately enclosed space. The light from the overhead milk glass window fills the room with a mystical and enigmatic atmosphere that sets it apart from its "secular" exterior. A painting by Jan Preisler on the wall and a heavy suite designed by Kotěra contribute to the ambience of the room.

The floor plan of these buildings retained the three-bay layout. The living quarters were mostly lined up along one side of the apartment—in Kotěra's own villa they all face the garden; in the case of Laichter's and Urbánek's villa, they face the street. In the latter building, this layout inspired Kotěra to make large openings in the partitions separating individual rooms—the dining, living, and drawing rooms—bringing them together in a rhythmically organized spatial whole. Space, the creation of which Kotěra discussed in *Volné směry* already in 1900, gradually became an independent artistic medium, and as such it began to compete in significance with the decoration of walls and with the tectonic, constructive aspects of a building, which probably still played the main role in the geometrical modern style. Once awakened, space gradually asserted itself, and, apart from bringing about further integration of the interior, it expanded outward, uniting the active space of the interior with the exterior. The bodies of Kotěra's buildings were still too material, too solid to allow such an expansion. However, the open ground floor and the band window on the first floor of the Mozarteum suggest future developments in this direction.

This new architectural problem was tackled even more vigorously by Otakar Novotný (1880–1959), one of Kotěra's most gifted students, whose major Prague building was the house of the art publisher Jan Štenc in Sal-

Jan Kotěra. Architect's own family villa, drawing room.
Vinohrady, Hradešínské 6. 1908–1909.

vátorská Street (1909–1911). Its elongated facade rendered in red brick is divided into two independent sections, each with its own rhythm of fenestration. Except for the rounded glass awning above the main cornice, the unifying element is the ground floor blind arcade, this time finished in white bricks, which are also used on the columns in the vestibule and on the staircase. In the interior, the graphic design studio provides an element of surprise: its large space is horizontally divided by means of a gallery, and it opens into the courtyard through an ample elongated window. In his study "Shody a rozpory" (Harmonies and Dissonances), written in 1915 and influenced by his reading of the outstanding German historian of architecture Paul Frankl (1879–1962), Otakar Novotný speaks of the "aerial form of space" and "aerial space filled with life," "the organism of space," "live space," and "the spirit of space."[35] A statement from the same study — namely, that if space is

Otakar Novotný. Štenc Building. Staré Město, Salvátorská 8, 10. 1909–1911.

Otakar Novotný. Štenc Building, view from the courtyard. Staré Město, Salvátorská 8, 10. 1909–1911.

Otakar Novotný. Štenc Building, graphic designers' studio.
Staré Město, Salvátorská 8, 10. 1909–1911.

*Otakar Novotný. Štenc Building, courtyard. Staré Město,
Salvátorská 8, 10. 1909–1911.*

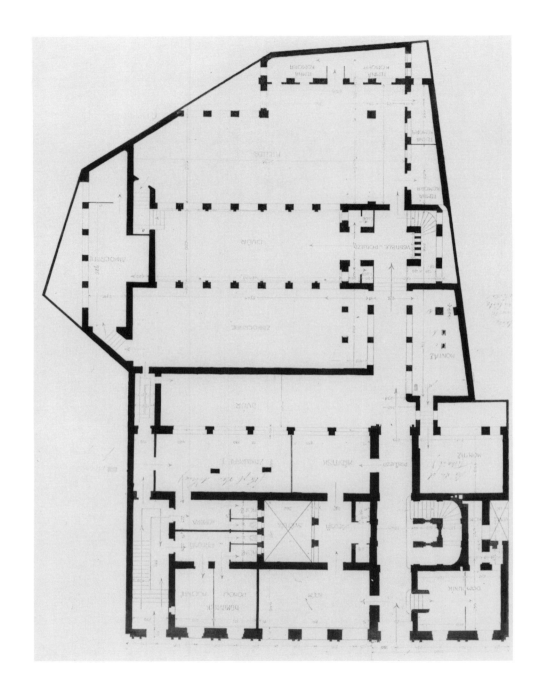

Otakar Novotný. Štenc Building, floor plan. Staré Město,
Salvátorská 8, 10. 1909–1911.

"indeed created as aerial space, then the bounding elements lose their importance," could serve as a theoretical parallel of the open type of space as it can be seen in the Štenc House design studio.

The designs produced in this period for various Prague locations by Josef Gočár (1880–1945), another outstanding pupil of Kotěra, were never realized, probably due to their daringly provocative artistic spirit. There are, however, two works outside Prague that attest to Gočár's remarkable talent. One is the reinforced concrete staircase to the Church of the Virgin Mary in the historical center of Hradec Králové, 1910; the other is the Wenke department store in the nearby East Bohemian town of Jaroměř, 1910–1911, with its glass facade projecting from the body of the building on cross-beams. In 1901, the Prague public was shocked by Gočár's project for the completion of the Old Town City Hall, conceived as an abruptly receding stepped pyramid. "My City Hall substantially changes the skyline of the Old Town," Gočár admitted innocently — and probably even with some pride — in *Styl*, the architectural review promoting the modern movement in architecture.[36] Other former students of Kotěra — Antonín Pfeiffer, Bohumil Waigant, Jaroslav Vondrák, Jan and Josef Mayer — enjoyed relative success with their buildings in Prague, partly due to the fact that in comparison with Gočár, their designs were less radical.

Apart from Kotěra and his school, the geometrical modern style was embraced by some of his younger contemporaries who had also studied under Wagner at the Vienna Academy. Among the works of the prolific architect Bohumil Hypšman (1878–1961), one worth mentioning is the Matějovský building on Národní Street, 1910–1912, notable for its facade articulated by means of three cylindrical projections that penetrate the overhanging main cornice. A similar formal elementarism and related chessboard detail characterized his Jewish Funeral Brotherhood apartment building on Široká Street, 1910–1911. The outstanding town planner Antonín Engel (1879–1958) designed only two realized buildings before the first world war: the apartment block in the street U starého hřbitova, 1910–1911, with its extremely austere, dryly schematic surface decorations and the family house on the neighboring Břehová Street, 1913–1915, which gave the im-

pression of having been assembled from solid blocks. Similarly reserved was the apartment building designed by another of Wagner's students who worked in Prague, František Roith (1876–1942), on the corner of Dřevná Street and Rašín Embankment, 1911–1912.

A special position among Wagner's disciples was held by Pavel Janák (1882–1956), an outstanding theoretician of architecture whose thinking at that time revolved around the idea of the visual harnessing of functional and constructive elements. In 1909, he entered the Old Town City Hall competition with one of the most successful projects based on the traditional motif of a light, floating renaissance *loggia*, which embraced the whole northwest corner of Old Town Square, being traced by a beveled, richly decorated cornice situated just under the roof. It was, however, in the rebuilding of Hlávka Bridge, 1909–1911, that Janák's control over construction became fully evident. The sensitive decorations and the flowing curves of the bridge, as remodeled by Janák, capture not the external face but the "spirit" of the early lyrical phase of Wagnerian modern style.

82

Josef Gočár. Competition project for the completion of Old Town City Hall. 1909.

Bohumil Hypšman. Jewish Funeral Brotherhood apartment building with the Jewish Cemetery in the foreground. Josefov, Široká 5, 7. 1910–1911.

In 1911, two schools of architecture in Prague subscribed to the modern style: Kotěra's Special School at the Academy of Fine Arts and the Department of Architecture at the School of Applied Arts, headed from 1911 by one of the best known students of Wagner and a close friend of Kotěra, Josip Plečnik.[37] Yet, at the Prague Polytechnic the architectural course remained so conservative, that, as late as 1914, it was described by Josef Chochol, who had graduated from there and who later also studied under Wagner, as a "seedbed of diehard reaction." Nevertheless, it was the same conservative attitude and respect for good manners that made the Polytechnic professors tolerate the excesses of their students, many of whom became interested in the modern style while still undergraduates and turned into enthusiastic supporters of the style when they left the school. Among others, they were Theodor Petřík, Rudolf Stockar, Vladislav

Pavel Janák. Competition project for the completion of Old Town City Hall. 1909.

Martínek, Bohumil Kozák and Josef Rosipal (d. 1915) whose cubic, flat-roofed building of the orphanage on Milady Horákové Street, 1912–1913, showed that he had mastered the fine points of Hoffmann's Viennese style with confidence that could have been envied even by the students of Wagner.

Some interesting buildings in the geometrical modern style were designed also by architects of the older generation, for instance the graduates from Ohmann's course Alois Dryák, Bedřich Bendelmayer, and Ladislav Skřivánek, and by builders and developers such as Václav Havel (grandfather of the playwright and current president), František Novotný, Josef Kovařovic, and Matěj Blecha, whose buildings still impress with their artistic quality and conceptual boldness. In the years 1907 to 1921, Václav Havel built the grandiose Lucerna Palace, situated between Vodičkova and Štěpánská, with its stunning internal arcade lined on both

85

Pavel Janák. Hlávka Bridge. Holešovice. 1909–1912.

sides with shops and cafés. Among the best designs by Matěj Blecha (and, of course, the architects who worked for his firm during this period), was the Kalous pharmacy in Wenceslas Square, 1911–1913, a successful imitation of Kotěra's style, and the large Šupich Building on the corner of Wenceslas Square and Štěpánská Street, 1913–1916. Otakar Novotný criticized the latter building in 1915 in the review *Volné směry*, describing it as an "architectural monster . . . a huge colossus in a repulsively inflated pose,"[38] but it seems that his criticism was not entirely justified. Despite its colossal scale, the front of the building is skilfully and rhythmically articulated. Its most remarkable feature, however, is the machinist corner with a cupola resembling a huge ball bearing.

       In its first years, the influence of the modern style in Prague was limited to designs for individual buildings. This did not mean, however, that

Josef Rosipal. Orphanage. Hradčany, Milady Horákové 139.
1912–1913.

Matěj Blecha, Petr Kropáček. Šupich Building. Nové Město,
Václavské náměstí 38. 1913–1916.

Prague modernists were not interested in treatments of larger urban areas or that they did not have their own concept of urbanism. In the redevelopment of inner city areas with continuous blocks of buildings, they were guided by the views of Otto Wagner, who routinely assigned all his students tasks in town planning, and they would later apply Wagner's principles when working in Prague.

Wagner's urbanistic program, set out in his books *Moderne Archi-tektur*, 1895, and *Die Großstadt*, 1911, was characterized by rationalism. Contrary to the principle of picturesqueness of winding, medieval streets, promoted by Sitte and Gurlitt, it returned to a strict geometrical order of the street network, to which the additional squares, porticos, arcades, tree-lined avenues, and pavilions were secondary features, designed merely to brighten up the grid system.

Wagner's second book provoked a polemical response from Cornelius Gurlitt himself. This polemic had its impact in Prague as well, where in 1911 Wagner's student Josef Chochol, seemingly impartial but making his con-tribution with remarkable precision, gave an account of Gurlitt's objections against the excessive uniformity of Wagner's vision of the modern metropolis.[39] On the other hand, Vladimír Zákrejs (1880–1948), the civic engineer, town planner, and graduate of the Prague Polytechnic, accepted this new uniformity as a historical necessity, required—as Wagner had already stated—by the democratic nature of social life of the time. Yet, according to Zákrejs, the modern urbanist should also be an artist, so that this "new necessary uniformity" does not become a mere stereo-type in his hands, but acquires aspects of monumentality.[40] Town planning proj-ects of the Prague-based students of Wagner—Jan Kotěra, Bohumil Hypšman, Antonín Engel, and Pavel Janák—which focused on the redevelopment of the embankments along the Vltava river and on the area connecting Staré Město with Letná, surely possessed such monumentality but none of them had been realized during the prewar period. The real era of Wagnerian urbanism did not start in Prague until 1918.

The views of modern urbanism on how to deal with the outer, not as densely built-up areas of Prague, fared only slightly better. In this respect, a pivotal role was played by the theory of garden cities, developed at the turn of the

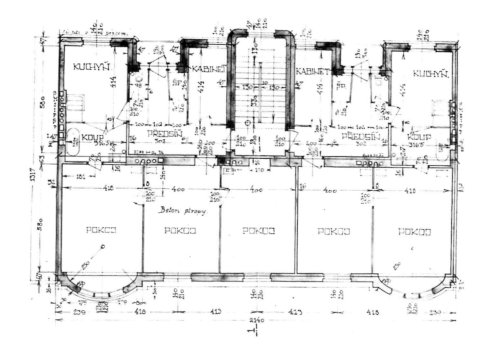

century by English architects and social reformers Ebenezer Howard and Raymond Unwin and made popular on the Continent by the German architect Hermann Muthesius (1861–1927). The starting point of this theory was the critical attitude of social reformers toward large industrial cities with their inadequate transport facilities and sanitary and social conditions, against which the urbanists posed the ideal of small satellite towns with family houses surrounded by gardens. Garden suburbs with villas had been, of course, already established by the historicists. In Prague, the first garden suburbs grew during the last two decades of the nineteenth century in Bubeneč, Vinohrady, Strašnice, and Smíchov. Although Jan Koula, for example, imagined Bubeneč as a "*villeggiatura* . . . of family houses for the affluent,"[41] the social aims of the modern garden city were far more democratic, at least in theory. In 1912, Rudolf Stockar characterized the garden city in the review *Styl* as a settlement designed for the neediest classes as well as for those

František Velich, Jan Žák. Apartment buildings, apartment floor plan. Hradčany, Na valech 24–28. 1912–1914.

The Modern Style in the Streets of Prague

with lower income, the clerical and working classes, and he considered it essential that a garden city should be established on publicly owned land "so that any exploitation of the property market is excluded once for all."[42]

In this case, however, theory clashed with practice. As could have been expected, the garden cities actually built in Prague in the twenties were occupied by the middle class rather than workers—and the situation was no different in Great Britain or in Germany. Prior to World War I, and in spite of vigorous promotion of garden cities, there was only one such complex built in Prague, which in its formal—but not social—aspect came close to the British ideal. This was the part of Hradčany around the former Bruská Gate, between Mariánské hradby, Tychonova, and Na valech streets. The building plan for this area, at that time an important center of Prague's intellectual and artistic life, was developed by the employees of the Municipal Construction Authority, Vladimír Zákrejs and Vlastislav Hofman, in 1911, and among the architects who designed the individual houses were also Kotěra, Gočár, Stockar, Petřík, and František Bílek. As with Muthesius's projects, the Hradčany garden city has an interesting asymmetrical layout that traces the lines of the former baroque fortifications. Following British examples, the family houses were usually linked by continuous terraces.

Under the northern edge of this settlement called U Bruské brány, on Na valech Street, the architects František Velich and Jan Žák built in 1912 to 1914 two apartment blocks in which modern architecture offered one more essential answer to the question of residential buildings. The relatively conventional facades designed in typical geometrical modern style conceal a remarkable floor plan. The motto "air and light," which had long figured in the vocabulary of Prague architects without prompting any particular changes in the basic apartment layout, made Velich and Žák abandon the traditional three-bay plan, with its core lacking in fresh air and natural light, and replace it with a two-bay one, in which all the rooms have natural light, either from the street or from the inner courtyard. The central bay was reduced to a small entrance hall that, although still hidden in the interior of the apartment, was directly connected with the outside by means of large balcony openings, which were also used to duct out bathroom

ventilation. Finally, the living quarters were designed so that the longer side always faced the street. The new blocks also had an innovative town-planning aspect. The architects enlarged their perimeter to achieve a more spacious and better ventilated central courtyard, where they placed small playgrounds in the midst of greenery. Such use of the building site, implying a smaller percentage of apartment space, was, of course, not very attractive to property developers, who simply continued to employ the three-bay floor plan. Velich's and Žák's experiment, which was hardly surpassed by later developments in apartment layout design, made little impact until after 1918, and even then it was used only in the building of government-sponsored estates or those financed by wealthy housing cooperatives.

The rationalist, geometrical second phase of architectural modern style suggested several logical developmental possibilities. Already before 1910, there was a tendency toward a traditionalist interpretation. The formal aspects connected with this line of thought readily fused with classical elements, particu-

91

František Velich, Jan Žák. Apartment buildings. Hradčany, Na valech 24–28. 1912–1914.

larly of the neobaroque and neoclassicist strain, and in place of the abstract "supports and weights," the buildings designed by former exponents of the geometrical modern style now displayed classical features such as tympanums, porticoes, columns, and pilasters with heads. The work of Josef Zasche, probably the most outstanding architect of Prague's German enclave, best illustrates this tendency. Zasche had studied under Wagner's predecessor at the Vienna Academy, Karl von Hasenauer, who favored the neo-Renaissance style, but he followed with interest the beginnings of the Viennese modern movement and quickly accepted Wagner's and Hoffmann's influence. The review *Volné směry* was right in commending Zasche's Vienna Bank Union Building in Na příkopě, 1906–1908, as being "noble in its simplicity, magnificent in its proportions."[43] The building's shiny stone-clad facade and beautiful white-and-gold interior became the first success of the geometrical modern style in Prague. Czech architects were, however, also quick to notice Zasche's return to the tradition of neoclassicism, most probably inspired by Hoffmann, which was in the following years combined with an interest in other historical styles and which before World War I unfolded into a particularly heavy, baroque-inspired variety of classicism.

Another potential direction for the future of the geometrical modern style, apparent during the preWar period, consisted in strengthening its constructivist aspects and in emphasizing the concept of architecture as a "tectonic organism" to which the exterior, with its accentuated tectonic features, was entirely subjected. This tendency had its starting point in Kotěra's Laichter House, as well as in the Hlava Institute of Pathology on Studničkova Street, 1913–1920, the work of a graduate of the Vienna Polytechnic, Alois Špalek (1883–1940). The front of the building facing the street has the air of a baroque palace, but the rear of this medical institution surprises the viewer with its large, metal-framed bay windows, the twenty-meter-wide ribbon windows of the autopsy rooms, and with its overall functional constructivist approach. After World War I, this approach found many followers among Prague architects who held little enthusiasm for the puristic and functional "new architecture" but who nonetheless wished to be seen as modern.

93

Josef Zasche. Vienna Bank Union. Staré Město, Na příkopě 1.
1906–1908.

*Josef Zasche, Alexander Neumann. Vienna Bank Union,
interior. Staré Město, Na příkopě 1. 1906–1908.*

94

Alois Špalek. Hlava Institute of Pathology. Nové Město,
Studničkova 2, 4. 1913–1921.

The Modern Style in the Streets of Prague

Yet another interpretation of the geometrical nature of Wagnerian modern style was presented by Pavel Janák. According to Janák, this style consisted in penetrating "as far as the unchangeable core of things," that is, to the geometrical forms of the prism and the cube, "the very essence of all forms."[44] This "Cézannesque," or neo-Platonic, interpretation of the geometrical modern style, whose ideological background has not as yet been sufficiently researched, contained the possibility that the architect might attempt to express the very essence of a given form without its tectonic skeleton, that he would imagine the geometrical form as entirely pure and bare. This approach may provide the basis for understanding the unrealized yet remarkable design for the Podolí Sanatorium, produced in 1909–1910 by Janák's friend, Josef Gočár. The compositional components of this building were smooth, white, cubical bodies with flat tops. When working on this project, Gočár most probably had in mind the similarly smooth and white walls of the sanatorium designed by Hoffmann for Purkersdorf, 1903–1904, but also the idea that the color of the building should contrast with the brick background of the baroque fortifications of Vyšehrad. However, Gočár's innovative contribution consists mainly in the functionally asymmetrical composition of the whole building—which had already been promoted by Kotěra—and also in details that appear to anticipate future developments, such as the ribbon window of the tower, the slanted concrete awning above the main entrance, and the round windows on the highest floors of the three large pavilions. Gočár's project remained rather isolated, and only five years later did Josef Chochol take it as a point of departure in several drawings of facades and factories. Its artistic significance, however, was not absorbed by Prague architecture in general until the 1920s.

The parallels between some of the buildings designed in the geometrical modern style on the one hand, and purist and functionalist architecture of the twenties on the other, make some art historians date the beginnings of the purist-functionalist era as far back as the end of the first decade of the twentieth century. The main argument in support of this hypothesis about "purism and functionalism appearing in architecture already prior to World War I"[45] is usually found in the prewar designs of Walter Gropius (1883–1969), whose architecture of

metal and glass was truly remarkable in its anticipation of future developments. One could also point to the work of the Viennese Adolf Loos (1870–1933) and the Californian Irving Gill (1870–1936), who first presented completely bare, unadorned, flat-roofed buildings that similarly pointed to future directions in architecture. In one of the first publications of the Czech purist-functionalist avant-garde, the anthology *Život II* (Life, 1922),[46] a photograph of Kotěra's own villa appears, and the first volume of the functionalist journal *Stavba* (Construction), published in the same year, featured Špalek's Institute of Pathology.

Although it cannot be denied that some projects designed by Prague's modern architects, in particular Gočár's Podolí sanatorium, were in their time true architectures of the future, on the whole, Prague's geometrical modern had by no means created a distinctly new style. Its individual gestures pointing toward functionalism had not yet succeeded in producing a new stylistic quality. In its totality, the stylistic character of the geometrical modern style, including the work of the assertive circle around Kotěra, undeniably sets it apart from functionalism. Against its own constructiveness and materiality stood the dematerialization and spatialism of purist-functionalist architecture; against the concept of architect's work as an individual manifestation of generally applicable architectural laws stood the functionalist bias toward typization and standardization; against architecture as art stood architecture as science. But, above all, there was a stylistic hiatus between Prague's geometrical modern style and the purist-functionalist "new architecture," the meaning of which consisted not in the logical development of the modern style but in its fundamental negation.

97

Josef Gočár. Competition project for Podolí Sanatorium.
1909–1910.

2 THE PRISM AND THE PYRAMID

The works designed by Jan Kotěra, Josef Gočár, Otokar Novotný, and Pavel Janák in the first decade of the twentieth century brought Czech modern architecture into contact with the latest European architectural trends of the time. But its great moment, the time when it would create its own modern architectural style instead of merely reworking foreign influences, was yet to come. Around 1909, opposition to Jan Kotěra was being articulated by some of the modernist architects of Prague whose spokesman was Pavel Janák, a reflective yet clear-thinking architect who also possessed a great educational talent. In 1910 Janák became convinced, as he wrote in the architectural magazine *Styl*, that the austere vocabulary of Wagner's and Kotěra's architecture no longer corresponded to the requirements of contemporary aesthetics and sensibility. The modern movement — or more precisely the geometrical modern style — was in Janák's view too sterile, too socially aware, too subservient to the common good, and therefore too utilitarian, materialistic, and constructive in character. Its materialism lacked spiritual values and beauty.[1]

When Janák formulated his program of opposition in 1910, he apparently aimed at enriching Kotěra's austere, geometrical style with elements that would be more poetic, expressive, and dramatic. Janák's and Gočár's designs for the completion of the Old Town City Hall, 1909, in which oblique and curved forms became more prominent at the expense of the purity of Wagner's and Kotěra's *Kistenstil*, were certainly already approaching this notion of a richer and more expressive modern style. The same notion also started gaining currency in the contemporary designs of Vlastislav Hofman,[2] and, above all, in the work of Josip Plečnik,[3] who succeeded Kotěra at the Prague School of Applied Arts, and whom Janák respected as an "artist of the plastic form ... an exotic and unorthodox romantic." Later events that revolutionized the Prague art world had a fairly reductive effect on Janák's originally much broader program. The key players in these events were the young Prague painters Bohumil Kubišta and Emil Filla and the sculptor Otto Gutfreund, who had become acquainted with the cubism of Picasso and Braque during their time in Paris in 1910–1911 and gradually began applying cubist elements to their own expressionistically oriented work. Between 1910 and 1914, their friend, the Vienna-educated art historian Vincenc Kramář, acquired one of the most beautiful collections of Picasso's and Braque's cubist paintings from the Paris dealers Clovis Sagot and Henry Kahnweiler.[4] And it was on the platform of cubism — initially called "New Primitivism" or simply "New Art" — that in 1911 Filla, Gutfreund, Kramář, and others founded the *Skupina výtvarných umělců* (The Group of Visual Artists), an association that was also joined by the architects Janák, Gočár, Chochol, and Hofman.

Janák's idiosyncratic interpretation of cubism made him exclude from his conception of the new architecture all elements that had so far provided a link with the geometrical modern style, leaving only those that he, together with Gočár and Hofman, initially used to enrich their own expressive style. "The modern will instinctively limits its own formal means" — was how the second theorist of the nascent style, Vlastislav Hofman, described this reductive process in *Umělecký měsíčník* (Art Monthly), a magazine published by the *Skupina* — "but at the same time it places an even stronger emphasis on the logic of form."[5] And so the orthogonality of the geometric modern style came to be replaced by a system whose logic of form consisted of a diagonal or triangular compositional plan, and the Wagnerian cubes gave way to tapered quadrilaterals, pyramids, and all kind of slanted forms. In his article "Hranol a Pyramida" (The Prism and the Pyramid), published in *Umělecký měsíčník* in 1912, Pavel Janák put forward the thesis that the orthogonal and constructive character of the geometrical modern style reflected its dependence on matter and its weight, whereas the new cubist style with its pyramids and slanted angles expressed the active nature of the human spirit and its ability to prevail over matter and creatively transform it.[6] In Janák's vision, matter figured as a monolithic, passive, dead substance, and it was not appropriate to emphasize its surface texture, let alone decorate it, whereas in Kotěra's work the same surface was still quite varied. It was the artist's creativity that invested this dead substance with spirit, reshaped it by means of various indentations and fractures, wrestled with it, even wished to destroy it, as Janák's friend, the sculptor Otto Gutfreund, wrote in an unpublished text.

Cubist architects were aware that mere transposition of the cubist approaches from painting into architecture would give their style a far too calcu-

101

lated impression. For this reason, they emphasized in their texts the contemporary spiritual climate as the source of their architectural designs, trying to convince both themselves and the public that these designs were produced in accordance with the evolutionary laws about which they had read in the writings of the German art theoretician Wilhelm Worringer or of the great Austrian art historian, Alois Riegl (1858–1905). The extraordinary ability of cubist architecture to integrate harmoniously with historically valuable parts of Prague and other Bohemian cities provided a strong argument in contemporary discussions on cubist architecture. Janák, Gočár, Chochol, and Hofman were all active members of the *Klub za starou Prahu* (Club in Support of Old Prague), an association of Czech artists and intellectuals that was formed in 1900 in protest against the planned modernization of Staré Město and Josefov. These architects would submit to the club's general assembly projects for the renovation of relevant historical buildings and monuments, and, in time, they became experts in this particular field. In their work, of course, they rejected the imitation of historical buildings and styles: Janák, for instance, declared such practice to be "highly immoral," and the other cubists hardly differed in their views. But they concentrated all the more on the study of architectural traditions through which they would achieve an understanding of universal laws of architecture on which they could draw in their work.

Pavel Janák, the ideological leader of Prague's architectural cubism, stood at that time closest to the tradition of the dynamic style of Prague baroque, to "that turning and bending of whole forms from their original, still, classical position into positions which went against the core of the building in an oblique and dramatic fashion."[7] Janák attempted to reconcile this baroque "manipulation of matter" with lessons learned from Picasso's analytical cubism, which captured his imagination both with its deconstruction of objects into slanted facets and with the way in which cubist painters wrapped space around these objects. Janák's ideas about matter diluted by space are most eloquently expressed in his essay "O nábytku a jiném" (On Furniture and Other Matters) in which he wrote about architectural surface that, with its cubist folds, fractures, and waves, became a "mixture of the matter existing inside and the space on the outside."[8] Janák then

102

Pavel Janák. Competition project for the Žižka Memorial on
Vítkov Hill. 1913.

The Prism and the Pyramid

put his ideas into practice in his suburban villas, in his monuments, and in the townhouses built for enlightened country intellectuals in Jičín, Kutná Hora, and particularly in Pelhřimov, where in 1913–1914 he rebuilt an old baroque house standing in the town's historical square in the style of baroque-inspired cubism. In Prague, however, Janák did not succeed in making a name as an architect, and he was known there only as a designer of cubist furniture, lighting, and ceramics, and perhaps as the author of unrealized cubist projects. The best known of these was the design for a memorial to the Hussite military leader Jan Žižka (d. 1424) to be located on the hill of Vítkov, which Janák submitted in an open competition in 1913. Other architects who participated with their cubist projects were Gočár, Hofman, and the young Bedřich Feuerstein. The compositional basis of Janák's design was a large pyramid on a rectangular base penetrated from above by another pyramid placed on its point. The longer sides of the monument were faceted to form the characteristic mixture of space and matter, and in the narrower frontal space Janák placed a figure of Jan Žižka, rendered in cubist style.

Characteristic of Janák's designs were the dominant, horizontally elongated facades that served to convey the idea that it is precisely the facade and its spatially modeled surface that should express the content of the building's inner space. This thesis was expounded in Janák's essay "Obnova průčelí" (Renewal of the Facade).[9] The second significant Prague cubist architect, Vlastislav Hofman (1884–1964), was on the other hand convinced that architectural space should not be denied any of its three dimensions, and this three-dimensional spatial sensibility is evident in his designs in which forms are based on a central ground plan as regular or elongated polygons. If Janák felt an affinity with the baroque, Hofman was more attuned to the Gothic style, which he valued for its constructive qualities. He was also interested in simple neoclassical buildings and in industrial architecture in which he admired the "clear, almost sharp expression."[10] The only one of Hofman's cubist projects ever realized was the wall and the gate of the Prague municipal cemetery on Ďáblická Street, 1912–1915, and even this project was considerably simplified in comparison with the original design. Its twin kiosks were inspired by a type of Gothic central chapel, and the gate in the middle illustrated

Pavel Janák. Study for a facade. 1912.

The Prism and the Pyramid

106

Vlastislav Hofman. Cemetery gate. Ďáblice, Ďáblická Street.
1912–1914.

Vlastislav Hofman. Cemetery gate. Ďáblice, Ďáblická Street.
1912–1914.

what a powerful subject the simplest concrete architrave could become in the hands of a cubist architect.

Although Hofman spoke of his interest in neoclassical architecture, it was not evident in his designs. When he noted the influence of the "traditional, heavy neoclassicism"[11] in the cubist works of Josef Gočár, he perceptively captured their unusual blend of style, which in Gočár's hands rarely resulted in a contradictory appearance. Unlike other Czech cubists, Gočár never wrote about his own work, nor did he formulate any theories. But when interviewed about a cubist project for a spa building in the country town of Bohdaneč and about the landscaping of its surroundings, he admitted that the inspiration for this design came from the neoclassical architecture of Františkovy Lázně, the West Bohemian spa town made famous by Goethe.[12] Gočár's two cubist designs that were realized in Prague also reveal the same source of inspiration. The double family house on Tychonova Street, 1912–1913, a white building with a smooth facade free of the usual cubist distortions, displays two porticoes, to which the aedicules of the entrances, with their cubist indentations and triangles, appear to have been added almost as an afterthought. A magnificent achievement of Prague cubism was Gočár's Black Madonna Building, 1911–1912, placed in a prominent position in a small square between the historical spaces of Ovocný trh (Fruitmarket) and Celetná Street. The cubist aesthetic of triangles and pyramids is echoed in the pyramidal outline of the building, its split facade, and in the many masterly details, while the fluted columns between the third-floor windows and the whole composition of the main cornice give a neoclassical impression. At the same time the building does not conceal its skeletal character inherited from Kotěra's modern style, or the architect's interest in open space, which flows freely into the building through the large windows.

However, the most impressive cubist buildings in Prague were built by Josef Chochol (1880–1956), the wayward and slightly eccentric student of Otto Wagner. The form of his cubist designs was determined by the means of a sparse, rhythmically set out grid in which Chochol marked the points where the surface of his facade would be fractured. This principle had not yet been fully

Josef Gočár. Family duplex. Hradčany, Tychonova 4, 6. 1912–1913.

Following pages: *Josef Gočár. Black Madonna Building. Staré Město, Ovocný*
trh 19. 1912.

Josef Gočár. Black Madonna Building, entrance. Staré Město,
Ovocný trh 19. 1912.

The Prism and the Pyramid

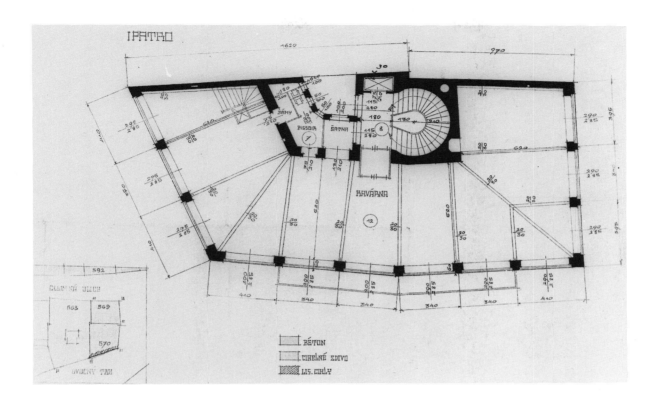

*Josef Gočár. Staircase in the Black Madonna Building. Staré
Město, Ovocný trh 19. 1912.*

*Josef Gočár. Black Madonna Building, floor plan. Staré
Město, Ovocný trh 19. 1912.*

The Prism and the Pyramid

Josef Chochol. Family house triplex, Vyšehrad, Rašínovo nábřeží 6–10. 1912–1913.

Josef Chochol. Family house triplex. František Hodek's house. Vyšehrad, Rašínovo nábřeží 10. 1912–1913.

117

*Josef Chochol. Villa Kovařovič. Vyšehrad, Libušina 3. 1912–
1913.*

*Josef Chochol. Villa Kovařovič, side facade. Vyšehrad,
Libušina 3. 1912–1913.*

The Prism and the Pyramid

developed in his family-house triplex on Rašín Embankment, 1912–1913, de-signed along the lines of a baroque palace with central *avant-corps* and gables. In his design for the villa on Libušina Street, 1912–1913, Chochol achieved an almost crystalline purity, and in the apartment block on Neklanova Street, 1913–1914, he boldly added further complexity to his original conception. The buildings on Rašín Embankment and on Neklanova Street with their predominantly vertical layout give the overall impression of giant pilaster order. Chochol paid particular atten-tion to the shaping of the basement facets and of the monumental main cornice. The slender column of the corner balcony looks as if it had been transferred from some late Gothic church, complete with the appropriate fragment of a diamond vault.[13]

The jagged formations of cubist buildings primarily reflect the imaginary struggle of the cubist architect with matter. However, they were also the outcome of speculative thinking about the optical effect of a building whose sur-

Josef Chochol. Villa Kovařovič, garden gate. Vyšehrad, Libušina 3. 1912–1913.

faces, according to Janák's principle of "frontality,"[14] turn outward to face several frontal and side views simultaneously, and to be fragmented and distorted in the same way as objects represented by analytical cubism. The facets of Chochol's facades turn frontally when viewed obliquely from the left, right, as well as from below, and in a similar way, Gočár's facade of the Black Madonna Building splits under the pressure of two lateral views. Unlike Kotěra's geometrical modern style, in which buildings were constructed in accordance with objective physical laws, architectural cubism turned the building into a subjectively viewed phenomenon.

No matter how we explain the origin of cubist distortions, it seems clear that the effectiveness of cubist buildings stems from qualities other than those affected by mere optical tricks. The perceptive viewer was probably able to appreciate their capacity for nonimitative evocation of the Gothic, baroque, or neoclassical styles, but would have been most immediately addressed by their ability to express certain moods, emotions, and concepts characteristic of the time, through more or less abstract configurations of forms. In 1912, Pavel Janák spoke of the possibility of evoking "dramatic feelings" through the use of oblique and pyramidal cubist forms.[15] At the same time, Vlastislav Hofman was reflecting on the "new content of emotional poetry that lives inside forms,"[16] and Josef Chochol, who in 1913 translated texts by Theodor Lipps, an important exponent of the German "aesthetic of empathy," for the architectural journal *Styl*, declared on the pages of the same journal his partiality for the "excitedly felt and presented overall form."[17]

These ideas, as well as their manifestations in the work of Prague architects, placed Czech architectural cubism close to other architectural directions of that period, such as the work of the Dutch group *Wendingen*, Italian and Russian futurism, and above all, the architecture of German expressionism that was developing around the same time. Cubist architects first heard about expressionist architecture in 1914, in relation to the Werkbund Exhibition in Cologne. However, information about Czech architectural cubism appeared in German art magazines several months earlier. In 1913, the Berlin-based expressionist critic Victor Wallerstein reported extensively on Janák's and Gočár's work in the magazine *Kunstge-*

120

Josef Chochol. Project for Hodek's apartment building.
Vyšehrad, Neklanova 30. 1913.

Josef Chochol. Hodek's apartment building. Vyšehrad,
Neklanova 30. 1913–1914.

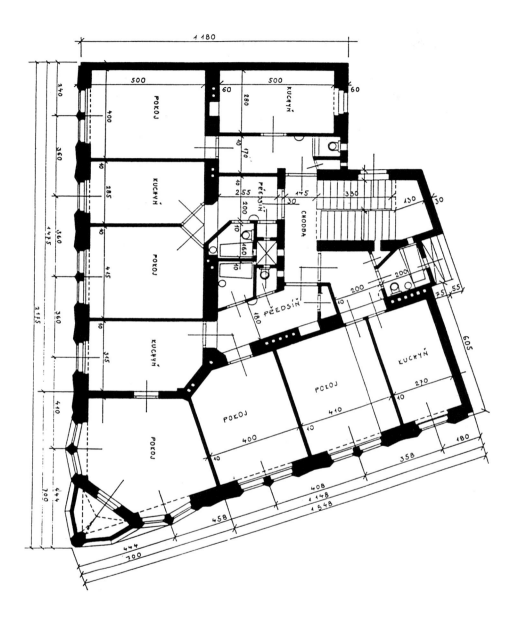

123

Josef Chochol. Hodek's apartment building, foyer. Vyšehrad,
Neklanova 30. 1913–1914.

Josef Chochol. Hodek's apartment building, floor plan.
Vyšehrad, Neklanova 30. 1913–1914.

The Prism and the Pyramid

werbeblatt,[18] and many of Hofman's projects were published during World War I in the magazines *Der Sturm* and *Die Aktion*. This opens up the interesting question of mutual influence between these two architectural directions. In comparison with expressionist designs, Czech cubist architecture appears to be stylistically purer but less visionary. We would not find in it the apotheosis of glass and light inspired in German expressionists by the poet Paul Scheerbart. Also, Czech architects had fewer opportunities to realize their new ideas concerning space, and they did not create spaces that would express the new cubist aesthetic in the same way that German architects manifested the spatial achievements of expressionism in Bruno Taut's Glass Pavilion in Cologne, 1914, in Hans Poelzig's Berlin hall Grosse Schauspielhaus, 1918–1919, or Walter Wurzbach's Berlin wine bar Skala, 1920.

Czech cubists, however, examined space as an artistic category with the same intensity as the modernists Jan Kotěra and Otakar Novotný. In 1912, Pavel Janák spoke about the "spatial expressions of emotion,"[19] and we would find mentions of the "spatiality" of architecture also in Chochol's writings from 1913. But it was Vlastislav Hofman who was most concerned about the problem of architectural space, and who in 1913 pronounced the "purely effective and creative sense for the space of geometrical bodies" to be the basis of architecture,[20] and in 1915 formulated his thesis on the "self-serving function of space."[21] It was with scorn that Pavel Janák rejected in his essay "O nábytku a jiném," published in 1912, everything in an apartment that gives the impression of a "case," that is, everything simply rectangular, and began to explore the idea of a more plastic and dramatic shaping of the inner architectural space. A year later, however, he moved in the wrong direction in his text "Obnova průčelí," pursuing the idea that the inner, three-dimensional space of a building was a simple fact, whose function was to provide a place for something far more artistic and spiritual that would be achieved by a new approach to the shaping of the walls of individual rooms, by a "spatial formulation of their surfaces."[22]

Fortunately, Janák was not dogmatic in his sketches and drawings, and it was through them that he managed to express the ideas of cubist architects about space in a new spatial type. His sketches from 1912–1913 present

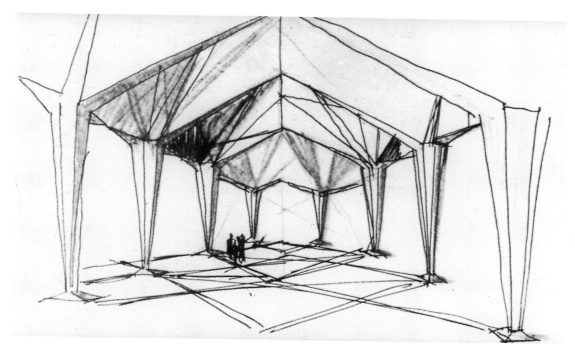

this type as a kind of crystalline canopy, "crystal viewed from inside." For its realization, the architect could find inspiration in the late Gothic chamber vaults and in the marvellous baroque-Gothic church interiors of Jan Santini (1677–1723), which Janák studied in 1909, and also in his own cubist method of beveling and faceting, transported into a three-dimensional system. However, none of the Czech cubist architects was commissioned to design anything that would provide an opportunity to integrate this new spatial type into the organism of a building, except for the tiny vaulted ceilings that Chochol used in the corridors of his apartment blocks, or the decorative variations on the same theme in the block of flats on Karmelitská Street, designed by Ludvík Kysela between 1912 and 1913.

And so the only realized examples of Janák's cubist space-canopy remained the constructions of cloth and timber used by Janák and Gočár to create a vaulted ceiling in the exhibition hall of the Municipal House for the shows of the

125

Pavel Janák. Studies of interiors. 1912.

CHAPTER 2

127

The Prism and the Pyramid

Group of Visual Artists between 1912 and 1914. Under these crystalline cubist vaults it was possible to see many remarkable artworks, including paintings and sculptures by Czech and French cubists and cubist furniture designed by Janák, Hofman, Gočár, and Chochol, which was as interesting as their cubist architecture. The stylistic purity of this cubist *Gesamtkunstwerk* was almost too rigorous, too grim, and uncompromising; its endless repetition of formal formulas, too narrow in their emotional mood, practically excluded the possibility of harmonization with art of a different style. Among the sculptors it was only another cubist, Otto Gutfreund, whose work was ideally placed to meet the demands of cubist architecture; any collaboration between artists working in a more traditional figurative vein turned out unfavorably for cubist architects. The art historian and collector Vincenc Kramář referred in his writings to the "spectral space of analytical cubism,"[23] a comment made in relation to Picasso's paintings in 1937, which could be equally used to describe the pitfalls threatening the Czech cubist synthesis of artforms in the period between 1911 and 1914.

RONDOCUBISM VERSUS PURISM

The ambition of Kotěra's modern style was to improve and reform Czech society. The cubists, on the other hand, often stated in their writings their desire to distance themselves from society. Above all, they rejected any notion of servitude on the part of art. In his essay "O nábytku a jiném," Janák wrote about the new art being elevated above both man and nature and described it as an "independent activity that has no obligations except to itself."[24] A year later, Josef Chochol offered a similar view, namely that "true art never tries to please or feels obliged for the attention given to it, it knows no concern except its own laws, and continues to live its imaginary life even against general lack of understanding."[25] Cubist architects knew, of course, that they could not entirely dispense with their audiences. But they were satisfied to produce work for only a small elite of connoisseurs who were able to understand the aims of the new art and commissioned it in its purest form, untainted by compromise.

When one examines the emphasis the cubists placed on the public's strong resistance against their art, it becomes obvious that while this was

Preceding pages: *Ludvík Kysela. Apartment building, foyer. Malá Strana, Karmelitská 30. 1912–1913.*

Pavel Janák. Exhibition hall of the Skupina výtvarných umělců in the Municipal House. 1911.

Josef Gočár. Exhibition hall of the Skupina výtvarných umělců in the Municipal House. 1912.

Vladimír Fultner. *Study for an apartment building. 1913.*

The Prism and the Pyramid

to some extent true, it was also a self-promoting maneuver aimed at proving their artistic heroism. Conservative architects and critics were outraged by the "mad dance of cubism" and in 1913–1914, cubism was attacked in journals such as *Architektonický obzor* (Architectural Horizon), *Moderní revue* (The Modern Review), and *Dílo* (Work),[26] and was strongly condemned by a segment of the public. But the cubists did find their clients, while more and more architects began to see cubism as an opportunity for artistic self-expression. The four architects Janák, Hofman, Gočár, and Chochol were in the years 1912–1913 joined by Vladimír Fultner, Petr Kropáček, Čeněk Vořech, Ludvík Kysela, Bedřich Feuerstein, and several others. The General Pensions Institute on Rašín Embankment, 1912–1914, designed by Jan Kotěra against whose work the new movement reacted, imitated some details from the cubist Black Madonna Building designed by his pupil Jan Gočár. The flat and decorative cubist vocabulary soon began to appear in the projects of building contractors and property developers Karel Hannauer Snr, Václav Hortlík, Bohuslav Homoláč, Jan Petrák, František Štorch, and Václav Zákostelna, none of whom had any qualms about mixing this vocabulary with elements of the geometrical modern style. Several significant works were designed by the builder Antonín Belada, whose 1913 project for the block of apartments on Neklanova Street was probably assisted by Josef Chochol, and by Matěj Blecha, whose office was responsible for the cubist Diamant department store building on Spálená Street, 1912–1913, and for the neighboring cubist canopy covering the baroque statue of Saint John Nepomuk. Another remarkable cubist project, the stone lamppost situated on the corner of Jungmannovo Square, in front of the back facade of Kalous Pharmacy, was also designed under Blecha's supervision, although it had been for a long time attributed to Vlastislav Hofman. The surviving drawings for this project show that its actual designer, Emil Králíček, was well aware of the heterogeneous surroundings in which the post was to be placed.[27]

The position of cubist art was not damaged even by the conflict within the Group of Visual Artists, which made the painters Josef Čapek and Václav Špála, the writer Karel Čapek, and architects Vlastislav Hofman and Josef Chochol leave the Group. The disputes within the Group were exacerbated by statements of the painters Emil Filla and Vincenc Beneš and art historian Vincenc

Josef Chochol(?), Antonín Belada. Apartment building.
Vyšehrad, Neklanova 2. 1913.

Chapter 2

The Prism and the Pyramid

Kramář who condemned the "renegades" for their unwillingness to follow nothing but the highest models of the new art such as Picasso and Braque, and also for taking seriously other directions like futurism, Orphism, and the work of minor cubists like Gleizes and Metzinger. The polemics among Czech cubists occasionally descended to the level of personal attacks, but the discussions forced those involved to think about their views and hastened the process of forming their individual styles.

The outbreak of World War I in the summer of 1914 had a serious effect on Czech cubism. Power was seized by a militaristic-bureaucratic clique that began to suppress the political life in Bohemia and thus unwittingly elicited another powerful wave of Czech nationalism. The impact of the war was far reaching: building development in Czech towns all but came to a halt, contacts with Paris and other centers of modern European art were severed, and art magazines such as *Umělecký měsíčník* ceased publication. The war also dispersed the clientele of cubist art and changed the taste of art audiences, who began to value traditional qualities of Czech folk art over modernity and originality. Some cubists, among them architects Chochol, Gočár, and Janák, were drafted into the Austrian Army, which made it somewhat difficult for them to maintain contact with Prague. Others preferred to emigrate and participate in anti-Austrian activities of the exiled future president T. G. Masaryk.

The cubist Group of Visual Artists also ceased to exist at the beginning of the war. Pavel Janák and Josef Gočár therefore transferred their activity to the arts and crafts cooperatives of the *Pražské umělecké dílny* (Prague Art Workshops) and *Artěl*, which specialized in the production of cubist furniture and luxury *objets d'art*. In 1914, artists who collaborated with these workshops began to be concerned about the continuing resistance of a large part of the public to cubism, and they set out to give the new art a form that would regain the public's interest. For instance, in his architectural sketches from 1914 to 1916, Pavel Janák experimented with rectangular shapes placed in thick layers on his facades, and in their furniture design, both Janák and Gočár introduced rounded forms, circles, and annular sections.[28] However, it was their attitude toward decorative ornament,

134

Preceding pages: *Emil Králíček, Matěj Blecha. Diamant department store, entrance. Nové Město, Spálená 4. 1912–1913.*

Emil Králíček(?), Matěj Blecha. Lamppost. Nové Město, Jungmann Square. 1912–1913.

Pavel Janák. *Study of architecture. 1915.*

The Prism and the Pyramid

which they had so far rejected, that underwent a remarkable change: they began to view ornament as the very element that would help them reestablish contact with the public, as well as a means toward expressing the national and folkloric aspect of their work.

The same direction was taken by the chairman of the *Artěl* cooperative, the cubist architect Rudolf Stockar (1886–1957), who in 1916 designed the new patisserie in the department store Ligna in Wenceslas Square in collaboration with the painter František Kysela, a former member of the Group. The spokesman of this newly born tendency, Václav Vilém Štech, also a one-time member of the Group, described Stockar's interior as a "fresh, happy, and cheerful improvisation, which creates the impression of folkloric art."[29] In December of the same year, Pavel Janák commented with obvious delight on the new "healthy sense for strong, full-blooded colors," especially the striking red and yellow, which

Rudolf Stockar, František Kysela. Patisserie in the Ligna
department store. 1915.

apparently reflected the Czech national temperament and were in harmony with the old baroque and neoclassical character of Prague. "Color to the facades!" was his motto at the time.[30] Following the creation of an independent Czechoslovak Republic in October 1918, this tendency developed into a very original and colorful style named *rondocubism*, whose language was used to the best effect by Josef Gočár.

The work of Vlastislav Hofman also began to follow a very individual direction around 1914. Initially, Hofman's views rarely differed from those of Pavel Janák, but as a theoretician, Hofman developed some original ideas concerning the spatial aspect and the "objectivity" of cubist architecture, a term most probably borrowed from contemporary German writing on art: *Die Sachlichkeit*. After Hofman left the Group, and particularly in 1913–1914, his writing acquired a polemical edge aimed against Pavel Janák. Above all, Hofman rejected Janák's concept of inert matter that comes to life only as it is formed by the active force of the architect's spirit. According to Hofman, matter was alive and moved of its own accord. In his 1913 essay "K podstatě architektury" (On the Essence of Architecture), Hofman set himself the task of shaping the "inner form" of matter and artistically capturing its "inner capacities."[31] Hofman's belief in the "movement of matter" soon began to manifest itself in a number of his drawings and woodcuts, which, beside the characteristic crystal-shaped forms, show also organic spirals and almost plantlike coils.

A different architectural approach is evident in the grandest of Hofman's wartime projects, a series of unrealized plans for the modern development of the baroque citadel of Vyšehrad, which the Prague municipality bought from the Viennese military authorities in 1910.[32] In Hofman's plans, completed in 1915, Vyšehrad was turned into a kind of English garden suburb with rows of family houses following the baroque layout of the fortifications, which naturally lent them the proper angular cubist lines. Part of the Vyšehrad site was reserved by Hofman for the new section of the Slavín Cemetery, the burial place of the most outstanding Czech artists, scientists, and scholars since the end of the nineteenth century. Above the low residential housing of this gloomy cubist acropolis, Hofman raised several large public buildings. Their lines exemplify the striving for massive

137

138

Vlastislav Hofman. Study for a pergola. 1914.

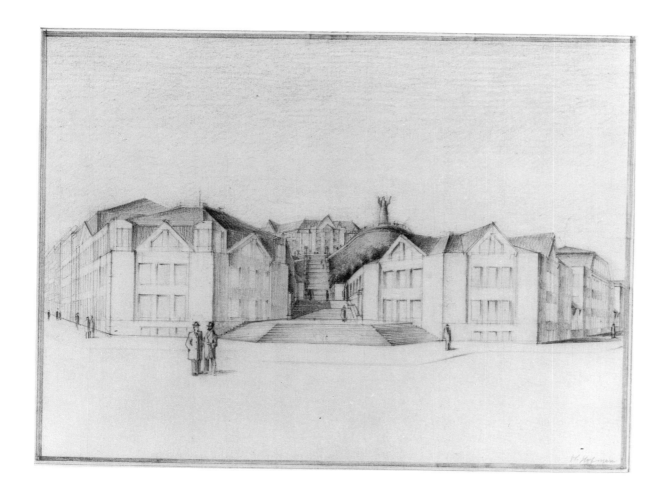

*Vlastislav Hofman. Project for a monumental staircase leading
to the Vyšhrad Citadel. 1915.*

139

The Prism and the Pyramid

monumentality that Hofman mentioned in his writings in 1915.[33] He took particular care to avoid contrived shapes and left the surfaces bare. During the war, Hofman too was swayed by the nationalist propaganda and began to dream about the creation of mysterious, prehistoric Slavic forms, while he described the simple lines of Gothic Hussite country churches as one of the sources of inspiration for Czech cubism.[34] But not even then did Hofman abandon the essential tenets of cubism, and the new curvilinear style embraced by Janák and Gočár remained alien to him.

Even further removed from Janák's and Gočár's quest for a new national style was Josef Chochol, whose negation of the original pyramidal cubism was the most radical and of the greatest European significance. The most important of Chochol's designs from the period of pyramidal cubism, the apartment block on Neklanova Street, 1913–1914, displays references to the Gothic style. In 1913, however, in his essay "K funkci architektonického článku" (On the Function of the Architectural Component), Chochol acknowledged his personal taste for the Gothic style but declared it a "closed chapter," and expressed the wish to create something new and individual. The cubist facets of his apartment block on Neklanova Street have a clearly visible ornamental character, particularly in the basement band and in the tilted main cornice. Yet, in the same essay Chochol repeatedly rejected decorative ornaments as something totally unacceptable, something that would interfere with "the precious, pure, and smooth effect of the modern work, austere and fantastic at the same time, making it stumble unbearably over a multitude of indifferent little ornaments and details." In Hofman's polemic

140

Vlastislav Hofman. Study for standardized houses. 1914.

against Janák, Chochol took Hofman's side. He too could not imagine architecture without a third dimension, he too reflected upon the interior structure of matter, which, like Hofman, he wanted to capture in its growth and movement. According to Chochol, the characteristic trait of the new architecture would be a "taste of mathematical precision, harsh austerity, and coarse-grained robustness."[35]

The effort to bridge the gap between theory and practice led Chochol to a kind of "straightened cubism," which he kept consistently free of any references to historical styles and ornamental deformations. Chochol expressed his vision of new architecture in a series of carefully hatched drawings and sketches, begun in 1914, some of which were drawn in the trenches of wartime Galicia. Although Chochol was the only cubist architect who strictly rejected any notion of transferring the methods of cubist painting into architecture, it is possible that the new stage in the development of his work was underpinned by his interest in synthetic cubism's new solidification of the object, the influence of which was also becoming apparent in 1913–1914 in the paintings of Josef Čapek and Emil Filla. Chochol probably also found inspiration in the sparse and down-to-earth qualities of industrial architecture, to which he dedicated a special issue of his review *Styl*, and which featured in many of his sketches produced between 1912 and 1919. In this context, it is interesting to consider the back facade of the building on Neklanova Street. Other architects would have possibly designed it the same way, bare and free of decorations, but this would have been done to economize on the part of the building that was not readily visible. Unlike Chochol, they would not have sensed a new stylistic quality in this undecorated bareness. The pristine, rectangular forms of buildings featured in Chochol's architectural drawings, accentuated by sharp, lateral illumination, were initially rather flat, and the architect stacked them one behind the other to capture in their layers the phases in the movement of matter. Gradually, the illusive movement died down, the shapes became more and more curved, their reliefs deepened, and the inner spatiality of their volume increased.[36] In this way, in the years between 1914 and 1920, Chochol progressed from the subjective breakdown of shapes—characteristic of analytical, or rather pyramidal, cubism—to the cubism of objective things, a style that was at that time named purism by Ozenfant and Jeanneret.

141

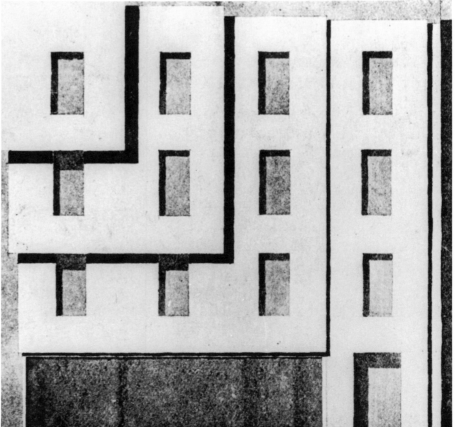

CHAPTER 2

Josef Chochol. *Study for a facade. 1914.*

Josef Chochol. *Study for a facade. 1914.*

Josef Chochol. *Study for an apartment building facade. 1920.*

3 TOWARD A NEW PRAGUE

With the support of France, Britain, and the United States, an independent Czechoslovak Republic was established in autumn 1918 on part of the territory that had previously belonged to the defeated Austro-Hungary. From its birth on October 28, 1918, until the events following the Munich Agreement in September 1938, Czechoslovakia was the most democratic state in Central Europe, maintaining close economic, political, and cultural links with France. In the large industrial centers of Czechoslovakia, voters mostly supported the social democratic workers' parties, which were the main political force behind the first president of the new republic, Tomáš Garrigue Masaryk (1850–1937). However, in the first years of the independent state it was the right-wing politicians who proved to have more initiative and political know-how, and so managed to overcome the growing power of the radical left in the 1920s and maintain a majority until the annexation of Czechoslovakia by Hitler in 1938–1939. In the interwar period many young artists and intellectuals sympathized with the program of the Czechoslovak Communist Party, established in 1921, and followed with keen interest the cultural developments in the Soviet Union, nurturing a somewhat naive hope that Czechoslovakia, too, would soon have its own socialist revolution. Masaryk's model of a democratic state displayed a great deal of tolerance toward the extreme left, and the revolutionary cultural avant-garde shared with Masaryk's democratic socialism the notion of modern architecture as a means toward resolving social problems. This notion comprised provisions for economical yet perfectly functioning housing, which would reflect the democratic character of the new republic and its respect for the working man and woman.[1] The left-wing avant-garde saw modern architecture as a "proto-image," a model of life in the new society to come. To them, modern buildings were "islands of the future," expressing the ethical and aesthetic ideals of the forthcoming socialist order despite the prevailing contemporary capitalist conditions of the time.

Prague became the capital of the new republic, and it was necessary to modernize its architectural resources if the new state institutions were to begin functioning properly. From 1920, work began at the Prague Castle, which was being rebuilt into a representative seat housing the office of the President of the Republic. The new political order was also symbolized by the Liberation Memorial erected on the hill of Vítkov between 1926 and 1933. Several new ministry buildings were soon under construction, and a competition was announced for the parliament building. New buildings for the schools of the Czech Polytechnic and of Charles University appeared in Dejvice and in sites around the Old and New Town; a new Technical and Agricultural Museum was built in Letná in the thirties along with the monumental Strahov sports stadium. An international airport was opened—temporarily in Kbely in 1918, then in Ruzyně in 1937. To these new developments the Prague municipality added a considerable network of modern schools and large buildings such as the social and medical care complex in Krč, the gas works in Michle, the filtration station in Podolí, the administration building of the City Power Company in Holešovice, and the new Municipal Library in Staré Město. However, the event that would crown the twenty-year effort of the Prague municipality, the competition for the completion of Old Town City Hall, announced for 1937–1938, proved yet again fruitless.

During the twenties and thirties, Prague attracted thousands of people from all social classes and all trades and professions who were drawn by the promise of good employment. Consequently, the municipality was faced with the increasingly urgent need to provide adequate housing and transportation for the rapidly growing population.

The position of Prague as capital of an independent republic appeared to make solutions to these problems easier than when its role was as a provincial center permanently out of favor with the Viennese authorities. The new administration therefore made an effort to create the best possible conditions for the development of the city. One of the first such measures was the Construction Act of 1919, which favored the building of blocks containing small, low-rent apartments; the second was the establishment of the State Planning Commission for Prague and Environs in February 1920, and finally the Greater Prague Act, which took effect January 1921. The Greater Prague Act added to the existing seven Prague districts ten smaller municipalities, including Vinohrady, Žižkov, Vysočany, Karlín, Bubeneč, Břevnov, Košíře, Smíchov, Nusle, and Vršovice, as well as twenty-seven small towns and villages. This extensive area with a perimeter of 24 kilometers and almost 700,000 inhabitants finally became one administrative entity.

The nine-member State Planning Commission, responsible to the Ministry of Public Works, was assigned the task of formulating town planning regulations that would apply to the whole area of Greater Prague. Along with architects–town planners, the commission included transport and civil engineers, one public health expert, and representatives of the municipality and of industrial associations. The first Chairman of the commission was the conservative architect Josef Sakař, supported by Antonín Balšánek, Jiří Stibral and other members of his generation who belonged to the late historicist circle. Following Balšánek's death in 1921, the historical orientation was countered by the growing influence of Wagner's pupils Antonín Engel and Bohumil Hypšman. Modernist views were brought into the commission only after the mid-twenties by Pavel Janák and in the thirties by Ladislav Machoň. From 1923 until the abolition of the commission by the Germans in 1939, it was chaired by the transport engineer Eustach Mölzer, who had worked for the government before the war on the construction of waterway locks, bridges, and power plants on the Labe River, and in the course of his work became friends with Engel and Janák. Mölzer followed the early modernist and cubist developments in Czech architecture with great interest, and in his role as chairman of both the State Planning Commission and the Power Company, he began to support other modern architectural styles, as can be seen in the beautiful functionalist building of the Power Company on Bubenská Street, designed by Adolf Benš and Josef Kříž, 1927–1935.

The brief of the commission was to work out a detailed plan for the development of Greater Prague, "within the widest possible context of economy, social and educational aspects, public health, technology and the arts."[2] The focus of this project was the planned transport network, around which the commission would further designate industrial zones, green areas, and residential and business districts. The commission would likewise determine the position of the most important public buildings, parameters of streets and squares, and, finally, the nature of housing to be built in the individual suburbs: apartment buildings or family houses, detached or in blocks. The planning stage, originally intended to take three years, was hampered by inadequate existing topographical surveys as well as by the immediate need to begin construction work. Therefore, the plan had to be developed in small sections that often comprised only several streets. By 1920 the commission decided to make its task easier by dividing the area into four sectors and by comparing its own planning ideas with plans submitted by other town planners for a series of well-prepared competitions announced between 1920 and 1924. The overall urban plan for Greater Prague, based on these preliminary activities, was finally published in 1928.

As for the aesthetic aspects of the plan, the planners found valuable inspiration in the uneven, hilly terrain, sloping down to the monumental meandering flow of the Vltava River. On the other hand, the same terrain proved to be a serious stumbling block for attempts to develop a balanced, functional infrastructure. At least four of the large competitions announced by the commission in the twenties tried to resolve the problem of linking the city on the right bank with the elevated suburbs lying west and north, while the 1927 competition for the Nusle Bridge tried to open up the center southward, where its expansion was restricted by the deep gorge of the Nusle Valley.

But it was the old problem of the Letná slope, beyond which a new satellite center was under construction, that remained the most difficult to resolve. Moreover, the problem was complicated by the commission's decision — from today's point of view a wise one — to keep the historical Old Town intact. This area, inserted between the rapidly growing northwest sector and the business and office district around Wenceslas Square, thereafter became an untouchable buffer zone in front of the steep slope of Letná. Many young architects saw this "Old Town taboo" as a major obstacle to the modern development of Prague and disapproved of the excessive concern about the historical character of the city. This was, according to Jaromír Krejcar, "something very vague, existing only in the alarmed imagination of the Club in Support of Old Prague, rather than in reality,"[3] and of "the reign of terror ... imposed by several sentimental art historians, not

149

only over architects with modern views and sensibility . . . but also over the population of the city, by forcing their lives into a tangle of old, narrow streets."[4] The commission stood up to this pressure, although its members were far from clear about ways in which the historical center could be used. Various suggestions were put forward by Josef Chochol, Josip Plečnik, and a member of the commission, Antonín Engel, who around 1922 recommended that the historical Old Town should be divided by a direct communication between the city around Wenceslas Square and either the Svatopluk Čech Bridge or Mánes Bridge. Countering these suggestions, the commission decided to protect the Old Town from the impact of city transport by means of a circular road that would detour the traffic and channel it out onto the steep left bank of the river.

However, this proposal still left open the question of how to connect the center with Letná. Several solutions to this problem were proposed. In 1922, Bohumil Hypšman suggested that the traffic should ascend by means of left- and right-sided serpentines leading from both Svatopluk Čech and Šverma Bridge. A year later, Antonín Engel returned to the old idea promoted in 1909 that proposed a tunnel combined with a pass to be constructed along the axis of Pařížská Street. The three most successful projects in the 1928 competition inviting plans for the buildings of the Parliament and several ministries to be situated in Letná, were those submitted by architects Štěpánek, Krejcar, and Roškot. All three proposed a system of surface ramps requiring extensive adjustments to the terrain.

In their search for solutions to these town-planning problems, the creators of new Prague took guidance from several urbanistic theories. The winning proposals for the four Prague sectors from 1920 to 1924 shared several common principles: the parts of the city nearer the center and standing on even terrain were designed in blocks—some compact, some open—while the parts lying in the surrounding hills were conceived as garden cities and designed on impressive fan-shaped or curved ground plans. The tops of the hills were used as sites for monumental public buildings, something the planners learned from the architects of the Gothic and baroque periods. Also the new squares, embankments, and avenues were intended to impress with their monumental character. These principles of the

150

official Prague urbanism of the early twenties can be traced back to the three main contemporary town-planning systems, mentioned in the historical introduction. The first was the town-planning program of Wagner's modern style, the second the English garden city, and the third the housing reform movement bringing a new concept of the apartment building block along with new solutions to the apartment layout.

Wagner's town-planning principles were most consistently and extensively applied in Engel's treatment of the new Prague quarter of Dejvice. The center of Engel's Dejvice became today's Victory Square, a spacious rectangle ending in a semicircle at its northwest side. The main avenues fan out from the square, opening up further down at their intersections into smaller spaces of various geometrical shapes. The star-shaped street network is complemented by a system of circular roads. Engel intended to surround the main square and avenues with monumental classicist buildings. As he put it, he had a vision of a "safe and definite style which disregards the passing fashionable and opportunistic ambitions, . . . a universal formal expression . . . indeed, monumental architecture which would maintain its pride and reflect the time of its birth."[5] Young architects from the circle around the functionalist review *Stavba*, however, considered Engel's definitive and universal project as the "result of outdated theories of classicism," which "may appear impressive on paper or, at best, in aerial perspective."[6] What diminishes the aesthetic impression of Engel's Dejvice is the fact that some of the most important parts of his project were never completed. This applies particularly to Victory Square where the missing west side, revealing the chaotic architectural mixture beyond, drains the space of all its energy.

The Wagnerian spirit — although not yet the spirit of Vienna's Ringstrasse — is also apparent on the embankments of the Vltava in the area of Old and New Town built in the twenties. Here, the monumental edifices of ministries and university faculties were erected in the same decade, according to plans by Josef Fanta and Josef Sakař, but above all by Wagner's students Roith, Engel, Hypšman, and Kotěra. The most successful of these projects was probably the new Palacký Square, established on the New Town bank of the river under the Gothic

151

Emmaus Monastery, in commemoration of the outstanding Czech historian and politician of the nineteenth century, František Palacký. The major problem facing the architects who had been dealing with this project already before World War I—for instance, Janák and Hofman—was how to design the square around the large statue of Palacký by sculptor Stanislav Sucharda, which had been standing in this space since 1912, and, at the same time, how to avoid obscuring the view of the facade of the Emmaus Monastery. Bohumil Hypšman, who was commissioned to design the square following his nomination as member of the State Planning Commission in 1923, was largely successful in his solution. The extensive cubic blocks of his new buildings, the Ministry of Social Welfare and the Ministry of Health, 1924–1931, were discreetly positioned away from the Emmaus panorama; the northmost of the two was situated on the axis of the statue, forming a suitable solid background for it, and under the monastery itself Hypšman placed the low wings linking the two buildings. Important elements of Hypšman's architectural vocabulary were pergolas, obelisks, and terrace ramps. His aim was to "clearly define and demarcate" the given space, and he used the various pergolas and balustrades to achieve an "impression of tranquillity in the square."[7] Hypšman's friend, the architect and art historian Alois Kubíček, later described the square as "arguably the only successfully completed urban area so far."[8] On the other hand the functionalist architect Jan E. Koula criticized the project in *Stavba*, stating that it "certainly complied with all sorts of absurd conservationist and scholarly-aesthetic requirements, but at the expense of economy, public health, and, above all, common sense."[9] Hypšman's square certainly lacks life and movement, mainly because there are practically no shops or services.

      Unlike the Wagnerian monumental blocks, the second urbanistic direction of the twenties, the garden city, was designed for the peripheral, satellite areas of the new metropolis. The main requirement Wagner's disciples had in mind was the representative function of the building, which was supposed to inspire respect, and this notion found its expression in the palace type of architecture. The promoters of the garden city, on the other hand, thought in terms of "idyllic coziness," of dwellings that would be "modest but would have sufficient space, ex-

Antonin Engel. Development plan for the suburb of Dejvice. 1921–1924.

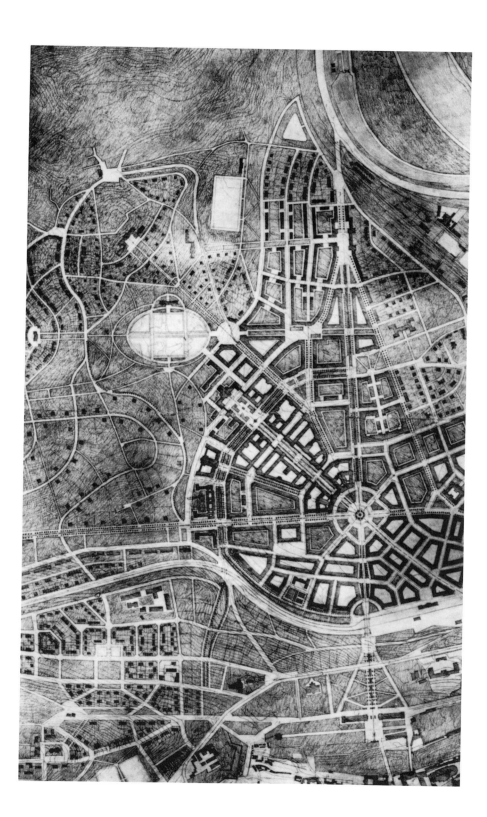

153

cellent services, and plenty of fresh air and sun,"[10] of housing accessible even to the "economically weaker classes." The ideal architectural type fulfilling their program was, according to them, the family house with a garden. The relatively extensive construction of garden suburbs in Prague in the twenties was generously subsidized by the government, which aimed to gain the support of the inhabitants of these new suburbs for the political directions of the Czechoslovak State.

The best known and probably the most successful garden suburb in Prague was Ořechovka in the municipality of Střešovice, the building of which began in 1919 by the Building Cooperative of Public Servants, according to a winning project by Jaroslav Vondrák and Jan Šenkýř. The center of the area focuses on a small square with a building housing various shops and a restaurant. The surrounding streets, some straight, some curved, are designed on a rectangular grid; others fan out from the square. The family houses in these streets are both detached and semidetached and are set in the middle of small gardens. Many of them are standardized, in terms of their ground plan as well as appearance, and groups of houses of one type alternate with groups of another. Their designers — beside Vondrák and Šenkýř, also Pavel Janák and Kotěra's pupils Jindřich

Freiwald, František Vahala, Eduard Hnilička, and Ladislav Machoň—applied the principle of diversity in harmony and unity, formulated by the pioneer of the garden city concept, Raymond Unwin.

The building of other garden suburbs began shortly after Ořechovka in Smíchov, Břevnov, Vinohrady, and Strašnice. The high standard achieved in Ořechovka was matched by another garden estate, Ve Stromkách, which was built between 1923 and 1928 in the area of Vinohrady between the streets Benešovská, Šrobárova, and Soběslavova, for the cooperative of senior administrative workers, journalists, and writers, according to plans produced by Tomáš Pražák, Pavel Moravec, and Ladislav Machoň. Pražák and Moravec designed several types of family houses for this project, assembled from standardized geometrical units into variable red and gray compositions. In the late twenties the era of garden suburbs came to an end with the establishment of the suburbs of Spořilov and Zahradní Město in the municipal area of Záběhlice. Spořilov was designed in 1924 by Josef Barek, professor at the Czech Polytechnic, who used eight different types of family houses, designed and built between 1925 and 1930 by Karel Polívka and Vlastimil Brožek. The author of the plan for Zahradní Město, 1928, was the architect Alex Hanuš.

The ground plan of the twenties-style family house belonged predominantly to the internally differentiated "regrouped" type, with living quarters facing south and into the garden, and the servicing spaces, kitchen, stairwell, and bathroom facing north and into the street. The two-bay plan, dividing rooms clearly into servicing and serviced, appeared in the more expensive houses of Prague's garden cities, where the chain of rooms along one side often inspired the architects to unite them into a single space, as well as in the more modest standardized houses, whether they had two stories or just a ground floor with an attic. A good example of an excellent larger family house layout are the semi-detached homes built in 1923–1924 by Ladislav Machoň on Bratří Čapků and Šrobárova streets on the Ve Stromkách estate. A more modest variation on the same theme was the standardized family houses on Bylanská Street in Strašnice, designed by Janák, Gočár, and Josef Zavadil from 1919 to 1921.

155

Bohumil Hypšman. Development of Palacký Square. Nové Město. 1923–1931.

Jaroslav Vondrák, Jan Šenkýř. Family houses. Střešovice, Lomená 15–36. 1920.

Ladislav Machoň. Floor plan of a standardized family house for the estate Ve Stromkách. 1922.

Josef Gočár, Pavel Janák, Josef Zavadil. Floor plans of standardized family houses. Strašnice, Bylanská 17–27. 1919–1921.

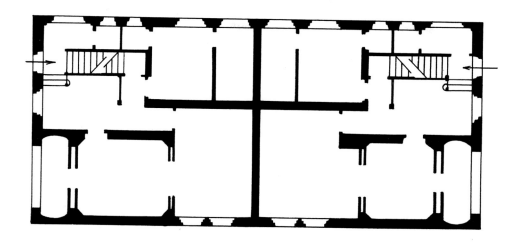

Toward a New Prague

The inner, more densely built-up residential suburbs of the city were affected by the third significant urbanistic direction of the twenties, the apartment block reform, which was supported by the state, the municipality, as well as by affluent building cooperatives. The aim of Prague reformers, who had learned their lessons in England, Germany, and the Netherlands, was to remove the shortcomings of the old, closed apartment block — in particular the inadequate access of fresh air and sun to the central courtyard and the rooms facing it. They saw the solution to this problem either in radically increasing the size of the block — a solution already proposed before the war by František Velich and Jan Žák — or in breaking the block up to achieve a result that contemporary architectural terminology named, not quite comprehensibly, "semiopen," "transitional," or "open" block. Variants of these reformed blocks, some more open, some more closed, were designed in the twenties by a number of architects including František Kavalír, Bohumil Sláma, Bohumír Kozák, Rudolf Hrabě, Josef Chochol, and František A. Libra.

Rudolf Hrabě (d. 1946), Head of the Municipal Construction Authority, focused in his experimental work of that time on the same problems as his contemporaries Theodor Fischer and Otto Haesler in Germany. In 1919 to 1922, Hrabě designed the apartment block between U Průhonu, V háji, Přístavní, and Na Maninách Streets. Two parallel, south-north oriented, three-story residential sections were on the long sides of the blocks linked by two ground-floor wings housing workshops. Between them were inserted two more detached three-story buildings on a square plan. If it were not for the low-level workshop wings, Hrabě would have arrived at the progressive system of row housing, made compulsory in the late twenties by the canon of functionalist urbanism. In his recently demolished housing estate for city clerks, built in approximately 1922 to 1925 on Úřednická Street in Dejvice, Hrabě, however, finally reached this functionalist solution, the prototype of which could probably be traced back to the makeshift barracks and hospital huts built during the war beyond the front line.

At the same time, Rudolf Hrabě made his contribution to the development of the floor plan arrangement of Prague apartment buildings. Being

158

*Bohumil Sláma, Jaroslav Pelc, Václav Vejrych. Apartment
buildings. Vinohrady, Slezská 99–105. 1920–1921.*

Toward a New Prague

*František Kavalír. Apartment buildings. Košíře, Píseckého
1–19. 1919–1922.*

*František A. Libra. Apartment buildings. Vršovice, Bulharská
29–41. 1925–1926.*

CHAPTER 3

CHAPTER 3

Rudolf Hrabě. Apartment buildings. Holešovice, U průhonu
44–52. 1919–1922.

Rudolf Hrabě. Family houses. Dejvice, Úřednická I–IV. Circa
1922–1925, demolished 1985.

Toward a New Prague

well aware of the economic disadvantages of Velich's and Žák's two-bay layout, which did not allow full use of the building lot, he also wanted to avoid the short-comings of the badly ventilated and dark apartments in the original three or multi-bay buildings. His answer to the problem was a kind of transitional form between a house and a block: a radically reduced block with an "airing courtyard," or rather a large skylight through which the central bays of the building gained access to light and fresh air. Hrabě built many such block-houses between 1919 and 1925 on Na Maninách, Tovární, Novovysočanská, and Na břehu Streets. For the blocks commissioned by the municipality on Radhošťská and Pod Plískavou Streets in 1925–1928, Hrabě's younger colleague from the Municipal Construction Authority, the architect Evžen Linhart, used the same plan for a more up-to-date, pristine white exterior that differed considerably from Hrabě's decorative red-and-yellow facades in the national style of rondocubism.

Hrabě's blocks in Novovysočanská, 1924–1925, however deserve attention for another reason. Their apartments, designed for low-income tenants, had only one bay, and in order to save space, the corridors were shifted outside in the form of an open balcony running around the courtyard, thus reviving a characteristic of nineteenth-century apartment buildings. Almost in the same period, František A. Libra also designed buildings with such open corridors in the courtyard, first in the blocks built for public servants on Podolské Embankment, 1924–1927, where they were duplicated by interior corridors, and then in his "open" block between Ruská and Bulharská Streets, 1925–1926.

The three main town-planning directions—the urbanism of Wagner's modern style, the garden city, and the approach resulting in the reformed apartment block—remained influential in Prague until the late twenties. During this decade, however, they were gradually displaced by functionalist town planning. In the twenties, functionalist urbanism formed a definitive view on all the important issues related to the development of new Prague, whether it was the functional structure of the city, its transport network, historically valuable architecture, ways in which individual areas would be built up, as well as the overall aesthetics of the new urban development. As for the first problem, the functional-

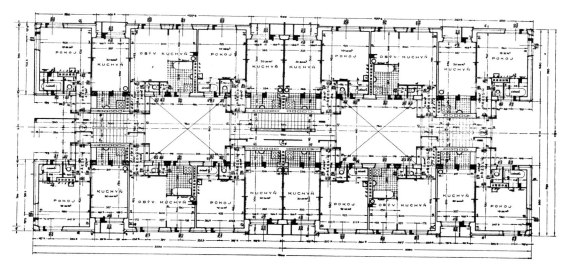

ists reached the conclusion that individual parts of the city should be monofunctional, and their functions should not be mixed. The shopping zone, for instance, should contain only shops and department stores, the business district only businesses and offices, the industrial zone only factories, whereas the residential zone was reserved solely for housing.

The need for special monofunctional "cities," for instance university or hospital cities, had been identified by many urbanists already at the beginning of the century. In Prague, such specialized areas became, for instance, the Vinohrady Hospital, designed by Josef Kalousek and under construction from 1904, or the university district at the southeast edge of New Town. Unplanned, spontaneously developed industrial zones had existed in Prague since the nineteenth century. The idea of the monofunctional city sector was consistently elaborated for the first time by the Lyon-based architect Tony Garnier in his famous project *Cité Industrielle* from 1901 to 1904 (published in 1917), which drew a distinct line between industrial and residential districts. Similar projects were conceived also by Prague urbanists. The most remarkable among them was the utopian *Ideální Velká Praha* (Ideal Great Prague), designed between 1915 and 1918 by Max Urban, who later became Secretary of the State Planning Commission.

165

Evžen Linhart. Apartment buildings, floor plan. Žižkov,
Radhošťská 18–22. 1925–1928.

This project goes into absurd lengths in dividing Prague, the metropolis of the future, into "the city — the government, business and office district, the diplomatic and cosmopolitan district, the garden suburbs, the middle class suburbs, the supply district, production district, and the district housing the working class."[11] In 1922, another important urbanist, Vladimír Zákrejs (1880–1948), proposed in his book *Praha budoucí* (Prague of the Future) the idea of a new industrial Prague, "the city of labor," established approximately 50 kilometers east of the Prague center, which was to become "the city of government."[12]

In the following years, especially after these ideas had been adopted by the influential Architects' Club, whose members were Oldřich Tyl, Oldřich Starý, and Ludvík Kysela, and the associated magazine *Stavba*, the notion crystallized in the minds of Prague urbanists into the concept of three essential monofunctional city zones: residential city, business city, and industrial city, separated from one another by green belts and lined up from west to east, following the direction of the winds. In Prague this principle, accepted even by the State Planning Commission, was manifested in the intention to move all the heavy industry into the northwest sector of the Prague agglomeration, while the center would retain its business, cultural, and representative functions, and the rest of the city, comprising the northwest area of Bubeneč, Střešovice, and Dejvice, would be reserved for residential purposes. The exponents of the monofunctional conception, codified later by Le Corbusier in his *La charte d'Athènes*, 1943, were unaware that this unnatural narrowing of the districts' functions would eventually have a detrimental effect on the harmonious running of everyday life and would excessively limit its formal and expressive possibilities.

The pioneers of functionalist urbanism paid unprecedented attention to problems of transport, which were becoming increasingly important not only due to the rapid increase in the use of automobiles in the postwar period but also due to the effect of the monofunctional zones that forced inhabitants of large cities to commute daily to work and back. The interest of the first functionalists in the problems of transport sometimes appeared almost exaggerated and self-serving, particularly in cases where it focused on the historical center of Prague. According to early functionalism, city communications were to be wide and direct, as purposeful and economic as possible. In this respect, Prague's functionalists paid attention to Le Corbusier, whose views were presented between 1923 and 1925 on the pages of *Stavba* by the theoretician of architecture Karel Teige. Although these ideas were relatively easy to realize in the peripheral, as yet sparsely built-up areas, the center of Prague, and particularly its historical nucleus, resisted modern transport theories like an invincible fortress. Most functionalists agreed that it was not enough to make minor changes to the historical center, merely adjusting some of its streets and intersections; it was necessary to rebuild it without compromise. But here the functionalists clashed with the State Planning Commission, which otherwise showed a great deal of understanding for the transport problems of the capital.

Against the "superstitious belief in *genius loci*" and the notion of "preserving the character of the city," which today probably represent values we can all share, the functionalists associated with *Stavba* demanded "radical modernization."[13] They recommended that from the unique historical ensemble of old Prague only the most significant parts should be preserved, and even then this should apply only to "certain outstanding works of architecture," as it was expressed in 1925 by Jaromír Krejcar, whose vision echoed the frenzied modernizations carried out at the turn of the century.[14] The prewar cubists' attempts to design new buildings so that they would harmonize with the picturesque old areas of the city were considered by the functionalists as unacceptably irrational. According to them, the wealth of historical architecture had to make way for architecture of the new rational order, for the principles of purpose, economy, and new life — probably the favorite concept of functionalism, which sought to subject everything "to the interests of city life," "the needs of life," "transformations of modern life," "tempo of modern life," and "the suppressed modern life," and "the struggle between the old and new life."[15]

It was to serve this concept of new life that the narrow streets of old Prague were to be opened up and widened. However, when we try to establish a closer definition of this notion, we find nothing more specific than the loud flow of traffic, rushing down the road. "Crowds of pedestrians, automobiles, trams and buses, perilous intersections, the fast rhythm of life punctuated by advertising slogans," summed up his vision of modern life the functionalist architect Josef K. Říha in 1929.[15] But thanks to concentrated protests by the public, the municipal and heritage authorities, the State Planning Commission, and to the resisting organism of the city itself, the historical center escaped the onslaught of "functionalist life." Only several isolated functionalist buildings made their way into the center of Prague, where they had to come to terms with the urbanistic dimensions of several centuries, and where, incidentally, they still make a far more interesting impression in the midst of their historical surroundings than in the modern suburbs where their authors had to assemble them into the schematic patterns of functionalism.

Having formulated the requirement of the "systematic division of city areas according to their functions and their organic interlinking,"[17] Prague's functionalist urbanists faced the question of how to build within these zones. In this respect, their program was not very clear. They rejected the monumental compositions of Wagner's disciples, which they considered outdated and too dependent on a priori aesthetic speculation, as well as the notion of the garden city, which they saw as uneconomical and suitable only for peripheral suburbs. The reformed apartment block was the only type the pioneers of functionalist urbanism approved of — to some extent — but from the early twenties they tried to develop their own town-planning systems, which were to be as independent as possible of previous urbanistic theories.

The first such systems were part of a wave influenced by American developments in architecture, which swept Europe from Moscow to Paris after World War I, and which characteristically showed a preference for skyscrapers in city centers. Apart from Gočár's 1909 plan for the rebuilding of Old Town City Hall, the first buildings of this type were designed by Jaromír Krejcar (1895–1949). His final student project at the Academy of Fine Arts, where he studied under Kotěra, was a plan for a large indoor market in Žižkov, 1921, the front of which was flanked by two office towers. According to Krejcar, the skyscraper, "a true marvel of technical construction" had the capacity to bring together a "whole

Jaromír Krejcar. Project for indoor market in Žižkov. 1921.

Toward a New Prague

apparatus of life's administration" within its walls.[18] The skyscraper became a particularly popular architectural type after 1922, the year when Le Corbusier, the pioneer of the new architectural movement, exhibited in Paris and then published worldwide his project *Ville Contemporaine*, which placed twenty-four skyscrapers in the city center. This project, which was known in Prague by the end of 1922,[19] became the model for tower buildings designed by František M. Černý, Vít Obrtel, Arnošt Mühlstein, Jan Gillar, and others. Significantly, only one of these projects was ever realized. It was the twelve-story office building designed by architects Havlíček and Honzík for the General Pensions Institute from 1929 to 1934, in today's Winston Churchill Square.

Not long after Krejcar's "skyscraper offensive," another more successful building system made its appearance. It was the system of row housing, the beginnings of which have been mentioned in the context of the work of Rudolf Hrabě. Hrabě's experiments from 1919 to 1925 were taken further by Bohumír Kozák, whose public health complex in Krč was realized between 1925 and 1940. The elongated rectangle in the oldest part of the complex is surrounded by symmetrically placed pavilions in five or six parallel rows; the longer side of the pavilions faces southwest toward Vídeňská Road. Janák's plan for the new suburb of Pankrác, 1927–1929, uses row housing of alternating orientation with the longer sides facing southwest, then southeast.[20] However, because the flats in the first row, which was closest to the road, were bound to suffer from excessive noise, while the southward orientation meant that only one part of the flat would have sun during the day, it was the north-south orientation that became the most common with the row housing systems in the mid-twenties. The main facade of the rows of houses faced east or west, and the shorter sides faced the adjacent communications. Already in 1926–1927, Gočár's students at the Academy of Fine Arts Ladislav Žák and Josef Havlíček produced drawings incorporating this approach to row housing. Yet, the most outstanding example of the system of north-south rows became Krejcar's acclaimed entry in the 1928 competition for the Parliament and ministry buildings in Letná, which literally stole the limelight from the winning project designed by Josef Štěpánek.

Bohumír Kozák. Public health complex. Krč, Vídeňská 5.
1926–1930.

Toward a New Prague

172

*Jaromír Krejcar. Competition project for the development of
Letná Plain. 1928.*

In his project, Krejcar proposed a wide avenue leading up to Letná that would join Kostelní Street at the intersection in front of Bílek's villa. The low-level buildings of the Parliament were situated along the right-hand side of the avenue, above the Letná slope, while the left-hand side opened up toward a remote row of free-standing pavilions of the ministries, lined up along the north edge of the Letná grounds. These buildings were united by their detailing in the elegant style of technicist functionalism. Krejcar himself described his design as "an open system allowing perfect access of light and fresh air."[21] Critical voices, however, objected to its "international layout, with facades designed in the same style," or to its barracklike appearance, reminiscent of old Austro-Hungarian government buildings "which violated life's needs."[22]

But the majority of informed contemporaries favored the magnificent discipline of Krejcar's design. It was precisely its unusual spatial generosity that inspired Ladislav Žák's view that it might often be preferable "to build nothing" in Prague, because "empty space is also architecture."[23] And it was probably this "open space aesthetic," whose influence the functionalists were sometimes hard-pressed to admit, masking it with their slogan "air-sun-light," which proved to be one of the most significant causes of the gradual dismantling of the traditional apartment block, as well as the source of the functionalist preference for free-standing planning systems. As for Letná, due to Janák's town-planning efforts "nothing" was indeed built there, except for two museums and the building of the Ministry of Interior Affairs at the northeast edge of the grounds. It is therefore possible to pose the question whether we should not consider the empty space of the Letná plain as the purest result of functionalist urbanism in practice.

Toward a New Prague

NEOCLASSICISM

In the early twenties, several architectural styles competed for the privilege of becoming the official style of the new republic. The most prestigious commissions went to neoclassicists, and in particular to that variety of neoclassicism that could be traced back to the work of Wagner's pupils and one-time orthodox exponents of the modern style Engel, Roith, and Hypšman, or even to the work of Plečnik, who had remained on the margins of Prague's architectural activity until 1920. The original rationalist thrust of Wagner's modern style all but disappeared from this direction during the second decade of the century; its vocabulary acquired a classicist character and adopted a number of elements pointing to classical antiquity. The exaggerated dimensions and monumental character of Wagner's classicism with its intimations of an unchanging world order probably best suited the taste of Prague's conservative financiers and high government officials whose ambition was to "preserve" the political status quo. As a result, in the twenties, Wagnerian classicism was almost exclusively appropriated by the most powerful of Prague's institutions: banks, insurance companies, and government offices.

Yet, among Prague's architects of that period there was probably only one who could identify with the artistic language of classicism and at the same time find in its forms a new poetry and new creative possibilities. It was the Slovene Josip (Jože) Plečnik (1872–1957), professor of decorative architecture at the School of Applied Arts between 1911 and 1921. When the decision was made in 1920 to rebuild the Prague Castle into a presidential palace, the new president T. G. Masaryk chose Plečnik for this task over local architects such as Jan Kotěra or Josef Bertl, then Director of the Czech Polytechnic.[24] It is possible that in this gesture Masaryk expressed his desire to establish closer political links with the Southern Slavs. From the year of his appointment until his return to Ljubljana in 1934, Plečnik worked on the reconstruction of the Prague Castle in a manner that placed his work "outside all that activity, outside time," as it was described by Pavel Janák who became his successor in the role of presidential architect.[25] Apart from reconstructing the gardens Rajská, 1920–1925, Na Valech, 1920–1925, and Na baště, 1927–1928, and renovating the presidential apartment, a project that began in 1921, Plečnik decorated the Prague Castle with many small architectural

gems designed with an unusual formal sense and a feel for the noble materials, metal and stone, as well as with a rare understanding for the unique historical nature of the site that found in Plečnik a worthy interpreter. He studded the spaces of the castle, which he probably perceived as some kind of a sacred area, an agora or forum designed for public gatherings, with antiquizing temples, pillars, and obelisks and with pergolas, awnings, fountains, staircases, and railings in the modern style. Their forms were nevertheless always imbued with a particular stylistic duality of "antiquity seen through modern eyes and modernism seen through the eyes of antiquity." The single building Plečnik designed during the interwar period when he was working on the Prague Castle, the Catholic Church of the Sacred Heart in Jiřího z Poděbrad Square, 1928–1932, has a similar character. Originally, Plečnik wanted to place a series of columns around the rectangular space of the church,

Josip Plečnik. Table in the White Tower. Hradčany, Prague Castle. 1923–1924.

Toward a New Prague

both on the inside and on the outside, as he did in the church of Saint Francis in Ljubljana, 1925–1927, which he was designing at the same time. In the final version of the Prague church from 1928, he decided to shape the interior as a simple cell, enclosed within bare brick walls and capped with a flat timber ceiling. In comparison with the church in Ljubljana, which had been apparently influenced by the tradition of neoclassicist architecture from around 1800, the vocabulary of Plečnik's Prague church presents a far more complex stylistic synthesis, the sources of which include classical architecture, as well as cubism and purism.

President Masaryk proved to be a dedicated client. "I have visited the garden—it is going to be very lovely!" he wrote to his architect in a letter dated September 4, 1924.[26] In spite of that, Plečnik's work was often criticized from a variety of positions: the conservatives criticized its "supranational" character, the functionalists considered it too conservative, and the supporters of Riegl's conservation program aimed at protection of historical buildings resented the courage with which Plečnik completed architecture of the past. The only architect who remained faithful to Plečnik's artistic legacy was his pupil and collaborator Otto Rothmayer (1892–1966), who worked at the Prague Castle independently from 1930. The most significant of Rothmayer's designs in Plečnik's style was the reconstruction of the Theresian wing of the castle, 1930–1951, to which he added a curious mushroom-shaped self-supporting spiral staircase.

However, many edifices designed during the interwar period by other disciples of Wagner have to be credited with a certain distinguished and noble discipline. What the classicists of the twenties lacked in comparison with Plečnik was his elegant irony and sense of space; for them, architecture was a matter of monumentality expressed by means of mass. The most exaggerated classicist vocabulary of the time was used by the planner of the Dejvice suburb, Antonín Engel, who was from 1922 professor at the Czech Polytechnic where he continued teaching in the conservative tradition, in spite of his reputation as a pioneer of modern rationalism. His most significant neoclassicist buildings, the filtration station in Podolská Street, 1923–1928, and the building of the Ministry of Railways on the Ludvík Svoboda Embankment, 1927–1931, were composed of

Following pages: *Josip Plečnik. Staircase in the garden Na valech. Hradčany, Prague Castle. 1924.*

Josip Plečnik. Living room in the presidential apartment. Hradčany, Prague Castle. 1925–1927.

Josip Plečnik. Obelisk in the garden Na valech. Hradčany, Prague Castle. 1925.

monumental, clearly defined blocks, assembled according to the classicist rules of balance and symmetry. The facades were placed on a robust supporting wall of stone and articulated by means of giant pilasters in an entirely monotonous fashion, without departing in any way from the predesigned scheme. Architectural monumentality remained in the center of Engel's interest: he believed that monumentality is of "metaphysical origin" and considered it to be the "highest expression of striving for all the stable, lasting, eternal qualities that stand above the ephemeral nature of things quotidian."[27] Considering the almost inhuman, inaccessible lithic order of his architecture, the question inevitably arises whether Engel included among the "things quotidian" also man himself.

Marginally more congenial were the classicist edifices designed by another of Wagner's pupils, František Roith, whose position as the architect of large financial institutions and government buildings was similar to that of Osvald Polívka. Among the most significant of Roith's interwar works were the complex of the Ministry of Finance on Letenská Street and in Dražické Square, 1926–1934, the bank building in Wenceslas Square, 1924–1931, the Municipal Library in Mariánské Square, 1924–1928, and the Živnostenská Bank in Republic Square, 1928–1938. The volumes of Roith's buildings were always organized in a very simple manner, and their floor plans were well thought-out. Their facades were stone-clad—employing material symbolizing "solidity"—and articulated by means of pilasters and relatively large windows, which were probably designed to achieve maximum contrast between the fragility of the glass panes and the massive nature of their stone surrounds. In the interior of the library, Roith designed impressive halls and staircases whose walls, ceilings, and windows were decorated in the style of art deco. The building faces the square with its shallow *court d'honneur*, while the side facades are rhythmically articulated in accordance with the various purposes of the inner sections, something that brought the character of the building closer to the rich vocabulary of the surrounding neo-Renaissance and neobaroque apartment blocks.

Immediately after the war work began on the construction of the group of mills and bakeries around U továren Street, 1919–1922, designed by

Josip Plečnik. Church of the Sacred Heart. Vinohrady, náměstí Jiřího z Poděbrad. 1928–1932.

Bohumil Hypšman in a somber geometrical style, as yet untouched by classicism. In the following years, Hypšman worked on the reconstruction of the Ludvík Svoboda Embankment, and, most importantly, on the plan for Palacký Square with its two ministerial buildings, 1924–1931. Here, his architectural expression was subjected to a classicist symmetry and enriched with the characteristic columns, pergolas, and obelisks. Unlike Roith and Engel, Hypšman did not use the giant pilaster order, and he preferred to leave the facades of his buildings smooth and bare. Among Hypšman's smaller works, one worth mentioning is his own family villa on U laboratoře Street, 1926–1927. The composition of masses in this building is reminiscent of the functionalist demarcation of independent volumes according to their interior purpose, and its flat roofs and smooth white walls also point toward the achievements of the new architecture. Yet, the small lozenge patterns that decorate the projecting cornice betray the extent to which Hypšman's work was firmly rooted in the tradition of Wagner's and Hoffmann's modern style.

184

Preceding pages: *Antonín Engel. Filtration station. Podolí, Podolská 17.*
1923–1926.

František Roith. Municipal Library. Staré Město, Mariánské
náměstí 1. 1924–1928.

*Bohumil Hypšman. Architect's own family villa. Střešovice,
U laboratoře 4. 1926–1927.*

*Jaroslav Rössler. Workers' Accident Insurance Company.
Holešovice, náměstí kapitána Jaroše 1000. 1926–1929.*

Apart from Wagner's followers Engel, Roith, and Hypšman, who were joined after 1918 by František Krásný, another of Wagner's pupils who had until then worked in Vienna, and who rebuilt the early baroque Michna Palace in Újezd for the seat of the sports organization Sokol, 1922–1926, classicist buildings were being designed also by other architects of the older generation as well. Among them were, for instance, Bedřich Bendelmayer, Josef Sakař, Josef Fanta, Antonín Pfeiffer, Ladislav Skřivánek, and one of the oldest pupils of Kotěra, Jaroslav Rössler (1886–1964), whose essentially classicist Workers' Accident Insurance Building, 1926–1929, achieved an almost modern abstraction of tectonic forces. However, with the exception of Krásný's and Rössler's work, the buildings designed by the majority of these architects suffered from dry schematism and lack of any substantial architectural ideas. On the whole, the work of Prague's classicist architects never rose to match the inimitable example set by Josip Plečnik.

LAST STAGES OF THE MODERN STYLE AND CUBISM

During the interwar period, the architectural vocabulary of Josip Plečnik, Antonín Engel, František Roith, Bohumil Hypšman, and most other architects mentioned here remained within the boundaries of neoclassicism, and, despite marginal vacillations in other stylistic directions, its essence never truly changed. In addition to the Prague neoclassicists, there were other architects of the older generation, especially members of Kotěra's circle, who were seeking large commissions in the capital. Typically, their work oscillated between several styles, which were often brought together in the design of individual buildings and could in itself be considered a specific style, an original Czech version of the Euro-American art deco. Neoclassicism still formed one of the points of departure for this style, but it was interpreted from a point of view that differed from Engel's or Plečnik's approach. A far more important role, however, was played by the two Cubist styles — the newer rondocubism and the older pyramidal mode, along with the revived geometrical modern style.

The earliest history of rondocubism between 1915 and 1918 has been outlined in chapter 2 along with the nationalist background of this style

186

whose crest-shaped, circular, and rectangular ornaments with white-and-red or yellow-and-red color schemes evoked Czech folk art and appealed to the patriotic circles in Czech society. For these reasons, in the new independent state, rondocubism seriously competed with neoclassicism, at least for some time. At the beginning of the twenties, it was used in the design of several ministries, insurance companies, and bank buildings, and thanks to Rudolf Hrabě, it became the trademark of apartment blocks built by the municipality. The winning quality of rondocubism was its accessible vocabulary, its apparent folkloric and patriotic character, for which it was often referred to as the "national style." On the other hand, this meant that its popularity was too closely dependent on the wave of patriotic enthusiasm and thus faded along with it.

In 1922, art historians Antonín Matějček and Zdeněk Wirth, who shared their views with the creators of rondocubism Pavel Janák and Josef Gočár, characterized this style as architecture "which subjects the mass of the building to imagination and turns the facade, as well as the space itself into a plastic body." In their view, the color schemes applied to the facades by architects working in this style increased "the plasticity of the surface and its individual elements."[28] This view of architecture as a problem of the plastic treatment of the surface, similar to the architectural thinking of postwar classicism, did not encourage interest in the shaping of the interior space. Despite the fact that Pavel Janák spoke as early as in 1918 about the quest for a type of dwelling whose spatial composition would reflect the national character, even about specific types of national "architectures-dwellings . . . just as each species has its specific type of burrow,"[29] apart from creating several interesting interiors, rondocubism never quite developed its own type of architectural space. At best, the characteristic spaces associated with this style were richly decorated with ornaments designed by professors from the School of Applied Arts and filled with furniture that was also fashioned in the style of rondocubism or in an overtly pseudo-folkloric style. And, when the functionalist Karel Teige commented in 1930 on the folkloric or rondocubist interiors by saying that "modern architects design peasant cupboards and baroque chests,"[30] while being perhaps too critical in denying this style some of its indisputable artistic value, he nevertheless captured its essence.

On the other hand, the pyramidal variety of cubism went through a more complex development around 1920, when it was revived in the work of some leading architects, and so became once more a pioneering style. After World War I, an important role in the development of pyramidal cubism was played by Vlastislav Hofman, "a most stubborn Cubist," who published some of his crucial projects in the socialist review *Červen* (June) and who was the only architect to join the cubist group *Tvrdošíjní* (The Stubborn Ones), which was formed in reaction against the official, patriotic direction of descriptive realism in art. Hofman's influence made its mark on the first architects of the association *Devětsil*, on the members of the group *Puristická čtyřka* (The Purist Four), as well as on some architects from the *Stavba* circle.

An even more remarkable contribution to the further development of pyramidal cubism was made by Jiří Kroha (1893–1974), graduate of the Czech Polytechnic, who drew many essential cubist methods to their logical conclusion in his theoretical manifestos, drawings, and projects from 1917 to 1922, the time before he left Prague for Mladá Boleslav and Brno. In his theory of the so-called form sequences, Kroha systematized the ideas of cubist perspectival illusionism, which had so far appeared only sporadically in texts written during the height of the cubist period, that is, between 1911 and 1914. According to Kroha, form sequences were created as individual phases of optical perspectival fragmentation of the "basic form," and it was necessary to change this a posteriori "transcription," which was performed unwittingly and automatically, into a conscious principle.[31] Kroha's ideas about the cubist concept of space were no less interesting. His view was that at the birth of every building stands an idea, "a creative thought," which in his theory possessed strongly spatial qualities: it made space expand and was manifest in the walls marking its boundaries; it gave life to forms that were its "channel, the conduit of the creative tendency."[32] According to Kroha, the work of architecture was an expression of a spatial idea that preceded even the conception of its layout and plastic shape, and which did not simply attack matter in the sense of the deformations of prewar cubism but permeated it and coalesced with it.[33] These principles, much closer to Janák's concept of cubist ar-

chitecture than to the thinking of Hofman or Chochol, were illustrated in Kroha's competition project for the Catholic church in Vinohrady, 1919, in his renovation of the later destroyed cabaret hall Montmartre on Řetězová Street, 1918, and in his sketches of enigmatic interiors with dramatically fractured plastic forms breaking out of numerous cavities and being in turn broken up by space.

Beside pursuing this cubist-expressionist line, Kroha had been working from 1917 on projects in an almost purist style, the so-called proto-designs, which, like Chochol's drawings from 1914 to 1920, responded to the impulse of synthetic cubism and the way in which it reinforced the reality of things by giving them a new, autonomous constructive organization. Independent of Kroha's work, Bedřich Feuerstein, and later some of the youngest architects of the period — those born around 1900, like Jaroslav Fragner, Evžen Linhart, or Vít Obrtel — learned similar lessons from the evolution of cubism. The cubist designs of these architects lacked the pyramidal and crystallic forms characteristic of archi-

189

Jiří Kroha. Competition project for a church. Vinohrady, náměstí Jiřího z Poděbrad. 1919.

tectural cubism before World War I. Their forms were relatively robust, predominantly cubic or cylindrical, and were assembled into very original asymmetrical compositions.[34] Their work bore some similarities with rondocubism, instead of with pyramidal cubism, but without its patriotic undertones.

The last important architectural style born in the prewar period was the geometrical modern style, which came to a new prominence after 1922, partly due to the crisis of cubist architecture and partly in response to the arrival of various new rationalist directions. Furthermore, the modern style presented an alternative to purism and functionalism, and it was adopted by architects who were not adventurous enough to respond to the latest impulses of the purist-functionalist new architecture but who nevertheless wished to be considered as modernists. This was primarily the attitude of Kotěra's students. Like late cubism, the modern style of the twenties differed from its original prewar stage. When Pavel Janák

190

Evžen Linhart. Study for a church. Circa 1920.

Jaroslav Fragner. Study for an apartment building. Circa 1921.

defended it in 1925, along with the last vestiges of cubism, against the austere, rationalistic, and pragmatic theories of functionalism, he used almost the same arguments with which he opposed the modern style in 1910–1911. He suggested that architecture should not limit its expression to mere constructiveness but that it should be "something more ... creation ... an activity that stands above its practical purpose," because only the creative "spirit" is able to breathe life into passive matter.[35] The buildings of this "spiritualized" modern style, which reflect Janák's ideas, often reveal their authors' earlier experience of cubist expressionism. Their volumes tend to be dramatically shaped, and a particular emphasis is placed on color harmony of the surfaces and on the abstract patterns of light and shadow in the numerous indents and under the prominent cornices.

Jan Kotěra, the founder of modern Czech architecture, experienced a deep creative crisis during the last five years of his life, before his untimely death in 1923. He was bitterly disappointed by the fact that the new government failed to entrust him with monumental projects in recognition of his merits. Furthermore, he found it difficult to come to terms with the new stylistic expectations that went against the grain of his earlier tectonic style and its austere purity. Kotěra's best project, designed in Prague at the beginning of the twenties, was the office building of the ironworks Vítkovické železárny on Olivová Street, 1921–1924, conceived in a classically oriented modern style whose architectural elements provided the basic framework for its rational composition, softened by the play of light and shadow in the curved cubist details around the entrances. A harsher and less outstanding example of the same stylistic mixture can be found in Kotěra's Charles University Law School. He produced a series of plans for this building in the years 1909, 1911, 1914, and 1920, but did not live to see the unsuccessful realization of his last version.

Kotěra's place as professor at the Academy of Fine Arts, and also as the leading figure in the mainstream of Czech architecture of the twenties, was taken over by Josef Gočár, whose working life was at that time divided between Prague and Hradec Králové. Gočár's creative personality was not theoretically oriented, and his approach was largely instinctive, but because he was a man of

Jan Kotěra. Office building. Nové Město, Olivova 1, 3.
1921–1924.

"infallible artistic instinct"—as his student Jan Sokol described him—he was able to produce strong works even at a time of unsettled stylistic and aesthetic norms. In the timber huts at Kbely Airport, 1920–1921, today situated in the Prague Zoo, Gočár tried out for the first time the loud, multicolored ornamental style of national rondocubism. In the key building designed in this style, the Czechoslovak Legiobank on Na poříčí Street, 1921–1923, the new architectural vocabulary is rendered in noble stone. The facade of the building is divided into three horizontal bands of different height. The lowest one comprising the entrance was conceived as an original three-part triumphal arch: on four partially sunken columns, Gočár placed figurative reliefs of bearers by the sculptor Jan Štursa, and above them, a long figurative frieze by Gutfreund depicting the victorious struggle of the Czechoslovak voluntary legions that were organized in France, Italy, and Russia by T. G. Masaryk during World War I. The four office stories above present a colorful mosaic of cylindrical supports and semicircular lintels, topped with a monumental projecting cornice decorated with semicircular patterns. The building is completed with a substantial attic. The same circular geometry appears also in the interior of the building, mainly in the central hall, where it is employed not only in the flat decorations on the counters, columns, and walls but also in the curves of the glass ceiling, constructed from three intersecting horizontally suspended cylinders. It may seem that here rondocubism developed its own spatial type that had logically evolved from its idiosyncratic vocabulary. This idea must, however, take into consideration the singularity of this approach among the interiors of buildings designed in the style of rondocubism, as well as the conspicuous similarity between Gočár's interior and the hall of the Post Office Savings Bank built in Vienna by Otto Wagner in 1904.

In the light of contemporary—and in particular functionalist—criticism, the Czechoslovak Legiobank appears to be the most problematic building erected in Prague in the twenties. Oldřich Starý described it in *Stavba* as an expression of the "chaos of the time," and according to Karel Teige there was no evidence of "programmatic nationalism" in the appearance of the Legiobank—a dubious assertion, considering the historical context of the building and the themes

Josef Gočár. Czechoslovak Legiobank. Nové Město, Na poříčí 24. 1921–1923.

Toward a New Prague

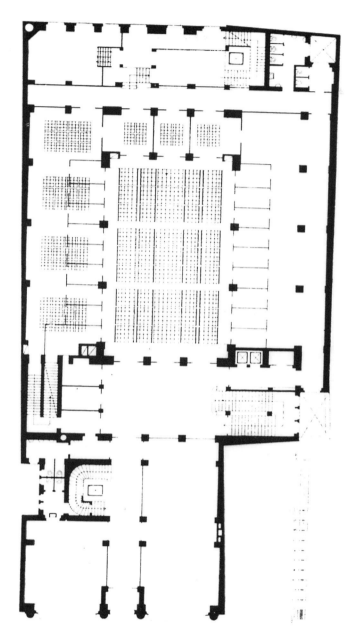

Josef Gočár. Czechoslovak Legiobank, interior. Nové Město,
Na poříčí 24. 1921–1923.

Josef Gočár. Czechoslovak Legiobank, floor plan. Nové
Město, Na poříčí 24. 1921–1923.

of its sculptural decoration—but it made an "unpleasantly baroque impression with its clumsy, overcrowded appearance and with the heaviness of its color-scheme and form."[36] Orthodox functionalists could not, of course, show any understanding for Gočár's individualistic interpretation of the classicist syntax or for the almost childlike absence of artificiality in his compositional method. In the years following the building of the Legiobank, Gočár himself became interested in the developmental possibilities of the geometrical modern style combined with influences from contemporary Dutch architecture and especially with Dudok's style, which he was studying at the time. This can be seen in his Rural Education Building on Slezská Street, 1924–1926. For all the rationalism of its plastic composition and organization of its surfaces with the striking use of red-brick facing, this work is full of lively expressiveness that points to cubism: it is apparent in its energetic silhouette, as well as in the unobtrusive use of oblique lines instead of the expected right angles, both in the floor plan and in the contouring.

The work of Pavel Janák, who in 1921 became Professor at the School of Applied Arts and whose influential theoretical texts to some extent reflected also Gočár's contribution, evolved in the first half of the twenties along similar lines. In 1920–1921, Janák designed the family villa on Na lysinách Street in the style of ornamental rondocubism, and in the same period he also designed the facade of the Juliš Patisserie in Wenceslas Square. As the architect Karel Honzík wrote later, young architects came to consider its "primitivist pink curves boldly placed on the white facade" as a "challenge to all the exhausted laws set down in academic recipe books."[37] The excitement of the future members of the group *Puristická čtyřka*, however, did not last for long. From 1922 to 1925, Janák in collaboration with Josef Zasche built his most important work in the style of rondocubism. It was the office building of the Italian company Riunione Adriatica di Sicurtà, also called Adrie, in Jungmannovo Square. Here, the architect had to come to terms with a difficult building program, and in particular with the requirement for a series of stepped terraces on the side facing Národní Street. Furthermore, he chose a demanding silhouette for this building by crowning it with massive battlements, a motif imitating the town halls of the Italian Renaissance city republics.

Following pages: Pavel Janák. The Juliš Patisserie. Nové Město, Wenceslas Square 22. 1920, demolished 1928.

Josef Gočár. Rural Education Building. Vinohrady, Slezská 7. 1924–1926.

Pavel Janák. Villa Hořovský. Hodkovičky, Na lysinách 2. 1921–1922.

Pavel Janák. Villa Hořovský, entrance hall. Hodkovičky, Na lysinách 2. 1921–1922.

Pavel Janák, Josef Zasche. Adrie building. Nové Město, Jungmannova 31. 1922–1925.

Toward a New Prague

The rich, detailed relief only reinforces the pomposity of this intentionally historicizing form, which was in grotesque contrast with the prosaic, bureaucratic purpose of the building.

Jaromír Krejcar adopted a purist point of view when he wrote in 1923 that in Gočár's contemporary work the cubist ornament only hides "a healthy plastic strength" whereas Janák's works drown in "historicism, idle nationalist traditionalism, and eclecticism."[38] Despite its controversial nature, Janák's Adrie is an original, inimitable work of architecture without which we can no longer imagine one of the busiest intersections on the boundary of Old and New Town.

After the Adrie project, Janák abandoned rondocubism, and his work began to move in two different directions. The first, "intimate" direction is represented by three family villas designed in the years 1923 and 1924 for friends of the architect, the sculptor Kafka, the painters Beneš and Filla, and the philosopher Krejčí, between Cukrovarnická, Lomená, and Na Ořechovce Streets. Their style could be described as "expressive modern style." Here again Janák used the red brick facing, evocative of homely coziness, combined with very steep pitched roofs, and he carved out the buildings' volumes in several places. The second, "monumental" direction of his work began with the administrative building of the Škoda works, 1924–1926, next to Adrie on Jungmannova Street. On the facade of this "strange heavy sculpture"—as the functionalist J. E. Koula described its barbaric, lithic classicism[39]—Janák placed monumental granite blocks in gradually thickening layers. The spaces between the blocks thus become deeper the closer they are to the main cornice, intensifying the depth of the shadows they cast.

Kotěra's pupil Otakar Novotný, Janák's colleague at the School of Applied Arts from 1929, always reacted to new developments in contemporary architecture with a certain delay. In this way he avoided taking risks, but on the other hand his reserved attitude meant that in his postwar work he had the opportunity to put up a persistent fight in an ideological battle that had been fought long ago by others. From 1919 to 1921, Otakar Novotný built apartment blocks for the Association of State School Teachers on Elišky Krásnohorské Street. Designed in the style of slightly decorative pyramidal cubism, these buildings use the

Pavel Janák. Villa Beneš. Střešovice, Cukrovarnická 24.
1923–1924.

205

modern two-section floor plan, and their colorful facades are bordered with fan-shaped ornaments. In the apartment block on Kamenická Street, 1923–1924, Novotný employed the expressive means of rondocubism, and the facade shows his unique understanding of the possibilities offered by this style with its plastic qualities and visual effects of light and shadow. Later Novotný also returned to the principles of the modern style, using the experience he had gained while designing the Štenc House before the war.

Important cubist buildings were also designed by Kotěra's student Jaroslav Vondrák at the beginning of the twenties. On Bubenečská and Českomalínská Streets, Vondrák built a series of apartment blocks in 1922–1923, the facades of which were decorated with small pyramidal and circular motifs, which again made an impressive use of the play of light and shadow. From this cubist point of departure, Vondrák developed his modern work. The standardized houses on Lomená, Západní, and Východní Streets in the suburb of Ořechovka, 1920–1922, with their characteristic triangular gables, long narrow windows, high chimneys and timber-frame masonry, imitate the vocabulary of the English cottage in the garden cities of Bedford Park, Hampstead, and Letchworth. On the other hand, the dynamic asymmetrical composition and brick facing of Vondrák's own house, built in 1923–1924 in nearby Machar Square, seems to follow the models of contemporary Dutch architecture.

The English orientation of the late modern style was also apparent in some of the works of Kotěra's student and colleague Ladislav Machoň, 1888–1974, who between 1918 and 1922 adopted both pyramidal cubism and rondocubism. Machoň's creative nature, however, was inclined toward the muted, less expressive styles of the time. The standardized family houses on the Ve stromkách estate, situated on Šrobárova and Bratří Čapků Streets, 1922–1924, which were designed on the basis of an ingenious two-bay ground plan, refer in a cultivated manner to the English domestic revival movement, recognizable by the cantilevered masses of their walls, the steep pitched roofs with gables, and picturesque attics. In the apartment blocks on Korunní Avenue, 1923–1924, and in his numerous family villas from the twenties, Machoň returned to Kotěra's modern

Pavel Janák. Škoda office building. Nové Město, Jungmannova 29. 1923–1926.

Otakar Novotný. Apartment buildings for teachers. Staré
Město, Elišky Krásnohorské 10–14. 1919–1921.

Otakar Novotný. Apartment building. Holešovice, Kamenická 35. 1923–1924.

Ladislav Machoň. Family duplex. Vinohrady, Šrobárova 30–
32. 1923–1924.

style. In his most interesting project from this period, the completion of the early baroque educational complex Klementinum that was to house the university library, 1923–1922, Machoň turned this reclaimed style into an austere and inconspicuous classicism, intended to attract as little attention as possible to these new buildings in their baroque surroundings.

Somewhere between cubism, the modern style, and classicism stood the work of several other architects of the period, all of them Kotěra's contemporaries, collaborators, and pupils of secondary importance. Among them were, for instance, František Kavalír and František Vahala, the authors of the fine neoclassicist school buildings on Sázavská Street and Žižka Square, and Rudolf Stockar, Bohumír Kozák, Jan Chládek, Eduard Hnilička, Josef Francŭ, Jindřich Freiwald, Theodor Petřík, and his architect-wife Milada Pavlíková-Petříková, whose rondocubist houses appear to be almost as impressive as those designed by Pavel Janák and Josef Gočár. The only older architect who kept up with the younger generation was Alois Dryák, former disciple of Friedrich Ohmann and one of the first Prague architects to work in the modern style, who designed the Trade Union Building on Na Perštýně Street, with its facade decorated with a cubist relief.

The majority of Prague architects whose work shifted between different styles — sometimes intentionally, sometimes with a modicum of confusion — published in the twenties in the review *Styl*. The title fits the nature of their endeavors and the type of problems on which they concentrated. For most of Kotěra's pupils and their contemporaries, form remained the main concern of architectural creation that was seen in terms of generating artistic ideas governed by the rules of style, which would in turn influence and create these rules. They still accepted Janák's theories formulated at the dawn of cubism in 1910–1911 and his words about the creative spirit overcoming matter, which Janák had the opportunity to repeat again in 1925. Talented architects, guided by his program, created works whose indisputable originality still appeals to us today, and even their less-gifted colleagues designed charming and unusual buildings on the basis of this program. However, it had its weak points that lay in its latent self-serving nature

211

and in the consequent production of new forms that were increasingly more difficult to justify. Janák's creative spirit could not continue to rely on itself; it was in need of corrective and counterbalancing measures. Vlastislav Hofman sought such measures already in 1913 in the properties of matter. At the beginning of the twenties, architects began to discuss the requirements of construction, as well as the purpose, functions, and the very life to which architecture must be subjected and which it should serve. Reliance on an intrinsic regulative capacity of a style—that is, style perceived as a series of rules—apparently carried the risk of entering a vicious cycle that could be broken only by artists of Plečnik's stature.

PURISM

The new look of Prague from 1918 to 1925 was largely determined by architects such as Josip Plečnik, Antonín Engel, Bohumil Hypšman, Pavel Janák, Josef Gočár, and other members of the generation born between 1870 and 1890, as they were the ones entrusted with the largest and most prestigious commissions. The future appearance of the city, the way it would look in the late twenties and thirties, was also being decided during this period in as yet unrealized projects and drawings produced by the forthcoming generation of young architects. The earliest projects of the period immediately following World War I were mostly designed in the cubist style. However, as Karel Honzík recorded in his memoirs, some architects were "dazzled" by the formal clarity and simplicity of Josef Chochol's purist projects shown in the exhibition of the group *Tvrdošíjní* in 1921 and published simultaneously in the review *Musaion*. In his new department store and office building on Jindřišská Street, 1920–1921, Chochol demonstrated these qualities in practice. In the same year, the news of parallel endeavors on the part of foreign architects such as J. J. P. Oud in Holland and Le Corbusier in France reached Prague. These local and international developments combined to create a stimulating environment from which Prague emerged as one of the European centers of purist-functionalist architecture.

The base of Czech purism was formed by three architectural groups. The first comprised the members of *Devětsil*, an avant-garde, left-wing association founded by a group of young poets, writers, painters, graphic artists, and architects in 1920. The second was born within the framework of the Club of Architects incorporating graduates of the Czech Polytechnic, which concentrated around the review *Stavba*. The third of the purist-oriented groups brought together the pupils of Kotěra and Gočár, who were mostly members of the *Sdružení architektů* (Association of Architects), which published the review *Stavitel* (The Builder). The three groups coexisted in an atmosphere of quiet competition, as well as collaboration, and there were no strict demarcation lines among them.

The original program of *Devětsil* from 1920 to 1922 opposed the glorification of modern technical civilization. The spokesmen of this group, the art theoretician Karel Teige (1900–1951) and the poets Jaroslav Seifert (1901–1986) and Jiří Wolker (1900–1924), were convinced that not only had modern technology so far exclusively served the capitalist entrepreneurial class but that it had also equipped the same class with weapons of mass destruction. According to them, the focus of the new progressive art would be the working man and woman, their social sensibilities, and their way of seeing and experiencing the world. In the essay "Nové umění proletářské" (The New Proletarian Art), published in 1922 in the *Revoluční sborník Devětsilu* (Revolutionary Anthology of Devětsil), Seifert and Teige wrote about the new beauty of popular, working-class entertainment which encompassed the circus, football, early film comedies, and dime novels set in the Wild West and other faraway places. In other essays from this period they discovered the poetry of the festive boulevard with its advertising signs, fluttering flags, and striped awnings of cheap cafés.[40] In the beginning, the poets of *Devětsil* devoted themselves to writing what they called proletarian poetry. Characterized by artlessness and innocence, this poetry celebrated the working people's sense of collectivity and brotherhood and sought beauty in the simplest things of life. The painters of *Devětsil* were trying to depict the same values through visual means borrowed from Douanier Rousseau. This program of "poetic primitivism," as it was later appropriately named, was joined also by Alois Wachsman and Josef

Alois Wachsman. Study for a tombstone. 1920.

Havlíček, two architects who had been active in the group from its inception. Both were impressed by Vlastislav Hofman's cubist projects, and both tried to render Hofmanesque forms in solid, precisely carved volumes, which they sketched in a naive style resembling children's drawings.

Wachsman and Havlíček left *Devětsil* for a long time in 1922, following a disagreement with Teige, and their place was taken by Bedřich Feuerstein and Jaromír Krejcar. In Bedřich Feuerstein (1892–1936), a graduate of the Czech Polytechnic who also briefly studied under Plečnik and who became known as architect, painter, stage designer, and essayist, *Devětsil* gained an artist who was well informed about worldwide developments in art and architecture. In 1912 Feuerstein made a trip to St. Petersburg to study Russian neoclassical architecture, and from 1921 to 1922 he lived in France where he became acquainted with Le Corbusier's purism and with the classicizing modern style of Auguste Perret, in whose office he worked between 1924 and 1926. Later, he was employed in Japan by the Czech-born architect Antonin Raymond. In comparison with the work of his predecessors in *Devětsil*, Feuerstein's designs were more mature and sophisticated. Stylistically, his work did not differ from Wachsman's and Havlíček's: he too aimed at a synthesis of the pyramidal and circular geometry of cubism and the neoclassicist sense for solid form. Feuerstein's architectural drawings from 1918 capture one of the stages in these endeavors, showing a crystal-shaped building with two recessed terraces. The plastic grill of the facade consists of circular and cylindrical sections, the flat roofs are surrounded by bar railings with flags flying above. The white cylinders and cylindrical sections, inviting the viewer to delight in their curved shapes, were the dominant elements of Feuerstein's best-realized project from the time of his membership in *Devětsil*: the crematorium in Nymburk, 1922–1924. In Prague he designed the Geographical Institute on Roosevelt Street, 1921(?)–1925, a monumental three-wing edifice whose precisely shaped pilaster-strips and cornices are a distillation of all the lessons he had learned from classicist architecture.

During 1922, *Devětsil*'s original program of opposition to technical civilization was replaced with the belief in the "art of living" and "enjoying all the

beauties of the world." The spiritual leaders of *Devětsil* became aware that life in the twentieth century would no longer be possible without modern technology, which, after all, belonged to its most prominent characteristics, along with modern art. The revolutionaries among *Devětsil* members were impressed by news of Lenin's plan for the electrification and industrialization of Soviet Russia. They began to study Marxism—which they also called "technical materialism"—and showed an increasing admiration for Soviet constructivism and other avant-garde currents inspired by modern technology. In summer 1922, Teige and Seifert went to Paris where they enthusiastically viewed new works of Orphism, neocubism, and purism, described by Teige as "the scientific climax of cubism."[41] Back in Prague, the ground for the introduction of similar directions was being prepared by the archi-

216

Bedřich Feuerstein. Architectural study. 1919.

tect Jaromír Krejcar, who had designed a large indoor market with two genuine American-style skyscrapers already in 1921, at a time when Teige still condemned futurism as art for the American industrialist. "Technology which has influenced the life of modern man to the extent that it has become unimaginable without it, could not remain unreflected in art," Krejcar wrote on September 3, 1922, in the newspaper *Československé noviny*.

The manifesto of *Devětsil*'s new program became the anthology *Život II* (Life II), edited by Krejcar in autumn 1922 and published in the beginning of the following year.[42] The anthology, reminiscent of the Paris review *L'Esprit Nouveau* both typographically and thematically, contained original essays on purism by Le Corbusier and Amedée Ozenfant, examples of Le Corbusier's latest projects, poems by Jaroslav Seifert and Vítězslav Nezval, an extract from the constructivist book by Ilja Erenburg *Yet It Does Move*, portraits of American film stars, and photographs of airplanes, steamships, skyscrapers and machines, accompanied by informative essays by Krejcar and Teige. The iconography of Czech purist architecture, which already included machinist elements, was now being programmatically enriched with nautical motifs, the unexpected beauty of which Krejcar highlighted in his article "Architektura transatlantických parníků" (The Architecture of Transatlantic Steamships), and with industrial motifs that were the theme of Krejcar's essay "Architektura průmyslových budov" (Architecture of Industrial Buildings), published in the beginning of 1923 in the magazine *Stavitel*. The new architectural attitude conveyed in *Život* was also reflected in Krejcar's sketches of a skyscraper, hotel, and country railway station. In his first realized project, the apartment building on Domažlická Street, 1923–1924, Krejcar cloaked in purist white the formal apparatus developed by his teacher Kotěra, whose work he commemorated in *Život* in a short biographical sketch written in French.

When in 1922 Kotěra assessed Krejcar's study results at the Prague Academy of Fine Arts, he said about his adventurous and anarchic student that "above all, he aimed at the application of his artistic convictions, which made the result of his studies somewhat one-sided."[43] The four students of the Czech Polytechnic who joined *Devětsil* in 1923 met with even greater disapproval from

217

Following pages:

Jaromír Krejcar. Study for a skyscraper. 1922.

Jaromír Krejcar, Kamil Roškot. Apartment building. Žižkov, Domažlická 10. 1923–1924.

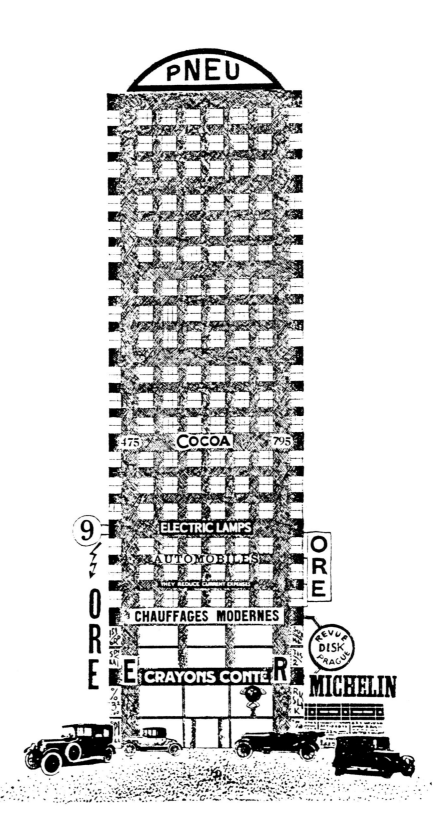

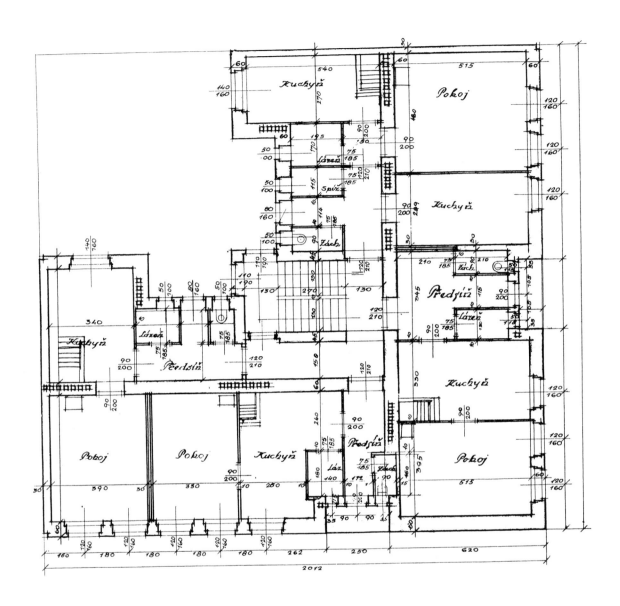

Jaromír Krejcar, Kamil Roškot. Apartment building, floor plan. Žižkov, Domažlická 10. 1923–1924.

220

their professors. The conflict between professors and students at the polytechnic stemmed from the old-fashioned concept of teaching whereby students were expected to produce meticulous drawings in various historical styles. A spa pavilion designed in 1921 by Karel Honzík (1900–1966) apparently prompted the following comment from his teacher Antonín Engel: "If you lit a fire underneath, it would set off like a locomotive."[44] Engel also protested against the publication of purist designs by his students Vít Obrtel (1901–1988) and Evžen Linhart (1898–1949) in the magazine *Stavba* in 1922, and he exhibited Obrtel's projects on the school notice board as an example of a badly executed assignment to be avoided by other students. The last of the four pioneers of Czech purism, Jaroslav Fragner (1898–1967), was so disillusioned with the teaching methods at the polytechnic that he left without graduating and set up his own architectural office in Prague around 1923.

The projects of the group *Puristická čtyřka* (The Purist Four), as these architects were called, endeavored to present the beauty of the simplest cubic and cylindrical volumes enriched with more complex symmetrical and asymmetrical figures of balconies, terraces, bow windows, and *avant-corps*. An important role in the overall effect of these designs was played by carefully plotted patterns of shadows, which the architects of *Puristická čtyřka* learned to draw so well from their unpopular teachers at the Polytechnic. The members of this group shared a liking for the simplicity of classicist architecture of the late eighteenth century and of the buildings commissioned by the enlightened Austrian Emperor Josef II, as well as for designs from the time of the French Revolution, which Karel Teige described as "advanced revolutionary neoclassicism."[45] They also shared a passion for the simplest objects that served as components of the new architecture: round lampshades, lightbulbs, metal railings made of wire and tubing, gutter pipes. Their fellow member in *Devětsil*, the poet Jiří Wolker, expressed their attitude in the famous line "I love things, the silent comrades." Characteristic for the style of *Puristická čtyřka* was also the naïve air of their projects, another legacy—along with the love of things simple—of *Devětsil*'s original program of poetic primitivism, which was probably reinforced by their awareness that, in a small Central European country,

221

the icons of new architecture did not have to be the monumental ocean liners fancied by Le Corbusier and his follower Krejcar, nor even the menacing steel battleships of the Russian Revolution that had undoubtedly served as a source of symbolism and formal experience for Soviet constructivism, but rather the little pleasure steamboats that made their Sunday excursions on the Vltava. The favorite theme of Czech purists' projects were buildings for special occasions—cafés, spa and exhibition pavilions, sports clubs—in other words, places associated with "sitting, sipping a drink and listening to the gramophone, while fountains whisper in the gardens and lanterns light up one by one."[46]

    The projects designed by the four architects between 1921 and 1925 displayed a uniform style and consistent artistic quality. Outstanding among them were the designs of Evžen Linhart with their sophisticated composition and an almost magical aura emanating from every shape. In his municipal apartment buildings on Radhošt'ská and Pod Plískavou Streets, 1925–1928 and 1925–1927,

Karel Honzík. Study for a spa pavilion. Circa 1921.

Linhart had the opportunity to apply some of the characteristics of Czech purism in practice. Only a few other architects were equally lucky — Karel Honzík with his renovation of a family house in Za Strahovem, 1925–1926; Linhart's friend and epigone Jan Rosůlek with his municipal apartment buildings on Zikova and Radlická Streets, 1925–1928; and Jaroslav Fragner in his hospital pavilion in the remote Mukačevo (now in the Ukraine), 1924–1928, whose exaggerated industrial motifs already suggest a new stage in the development of purist-functionalist architecture.

Among the architects associated with the review *Stavba*, it was Jan E. Koula (1896–1975) whose work placed him closest to the philosophy of *Devětsil*. His project for a waterfront café from 1923 could well have been designed by any of the members of the *Puristická čtyřka*. Koula also participated in *Devětsil's* exhibitions and published his designs in one of the short-lived reviews of *Devětsil*, *Pásmo* (Zone), 1924–1926. Other architects around *Stavba*, such as Oldřich Starý,

223

Vít Obrtel. Study for a family house. 1921.

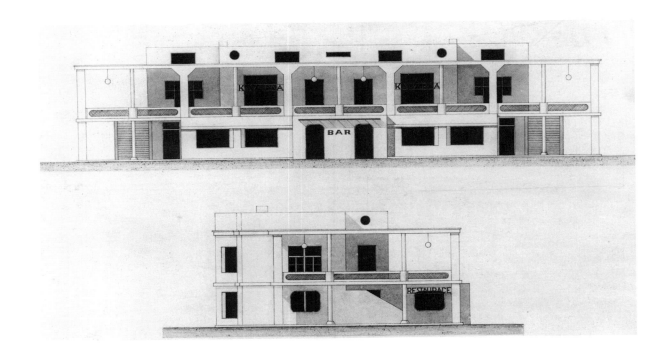

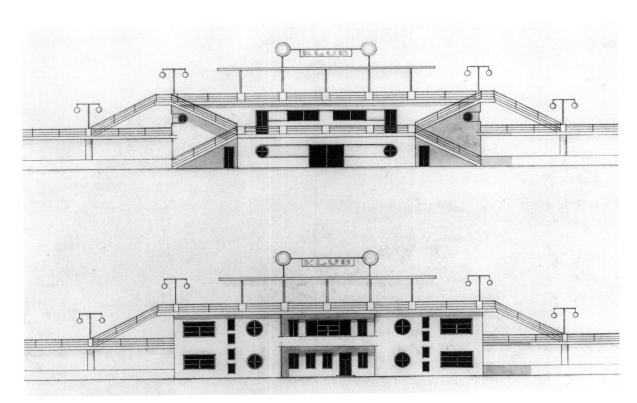

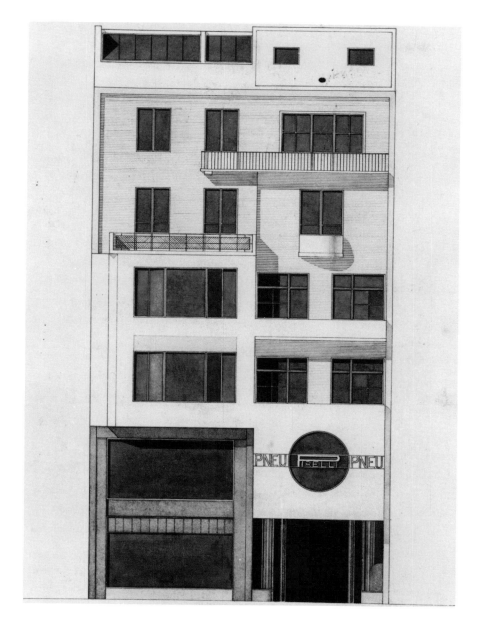

Evžen Linhart. Study for a bar pavilion. 1923.

Vít Obrtel. Study for a rowing club building. 1922–1923.

Evžen Linhart. Study for the Pneu Pirelli commercial build-ing. 1923.

Toward a New Prague

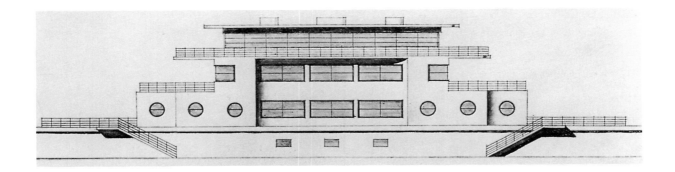

František A. Libra, František X. Čtrnáctý, Ludvík Kysela, Bohumil Sláma, and Bohumír Kozák, mostly lacked Koula's romanticism. Nevertheless, the first volumes of *Stavba* contained some remarkable examples of purist architecture. Very interesting, for instance, were the designs of Oldřich Tyl (1884–1939), who first worked in the architectural office of Matěj Blecha and who later employed in his own office several talented Prague purists and functionalists including Jan E. Koula, Ferdinand Fencl, Antonín Černý, and others. The facades of Tyl's apartment buildings on Nezamyslova Street, 1922–1923, perforated with a monotonous pattern of square windows, were still fashioned in the cubist mode and were brought to life by the subtle play of light and shadow achieved by lateral illumination. From a distance, however, these facades look rather flat and bare. Oldřich Tyl came into close contact with the austere classical architecture that proved so stimulating for many of his contemporaries when he was commissioned to design a vertical extension for the neoclassicist administrative building of the Ministry of Education on Karmelitská Street in 1922. The precise quadrantal ground plan of his YWCA hostel on the corner of Kubelíkova and Žižkova Streets, 1923–1926, necessitated its magnificently curved purist volume and rounded facade, which was again studded with relatively small square windows.

Some architects congregating around *Stavba* looked to the example of the Paris architect Auguste Perret, preferring his rationalist modern style based on the constructive possibilities of reinforced concrete to the radical experi-

Jan E. Koula. Study for a waterfront café. 1923.

ments of Le Corbusier or Walter Gropius. Within *Devětsil*, the follower of Perret was Bedřich Feuerstein; in the *Stavba* circle it was, above all, Alois Špalek, already known as the author of the preconstructivist building of the Hlava Institute of Pathology on Studničkova Street, 1913–1920. On nearby Albertov Street, Špalek built from 1923 to 1925 another large teaching hospital, the Purkyně Institute, whose formal composition combines Perretian tectonics and the purist sense for large, simple volumes with cubist richly patterned portals and entrances. Another design that followed Perret's example was one of the most beautiful purist interiors, the exhibition hall of the Museum of Agriculture, 1923–1924, situated in the Kinský Garden in Smíchov, which was designed by Jan Víšek (1890–1966) as an extension to its neoclassicist garden house.[47] Víšek conceived the hall in the form of a tunnel-shaped cylindrical section, illuminated through a glass strip placed in the arch of the reinforced concrete vault. The milky white light subtly contours the interior of this refined space, suffusing its Perretian construction with the mysterious atmosphere of a science laboratory.

The Academy of Fine Arts' Department of Architecture, headed first by Kotěra himself and later by Gočár, adopted purism along with its official style, which derived mainly from Kotěra's pre–1910 work and from contemporary Dutch examples. The characteristic feature of this style, applied for example in the cooperative housing on Kafkova Street designed by Josef Havlíček and Vladimír Wallenfels (1925–1927), was the reduction of the modern syntax to several logically justifiable tectonic elements—base, pilaster, architrave. Purism was programmatically adopted by the school after 1925, when Josef Gočár employed the new style ahead of many of his students in the design of the first purist villa in Prague, commissioned by the building contractor Strnad on Na Marně Street. Interesting purist projects were produced in Gočár's department by Pavel Smetana, Karel Seifert, František M. Černý, and Josef Havlíček, who all joined *Devětsil* around 1926 as a third wave of architect members. The best Purist building that in its conception points to Gočár's "Dutch" interpretation of this style was, however, designed by František Bartoš, Gočár's favorite pupil who left Prague for Hradec Králové in 1926. Bartoš's Institute of Hydrology on Papírenská Street in Bubeneč,

227

Following pages: *Oldřich Tyl. YWCA hostel. Žižkova, Kubelíkova 16. 1923–*
1926.

Alois Špalek. Purkyně Institute of Physiology. Nové Město,
Albertov 4. 1923–1925.

Jan Víšek. Exhibition hall of the Museum of Agriculture.
Smíchov, Kinského zahrada 97. 1923–1924.

CHAPTER 3

*Josef Gočár. Villa Strnad. Bubeneč, Na Marně 5. 1925–
1927.*

1925–1929, was designed as an abstract composition created out of a solid orange mass of rectangles, placed both vertically and horizontally, and finished in fired bricks.

Another example of how Kotěra's last pupils interpreted purism were the designs of Kamil Roškot (1886–1945), whose early work could be described as purism cloaked in Kotěra's tectonic modern style. His first architectural works from the twenties—when he also designed the outstanding family villas on Chorvatská and Čechova Streets, 1923–1924,—were enclosed in a layer of plastically accentuated Kotěresque tectonic, whose shapes, projecting from the body of the building, cast shadows on its surfaces. The combination of external modern tectonic and internal purist volumes led Roškot to an unprecedented monumentality of expression. Later, he gradually rid the solid core of his buildings of the tectonic outer layer, bringing out their simple purist essence. Another work displaying this tendency toward abstraction, which was typical also for other architects of Kotěra's and Gočár's school, was Roškot's 1928 competition project for the parliamentary buildings in Letná.

Stylistically close to Roškot's architecture was the work of another of Kotěra's pupils, Jan Zázvorka (1884–1963), author of the winning project for the Liberation Memorial on Vítkov hill. Visitors to the memorial first encounter the Military Museum at the foot of the hill, on U památníku Street, 1926–1930. It is a group of buildings designed in a neoclassical vein, with facades either smooth or articulated by means of pilaster strips. The main body of the memorial on top of the hill, built in 1926 to 1932, was conceived by Zázvorka as a dynamic composition of solid plastic bodies—tall prisms and low semicylinders clad in white limestone—gradated in height toward the city center. Formally, the monument points to neoclassicism, tracing it back as far as Friedrich Gilly's designs for the Berlin National Theatre from 1797–1798. The interior of the memorial, richly decorated with mosaics, sculptures, and frescoes, was designed as a three-aisle hall, lit through tall, narrow windows in the side walls.

Another interesting variety of purist architecture developed in Kotěra's school is represented by the work of Josef Štěpánek (1889–1964). Ště-

232

BUDOVA PARLAMENTU.
NA SVAHU LETNÉ

Kamil Roškot. Competition project for the development of
Letná Plain. 1928.

Toward a New Prague

234

Kamil Roškot. Project for the Ministry of Public Works in Těšnov. 1929–1930.

Jan Zázvorka. Liberation Memorial. Žižkov, Vítkov Hill. 1926–1932.

Toward a New Prague

pánek participated in the 1922 competition for the rebuilding of the Michna Palace for the sport organization *Sokol* — known also as the Tyrš House Competition — with a strictly purist project, inspired by earlier drawings by Josef Chochol and enriched with interesting new forms such as gothicizing pointed arches and their fragments. The interior was also designed in the purist style: pristine barrel-vaulted ceilings with supporting arches. Here Štěpánek expressed his vision of a purist space by means of a tunnel-like shape, similar to Jan Víšek's exhibition hall in the Museum of Agriculture, which in his case derived from the monumental public spaces of neoclassicist architecture and was composed of the ideal geometrical forms — the prism and the cylinder. A similar hall with a barrel-vaulted ceiling, this time made of glass, can be found in another original purist building designed for the cultural society *Umělecká Beseda* by Kotěra's pupils Čeněk Vořech and František Janda in 1923 to 1925, which sensitively complements its historical surroundings on Besední Street in Malá Strana.

In some of their projects, the creators of Czech purism, and in particular the members of *Devětsil*, attained a level of quality and originality that matched the achievements of Czech cubism. However, the historical significance of this style is diminished by the fact that only a small number of the buildings designed during the legendary period of Czech purism that ended around 1925 were realized. Purist buildings continued to be designed after this date, but the style often served as a substitute for more radical approaches, which after 1925 began to take a functionalist direction. Some of the most interesting of these late purist

Josef Štěpánek. Competition project for the Tyrš House in Malá Strana. 1922.

buildings were designed, for instance, by Petr Kropáček, a member of the prewar cubist generation; Josef Kalous, a graduate from Kotěra's department; Plečnik's pupils Ludvík Hilgert and Alois Mezera; and two architects from the circle of the Polytechnic, Miloš Vaněček and Václav Křepel.

The word that frequently appeared in the theoretical programs of Czech and European purism was the adjective "new": "new art," "new forms," "new architecture," "new aesthetic," "new creative beauty," "new style," "new Prague."[48] It is true that the term "new art" had already been used by the cubists and before them by the pioneers of the modern style. They used it, however, for want of a better designation and did not insist on it in the same way as the purists who considered novelty to be the most essential quality of their art. The most important European purist review was called *L'Esprit Nouveau*; *Devětsil's* collection *Život* (Life) was subtitled *Anthology of New Beauty*; the essays written by Karel Teige and Oldřich Starý for the first volumes of *Stavba* had the titles "Toward a New Architecture" or "Developments toward a New Architecture."

The requirement of novelty meant, above all, a break from what was perceived as old. In this spirit, Karel Teige advocated in 1922 a complete purge of architecture of the "old, moldering culture," of the "senile impotence" of architectural directions developed in the nineteenth century and in the first decades of the twentieth.[49] Purism approved only of the simple forms of classicist architecture from the time around 1800 and, at best, the most rationalist creations of the geometrical modern style. In the purist manifesto "Oč usiluji" (What I Strive For), published in 1921 in *Musaion*, the review of the group *Tvrdošíjní*, Josef Chochol demanded that the new architectural form should "be an empowered expression of the purpose whose face it is," it should "stop at the precise function of this purpose and be free of anything that is superfluous," it should be "liberated at last from all the archaic influences, epigony, and eclecticism and never be touched by the poisonous stench of the decaying corpses of yesterday's styles."[50]

The artistic thinking of the purists was not limited to aesthetic visions of purified elementary forms. Their admiration for the "naked, pure, and austere beauty" of "new architecture" did not mean that they created something new merely for the sake of novelty. If we set aside the occasional flashes of purism before 1914, we must concede that the true beginnings of purism only date back to the time immediately following World War I and the Russian Revolution, that is, the events that gave rise to the independent Czechoslovak Republic. In the minds of young progressive architects, the "new" purist architecture was associated with a new social order that prevailed in postwar Europe.

Explaining the genesis of purism's expressive means, some theoreticians, and especially Jan E. Koula, emphasized the cathartic effect of war, or rather of the postwar atmosphere: the horrific experiences that bared the basis of human nature, the irrationality of war to which humankind reacted with the decision to start living differently, from a new and better beginning. "We have understood that we cannot do without light, air, water, and purity—purity of thought and form—if we are to overcome the postwar depression, if we are to reclaim the material and moral values lost to the war" wrote Jan E. Koula in his book *Obytný dům dneška* (The Residential Building of Today), published in 1931.[51] Initially, many purists associated the birth of the independent republic with a "new beginning" and hoped that it would be organized on a far more rational and socially just basis than the former Austro-Hungary. For the majority of theoreticians around the review *Stavba*, the functionality and rationality of purism reflected the capitalist order reformed in a functional and rational manner: when in 1924 the editors proclaimed their ambition to be "above all, an improvement in the living standard and in the standard of housing in particular, so that healthy living would no longer be the privilege of only some members of our society," they reached an extreme position in their social vision of the time.[52]

A far more radical attitude in interpreting the social significance of purism was adopted by the architects and theoreticians of *Devětsil*. To them the artistic innovations of purism were an expression of a revolutionary stance. The force which, according to Teige, gave rise to the purist new art, was "modern life and its social structure resulting from class struggle, revolution, and the purple dawn of a future that shall arrive, sooner or later." Above all, however, this force was the proletariat, "the bearer and creator of new social and political forms."[53]

Next to the principle of functionality, *Devětsil* architects adopted as their aesthetical basis the "method of constructivist purism" as it was characterised in 1924 by another theoretician of *Devětsil*, Josef Jíra, while "Marxism as technical materialism" provided the basis and meaning for their creative efforts.[54]

In the minds of *Devětsil* members, purist new art therefore became a symbol of a new revolutionary and socialist society. "[This art] presumes and is contingent on a new social organization of life, a newly consolidated society, in short—on social revolution"—pronounced Karel Teige in 1922. *Devětsil's* rejection of older styles is to be understood primarily as a rejection of everything that represented the old social order that, according to its theoreticians, was hopelessly outdated.

The most radical of *Devětsil's* left-wing members were, however, soon concerned about the gap between the function of their architectural experiments and the real needs of the workers, which were often limited to a simple requirement for shelter, for a roof over their heads. It is true that in 1926, Vít Obrtel wrote in the sixth issue of the periodical *Tam-tam* that it was more beautiful to have one's head above the roof,[55] and it was probably this and similar comments that prompted Teige's long-term hostility toward him. *Devětsil's* left-wing avant-garde architects found it equally difficult to come to terms with the fact that their revolutionary "new architecture" was not commissioned by the workers themselves but by state institutions or individual wealthy clients. This situation naturally made *Devětsil's* purism appear as a somewhat utopian laboratory experiment. The theoreticians of *Devětsil* tried to resolve these contradictions by developing the concept of "proto-images" or models.[56] In the context of this concept, purist architecture became a prophesy about architecture of a socialist tomorrow, a repository of as yet nonexistent social and cultural needs that would become reality in a not so remote future.

The years 1924 and 1925 were crucial for further development of Prague's avant-garde architecture. By that time, Jaromír Krejcar, Jaroslav Fragner, and Oldřich Tyl had taken their personal concept of purist architecture to a stage where it had lost some of the characteristics of Czech purism and began creating a new, more modern style in its place. This development was probably motivated by their attempt to come to terms with the ideological system of functionalism in which they recognized a formal and stylistic parallel and whose name they therefore adopted.

It was also on the basis of functionalism that around the same time Karel Teige formulated his theory about the death of architecture as an artistic discipline and the birth of architecture as science. In the process of forming a new style, this theory acted as a dividing force: there were those architects who agreed with Teige, and there were others who continued to consider themselves as artists and who therefore entered into a polemic with him. In the beginning, both sides thought of this dispute in rather theoretical terms, and even today it is possible to tell whether this or that architect belonged to the scientific or artistic camp from his theoretical views rather than from his architectural practice. However, both sides soon began to look for heroes who would exemplify one of their own stances, and for projects or existing buildings whose characteristics they could imitate and develop. In this way, theory gradually found its practical expression in the early buildings of Czech functionalism.

Functionalism as a system of ideas was born from the modern organization of factory work, from the contemporary cult of engineering and machine technology, and from the appreciation of purposeful activity expressed so clearly in American pragmatic philosophy. Another important center of functionalist theory was postrevolutionary Russia, where around 1920 Tatlin's and Rodchenko's circles created analogical concepts of productivism and constructivism. According to functionalist theory, the floor plan of a building, the positioning of individual spaces, and their mutual relationships and size corresponded to the function and purpose the building and its parts were to serve. The form of the building was not an a priori given: it was based solely on its functions. That is why, for instance, many functionalists avoided symmetry, which they suspected to have

Jaroslav Fragner. *Study for a villa. 1923, 1924.*

Toward a New Prague

its roots in formal apriorism. Form had to follow function. The example of situating and connecting factory spaces according to the stages of the production process led to the functionalist emphasis on the logical linking of individual rooms — the kitchen was placed next to the pantry and the dining room, the dining room next to the living room, the living room next to the study, the bedroom next to the bathroom and terrace, and so forth — on the orientation of the spaces, and on avoiding unnecessary and chaotic movements around the home. To the functionalist mind, the house became a machine — or more precisely a factory — for living. The functional layout of the building was to be designed in an analytical and scientific manner, with extreme precision but at the same time with creativity and intelligence matching the complexity of chess moves. A good layout required "lyricism" or at least "taste," which was defined by Karel Honzík in 1926 as "the ability to guess the form appropriate to the given solution."[57]

Functionalist principles were undoubtedly followed already by the pioneers of Czech purism. In the manifesto "Oč usiluji" from 1921, Josef Chochol called for the strengthening of the relationship between form and purpose, and similar demands appeared in later years in the writings of Karel Teige and Oldřich Starý. Characteristically, between 1914 and 1920, Chochol's purism was manifested only in the facades of his buildings and not in the internal arrangement that should have been the first indicator of a functional solution. In this respect the members of the *Puristická čtyřka* were far more active, but they too displayed a greater interest in the external appearance of a building rather than in its internal organization, which was often stereotypical and old-fashioned in comparison with the radical nature of the facade. As the Čtyřka's theorist Karel Honzík put it: "The facades were constructivist before the interior."[58]

One of the architects who tried to absorb functionalist principles already in 1924 and 1925 was Jaromír Krejcar, "the initiator and foremost creator of the new movement in Czech architecture," as he was described by Karel Teige in 1930. In 1924 Krejcar designed a more or less ideal family villa to be built in Zbraslav near Prague for the writer and chairman of *Devětsil*, Vladislav Vančura. In this project, he wanted to incorporate several contemporary European influences,

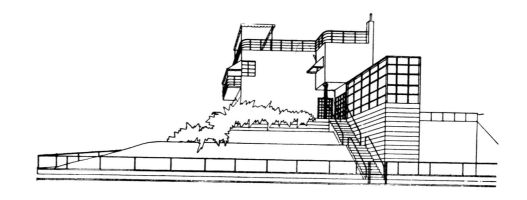

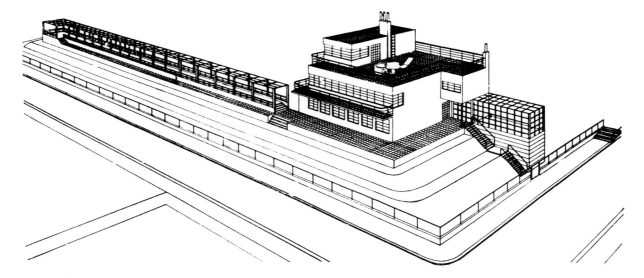

Jaromír Krejcar. Project for Vladislav Vančura's villa. 1924.

Toward a New Prague

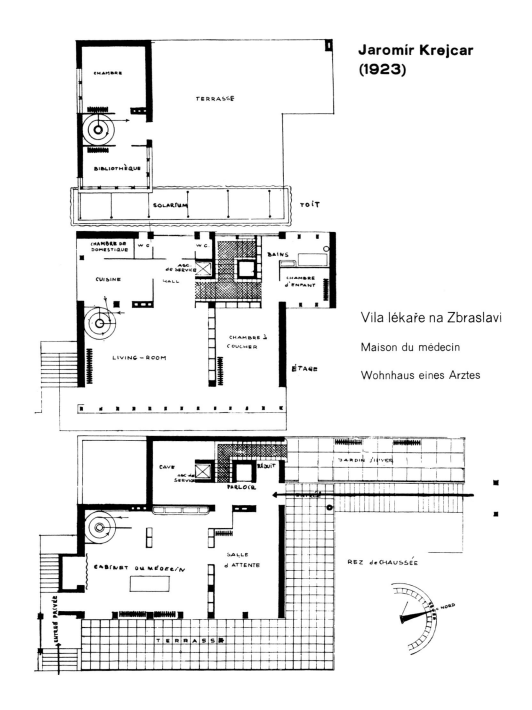

Jaromír Krejcar (1923)

Vila lékaře na Zbraslavi

Maison du médecin

Wohnhaus eines Arztes

Jaromír Krejcar. Vladislav Vančura's villa, floor plan. 1924.

244

and in particular that of Le Corbusier whose Vaucresson villa from 1922 he had obviously studied in great detail. It was Krejcar's ground plan and spatial layout that played the most important role in the overall appearance of the building. The floor plan of Vančura's villa represents an advanced example of the regrouped layout that uncompromisingly divides the individual spaces into the "servicing" ones, turned toward the slope behind the building, and the "serviced" ones, facing the southeast sun and the view of the Vltava Valley. On the first floor, Krejcar removed all divisions between individual rooms, creating a single, effectively unified space, and emphasizing the way in which the living quarters were conveniently ordered into one uninterrupted chain. The radical "spatialization" of the living interior of the villa not only abolished any demarcation lines between the rooms but was reflected also in the boxlike exterior, punctuated — in a manner typical for Krejcar — by a dense series of oblong windows with rounded corners and by long bands of windows running around the corners of the building. Krejcar's consistently spatial architectural thinking, his aiming at "the essence of architecture: space and its new solution" — as he himself described it at the beginning of 1923 — and his innovative discovery that "architecture is based on the interior,"[59] gave rise to a new type of architectural space: a large living room whose one side opened up into the garden and toward the south. Jaromír Krejcar laconically described this new type of space as "open space."[60] His younger colleague Ladislav Žák later spoke of "a kind of vitrine, open to the sun and the sweeping views."[61]

In his project Krejcar wanted to illustrate the effect of the expansive power of architectural space. Unlike Janák's or Kroha's cubist concept of active space, Krejcar's space attacked the object not from the outside but from the inside. The subject of the attack was not some dead, amorphous mass that would be given form only by the architect's "spirit," but a rectangular, boxlike container, which had been already developed by purist architecture. However, Krejcar's project for the Vančura villa no longer corresponded to the principles of Czech purism either. The walls, as he drew them, were not the strong and thick walls promoted by Czech purists, following the example of neoclassicism. Here they became a thin coating enveloping their rectangular spatial contents. Nor were these

245

Following pages: *Jaromír Krejcar. Project for the Olympic Building. Nové Město, Spálená 16. 1925.*

Jaromír Krejcar. Project for the Olympic Building. Nové Město, Spálená 16. 1926.

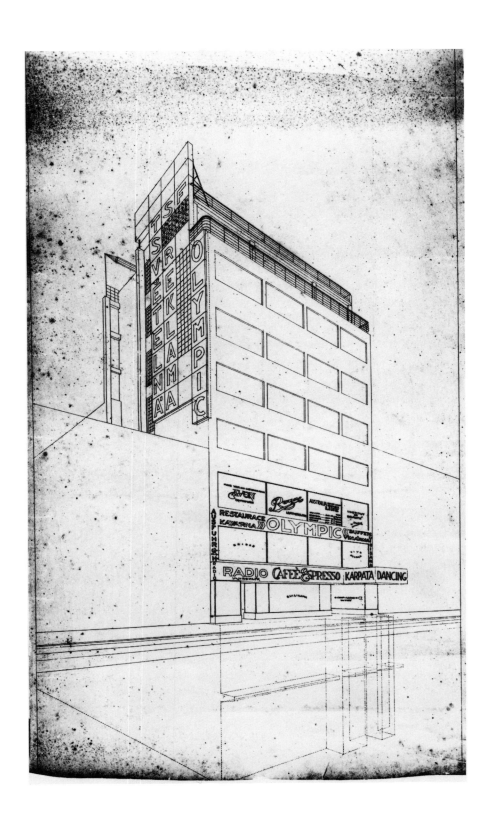

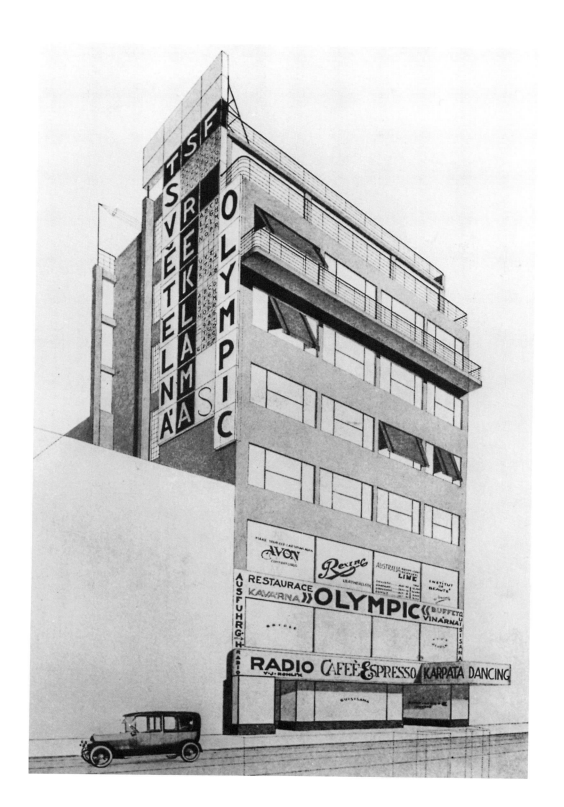

247

ČESKÁ STÁTNÍ POJIŠTOVNA

walls whole in the purist or neoclassical sense. The container of the building was broken from the inside by space, which divided it into alternating horizontal bands of masonry and glass. The spatial "vitrines" of the new style called for the characteristic ribbon windows — or the windows called for the form of the glass case — a feature functionalist architects borrowed from factory halls and ocean liners. Krejcar probably tried to express the lightness and thinness of the new style by means of a new drawing technique, different from the meticulous shading of purist drawings, and it was by means of the same shadowless lines that in 1924 Jaroslav Fragner captured his vision of the new functionalist style in his project for a villa published in the review *Veraikon*, and in the final designs for his hospital pavilion in Mukačevo.

The purist alternation of light and shadow was, however, a far too impressive device for the functionalists to discard. We can see this in Krejcar's Olympic Building on Spálená Street dating from the time of the transition from purism to functionalism. Krejcar began work on this project in 1923 and originally designed it in the same style as his apartment block on Domažlická Street, 1923–1924, with strong, plastic window ledges and relatively narrow elongated windows. However, only a minor part of his project, the now almost invisible north wing extending into the back courtyard, was eventually executed in this style. In 1925 Krejcar completely revised the plans for the remaining parts of the Olympic, the south courtyard wing and the main west wing that faces Spálená Street, creating one of his most impressive designs and the best example illustrating *Devětsil*'s architectural program. Unfortunately, the historical significance of this work was somewhat diminished by its heavy-handed realization in 1926 to 1928.

In spite of the purist shading, absent in the first version of the Olympic drawings from September 1925,[62] Krejcar's design yet again presented the functionalist concept of the building as a thin container, broken from inside by the active inner space. The three first floors were almost completely made of glass; in the higher ones the wide windows were aligned into continuous bands. Above all, the value of Krejcar's project lies in the way he succeeded in marrying the nascent functionalist aesthetic with those poetic elements that had been discovered

Jaromír Krejcar. Olympic Building. Nové Město, Spálená 16. 1925.

Jaromír Krejcar. Villa Gibian, view from the garden. Bube-
neč, Charlese de Gaulla 22. 1927–1929.

CHAPTER 3

Jaromír Krejcar. Villa Gibian, view from the street. Bubeneč,
Charlese de Gaulla 22. 1927–1929.

Toward a New Prague

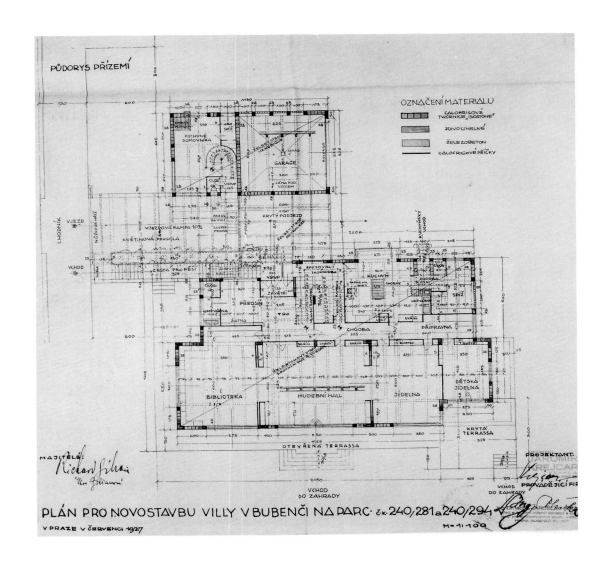

Jaromír Krejcar. Villa Gibian, floor plan. Bubeneč, Charlese
de Gaulla 22. 1927–1929.

252

for architecture in *Devětsil*'s early theories from 1920 to 1922, as well as in the later phase of *Devětsil*'s work heralded by Krejcar's anthology *Život*. Advertising signs, the use of different typography on the front facade and on the blind side wall of the Olympic Building, along with the striped awnings reminiscent of street cafés, all these features can be seen as a celebration of the metropolitan boulevard in festive garb, an image whose poetic power *Devětsil*'s theorists highlighted already in the early, naive stage of the group's activity. Antennas on the roof, wire mesh "ocean liner" railings of the balconies and terraces, the use of electricity for neon advertising, the total technicist conception of the building including the indispensable automobile parked on the street—all these features joined in a celebration of the poetry of modern technical civilization.

Krejcar's work from the second half of the twenties repeated and further developed the stylistic principles first expressed in the Olympic Building and in Vančura's villa. An example of this is the villa of the writer Grete Rainerová in Nad olšinami, 1926–1927, and, in particular, the large Villa Gibian on Charles de Gaulle Street, 1927–1929, in which Krejcar completely separated the servicing quarters by housing them in an independent north-facing wing connected with the south-facing living part of the house by means of a bridging ramp, probably following the example of Gropius's Bauhaus in Dessau. The boxlike building opens up southward through large windows. Transition between the closed volume of the building and the surrounding open space is mediated by the projecting, horizontal slabs of balconies and roofs, the terraces on the first floor and recesses on the ground floor, and by the mesh of timber pergolas and metal naval railings.

In several versions of the project for the cooperative house of the Association of Private Clerical Employees on Francouzská Street, 1927–1931, Krejcar worked his way from a playful technological romanticism of the version produced in 1927 to the final "matter-of-fact, restrained, sober, ascetic solution," evidenced by the realized building.[63] How far Krejcar took this cult of space—for which the German art historian Kurt Badt coined the fitting term "spacemania"—can be seen in the interiors of the recessed story, which was really a three-section residence where he lived with his wife, Milena Krejcarová-Jesenská.[64] "In the liv-

Following pages:

Jaromír Krejcar. *Building of the Association of Private Clerical Employees, view from the street. Vinohrady, Francouzská 4. 1930–1931.*

Jaromír Krejcar. *Building of the Association of Private Clerical Employees, view from the courtyard. Vinohrady, Francouzská 4. 1930–1931.*

Jaromír Krejcar. *Building of the Association of Private Clerical Employees, section. Vinohrady, Francouzská 4. 1930–1931.*

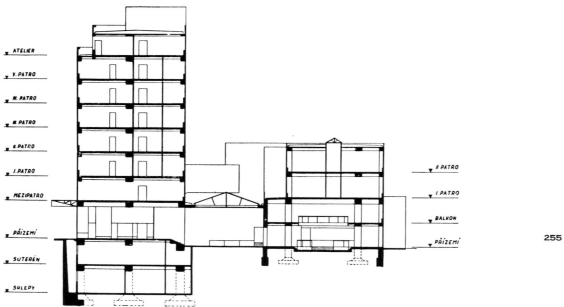

255

ing room, almost as large as a temple nave" — went the description of Krejcar's living hall in Gusta Fučíková's memoirs — "the three armchairs around the fireplace . . . and the dining table near the kitchen completely disappeared. An ample white sheet, thrown over a wooden pole, served as a wardrobe. . . . Jaromír had his room at the opposite end of the corridor, behind the office. He slept on mattresses which the maid, Mary, placed every evening on the floor and removed in the morning."[65] An empty space is also architecture would probably by the comment of Ladislav Žák, a young architect dazzled by the open spaces of Krejcar's urbanistic and architectural visions.

The capacity to express the poetry of the boulevard, the emphasis on the lyrical content of the technicist shaping of the building's total volume and details, the play of shadows against the bright white planes — all these made Krejcar's Olympic the best example of the direction in Prague's functionalism of the twenties that asserted its artistic character, intentionally stressing the emotional impact made by a work of architecture. The architect Karel Honzík, following Le Corbusier's arguments in *Vers une architecture*, 1923, later described this direction as "emotional functionalism." On the other hand, Krejcar's building designed for the Association of Private Clerical Employees, which Teige described as "matter-of-fact, restrained, sober, and ascetic," manifests the approach of an architect who no longer considered his profession as art but as science.

Karel Teige, the most influential of *Devětsil*'s theoreticians, stressed since 1922 that new art, and by extension also new architecture, would differ very little from the product of a factory worker or an engineer. He often quoted Flaubert's vision of an impersonal and scientific art of the future. The difference between the work of an engineer-technician and architect-artist was, according to Teige, historically conditioned, owing to the division of labor during the Industrial Revolution. New architecture would abolish this difference. The question of how this would happen was answered in his essay on modern Czech architecture published in *Veraikon* in 1924, and later again in the essay-manifesto "Konstruktivismus a likvidace 'umění'" (Constructivism and the Liquidation of 'Art') in *Devětsil*'s review *Disk*, 1925: architecture would become a science. "Ar-

256

chitecture, which in our time has been given an absolutely new technology, new materials, and constructive means, and which is being challenged with tasks quite different from those it performed in the religious, feudal Middle Ages, is also being separated from the fine arts; it ceases to be an art or a decorative craft and is becoming science, technology, industry," was how Teige clarified his thesis in the collection of essays *Mezinárodní soudobá architektura* (Contemporary International Architecture) published in 1930.[66]

This concept of architecture turned it into a precisely defined result of several abstracted functions — residential, working, sanitary, and communicational — a list to which a somewhat embarrassed Teige later added the aesthetic or "psycho-ideological" function, whose importance to a harmonious life he had never denied, believing as he did that this function would be fulfilled by other, "free" kinds of artistic creativity, primarily poetry and painting. Within the context of the contemporary ideological polarities, twenties' architecture was confined to the first of a series of opposites that were repeatedly formulated by Teige between 1924 and 1930: discipline versus freedom, precision versus lyricism, construction versus poetry, and constructivism versus poetism. Art with a capital A, as it had been so far understood, was seen by Teige as a bourgeois anachronism and a product of formalism. The new architecture was to be based on function, not on form. By extension, the task of the architect was to define these functions and to seek the most economical form to fulfil them, for "the law of economics is the law of all work."[67] In accordance with these views, Teige, enchanted by his vision of industrial mass production of building components, advocated their standardization, as well as the standardization of whole buildings. The monotonous repetition of one single element became in his thinking a positive aesthetic value; he sought the beauty of new architecture in "noble uniformity."

An integral part of Teige's program of scientific functionalism was his critique of monumentality in architecture and his polemic with those concepts that in the interest of artistic impression continued the tradition of nineteenth-century historicism with its reliance on the image of the palace, chateau, or temple. From this point of view, Teige considered the artistic aims of Wagner's classicism and of other conservative currents to be unacceptable. However, he also severely criticized Le Corbusier's book *Un maison, un palais* from 1928[68] and his project for the center of world culture, *Mundaneum*, which used references to the majestic architecture of palaces and temples as an indispensable element of its architectural vocabulary. "The error of Le Corbusier's *Mundaneum* is the error of monumentality . . . error of the palace," wrote Teige in 1929 in his famous critique of Le Corbusier's project, the significance of which has been pointed out by historians of modern architecture George Baird and Kenneth Frampton.[69] "Despite their understanding of important practical and utilitarian requirements," continued Teige "both Wagner and Le Corbusier see the ultimate aim of architecture, which they believe to be the supreme art, in the construction of some temple or tabernacle."[70] According to Teige, true modern architecture, subjected solely to the criterion of utility, had already abandoned the "mammoth body of monumentality" and instead of monuments began to create instruments. The advocates of scientific functionalism from Teige's circle no longer looked up to palaces and temples and instead adopted the down-to-earth and, as they believed, more economical and utilitarian forms of ships, railway carriages and industrial buildings, in a process that the Austrian art historian Hans Sedlmayr called "downward assimilation."[71]

"Whether the modern museum will look like a factory, whether the modern school will look like a rowing club, or whether the modern crematorium will resemble the hall of a power plant rather than the nave of a Catholic church—all this will depend on what the new society is going to be like," wrote J. E. Koula in *Stavba* in 1926.[72] Teige was, of course, aware that the success of the program of scientific functionalism was socially conditioned, and he also presupposed a change in the social role of the architect. The architect should no longer be just a creator of "proto-images" or models of future socialist construction, but should also be a "constructivist," that is, "an engineer in the sense of organizer of work and life"—wrote Teige together with the editorial board of *Stavba* in 1925.[73] The architect's task would be to bring a rational socialist order into the chaos of postwar capitalism. In the following years, however, the thinking of Prague's left-wing architects became radical to the extent that even Teige's constructivist con-

258

ception was in the end declared a product of the detested capitalism. "By reducing the dwelling space into a shelter from the elements, a place to sleep and eat in, by packing into a minimal space all the latest inventions and machines serving economy, the constructivist, having taken an all-too-easy path, has reached a position that is dangerously close to that of capitalist exploitation (economy of movement in the home = increased working energy in the factory)" was how Vít Obrtel angrily opposed Teige in 1930.[74]

With his definition of architecture as science — based on the views of Adolf Loos and primarily on the theories of Soviet productivism and constructivism, Teige found the most favorable response in the Club of Architects and its magazine *Stavba*. He served as editor between 1923 and 1930 and made the publication into one of the most progressive European architectural reviews. Other architect-theorists who advocated the stance of scientific constructivism in *Stavba* were Oldřich Starý, Alois Špalek, and Vladimír Ježek. Exemplary works of scientific functionalism coming from the circle around *Stavba* were the projects of Oldřich Tyl, an architect whose work made the same progress from purism to functionalism in 1924–1925 as the designs of Jaromír Krejcar and Jaroslav Fragner.

Oldřich Tyl belonged among the most successful building contractors of the twenties. Outside Prague, he built mainly hospitals with his partners Josef Mikyna and Miloš Tereba from the construction firm Tekta. In Prague, he built apartment blocks distinguished by inventively designed ground plans and an overall sober approach to architectural treatment. The first of Tyl's functionalist buildings, which also became something of a model for Prague's scientific functionalist architects, was the large administrative building of the Prague Trade Fair in Dukelských hrdinů, designed in 1924–1925 and built between 1925 and 1928. In the first stage of the competition for this building, Tyl entered a design of classicist symmetry, albeit with ribbon windows, while his main competitor Josef Fuchs, who later coauthored the final project and who had received classicist training from Josip Plečnik, entered a design full of genuine functionalist asymmetry. As Teige pointed out, in spite of Fuchs's important contribution, the final

259

Oldřich Tyl, Josef Fuchs. Prague Trade Fair Building. Hole-šovice, Dukelských hrdinů 7, 1924–1928.

Oldřich Tyl, Josef Fuchs. Prague Trade Fair Building. Holešovice, Dukelských hrdinů 7, 1924–1928.

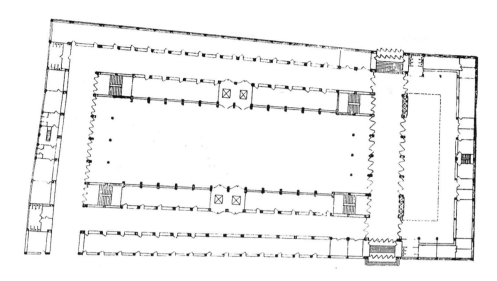

appearance of the building shows Tyl's "realistic, truly engineering mentality."[75] At that time, the Prague Trade Fair Palace was one of the first large functionalist constructions in Europe, a building where the founders of the international style could test the virtues and pitfalls of functionalism on a large scale. Its traditional layout with a covered central courtyard, and, above all, the imperfect proportions of the window bands and the bare wall facing Veletržní Street with its quadrangular windows set at a relatively large distance from one another, prompted Le Corbusier to make his well-known observation about a building that is not yet architecture when he visited Prague in 1928. "But I congratulate Prague and local architecture for being able to realize such a grandiose construction," declared Le Corbusier about Tyl and Fuchs's building in an interview with Teige. "When I inspected the Trade Fair Building, I understood how to create large constructions, having so far built only several relatively small houses on a limited budget."[76]

Tyl's indifference to traditional concepts of architectural beauty was close in attitude to the German functionalist movement *Die Neue Sachlichkeit*, which Le Corbusier detested, and his comment on Tyl's building seems to reflect this aversion. However, Tyl did not subject all the elements of his method to

263

Oldřich Tyl, Josef Fuchs. Prague Trade Fair Building, interior.
Holešovice, Dukelských hrdinů 7, 1924–1928.

Oldřich Tyl, Josef Fuchs. Prague Trade Fair Building, plan.
Holešovice, Dukelských hrdinů 7, 1924–1928.

265

Oldřich Tyl. The Black Rose commercial building. Nové
Město, Panská 4. 1929–1933.

Oldřich Tyl. The Black Rose commercial building, interior.
Nové Město, Panská 4. 1929–1933.

functionalist orthodoxy. During the twenties, his sense of proportion became more refined; it is said that Tyl exercised it by studying Prague's baroque houses and palaces and by measuring the proportions of their windows and doors in relation to the wall space. Also, his liking for symmetry did not correspond to the functionalist approach. His best buildings were therefore a mixture of asceticism and vitality, schematism and inner tension. For instance, the austere facade of the Black Rose commercial building on Panská Street, 1929–1933, concealed two large halls with elegant glass-floored galleries of reinforced concrete and a vaulted glass concrete ceiling. Round white lamps, suspended in space, used to add the finishing touch to this impressive interior. For his YWCA hostel in Žitná, 1926–1929, Tyl designed a bold facade, cold and aggressive in its puritanical forms, yet lively thanks to the syncopated shifts in the dimensions and relationships of the band windows, railings, and balconies, whose floor slabs jut out into space. Unfortunately, because Tyl's partners Tereba and Mikyna "did not comply with regulations" in the process of concreting—as it is reported in a document on Tyl's apartment block in Skořepka, built at the same time[77]—the facade of the hostel soon began to crack and immediate rebuilding was required. After this fiasco the firm Tekta went bankrupt, and Tyl spent the rest of his short life in courts and hospitals.

Ludvík Kysela (1883–1960) was another outstanding architect from the *Stavba* circle who suddenly stopped working at the beginning of the thirties, although for different reasons than Tyl. Yet, his large functionalist buildings from 1925 to 1929 left a lasting mark on the city center, more so than the work of many other modernist architects. In 1925 Kysela designed the administrative and office building for the insurance company Praha in Na příkopě (today's Children's House). He divided the lower part in a proper functionalist manner by means of large ribbon windows, and the upper office floors were conceived as a solid, white purist volume. In the plans used in the realization of the building in 1927–1928, Kysela enlarged the windows in the upper block and redesigned the wall between them as a constructive concrete grillage. At the same time, three other commercial buildings by Kysela were erected in Wenceslas Square, all of them designed on the same simple, spatially unified ground plan, determined by the pattern of reinforced

267

Following pages:

Oldřich Tyl. YWCA hostel. Nové Město, Žitná 12. 1926–1929, rebuilt 1929–1932.

Ludvík Kysela. Lindt department store. Nové Město, Václavské náměstí 4. 1925–1927.

Ludvík Kysela. Baťa department store. Nové Město, Václavské náměstí 6. 1927–1929.

concrete pillars: the Lindt department store, 1925–1927, with five wide horizontal window bands, and a rounded roof influenced by the machine aesthetic; the Stýblo Building, today's Alfa, 1927–1929, and finally Baťa, 1927–1929, which became Kysela's most outstanding work and one of the most impressive examples of Czech functionalism. The ribbon windows in the facade overlooking Jungmann Square almost swallow their ledges, so that all that remains are the shiny white strips between them. The facade, boldly suspended on a skeleton of reinforced concrete, is made completely of glass. The aggressive functionalist space surges out through all obstacles, admitting only the existence of the construction.

For the majority of architects around *Stavba*, Tyl's and Kysela's bold structures and refined style remained an almost unattainable ideal. Oldřich Starý and Alois Špalek had no clients in Prague after 1925, while others like Bohumír Kozák, Oktáv Koutský, Vladimír Ježek, and Vojtěch Kerhart struggled for a long time to free themselves from the influences of the modern style and purism. On the other hand, for František A. Libra (1891–1958), the second half of the twenties was a period of change. The first of his functionalist buildings in Prague was the Edison power station on Jeruzalémská Street, 1926–1930. It had an asymmetrical composition, consisting of several boxlike volumes, divided by ribbon windows and crowned with an abstract glass sculpture by Zdeněk Pešánek, originally illuminated with internal neon light. Other remarkable functionalist buildings created by architects around *Stavba* were Bedřich Adámek's family villas, Vladimír Frýda's school on Špitálská Street, 1927–1929, Václav Velvarský's building for the Czechoslovak Press Agency on Opletalova Street, 1928–1930, and Bohumil Sláma's Czechoslovak Radio Building on Vinohradská Avenue, 1927–1930, whose angular forms and windows, lined up in long bands, somewhat awkwardly imitated the style of Tyl and Fuchs's Trade Fair Palace.

Scientific functionalists from Teige's camp considered architecture to be a logical, almost mathematical result of precisely determined functional requirements. For architecture to be more than a sum of functions would breed controversy between function and form. Form will be found when it is not sought, was how Jaromír Krejcar expressed the scientific-functionalist attitude

270

František A. Libra. Edison power station. Nové Město, Jeruzalémská 2.

272

Vladimír Frýda. School building. Vysočany, Špitálská 700.
1927–1929.

Bohumil Sláma. Czechoslovak Radio Building. Vinohrady,
Vinohradská 12. 1927–1930.

274

toward this problem.[78] Within the framework of this conception, the architect was considered to be the recorder of requirements rather than the economist of expression, a role outlined for him by Teige. In this context, John Summerson pointed out that functionalists were not obsessed with architecture as such but with its position in relation to external determining factors, to "other things." "The result has been diagrammatic planning," added Robert Venturi.[79] By the twenties, some pioneers of the new architecture began to question the strict limitations imposed on their creativity. Within *Devětsil*, the first to admit such doubts was Bedřich Feuerstein, who in his letters to Josef Havlíček, written from Paris in 1925, condemned Teige's "critical extremism" and sowed the seeds of opposition to scientific functionalism in the minds of several others: Karel Honzík, Vít Obrtel, as well as Jaromír Krejcar, Teige's closest friend among architects.[80] In the French collection of articles *L'architecture contemporaine en Tchécoslovaquie* published in 1928, Krejcar described Teige's concept of scientific functionalism as a phase in the development of modern architecture that had its historical justification but had already been superseded. The architects of *Devětsil* still placed an emphasis on the creative nature of their work: they continued to "construct spaces by means of combining matter with will," to "create beauty with intention and awareness," as it was expressed by Vít Obrtel in 1930 and 1933.[81]

None of the proponents of scientific functionalism would ever deny that their work focused, above all, on people and their natural needs. However, they had the tendency to see humans schematically, as the sum total of several abstracted functions or as a kind of simple diagram, and most functionalists considered the psychological and aesthetic function of architecture as more or less superfluous. Central to the philosophy embraced by supporters of emotional functionalism, mainly Karel Honzík and Vít Obrtel, was man in all his complexity, man who "not only works but also sings."[82] In their opinion, the purpose of the architect's work consisted in repeated acts of restoration of harmony that had been disturbed: harmony between the objective and the subjective, the physical and the metaphysical, the rational and the irrational, the necessary and the random aspects of creation, and between humankind and the world as a whole.

275

Jaroslav Fragner, Josef Havlíček, Karel Honzík, Evžen Linhart, Pavel Smetana. Competition project for the Czechoslovak Press Agency Building. 1927.

Teige, who considered everything subjective, metaphysical, irrational, and random in architecture as a manifestation of right-wing, traditionalist attitudes, responded with a critical attack. The supporters of emotional functionalism defended themselves, claiming that they could not agree with his thesis of artistic qualities playing a role in architecture only at the expense of its purpose or outside it. New architecture, as they imagined it, would be harmonious, because it would serve its purpose absolutely, it would serve all the purposes required of a work of architecture, not only some of them. In his essay published in *Stavba* in 1926, eloquently called "Estetika v žaláři" (Aesthetics in Servitude), Karel Honzík proposed that intentional beauty amplifies the functionality of architecture, playing the role of an intermediary between the building and its users.[83] "Clear and functional organization of the ground plan is as important for the physical needs [of people] as is visual satisfaction for the practical hygiene of the spirit," was Vít Obrtel's view of the problem in the anthology *Fronta* (The Front) published by *Devětsil* in 1927.[94] Against Teige's ideal of objectivity, sobriety, asceticism, and "noble uniformity," Obrtel set an ideal of architecture that "being anchored in its artificial surroundings of gardens, fountains, lights, playgrounds, and swimming pools, in the midst of all the wonders of technology and poetry, would be a harmonious part of the world."

Yet, this ideal was difficult to apply in practice. Many new and older members of *Devětsil*—for example, Pavel Smetana, Karel Seifert, Karel Stráník, Jan Gillar, Josef Špalek, and Vít Obrtel—did not find any clients in Prague in the second half of the twenties. Josef Chochol, an honorary member of *Devětsil* from 1923, and others such as Jaroslav Fragner and Karel Honzík received commissions, but their clients did not allow them to express their artistic stance. Bedřich Feuerstein worked on projects in France and Japan, while Jaromír Krejcar gave the impression of being unable to decide which of the two functionalist directions he should embrace. In spite of that, Prague's emotional functionalism of the twenties did find its expression in realized projects, even though there were only a few.

At the upper end of the quiet street called Na viničních horách in the suburb of Dejvice, the architects Jan Rosůlek and Evžen Linhart built their

family villas in 1927 to 1929. Rosůlek's residence was later rebuilt in 1939 by Vladimír Grégr, who changed its stylistic character. Linhart's house, however, still provides an impressive testimony of its talented author's artistic orientation. The layout and proportions of his house were undoubtedly inspired by the family house of the German architect Ernst May, who was responsible for the new functionalist housing estate in Frankfurt in his role as city architect, and this may suggest that Linhart would have liked to follow May's example also in his own work at the Prague Municipal Construction Authority. The details of the house, however, were clearly influenced by the architecture of Le Corbusier, with whose work Linhart and Rosůlek became acquainted in Paris and Stuttgart during 1927.[85] The large ground floor living space was split into two levels connected by a sloping ramp and opened into the garden through a wide door and an enormous window divided into nine panes. The bedrooms on the first floor were designed in a similar way as

277

Jaroslav Fragner. Project for a neighborhood of family houses in Barrandov. 1927.

*Evžen Linhart. Architect's own family villa, view from the
garden. Dejvice, Na viničních horách 46. 1927–1929.*

Evžen Linhart. Architect's own family villa, view from the street. Dejvice, Na viničních horách 46. 1927–1929.

Toward a New Prague

functionalist "vitrines." The complicated volumes of Linhart's house, broken by means of a series of oblong and ribbon windows of various sizes, the glass "curtains" that challenged traditional notions about the weight of matter, the metal columns and railings, the fragile concrete frame of the pergola — all these features fitted Honzík's description of Linhart's work as having the "particular complexity of fine mechanisms."[86]

   When sometime in 1926 Evžen Linhart made a drawing of the first version of his villa, which was published the following year in the anthology *Fronta*, his approach was still close to the style of the *Puristická čtyřka*, including the unusual new shapes and the taste for the simple beauty of light bulbs and tubular railings. However, the final version of Linhart's residence has a somewhat international character, which shows that he had learned his lessons from the latest developments in European architecture. The work of other members of *Devětsil*

Evžen Linhart. Architect's own family villa, living hall.
Dejvice, Na viničních horách 46. 1927–1929.

Evžen Linhart. Architect's own family villa, floor plan.
Dejvice, Na viničních horách 46. 1927–1929.

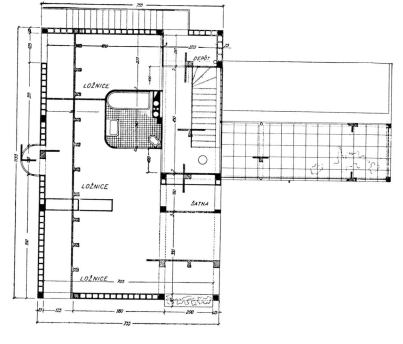

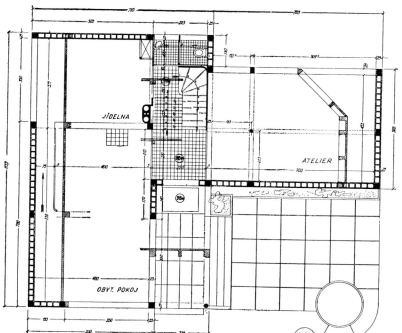

281

282

Jan E. Koula. Šalda's villa. Smíchov, Na Hřebenkách 12.
1928.

went through a similar process, which had been initiated in 1924–1925 by Fragner and by Bauhaus-influenced Krejcar. One of Josef Chochol's most interesting projects, the design for the Liberated Theater from 1927, testifies to the fact that he was inspired by Soviet constructivism, and in particular by the project for Lenin's House of Culture in Ivanovo-Voznesensk by Grigori Barkhin, published in 1925 in the magazine *Stavba*. Karel Teige even visited the Soviet Union in 1925, and since then he described Soviet constructivism as the paradigm of scientific approach to architecture. Chochol's drawing, however, while imitating the technique of contemporary projects by Barkhin and Vesnin with their dark tectonic components and illuminated windows, stressed the romantic aspects of constructivism. The octagonal ground plan of the theater reflected the star-shaped design of an aircraft engine, and the art historian František Šmejkal saw Chochol's perspective drawing as an evocation of a ship traveling toward new tomorrows.[87] A different kind of international new architecture was cultivated by Gočár's pupil František M. Černý (1903–1978), who as early as 1924 became interested in the neoplasticist notion of architecture as the materialization of the nexus between several infinite spatial planes, developed by the Dutch architects of *de Stijl*. Yet, Černý did not succeed in expressing this in his realized work as well as he did in his 1924 drawings for the Workers' Accident Insurance Company building or for the department store designed for Wenceslas Square, the latter showing a clear influence of Gropius's and Meyer's Chicago Tribune Building project from 1922. In his apartment buildings on Chrudimská Street, 1928–1929, the neoplasticist approach is evident perhaps only in the motif of the large chimney slabs turned vertically against the facade.

However, it was Le Corbusier who was most admired by the advocates of emotional functionalism in *Devětsil*, and he gradually became the hero of their faith in artistic architecture. Krejcar, Fragner, Obrtel, Honzík, Evžen, Linhart, and the young architect Karel Stráník who worked in Le Corbusier's studio in 1925–1926—all learned their lessons from his projects and theoretical views.[88] The most consistent follower of Le Corbusier was Josef Havlíček (1899–1961) who rejoined *Devětsil* in 1925 after his study with Josef Gočár. His competition entry for a bridge across the Nusle Valley with a motorway placed on top

283

Josef Chochol. Project for the Liberated Theater. 1926–1927.

František M. Černý. Competition project for the Workers' Accident Insurance Company. 1924.

František M. Černý. Project for a department store in Wenceslas Square. 1924.

Toward a New Prague

Toward a New Prague

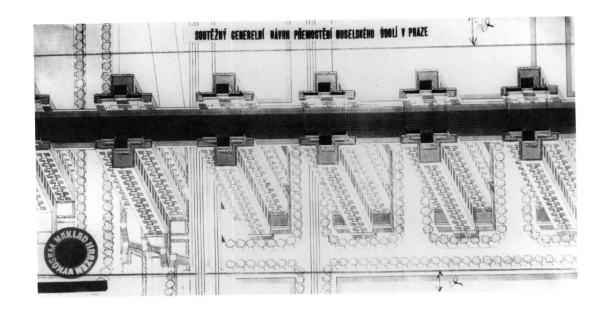

SOUTĚŽNÝ GENERELNÍ NÁVRH PŘEMOSTĚNÍ NUSELSKÉHO ÚDOLÍ V PRAZE

of nine residential skyscrapers attracted considerable attention in 1927. Le Corbusier's projects for the *Ville Contemporaine* and *Plan Voisin* influenced Havlíček's formal approach to this project, and he in turn may have inspired Le Corbusier in his vision for the reconstruction of South American cities, from 1929 to 1935. In the Habich department store on Štěpánská Street, 1927–1928, Havlíček tried to transfer the stylistic apparatus of Le Corbusier's purism into an architecture of monumental dimensions. In 1929, Havlíček, who had so far been working for the developer Jaroslav Polívka, joined forces with Karel Honzík, and they established their own architectural studio H&H. Their first project was the beautiful villa designed for the editor Jíše on U dívčích hradů Street, 1929. Both architects then concentrated their efforts on their project for the twelve-story administrative building of the General Pensions Institute in Winston Churchill Square. The concept for the largest functionalist building in Prague went through a process of dramatic changes between 1929 and 1932: the composition of the main office wings whose gigantic steps were originally meant to follow the steep terrain, the length of

288

Preceding pages: *František M. Černý. Apartment buildings. Vinohrady, Chrudimská 5, 7. 1928–1929.*

Josef Chochol. Competition project for the Nusle Bridge. 1927.

the lower wings housing apartments and shops, as well as the details of the whole project were simplified in each successive version. The only feature which remained constant until the realization of the building between 1932 and 1934 was the Corbusier-inspired cruciform ground plan.

        Devětsil with its architectural section ARDEV, headed from 1926 by Karel Honzík, was the main focus of Prague's emotional functionalism in the twenties. This direction also found support among other architects, for instance from some members of the artists' association *Mánes*, which regained its strength in the twenties after a pause following its era of fame at the beginning of the century, and among architects around the magazine *Stavitel*. Between 1928 and 1930, *Mánes* built its new headquarters on Masaryk Embankment. Judging from its striking design, the architect Otakar Novotný was familiar with the contemporary, sophisticated versions of the functionalist style. A similar youthful approach was taken by Josef Gočár in his project for the Catholic church in Svatopluk Čech Square, 1927–1930, and by the architect and town planner Max Urban (1882–1959), who, partly in opposition to Teige's criticism of monumentality in architecture, built the functionalist film studios in Lumièrů Square, 1931–1934, as a

Josef Havlíček, Jaroslav Polívka. Competition project for the Nusle Bridge. 1927.

Josef Havlíček, Karel Honzík. General Pensions Institute, model. Žižkov, náměstí Winstona Churchilla 3. 1929.

Josef Havlíček, Jaroslav Polívka. Habich department store.
Nové Město, Štěpánská 33. 1927–1928.

Josef Havlíček, Jaroslav Polívka. Habich department store
today. Nové Město, Štěpánská 33. 1927–1928.

Toward a New Prague

Karel Honzík. Langer's family house. Podolí, Nad cemen-
tárnou 23. 1929–1930.

CHAPTER 3

Josef Gočár. Project for the interior of the Church of Saint Wenceslas. Vršovice, náměstí Svatopluka Čecha. 1927.

293

Toward a New Prague

baroque château with a *court d'honneur* crowned by a tower in the middle section of the facade.

The leading architects of the group around the magazine *Stavitel* were the pupils of Kotěra, Gočár, and Plečnik: Adolf Benš, Josef Štěpánek, Ludvík Hilgert, J. K. Říha, Václav Kopecký, Vladimír Wallenfels, Josef Grus, and Jaroslav Kabeš.

Josef Štěpánek, whose designs were distinguished by subtlety comparable only to the work of Evžen Linhart, was one of the tragical figures of modern Czech architecture. In 1928 and 1929, he won the two most significant competitions of the end of the decade — one for the complex of parliamentary and ministerial buildings in Letná, the other for the sports stadium in Bráník. Due to the deepening economic depression, however, his plans were never realized. In the Letná project, supplemented by an alternative design for the parliamentary building, Štěpánek proved himself to be a master of perspectival effects who knew exactly how the appearance of a building changes from a moving point of view, as well as an inventive creator of various ground plan patterns in the shape of a square, cross, or the letters H, L, and E. In this respect his imagination remotely echoed the Czech baroque, and at the same time he showed himself to be a true poet of the radiant form.

In the second half of the twenties, Štěpánek became the editor of the magazine *Stavitel*, which he developed into serious competition for *Stavba*. In this effort he was helped by Adolf Benš (1894–1982), a pupil of Kotěra and Gočár, who used the pages of *Stavitel* mainly to promote the work of Le Corbusier. Compared to Štěpánek's designs, Benš's work tended toward the objective and the rational, while remaining firmly grounded in the program of emotional functionalism. In Prague, his work is represented by the villa on Trójská Street, 1928–1930, a complex system of intertwined spaces, terraces, ramps, and balconies, and, above all, by the office building of the Prague Power Company on Bubenská Street, 1926–1935, designed by Benš in collaboration with Josef Kříž, the author of the interesting functionalist factory Ferra on U Pergamenky Street, 1928–1929. Even in the functionalist era, large public buildings did not discard the notion of the

Josef Štěpánek. Competition project for the development of the Letná Plain. 1928.

Josef Štěpánek. Competition project for the new parliament house in Letná Plain. 1928–1929.

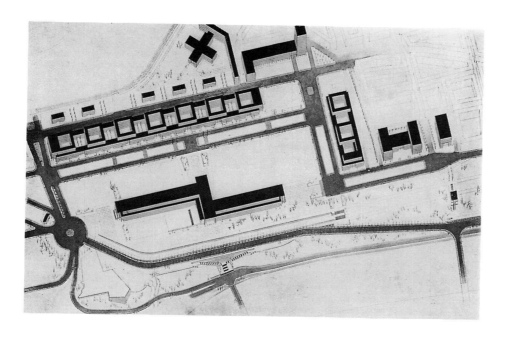

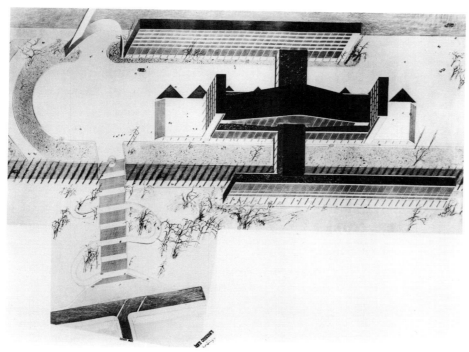

palace, a prototype that in Benš's and Kříž's work explains the origin of the symmetrical composition of the ground plan and volume, which gradually rises toward the central mass of the *piano nobile*. This traditional skeleton was then clothed in a polished functionalist exterior, whose effect was intensified by the radiant white ceramic cladding.

Among the architects around *Stavitel*, Josef K. Říha, 1893–1970, was the most commercially successful. He designed, for example, the large residential buildings on Zelená and Terronská Streets, 1928–1930, as well as two office buildings in the center of Prague—the Ferra palace on Na Florenci Street, 1926–1928, and the building of the Mining and Metallurgy Company on the corner of Lazarská and Jungmannova, 1928–1930. The latter, a remarkably elegant and generous functionalist edifice, benefited from the same prominent position on the corner of an extensive block as did Tyl's YWCA hostel on Kubelíkova Street, 1923–1926. This may have been the reason Říha chose a similar rounded volume, which in this case flowed into the longer rectilinear facade facing Lazarská Street. Tyl's full, purist plastic form had to make way for the forceful functionalist space, which, having emptied the volume of the building and leaving only a thin outer skin, began to peel it off in strips through which it surged outward.

The taste for the open space, and the consequent blurring of the boundaries between the interior of buildings and their surroundings, was a feature common to both the scientific and the emotional branches of functionalism. Moreover, it happened to be one of the important characteristics of the functionalist style, an element which gave the aesthetic of Czech purism a new content and, to some extent, even negated it.

The origins of the concept of the open space breaking outward from the interior was explained by some of its pioneers and proponents in the context of the technological inventions of the new architecture. In particular it was the introduction of skeleton constructions made of reinforced concrete or steel, whose "cage" directly invited the architect to open the building up. Functionalist publications also discussed at great length the functional opening up of the building to "air, sun, and light"—an architectural slogan that was already common at the end of the nineteenth century, which was, apart from this fact, questionable from

296

the point of view of the building's function of providing a shelter from the elements.

It appears, however, that the open space of functionalist buildings reflected the romanticism and exoticism characteristic of this era, which considered its opportunities, initially at least, as limitless. Jan E. Koula, whose essays often proved to be revealing probes into the thinking of the interwar architectural avant-garde, associated the open architectural space with the experience of those who no longer dream of "magical gardens" and "charming views of the landscape" — as did the romantics of the nineteenth century — but who "want to have everything in reality."[89]

In the work of Prague's purists, it was already possible to discern many intentionally romantic and exotic elements representing the world of technological civilization that united the continents, a world that, in the words of Krejcar's client, the writer Vladislav Vančura, "was bounded by distance in the North, the South, the East and the West."[90] Prague's purists resorted to transplanting the characteristic attributes of modern technology onto their buildings, and even to designing buildings that simulated these attributes in their entirety. And so a purist building would have the windows of an express train, whereas another was designed in the shape of a pleasure boat on the Vltava or a Mississippi steamer.

The functionalists used the same devices but, unlike the purists, they were unwilling to express their romanticism with the same naiveté and directness. Jiří Kroha, for instance, published a self-critical assessment of his very interesting machinist buildings in Mladá Boleslav in the review *Horizont* (Horizon) in 1927.[91] Around the same time, Krejcar warned against the tendency to "approximate the form of a little country villa on the Sázava River to the dynamic design of a car or a steamer, both of which fulfil entirely different functions."[92] The functionalist house — the *machine à habiter*, as it had been defined by Le Corbusier — was meant to function as a machine, but there was no reason for it to look like one. Modern architecture began to search for different means to express the exoticism and romanticism of the time and sought them in spatial qualities, which Jaromír Krejcar had considered to be the very essence of architecture already in 1923. Open space, it seems, was precisely what modern architecture was looking for.

297

298

Adolf Benš. Villa Diviš. Trója, Trójská 134. 1928–1930.

Adolf Benš. Villa Diviš, living hall. Trója, Trójská 134. 1928–1930.

Toward a New Prague

Adolf Benš, Josef Křiž. Office building of the power company. Holešovice, Bubenská 1. 1927–1935.

Josef K. Říha. Office building of the Mining and Metallurgy
Company. Nové Město, Lazarská 7. 1928–1930.

4 ARCHITECTURE AND THE GREAT DEPRESSION

The progress of Prague's functionalism was halted from 1929 by the economic depression, during which the volume of construction work sharply declined, especially in the mid-thirties. The crisis had a devastating impact on the building industry: it curbed the investment capacity of the clientele, both individuals and institutions, caused massive job losses, and deepened the shortage of housing that had already existed in Prague at the time of economic boom in the early twenties. It also brought unemployment to Prague architects. "Our hard times have changed the meaning of the word architect," commented the magazine *Architekt SIA* in 1934. "These days the architect becomes a sociologist, philosopher, and organizer, and most often an unemployed man."[1]

To deal with the new situation that gave rise to general feelings of sympathy toward the radical Left, the Czechoslovak government and the Prague municipality had to change their housing policies. The type of development most favored in the twenties was the garden city with its standardized family houses. But by having concentrated on the building of garden cities, the government obliged mainly the middle classes whose support it already had. In the thirties, however, the government and the municipality turned its attention to placating the disaffected "economically weak classes." The most characteristic outcome of the new housing policy were groups of apartment buildings containing small apartments accessible even to the very poor. Generously subsidized architectural competitions for such apartment complexes were in turn meant to provide support for the underemployed architects.

The year 1930 was a turning point in the development of the new housing policies: the Prague municipality and the state insurance company announced several competitions for the design of complexes with small apartments to be located in three different sites in Pankrác and Holešovice. Alongside the architects of the middle and older generation, several young members of the architectural avant-garde made their mark in these competitions. Among them were, for instance, František Jech, Antonín Černý, and, above all, the team Ossendorf, Podzemný, and Tenzer. The competitions resulted in the construction of apartment complexes on the streets Za Zelenou liškou, 1932–1938, and U staré plynárny,

1936–1939. In 1931, a similar competition was announced by the Communist workers' cooperative *Včela*. The 1936 Prague municipality competition concluded the series of these important efforts. The winners then prepared plans for apartment complexes in the suburb of Břevnov, around Nad Kajetánkou and Pod Marjánkou Streets, 1937–1947, and in Libeň, on U školičky Street, 1938–1940. This competition also helped establish new talent, including such architects as Hilský, Jasenský, Koželka, and Míšek.

　　　　All four competitions were meant to elicit the ideal project for a building with small apartments, affordable to poor tenants. The size of the apartments was around 25 to 40 square meters;[2] each had its own kitchen and a bathroom with toilet, and the living space usually consisted of a single room with a corner designed for sleeping accommodation. These requirements were best met by a block with open corridors, and especially by the type developed for the 1930 competitions by František A. Libra, whose three-bay layout, including an open corridor, an eat-in kitchen with adjacent sanitary facilities, and a living space divided by a lightweight partition to accommodate a "bedroom corner," could hardly be improved on. Along with the advantages for which it had been selected, however, the open corridor had its shortcomings. It offered little privacy to the residents, in winter it could not be used, and in summer it let in too little sun. For these reasons some participating architects tried to find different solutions. The most common one was a five-bay floor plan with a connecting corridor along the long axis of the building, which unfortunately provided less air and light for the adjacent rooms; another was a two-bay layout with the traditional ventilation conduits and fewer staircases, which accessed at least four apartments each. Both layouts, however, merely improved on types already known in the twenties.

　　　　But the Prague small-apartment competitions also generated brand-new ideas. One of the variants of the project designed in 1930 by the team Ossendorf, Podzemný, and Tenzer featured a glazed open corridor on alternate floors with split-level maisonettes. Similar designs were entered in the same competition by Jan Gillar and Josef Špalek. The magazine *Stavba*, which criticized these designs for being uneconomical, associated them with Adolf Loos's *Raum-*

305

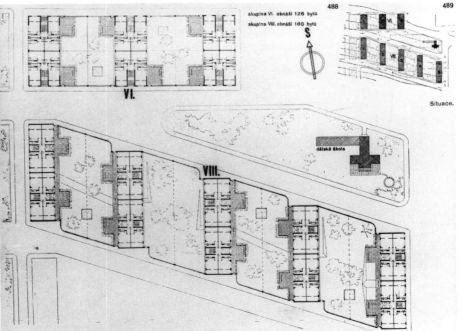

skupina VI. obnáší 126 bytů

skupina VIII. obnáší 180 bytů

488

489

S

VI.

VII.

Situace.

VI.

dělská škola

VIII.

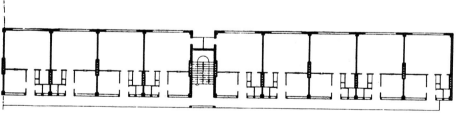

Opposite:

Václav Hilský, Rudolf Jasenský, Františerk Jech, Karel Koželka. Buildings with small apartments. Břevnov, Mládeže 2–10, Nad Kajetánkou 20–24. 1937–1939.

Václav Hilský, Rudolf Jasenský, Františerk Jech, Karel Koželka. Buildings with small apartments, plan. Břevnov, Mládeže 2–10, Nad Kajetánkou 20–24. 1937–1939.

František A. Libra, Jiří Kan. Buildings with small apartments. Krč, Obětí 8. května 2–6. 1935–1937.

František A. Libra, Jiří Kan. Buildings with small apartments, plan. Krč, Obětí 8. května 2–6. 1935–1937.

Architecture and the Great Depression

plan.[3] Comparisons could also be drawn with similar projects by Le Corbusier, Hans Scharoun, and the Russian constructivist Moses Ginsburg (1892–1946), whose collective houses designed in 1926–1929 were seen by the three-architect team as a prime example of formal solutions.

Some of the other projects entered in the 1930–1931 competitions were even closer to the housing concepts formulated after 1925 by Russian constructivism. They were mainly the project entered by Jan Gillar and Ladislav Žák in the *Včela* competition and projects entered by the teams Gillar-Špalek and Havlíček-Honzík in the Prague municipality competition. Finally, there was the so-called L-project, developed by the architect team of the association *Levá fronta* consisting of Peer Bücking, Jan Gillar, Augusta Müllerová, and Josef Špalek. This project, comprising fifteen large high-rise blocks, a complex of old people's homes, daycare centers, kindergartens, and schools, an office building, a house of culture, and a sports stadium, was designed to demonstrate a "new form of housing for the working class—collective housing."[4]

The meaning of this concept was best explained by the indefatigable Karel Teige, who cofounded *Levá fronta* in 1929 and became the ideological leader of its architectural section. Collectivized living and its concrete architectural form, the collective or communal house, an "integrated residential building," was seen by Teige as the necessary outcome of technological and social development heading toward general typization and standardization. One of the major factors contributing to this process was, according to Teige, the inclusion of women in the workforce and the ensuing need to emancipate them from the traditional burden of housework and from what he saw as amateur childcare. Another factor was the housing shortage among the working class, which led to many individuals living in temporary housing facilities and workers' hostels. Finally, the dissolution of the family as an anachronistic social unit was seen as playing its role. Teige's collective house as a dwelling type that would result from these historical changes was not supposed to contain traditional family apartments, which still reflected the bourgeois form of family coexistence, or the mini-apartments imposed by economic circumstances of the time, but individual residential units, a kind of "sleeping

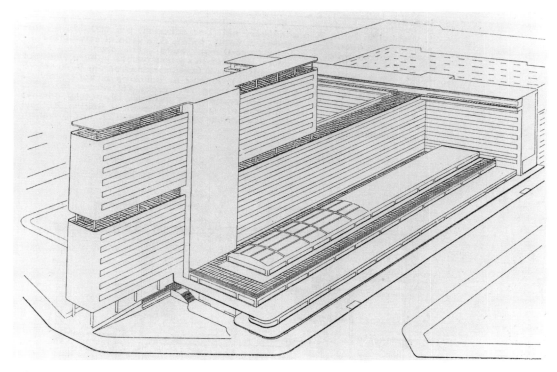

cabin" equipped with the most essential sanitary facilities. All the remaining functions — cooking and eating, washing, study, physical and mental activities, as well as the bringing up of children from the earliest age was to take place on a collective basis in specially designed spaces. This would create a new, truly proletarian form of living, appropriate to the "lifestyle of this class," a class that did not "demand particular rights" and therefore allowed for "perfect uniformity" in matters of living and housing.[5]

In some quarters Teige's concept of collective housing met with enthusiastic approval, which was not surprising at a time of remarkable political radicalization of Czech society during the Depression years. There was, however, also considerable criticism, voiced mainly by government authorities who considered such public manifestations of socialist living politically inadmissible, as well

*Ladislav Žák. Competition project for a collective building
for the Včela cooperative. 1931.*

Architecture and the Great Depression

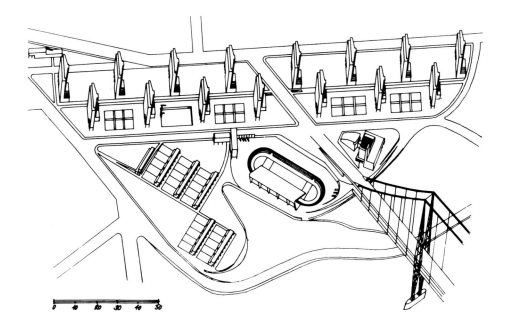

as by the very people whose needs it was supposed to meet. This became obvious during the competition organized by the workers' cooperative *Včela* where the winning project by J. K. Říha was based on a family mini-apartment of a conventional design, which included the traditional marital double bedroom and kitchen. Architects like Vít Obrtel considered Teige's concept of the uniform "minimum dwelling" an opportunistic makeshift solution enforced by unfavorable social conditions. Others again saw it as an expression of left-wing extremism that preceded the necessary stages in social development. Jaromír Krejcar made a tactful comment to this effect in an interview published in the Communist review *Tvorba* (Creation) in 1930: "The advantages of collective forms will certainly become clear in time"—he addressed his friend in a reconciliatory tone—"but I would not dictate them by means of housing design."[6] After all, Teige himself admitted that collective living was a project that was ahead of contemporary economic conditions and that could not be realized because the working classes had adopted the domi-

310

Peer Bücking, Jan Gillar, Augusta Müllerová, Josef Špalek.
Project for the development of the Nusle Bridge area with
collective buildings (L-project). 1930.

nant ideology as part of their own lifestyle and views. This, however, was no excuse for left-wing architects who had the duty to "provide architectural solutions that would contribute to the development of processes leading to collective forms [of living]."[7]

Such a program appeared to be somewhat more realistic and was even to some extent practicable. The housing competitions of the early thirties offered several points of contact, as, for instance, in the case of the open-corridor type of apartment block that, according to the idiosyncratic interpretation of its authors Havlíček and Honzík, "could be easily adapted to a collective house in the true sense of the word," as it "fully expressed the collective life in an apartment building."[8] It is also possible to consider in this context the various modern pensions and serviced apartment buildings, such as the outstanding pension Arosa on U Kavalírky Street by Karel Hannauer, 1931, and the one on Londýnská Street, built in 1938–1939 by Václav Kopecký. Some members of Prague's avant-garde pursued their ideals of collective living in more concrete forms. Among the first to do so was Karel Teige himself, whose attic apartment on Černá Street was designed in 1927 by Jaromír Krejcar to evoke a system of "sleeping cabins" in a collective house, complemented by a communal space for social activities. There were, however, only two cabins in the apartment. Ladislav Žák, an enthusiastic supporter of the idea of collective living, went even further when he rebuilt his neo-Renaissance building on Kornunovační Street as a true collective house, disguised in official documentation as a "hostel for single residents."

The town-planning schemes of the thirties still sometimes used the closed or semi-opened block. Far more popular was the completely open solution, designed on a pattern of parallel rows that corresponded to the contemporary notion of a "free, open prospect" as it was described by *Stavba* in 1931 in the context of small-apartment competitions.[9] This solution also reflected the collectivist and rationalist ideals of the time, and the contemporary passion for a mathematically precise regiment of rows and for the mechanical rhythm of the spacing between them, best illustrated by some of the designs produced by Krejcar, Gillar, and Špalek.

311

Karel Hannauer. Pension Arosa. Košíře, U Kavalírky 1. 1931.

A) Návrh na změnu přehledného regulačního a zastavovacího plánu pro část území Prahy XVIII-Břevnova mezi Bělohorskou třídou a Bořislavovou ulicí, západně od ulice Na Malovance. *Situace.*
Měřítko 1:2880.

Fortunately for Prague, the realization of these visionary projects often met with insurmountable obstacles arising from the hesitant attitude of the State Planning Commission, which was unwilling to change its existing plans due to lack of funds. In addition, Prague's hilly terrain proved unsuitable for the regularity of rows and spaces paramount in this type of housing. The small apartment complexes in Pankrác, Holešovice, or Libeň, built in the thirties on the principle of row housing, were always the result of a compromise between an ideal and reality. The less regular layout of the complex in Břevnov around Nad Kajetánkou Street, where the rows following the sloping terrain create a diagonal pattern, demonstrates that the functionalist "dogma of the right angle" was not respected even by its originator Ladislav Machoň already in 1935.

Individually designed buildings with apartments of average or above-average size still mostly used the three-section floor plan in the thirties. The disadvantages of this layout were criticized by left-wing architects: the entrance hall with no natural light and the sanitary facilities with no proper ventilation "ridiculed the endeavors toward healthy living."[10] But even these architects had to comply with the dictate of the developers, although this was often justified by the use of technically improved systems of artificial lighting and ventilation. The main reason for criticism was, however, that for all its advantages, the two-bay

313

Ladislav Machoň. Project for the development of the suburb of Břevnov. 1935.

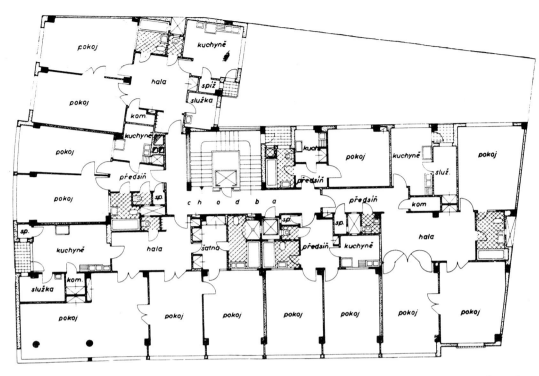

layout was too generous and uneconomical. Therefore, attempts were made to improve the three-bay layout. Sometimes this was done by means of strict rationalization, simplification, and better organization of the floor plan, as for instance in the house on Žitná Street, designed by Obrtel and Hölzel, 1937–1939. At other times the three-bay layout was improved by breaking up the floor plan pattern, as was done by Richard Podzemný in the so-called Glass Palace, 1936–1937, where the two types of layouts alternate.

A team of architects including Josef Gočár, Emanuel Hruška, Jan Gillar, Josef Chochol, and others, who in 1934 designed a group of electric-powered apartment blocks for the Prague Power Company, tried out an original solution to the lack of natural light. In the best designed buildings of this group, authored by Gočár's student Evžen Rosenberg and built from 1935 to 1937 on

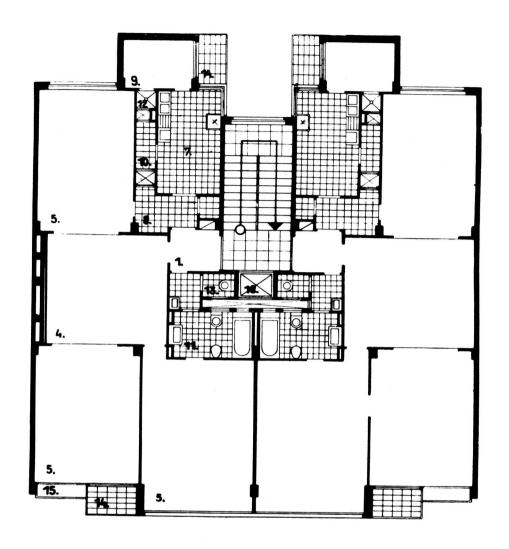

Vít Obrtel, Zdeněk Hölzel. Apartment building plan. Nové Město, Žitná 23. 1937–1939.

Evžen Rosenberg. Apartment building plan. Holešovice, Antonínská 4, 6. 1936–1937.

Architecture and the Great Depression

Letohradská and Antonínská Streets, the sanitary facilities were adjacent to large skylights. Inside the apartments, Rosenberg did away with the partitions that would normally divide the large hall in the center from the rooms on the outside, so that they formed a continuous naturally lit space.

An era of slogans proclaiming collectivization and rationalization of living did not favor the development of the family house. In his extensive essay "K sociologii architektury" (On the Sociology of Architecture), published in *Revue Devětsilu* and presented in 1930 at the Dessau Bauhaus, Karel Teige described the family house as a new form of the castle or the palace, a form that best suited bourgeois individualism, bourgeois social order, and its basic unit—"the family." Designing luxury villas was an "undignified" task for modern architecture, wrote Teige in the same year in *Stavba*.[11] Other Prague functionalist architects, for instance Oldřich Starý or Jan E. Koula, tried to counter these extreme views by making space at least for standardized family housing of the type realized in the twenties by Le Corbusier in Pessac, and later by May in the new suburbs of Frankfurt and by Gropius in the Dammerstock colony. In Prague, it was Jaroslav Fragner who promoted the construction of standardized functionalist housing already in 1927, when he designed three different types of small functionalist villas for the newly established Barrandov, a suburb intended for the film industry. However, the sponsor of the plan, the wealthy developer Václav Havel, who envisaged the new suburb as a romantic, rocky city, a "Czech Hollywood," was not convinced by Fragner's designs, and in 1929 hired two other architects, Max Urban and Vladimír Grégr, to realize his vision.

A greater success in standardized family housing was promised by the showcase Baba complex, established in Dejvice between the streets Nad Paťankou, Průhledová, Matějská, and Jarní. The construction of the complex had been planned from 1929 by the Czechoslovak arts and crafts association, *Svaz československého díla*, which commissioned the architect Pavel Janák.[12] Janák's plan sensitively transcribed the contours of the terrain into a system of streets and employed the method of so-called alternate building, which had already been applied on Písecká Street in Košíře by František Kavalír between 1919 on 1922. The plan

included several dozen terraced and free-standing standardized houses, occasionally combined with individualized ones. But when construction finally began in 1932, after a series of administrative and economic hurdles, the idea of standardized houses was abandoned. The complex was finally completed in 1940. The clients, mostly successful artists, writers, public servants, and university professors who formed a loose cooperative under the auspices of the *Svaz*, simply did not wish to live in houses that would look exactly like their neighbor's.

Functionalist architects therefore never managed to apply the principles commonly used in the construction of the garden cities of the twenties that incorporated dozens of standardized houses. It appeared that the concept of the standardized house was doomed, and Prague's left-wing architects considered it as such. It is important to ask whether the mass-produced standardized house, which would be repeated twenty times in one street, was necessarily the only appropriate option for functionalist architecture. According to Oldřich Starý, this requirement was based on misunderstanding: "Isn't it the case that in industry,

317

Pavel Janák. Model for the Baba estate in Dejvice. 1930.

there is also not only one single type of product, but many, each designed for a different purpose, price, and efficiency?"[13] Vít Obrtel considered standardization of whole buildings as a "tragic mistake": the fast development of technology should be reflected in variability, not in standardized uniformity. His motto was: "International style, individual buildings!"[14]

The architectural character of the Baba houses can be described precisely in such dialectical terms. They all originated from a single type of floor plan, the "regrouped" two-bay layout whose glassed living spaces opened up toward the south, the gardens, and the Vltava River. They were also all unified by their lightweight, boxlike functionalist style. This style was, however, applied in individual ways, from the fragile constructivist design by the Dutch participant Mart Stam, to the romantic "steamship" style of Ladislav Žák's villas, or the classical tone of Gočár's contributions. In comparison with the development of the family house in the twenties, two new tendencies were in evidence. In the family house in Na Ostrohu, designed by Evžen Linhart and Antonín Heythum, 1932, and the villa designed by Antonín Černý for his own family in Matějská Street, 1939–1940, both have a single-bay living space instead of the usual two-bay layout, clearly demonstrating the influence of functionalism and its spatial concepts. There was also a new approach evident in the splitting of the main space into several levels. Villas designed by Oldřich Starý on Průhledová and Na ostrohu Streets, 1932, feature large living halls and studios split by low galleries; and in Janák's own villa in Nad Paťankou, 1932, and one of František Kerhart's villas in Na ostrohu, 1935–1936, the interiors are designed in the form of a two- or three-step cascade. This solution may have been inspired by Le Corbusier's purist villas, as well as by Loos's *Raumplan*, known in Prague from the famous villa built by Loos for the developer František Müller in Nad hradním vodojemem, 1928–1930. But in comparison with Loos's complex composition, the spatial layouts of the Baba villas were mere suggestions, unreflected in the structure of the buildings.

The thirties highlighted the tendency to view the city as part of a larger organism that included its industrial, agricultural, and leisure areas. Even the State Planning Commission tried to break free from the limitations imposed by

Mart Stam, Jiří Palička. Palička's family villa on the Baba estate. Dejvice, Na Babě 9. 1929–1932.

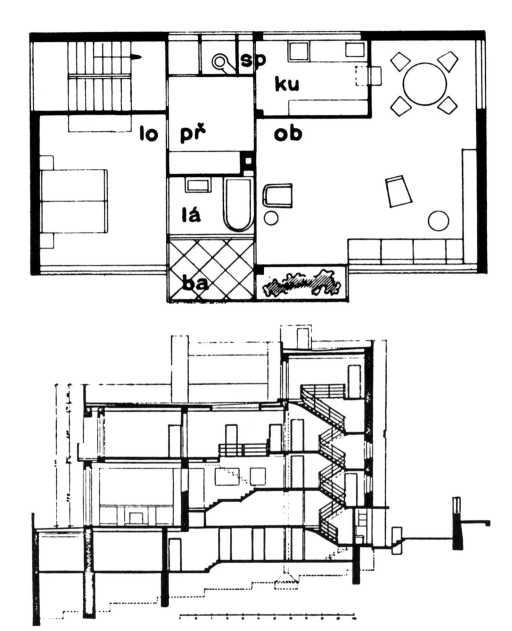

Antonín Heythum, Evžen Linhart. Lisý's family villa on the
Baba estate. Dejvice, Na ostrohu 50. 1931–1932.

Adolf Loos, Karel Lhota. František Müller's family villa, section. Střešovice, Nad hradním vodojemem 14. 1928–1930.

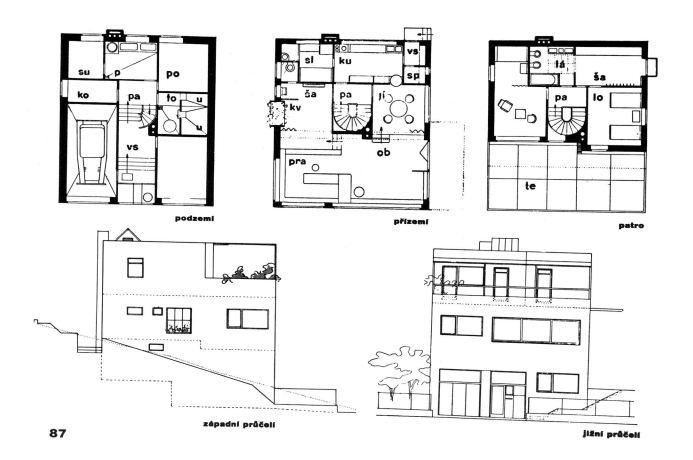

podzemí   přízemí   patro

západní průčelí   jižní průčelí

87

321

Pavel Janák, project for the architect's own villa on the Baba
estate. Dejvice, Nad Pat'ankou 16. 1931–1932.

its own policy that encouraged the approach "from parts toward the whole." In 1928, the commission published its development plan for the Prague region, and two years later, in collaboration with the power company, it announced a major international competition for an overall transport and traffic plan for Greater Prague and environs. The participants, mainly planning departments of large Czech and German transport manufacturing companies, faced the old problem of the historical center unsuitable for high-level through traffic. They focused on how to best utilize or even extend the system of traffic areas introduced by the commission, and suggested various solutions involving underground transport, tunnels, and new passages. Many Prague architects and town planners were disappointed by the results of the competition, which confirmed the view that focusing exclusively on the question of traffic not only leaves aside various other town-planning questions but ultimately does not resolve the problem at the very heart of the enquiry. In 1931, Alois Mikuškovic (1897–1952), a pioneer of regional planning and author of the slogan "from cityscape to landscape," sought to resolve the problems of Prague's urban development by "correct organization of municipal functions," which would follow from "sociological analysis."[15]

One such project based on sociological analysis, called *Veřejná především* (Public Transport above All), was in fact entered in the the city traffic competition of 1930 by Jaromír Krejcar and Josef Špalek. To all the discussions concerning the traffic capacity of the inner city, the necessity or impossibility of opening up new passageways through the center of Prague, the implications of increasing motor traffic, and the limitations of the tramway network, Krejcar and Špalek responded by proposing a total ban of private motorcars in the center and by "expropriating" the area for public transport. The city center was to be made accessible by surface express rail, complemented by streetcar and trolleybus services. Individual motorists traveling to the historical center would have to leave their cars in multistory parking garages on the periphery of Malá Strana, Hradčany, and Nové Město, and from there they would continue either by public transport or on foot.

322

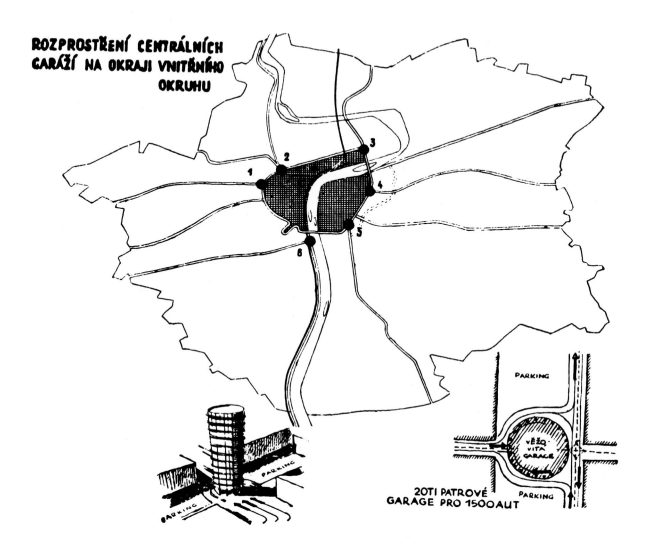

ROZPROSTŘENÍ CENTRÁLNÍCH
GARÁŽÍ NA OKRAJI VNITŘNÍHO
OKRUHU

PARKING

20TI PATROVÉ
GARAGE PRO 1500AUT

323

Jaromír Krejcar, Josef Špalek. Competition project for the
Greater Prague transport plan. 1930–1931.

Architecture and the Great Depression

The competition judges did not give Krejcar's and Špalek's plan the attention it deserved, mainly because they found its underlying social policy unacceptable. And yet, this was the only project that offered a comprehensive and to a large extent feasible solution that would have probably best served the future of Prague's historical architectural treasures. The value of the plan's proposed reorganization of city traffic and its social implications prompted Karel Teige to describe it as an urbanistic analogy of Engels's *Zur Wohnungsfrage*.[16] Yet, equally valuable was the potential new foundation for successful conservation that would have protected the historical center from its most powerful enemy—automobiles— without requiring any substantial changes to the area.

The new attitude of functionalist architects to the question of historical conservation was in the thirties still somewhat vague. The functionalists sensed that the early plans of the twenties for a radical rebuilding of the old part of Prague were no longer acceptable, but they did not know how to justify this in terms of rational functionalist theory. Their lack of clarity in this respect was obvious when their colleague Josef Havlíček published his project for a series of gigantic skyscrapers designed for the area of the New Town, 1937, 1943–1944, or when, in 1936, the group *Skupina architektů SIA* proposed that the eastern part of the New Town should be turned into a modern functionalist suburb with row housing. In a debate about this project, the art historian Zdeněk Wirth stressed that the whole center, not only its best-preserved parts, should be considered an area of historical importance, valuable by virtue of being a "document of the creativity of nature and human society alike."[17] The functionalists could have argued that a city must be organized to serve those living in it; it should not be a museum collection of architectural exhibits but a functioning, living organism. Even Wirth's concept of the historical center as a "large plastic whole" would not have justified architectural conservation because it would have sounded too formalistic. It was not until 1939 that the architect Jan Mannsbarth offered a more convincing functionalist defense of the value of the historical center. He pointed out that while it was possible to put aside "reasons based on aesthetic feelings," it should not be overlooked that historical Prague "has an economic significance as a place of tourist interest."[18]

It is not surprising that the functionalists had no clear-cut views on the historical areas of the city. Research into the irreplaceable value of old towns and their significance for the spiritual and intellectual life was initiated only by the postwar congresses of CIAM, and serious results appeared only in the sixties and seventies in the theoretical work of Kevin Lynch, Christian Norberg-Schulz, and others.[19] Functionalist architects and town planners had the tendency to leave the aesthetic and spiritual values of the Prague center aside. However, by the end of the thirties, when the generation pioneering the new architecture matured, became wiser, and began to fear the potential consequences of war for the city, Jan Mannsbarth admitted that these values were "shared by all."

This new and slowly emerging attitude about Prague was not yet enough to provide sufficient basis for a proper town-planning conservation program, which still had to be justified with reference to the traditional functionalist categories. This is where Mannsbarth's earlier point about economic profitability of the historical center became useful. For the center to be kept relatively intact while preventing it from becoming a mere museum collection, it was necessary to use it in some way, "even at the expense of the needs of contemporary life," as it was put by the architect and town planner Miloš Vaněček during the 1936 debate. But the question of a specific approach to this problem has not been properly answered even today.

Josef Havlíček. Study for redevelopment of the New Town.
1943–1945.

325

In 1928, when the Czechoslovak Republic celebrated the first decade of its existence, the architectural press began to publish assessments of the past developments, present state, and future prospects of modern Czech architecture. Among such appraisals looking into the future were Krejcar's French book *L'architecture contemporaine en Tchécoslovaquie*, published in the same year, Teige's volume *Mezinárodní soudobá architektura 2* (Contemporary International Architecture 2) from 1930, Zdeněk Rossmann's article *"Deset let tzv. československé moderní architektury"* (Ten Years of the So-called Modern Czechoslovak Architecture) published in the review *Stavitel*, and Teige's book *Práce Jaromíra Krejcara* (The Work of Jaromír Krejcar) from 1933.

Considering the success of functionalist architecture, these texts could well have been full of complacency. Yet, the opposite was true. As Zdeněk Rossmann wrote, the new stylistic form had succeeded, but at the expense of a far more significant social content. Architecture as art had not as yet become a social phenomenon. "Considering the seemingly record success of today's architecture, it is surprising that the number of homeless in our cities increases day by day, almost in parallel with the numbers of new and fashionable palaces and villas."[20] Teige's assessment of the past decade was similar. As he wrote in his book on Krejcar, already in the twenties, many members of the one-time Czech avant-garde "quickly became commercialists, have gone astray and colluded with official institutions and corporations."[21] Despite the successful initial years of 1922 to 1924, Czech architecture was soon overtaken by avant-garde groups in other countries. Both Zdeněk Rossmann and Karel Teige saw the only way out of this situation in complete negation of aesthetics, "for we have to be indeed entirely indifferent to form and aesthetic canon, even in case of the so-called new styles, as these represent non-productive superstructure," and in consistent industrialization of the construction business, "which can only bring down the prices." Finally, Rossmann recommended that truly modern architects should "organize and discipline themselves" as this was the only way to counter the power of private capital and assert the interests of the whole community.

It is obvious that Rossmann's program unequivocally subscribed to the scientific line of interwar functionalism. During the Depression, this line went through a process of renewal, its program tended strongly toward the left, and it gained many more supporters. Oldřich Starý and Karel Teige who fought for the ideas of scientific functionalism in the twenties, were around 1930 joined by the young left-wing group *Pracovní architektonická skupina* (The Architectural Working Group) known by its abbreviation PAS. The members were young graduates from the Polytechnic, Karel Janů, Jiří Štursa, and Jiří Voženílek. There were many others who also identified with scientific functionalism in the thirties: the former members of *Devětsil*, Jan Gillar, Josef Špalek, and Jaromír Krejcar; the younger generation around the review *Stavba*, including Josef Kittrich, Gustav Paul, Antonín Černý, and Ferdinand Fencl; and even the contemporaries of Kotěra's architectural revolt, Pavel Janák and Josef Chochol.

In his manifesto *Dva domy* (Two Houses) from 1929, Chochol juxtaposed "artistic pathos, based on the traditional irrationality of artistic methods" and the "totally nonpathetic construction, based on modern rationality of purely technical thinking." It need not be stressed which alternative was favored by an era striving to find its way out of the irrational chaos of the Depression.

At the beginning of the thirties, Jaromír Krejcar experienced a change of mind similar to that experienced by the former lyrical constructivist Josef Chochol. The well-known Tugendhat villa, 1929–1930, designed for the Moravian town of Brno by Mies van der Rohe—which is, with all due respect for the qualities of Czech functionalism, probably the most significant example of the international style in Czechoslovakia—was in 1932 described by Krejcar as being "far less significant, from the point of view of technological progress and public hygiene, than local council discussions in the remotest part of the country about the building of a primitive canal system in their village."[22] In the Depression years, the beauty of Mies's building, which had been achieved at great expense, appeared to Czech left-wing architects as something immoral and asocial. Finally, when in 1933 the spokesman of PAS, Karel Janů, reviewed the Prague exhibition of Soviet architecture, he confessed that he sympathized with the quantity and the mass-produced, provisional nature that characterized the constructivist development of new Soviet cities, rather than with the "unique monuments of Western architects, artists, and individualists."[23]

During the thirties, the forum for Czech scientific functionalism was the review *Stavba* along with *Stavitel*, which moved closer to *Stavba*'s direction in 1930 when it became the official voice of the Czechoslovak chapter of the international functionalist association CIAM/CIRPAC. Moreover, orthodox scientific views took hold among many members of the architectural section of *Levá fronta*, founded in 1929–1930, prevailed among the participants of the *Sjezd levých architektů* (Congress of Left-wing Architects) held in Prague in 1932, and began gaining ground within the *Svaz socialistických architektů* (Association of Socialist Architects), founded in 1933, and in the *Blok architektonických pokrokových spolků*, BAPS (The Bloc of Progressive Architectural Associations), which came into existence a year later. The very names of these associations suggest the direction adopted by many progressive Czech architects in an attempt to come to terms with the growing polarization of Czech society. Rossmann's call for organization and discipline had been heeded. And if architects were taking up the roles of sociologists and philosophers-organizers, prescribed for them by *Architekt SIA* in 1934, they were also becoming political activists. The best example was Jiří Kroha, professor at the Brno Polytechnic, who was sentenced to several months imprisonment for the promotion of the Soviet State in 1934, or the German architect Hannes Meyer who, having been forced to resign from his position as director of the Bauhaus in 1930 as a result of his Marxist convictions, settled in the Soviet Union and later worked in Mexico under the left-wing Cárdenas government. Another example was the Lithuanian architect Nusim Nesis, Meyer's student and later member of the architectural section of *Levá fronta*, whose contributions to the debates of the time were remembered in Karel Honzík's memoirs: "Sometimes it appeared that he would have architects abandon the drawing board to become professional revolutionaries."[24]

Fortunately, Prague architects never went that far, not even in the thirties. While they considered social change necessary, they tried to contribute to it primarily through their architectural work. In this way they fulfilled Teige's program of social critique by means of architecture, formulated already in the mid-twenties. Scientific functionalists from Teige's circle typically engaged in elaborating theories about socialist living, they constructed sociological analyses of living and architecture under capitalism and socialism, and developed ideal projects for buildings and complete new towns on the model of the *socgorods*, the socialist cities invented by the Soviet economist and urbanist N. A. Milyutin (1889–1941).

But it was the very concept of functionalist architecture as science that was meant to have the character of social critique, and it became a methodological or even philosophical basis for other related activities. Karel Teige, the author of this concept, demanded that functionalist architecture should precisely reflect the appropriate functions in its form; that it should be strictly rational and desubjectivized, in short, that it should become a completely scientific discipline. Such architecture would then naturally have a left-wing orientation. Against it, Teige set architecture disguised as modernism or functionalism, which had in reality become "commercialized and had gone astray" and thus began to express the interests of the political right — architecture, which, regardless of Teige's theories, did not give up its artistic aspect. This peculiar sociologizing was openly supported by Jaromír Krejcar in his essay "Architektura a společnost" (Architecture and Society) written in 1932–1933. According to him, there were two main directions in Czech architecture at the beginning of the thirties: the capitalist direction, derived from Le Corbusier's purism, and the socialist direction, based mainly on the work of Soviet constructivists.[25]

The role of left-wing architects, whose persuasion was unequivocally scientific and who were honest in their desire to come to terms with the problems of their time, was relatively easy. Those, however, who did not want to lose sight of the artistic aspect of their work, while at the same time subscribing to Teige's or Krejcar's views, had to make a difficult choice. Should they create as artists, that is, subjectively and therefore conservatively, or should they work in a scientific manner, that is, objectively and on the side of progressive forces? A synthesis of these two opposites was, at least at the beginning of the thirties, unthinkable: scientific functionalists saw the question as an either-or, just as they deemed impossible any reconciliatory settlement of class differences. Perhaps that was why Teige's opponent Vít Obrtel spoke about broken harmony, claiming that only the social order of the future would be able to create a truly harmonious architecture.[26]

Although in the early thirties many avant-garde architects considered the austere and impersonal concept of functionalist architecture as the only progressive alternative, there soon appeared attempts, both in theory and practice, to weaken its orthodoxy. It would be difficult to ascertain what initiated this turn in functionalist thinking. One important contributing factor must have been the news about the tragic fate of Teige's model of scientific-functionalist architecture — Soviet constructivism. Czech architects were aware that Stalinist bureaucracy was much to blame for its demise, but they also admitted that constructivist architecture undermined its own position by the lack of attention it paid to aesthetics — or as the contemporary term went — to the "psycho-ideological" impact of architectural form.[27] Another factor that made scientific functionalism lose its edge was the beginning of economic recovery, as well as the all-too-obvious discrepancy between the "scientifically" constructed notions of human needs and their true nature. Karel Teige, who in 1934 joined the Prague-based *Skupina surrealistů ČSR* (The Surrealist Group of CSR), and others including Jiří Kroha and the young PAS members, suddenly began to think about the subconscious impact of architecture on man, and their writings showed an attempt to reconcile the system of scientific functionalism with Freudian psychoanalysis and with the artistic theories of surrealism.[28] "Narrow, materialistic utilitarianism cannot continue to provide the only basis for architectural work," Teige admitted self-critically in his excellent book *Sovětská architektura* (Soviet Architecture) published in 1936.[29]

In the thirties the most active focus of Prague's scientific functionalism was the architectural section of *Levá fronta*, ASLEF, formed in 1929–1930. From 1933, its activities were continued by the scientific-functionalist faction of the *Svaz socialistických architektů*.

The most influential of ASLEF's members was probably Jan Gillar (1904–1967), former student of Josef Gočár and member of *Devětsil* who worked with Krejcar in the late twenties, and who probably succeeded him as the most affordable architect among the Czech avant-garde. In the early thirties Gillar designed several significant works, remarkable not only for their austere appearance, rationalized in the extreme, but also for their progressive concept of the "minimum dwelling." Together with Josef Špalek, another of Gočár's students and a colleague from *Devětsil* and from Krejcar's studio, Gillar developed a project for collective housing with maisonette-type flats for the 1930 small-apartment competition of the Prague municipality. He also participated in the 1930 small-apartment competition of the Central Social Insurance Company with the so-called L-project prepared by the architectural section of *Levá fronta*, and in the *Včela* cooperative competition for which he submitted his project for a collective house combining a flat, low wing with a tower building.

In 1931–1932, Gillar's project for the complex of French schools (kindergarten, primary, and secondary school) on Božkova Street narrowly won over Krejcar's equally excellent design and was realized in the following two years. Even here, Gillar made no compromise in his scientific-functionalist approach: the form relentlessly followed its functional content, probably on the model of the strictly functional buildings of Hannes Meyer, whose work apparently influenced other Gillar designs as well. In this case, however, the result was a rich and diverse composition of buildings with interesting details and with a range of differently shaped windows accentuated by means of the subtle pattern of window grills. L-shaped windows, windows with slanted corners following the incline of the staircase behind them, large windows with varied glazing bar patterns, architectural volumes arranged in steps — all these features could be explained in terms of functional requirements, while at the same time they defied the notion of the austere and strict look of functionalist architecture. Gillar did not abandon this notion all at once, and he incorporated it in the project for apartment blocks on Družstevní ochoz Street in 1936–1937. In other buildings of the second half of the thirties, his functionalist style became visibly aestheticized, as, for instance, in the striking ground floor of his apartment block in Vinařská Street, built in the same period.

331

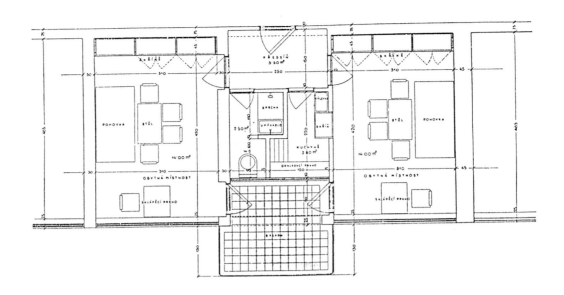

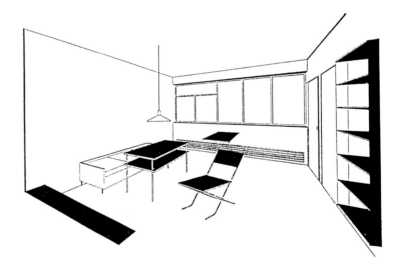

Jan Gillar. Project for a minimum dwelling interior for the
Ruzyně estate. 1932.

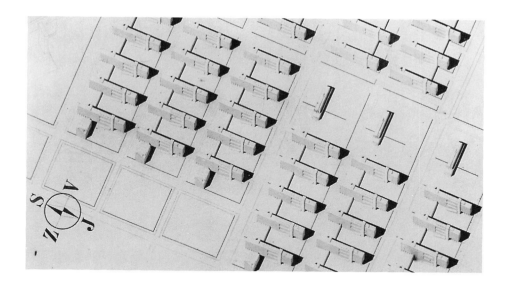

Prague's functionalists were interested in the work of the second Bauhaus director Hannes Meyer mainly because it offered the best example of a sophisticated and theoretically based design method of scientific functionalism. Meyer owed his popularity also to his frequent trips to Prague where he visited Teige and Krejcar, as well as to the mission of his students Peer Bücking, Nusim Nesis, Zdeněk Rossmann, Josef Hausenblas, and others, many of whom left the Bauhaus following Meyer's forced resignation and sought work in Czech cities. This was difficult, however, at the beginning of the thirties, and Bücking and Nesis then followed Meyer to the Soviet Union, where they were joined by Krejcar and Špalek in 1934, while Rossmann concentrated on typographical design. The only Bauhaus graduate who managed to get a good commission in Prague in the thirties was the little-known Václav Zralý, author of the villa in the street Nad Zámečnicí, 1932.

333

Jan Gillar, Josef Špalek. Competition project for municipal housing with small flats in Pankrác. 1930.

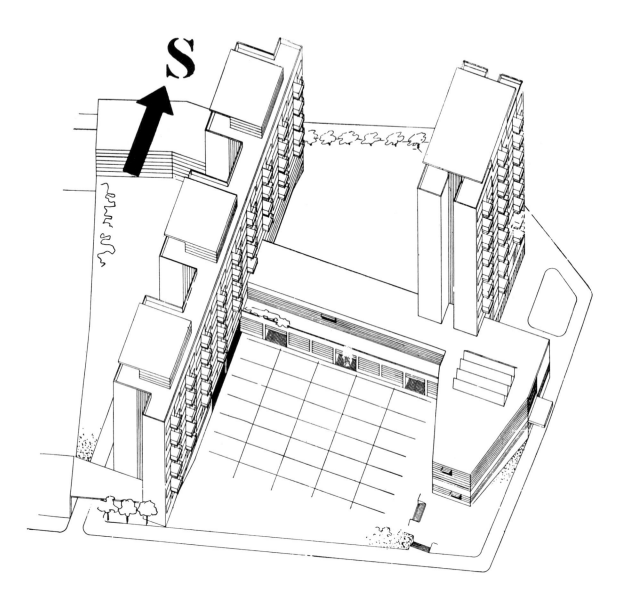

334

Jan Gillar. Competition project for a collective building for the Včela cooperative. 1931.

Jan Gillar. French Schools, view of the kindergarten. Dejvice,
Božkova 3. 1931–1934.

Architecture and the Great Depression

Jan Gillar. French Schools, gymnasium and kindergarten.
Dejvice, Božkova 3. 1931–1934.

Jan Gillar. Apartment buildings. Nusle, Družstevní ochoz
22–30. 1936–1937.

Following pages: *Jan Gillar. Apartment building. Holešovice, Vinařská 6.*
                     1936–1937.

                     Jan Gillar. Apartment building, entrance. Holešovice,
                     Vinařská 6. 1936–1937.   **Architecture and the Great Depression**

Theories and urbanistic visions of scientific functionalism were embraced by the PAS trio Karel Janů (1910–), Jiří Štursa (1910–) and Jiří Voženílek (1909–1987), who were later joined by Oldřich Stibor and Vlasta Suková-Štursová. The theoretical writings of PAS members were not as mature as Teige's work, being too limited by their authors' oversimplified, mechanical-materialistic sociological views. The value of PAS members' contribution consisted in their practical architectural and town-planning work. From 1931 to 1935, PAS developed plans for a large industrial satellite city to be situated between the small towns of Kralupy and Brandýs nad Labem near Prague. It was an innovative re-working of Zákrejs's idea of *Paralelní Praha* (Parallel Prague), conceived in this case as a linear city strictly following the formula prescribed in Milyutin's book *Socgorod*. Along with this project, PAS published designs for working-class children's schools and for collective houses. In Prague, they built several apartment blocks in the second half of the thirties, when their work already showed increased interest in the aesthetic aspects of architecture. An example of this is the subtle facade of the building in Milady Horákové, 1938–1939, designed by Karel Janů. The receding upper floor was undoubtedly inspired by Le Corbusier's Paris Salvation Army Building, 1930–1933, a model that had been practically banned by scientific functionalists in the early thirties.

In spite of that, the model was carefully studied. At the end of the twenties, there were several young polytechnic graduates in the *Stavba* circle who shared the ambition to give an emotive modern form to technically and socially progressive architectural works. The members of this loosely formed group were Josef Kittrich (1901–1968), who later became an official of ASLEF and of the Association of Socialist Architects and whose views placed him closest to the program of scientific functionalism, Josef Hrubý (1906–1988), whose work showed a strong artistic talent, and Karel Hannauer (1906–1966) who was also a building contractor, talented designer, theoretician of architecture, and researcher in the field of apartment lighting. From 1928 to 1930, these architects published their projects in the magazine *Stavební rádce* (Building Guide) and in *Stavba*. Together, they collaborated on the project for an air-conditioned glass family house in 1931.

Karel Janů. Commercial and apartment building. Holešovice, Milady Horákové 63. 1938–1939.

Josef Kittrich's work had an austere practical character whereas Hrubý's and Hannauer's designs showed the influence of Le Corbusier' aesthetic of the "play of volumes in sunlight," which remained present also in their later buildings and projects. Kittrich and Hrubý set up their own architectural practice in 1933. In the first works produced by this team, and particularly in the Březnice school building, 1933–1934, it was Kittrich's practical nature, in line with the contemporary program of ASLEF, that prevailed. Their Prague buildings, on the other hand, show Hrubý's artistic influence. For instance, the symmetrical stone-clad facade of the commercial building on the corner of Londýnská and Anglická Streets, 1938–1939, had a classicist character, while the facade of their elegant department store The White Swan in Na poříčí, 1937–1939, was made entirely of glass.

The program of *Stavba* was influenced by architects whose thinking was close to ASLEF members' scientific-functionalist stance but not their left-wing political views. These were Oldřich Starý, F. A. Libra, Bohumír Kozák, Gustav Paul, František Čermák, Antonín Černý, Ferdinand Fencl, Bohumír Kněžek, and Josef Václavík. These architects mostly took stock in the continuity of their scientific-functionalist views, and their work did not show a sudden break, unlike the work of ASLEF members around 1935. But even among them there were architects interested in the emotional aspects of architecture. Apart from Karel Hannauer, they were, for example, František Čermák (1903–   ) the author of the impressive "nautical" vertical extension of the apartment building on Americká Street, 1934–1935, František Zelenka (1896–1944), who started his career as stage designer for *Devětsil*'s experimental theatre and carried something of this experience into his Prague buildings designed in the thirties, or František Kerhart, whose villa on Nad Paťankou Street, 1935–1936, was undoubtedly meant as a manifesto of the importance of beauty in architecture.

The editor-in-chief of *Stavba*, Oldřich Starý, built eight family houses in Prague after 1928, including four on the Baba estate. His most significant architectural work from the thirties that best documents his continued effort to achieve "purity and truthfulness"[30] was the building of the *Svaz československého díla*, on Národní Street, 1934–1938. In this project, Starý had to come to terms not only

Josef Kittrich, Josef Hrubý. The White Swan department
store. Nové Město, Na poříčí 23. 1937–1939.

*Karel Hannauer. Apartment building. Nusle, Petra Rezka 16.
1938.*

*František Kerhart. Bělehrádek's family villa on the Baba es-
tate. Dejvice, Nad Pat'ankou 10. 1935–1936.*

Architecture and the Great Depression

346

with a very complicated building plan that included shops, exhibition halls, and office spaces of several major cultural institutions but also with the difficult L-shaped building site. He decided on a flexible layout designed around an internal court with elastically rounded corners and a retractable ceiling, which still works to this day, and the size and shape of all the rooms can be changed according to immediate need. The building's suspended facade facing Národní Street is made of large glass panes divided by the thin horizontals of the floors and even thinner vertical bars.

A similar minimalist approach, limited to a bare wall with a regular pattern of windows, was characteristic also of the work of Ferdinand Fencl (1901–1983) and Antonín Černý (1896–1976), who both gained their first working experience in Oldřich Tyl's office. Fencl specialized in large functionalist buildings — hospitals, sanatoriums, and schools — whose enormous volumes he skilfully harnessed and articulated despite the laconic nature of his architectural vocabulary. An example of his approach is, for example, the secondary school in Pátého května, 1937–1941, or the nursing school in Charles Square, 1937–1950. Vojtěch Kerhart, Fencl's colleague from the *Stavba* circle, later designed the polyclinic complex that was added to the back of the nursing school building in Malá Štěpánská Lane in 1937–1953. Antonín Černý established himself in the thirties as designer of small-apartment municipal housing, but he was also capable of designing the monumental functionalist building for the insurance company Assicurazioni Generali and Moldavia Generali in Na příkopě, 1936–1938, which he divided into three parallel wings connected on the ground floor by means of a beautiful vaulted passage.

The shift toward a sophisticated functionalist style in the work of Bohumír Kozák, the coauthor of this building, can probably be explained by the increasing influence of his younger brother, Ladislav Kozák, on the output of the family-owned architectural office. The best work designed by the two brothers was the women's pavilion of the Municipal Social Institute on Vídeňská Road, 1934–1940.

347

Oldřich Starý. Building of the Svaz československého díla.
Nové Město, Národní 36. 1934–1938.

A new face appeared also in F. A. Libra's office. It was the Latvian architect Jiří Kan (1895–1944), who had studied in the early twenties with Hans Poelzig in Berlin. Libra and Kan were the authors of the largest functionalist building in Czechoslovakia, the tuberculosis sanatorium in Vyšné Hágy in the Tatra Mountains, 1933–1939. Generous conception and a sense of monumentality characterized the work of Gustav Paul (1903–1974), who worked in partnership with František Čermák from the late twenties. In 1936, these architects won the competition for the teaching hospital in Motol with a project that displayed a rare harmony between the austere functional hierarchy of the individual pavilions and the aesthetically based gradation of their volumes.

The scientific-functionalist approach never became dominant within the circle of Kotěra's and Gočár's students around *Stavitel*, although it temporarily gained currency after 1930, when the magazine published projects and essays by Jan Gillar, Jaromír Krejcar, Josef Špalek, Zdeněk Rossmann, and other members of ASLEF and the *Svaz socialistických architektů*. Among the youngest graduates from Gočár's department who subscribed to scientific functionalism were, for example, Lev Krča, Stanislav Tobek, and Jaroslav Kincl, who in the thirties designed standardized family housing for the ironworks Vítkovické železárny using assembled steel construction, or Bohumil Steigenhöfer, the author of a large modern printing plant in the block between Na poříčí and Na Florenci Streets, 1938–1945. Among Kotěra's students, whose work in the thirties also showed aspects of austere, scientifically oriented asceticism, were Jaroslav Kabeš, Rudolf Stockar, Karel Caivas, Arnošt Mühlstein, and Ladislav Machoň, whose gymnasium in U branek, 1931–1933, belongs to the most sophisticated functionalist buildings of its kind in Prague.

Pavel Janák's progress toward scientific functionalism was planned and systematic, and had started already in the late twenties. This development was prompted by his membership in the State Planning Commission, whose work, as he believed, was to be based on objective criteria. This conviction led him to write a series of complex analytical studies, appendixed with mathematical calculations, tables, and diagrams, which were published in 1924 in *Styl* and to examine

SOUTĚŽ NEMOCNICE V MOTOLECH

the relationship between modern systems of developing urban areas and population density. In 1933, he also published a book on the history of Prague apartment floor plans.[31] His architectural work was, however, less orthodox than his theories, and several of his buildings from this period were undoubtedly designed to make an emotive impact, which is the case mainly with his elegant Hotel Juliš in Wenceslas Square, 1929–1933. On the other hand, Janák designed buildings that could be only described as manifestos of scientific functionalism. The building designed for the evangelical meeting house, the Husův sbor on Dykova Street, 1931–1933, is a well-thought-through composition of three basic elements: the ceremony hall, the residential quarters, and the bell tower, which surprises the viewer with its variable configurations of masses, the play of shadows cast on to the white surfaces, and the

349

František Čermák, Gustav Paul. Competition project for the teaching hospital in Motol. 1936.

Pavel Janák. Hotel Juliš. Nové Město, Václavské náměstí 22.
1931–1933.

Pavel Janák. Interior of the Hotel Juliš café. Nové Město,
Václavské náměstí 22. 1931–1933.

Architecture and the Great Depression

unexpected vistas. The scientific-functionalist character of the building is nevertheless underlined by the industrial shed roof of the hall, the glass brick bands in its base, and the constructivist structure of the bell tower, reminiscent of water tank structures of factories or railway stations.

At the turn of the twenties and thirties, the Viennese architect Adolf Loos (1870–1933) arrived on the architectural scene of Prague. Loos had become a Czechoslovak citizen in 1920 and had worked on commissions in Plzeň and Brno. Czech architects followed his work with great interest from 1922, and Karel Teige considered him as one of the fathers of his concept of architecture as science. The great Viennese architect indeed continued to deny the artistic character of his work and presented it as a perfectly mastered craft; he even liked to discuss the spiral-shaped *Raumplan* of his late buildings in terms of a mere device that enabled a better utilization of the interior space of a house. The two villas Loos built in Prague, the Müller House in Nad hradním vodojemem, 1928–1930, and the Winternitz House in Na Cihlářce, 1931–1932, nevertheless can hardly be fitted within the framework of scientific functionalism. Loos's ideas about the craftsmanlike, nonartistic nature of his architecture, which found its practical expression in the way he dispensed with ornament of any kind, and in the almost drastically discordant placing of windows in the side facades of his houses, were in striking contrast with his passion for expensive stone and timber materials with which he usually finished his interiors. Also Loos's interest in the compositional principles of classicism, whose syntax was always evident in the "face" of his buildings, was at odds with the doctrines of scientific functionalism.

Several students from Loos's private school of architecture, which had been active in Vienna before World War I, worked in Prague in the twenties and mainly in the thirties. They were, for example, the brothers Bedřich and Leopold Ehrmann, Rudolf Wels, and Jacques Groag. It cannot be said, however, that any of them applied Loos's methods in their realized Prague buildings. The same goes for the family house in Finkovská Street, built in 1936–1937 as the only Prague project of Karel Lhota, the coauthor of the two famous Loos villas. There is one building, however, that does appear to have been inspired by Loos's

Following pages:

Pavel Janák. Evangelical meeting house Husův sbor. Vinohrady, Dykova 1. 1931–1933.

Adolf Loos, Karel Lhota. Müller House, main facade.
Střešovice, Nad hradním vodojemem 14. 1928–1930.

Adolf Loos, Karel Lhota. Müller House, rear facade. Střešo-
vice, Nad hradním vodojemem 14. 1928–1930.

Adolf Loos, Karel Lhota. Müller House, living hall. Střešo-
vice, Nad hradním vodojemem 14. 1928–1930.

Adolf Loos, Karel Lhota. Müller House, dining room.
Střešovice, Nad hradním vodojemem 14. 1928–1930.

359

Adolf Loos, Karel Lhota. Winternitz House. Smíchov, Na Cihlářce 10. 1931–1932.

Adolf Loos, Karel Lhota. Winternitz House, living hall. Smíchov, Na Cihlářce 10. 1931–1932.

work. It is a villa designed by Arnošt Wiesner (1890–1971), who by coincidence also came from Brno, Loos's frequently visited birthplace. The keel roof of this villa situated in the street U Mrázovky, 1930–1931, as well as its symmetrically asymmetrical street facade in the shape of an upside-down letter T, are strongly reminiscent of Loos's Viennese Steiner House from 1910–1911.

Arnošt Wiesner, who was described by the art historian Zdeněk Kudělka as "the Loos of Brno architecture,"[32] took a rather romantic approach to his building. The arched outlines of the monumental roof with its slate covering and the picturesque grouping of tall chimneys point to the very beginnings of the modern style as exemplified in the buildings of Voysey and Baillie-Scott. At the same time these features linked Wiesner's work with those tendencies in Prague architecture of the thirties that took a critical view of the extremes of scientific functionalism and its denial of the "emotive" aspects of architecture.

EMOTIONAL FUNCTIONALISM: BETWEEN ORGANIC ARCHITECTURE AND CLASSICISM

Many exponents of scientific functionalism thought about architecture in terms that were too schematic and tended to oversimplify its problems. Scientific functionalism often "preferred to shut its eyes" to symptoms of "serious uncertainties and inconsistencies," so as not to let them "interfere with its ideal system," stated the historian and theoretician of architecture Oldřich Stefan in 1942.[33] A similar view rejecting orthodox functionalism was later adopted by Richard Venturi in his thesis about the "exclusive," eliminatory nature of functionalist methods, summed up in Mies van der Rohe's laconic slogan: "less is more."[34]

As the opponents of the scientific variety of functionalism had been aware from the outset, the considerations ignored by scientific functionalists were many indeed. Nearly all the extremes of the "scientific" theory and practice — from the exaggerated importance given to the objective over the subjective, the rational over the emotional, the collective over the individual, through the lack of communicativeness and preference for uniformity, to the overt lack of interest in the surrounding landscape or cityscape — could be summed up in one common denominator. This common denominator — or rather the common error — was the

Arnošt Wiesner. Pick House. Smíchov, U Mrázovky 7. 1930–1931.

absence of the psychological function, the absence of a psychological, or, in the words of Karel Honzík, emotional impact. The individual, denied his psychological needs by functionalist diagrams, "does not find full realization, nor is he realized in his totality," wrote Oldřich Stefan in 1944.[35]

Architects who subscribed to the second variety of Prague's functionalism, which mostly did not reject the scientific basis of creative processes but placed the dominant artistic or at least "emotional" intention above it, focused their attention on the carrier of the psychological and emotional impact in architecture, which was primarily the architectural form. "Today, we have reached a phase when the question of the architectural form needs to be addressed with new urgency" were the words with which Karel Honzík began his lecture on the problems of "physioplasticity" in 1937.[36]

What this form should look like and what was the role of its creation in the designing process were questions that have never been clearly answered by the supporters of the "emotional" direction in architecture. Karel Honzík's program, for instance, was in this respect very moderate. To him, form was created by following the purpose; in other words, there was no need to revise earlier functionalist theories. The final form, however, does not come into existence automatically, as its "finalization" and the full expression of the form-creating purposes in all their complexity depend on the subjective qualities of the architect. According to Honzík, an a priori formal intention, or the "effect desired in advance," would result in formalism. Honzík's recommendation to progress "from purpose to form" was not far from mechanicism and as such did not represent the only alternative available to the adherents of emotional functionalism. When in 1939 Josef Chochol published in the review *Architektura ČSR* his praise of the Glass Palace, 1936–1937, designed by his younger partner Richard Podzemný, he made the connection between this remarkable example of emotional functionalism and the notion of architecture that does not proceed mechanically from purpose to its formal expression but which pulsates between the two, oscillates between the technical possibilities and the individuality of the architect's creative energy. In the hands of an "artist-architect," such architecture should, according to Chochol, blossom into "the sublime flower of a lyrical poem."[37]

364

Around 1930, the review *Musaion* became the focus of Prague's emotional functionalism and a forum for former members of *Devětsil* who did not wish to be associated with the dogmas espoused by the ASLEF group. Among others, they were Josef Havlíček, Karel Honzík, Evžen Linhart, and Pavel Smetana. In 1931, *Musaion* published Le Corbusier's "Obrana architektury" (Defense of Architecture) in response to Teige's scientific-functionalist critique of the *Mundaneum* project.[38] The review, however, soon ceased publication due to financial difficulties, and the group later found shelter in the association of modern painters, sculptors, and architects, *SVU Mánes*. This association was experiencing a period of renewal in the thirties when it became the refuge for late lyrical cubism and surrealism and where architects like Josef Gočár, Otakar Novotný, Kamil Roškot, Josef Štěpánek, František Marek, Adolf Benš, and Ladislav Žák had already prepared the ground for the program of emotional functionalism.

The beautiful review *Volné směry* (Free Directions), published by *Mánes*, also adopted the cult of Le Corbusier that had been so characteristic for *Musaion*. In the eyes of Prague's architects, Le Corbusier's work epitomized a truly artistic architecture already in the twenties, and it continued playing this role well into the thirties, when the need for such models became even greater. The stylistic character of Prague's emotional functionalism of the thirties was nevertheless marked by the fact that the notion of a truly artistic architecture to which its leading proponents subscribed was far too closely associated with Le Corbusier's buildings from 1923 to 1929, which reflected his definition of architecture as the play of pristine white volumes in sunlight. The language of Le Corbusier's purism usually became dominant even in cases where Czech architects tried to come to terms with the influence of his later, stylistically more advanced buildings, such as the Swiss College, the Salvation Army Building, or the villa in Les Mathes. In this way, Le Corbusier's example lent support to the emotional, artistic tendencies in Czech architecture of the thirties but at the same time acted as an obstacle to their development.

The most successful examples of this brand of neopurism in Prague architecture admittedly possessed some stylistic novelty. The syntax of the

365

large Villa Šajn on U Ladronky Street, 1938–1939, designed by Pavel Smetana (1900–1986), is full of references to Le Corbusier's Villa Stein in Garches, 1926–1927. Smetana's touch, however, is evident in a new aspect of robustness and monumentality that was becoming more and more characteristic of Prague's emotional functionalism in the thirties. Evžen Linhart's subtle and fragile style, clearly inspired by Le Corbusier, was still manifest in his family villa on Na Ostrohu Street, built in 1932, but his secondary school building on Evropská Road, 1936–1937, already displayed a similar, and in this case perhaps too heavy, monumentality. The most conspicuous shift toward this new monumentality was apparent in the projects of Karel Stráník (1899–1978) who briefly worked in Le Corbusier's office in 1925, and who in 1929 created an interesting variation on the Maison Cook in a summer villa in Černošice near Prague.[39] But a typical example of Stráník's post-1930 work, the family villa in Na Podkovce, 1935–1936, is far removed from such experimentation. A similar robustness and monumentality combined with effective aerodynamic motifs characterize Adolf Benš's most significant work of the time, the departure hall of the Prague Airport in Ruzyně from 1932–1934. The effort to revive Le Corbusier's purism in its undiluted form, with all its lightness, compositional logic, and spatial transparency, was, on the other hand, typical of buildings designed by architects Jaroslav Čermák, Václav Kopecký, Čeněk Vořech, František Fiala, and Josef Fuchs, and of the family villas designed for the Baba estate by Janák's pupil Hana Kučerová-Záveská (1904–1944), which were built in 1932.

After 1930, Evžen Linhart, Adolf Benš, Pavel Smetana, Karel Stráník, and other architects, who all at some stage in their careers felt the need for Le Corbusier's influence, already belonged to the middle generation of Prague's architects. However, the tendency to "learn Le Corbusier by heart"[40] was apparent also with the young generation, whose leading architects were several former students of Janák who had graduated from the School of Applied Arts — Richard Podzemný, Kamil Ossendorf, Antonín Tenzer, Rudolf Jasenský, František Míšek, Bohumil Holý, Karel Koželka, and Václav Hilský, who had studied at the school under Otakar Novotný. Their older colleagues such as Josef Chochol, F. M.

Pavel Smetana. Villa Šajn. Břevnov, U Ladronky 31. 1938–1939.

Antonín Heythum, Evžen Linhart. Villa Lisý on the Baba es-
tate. Dejvice, Na ostrohu 50. 1931–1932.

Evžen Linhart. Secondary school building. Dejvice, Evropská
33. 1937–1938.

Adolf Benš. Departure hall of the so-called Old Airport.
Ruzyně, K letišti 2. 1932–1934.

Hana Kučerová-Záveská. Villa Balling on the Baba estate.
Dejvice, Na Babě 5. 1931–1932.

Following pages:

Hana Kučerová-Záveská. Villa Balling on the Baba estate.
Dejvice, Na Babě 5. 1931–1932.

Václav Kopecký. Apartment house-pension. Vinohrady,
Londýnská 28. 1938–1939.

Architecture and the Great Depression

Černý, Pavel Smetana, and Stivo Vacek sometimes sought collaboration with these talented architects.

During the thirties, the young generation took over from *Devětsil* in the sphere of creative initiative. At the beginning, they were often in contact with the ASLEF group and with the Association of Socialist Architects whose program concurred with their left-wing thinking. They also found their way into *Mánes*, which they saw as a base for their efforts to create an aesthetically effective architecture that, in the words of Karel Koželka, should possess "all the human aspects given by civilization and culture."[41] They decided to do so regardless of Teige's warning that creating such architecture would turn them into retrograde bourgeois subjectivists. They were convinced that the aesthetic aspect was indispensable for truly progressive architecture. But it seems that they did not entirely accept the utopian concept of emotional functionalism being the "proto-image" of the socialist future of their dreams. They preferred to apply their program wherever it could bring an immediate solution to social problems. The most attractive of such solutions was the concept of "minimum dwelling" for the poor. "Housing competitions and buildings designed for mass accommodation were forms that gradually became the most recurrent focus of an architect's work and ones that were closest to his heart," was how Karel Koželka described the tendency of this group in 1940.

The first work that guaranteed the young generation a place in the history of Prague's functionalism was the project for a series of blocks with small maisonette units entered in the 1930 Prague municipality competition by the trio of architects Richard Podzemný, Kamil Ossendorf, and Antonín Tenzer. Formally, this project had been inspired by the constructivist collective houses of Moses Ginzburg, who was the main propagator of Le Corbusier's style in Soviet architecture. The terrace gardens and pergolas of another project entered by this team for the 1931 competition of the workers' cooperative *Včela* again clearly point to the influence of Le Corbusier and Ginzburg. Its particular quality consisted in the subtle height gradation of the whole structure and in the articulation of the facade by means of the sharp recesses of the balconies. The visual effect of the small-

František Jech. Commercial, office, and apartment building.
Nové Město, Jungmannova 16. 1937–1938.

374

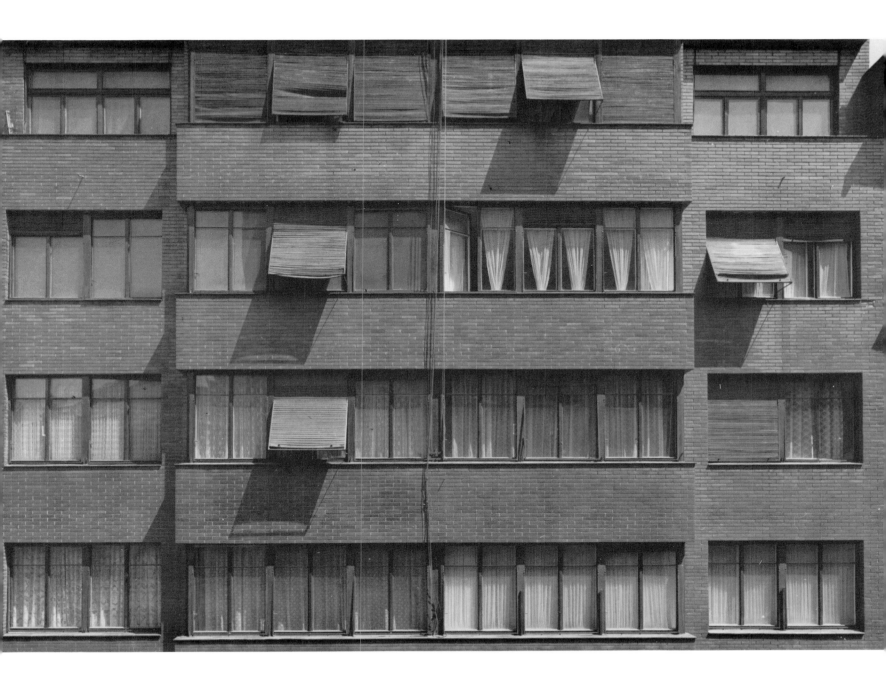

Architecture and the Great Depression

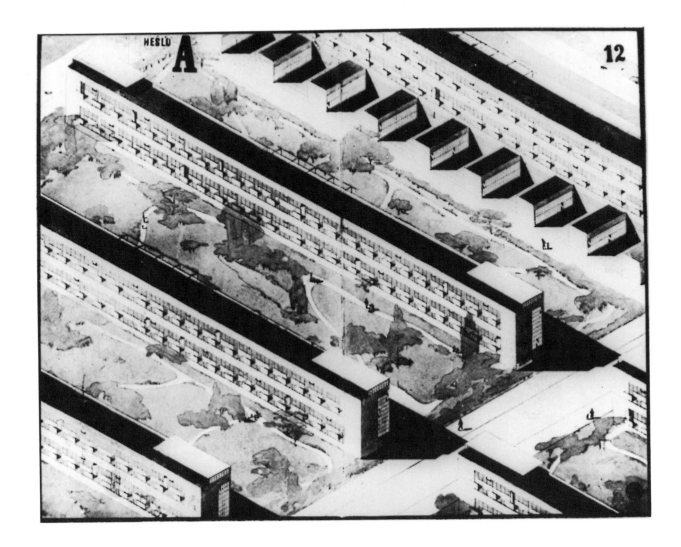

Kamil Ossendorf, Richard Podzemný, Antonín Tenzer.
Competition project for municipal housing with small
apartments in Pankrác. 1930.

CHAPTER 4

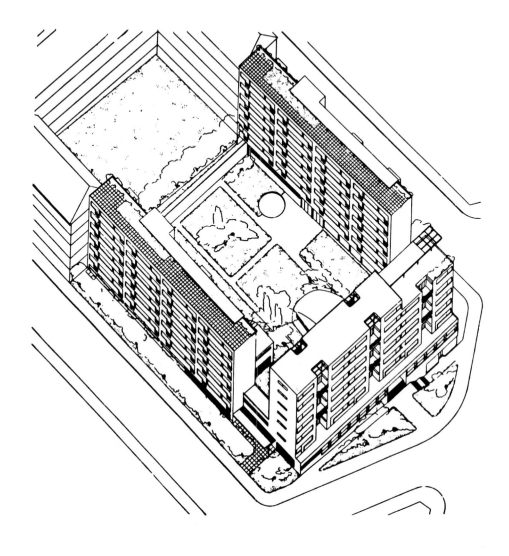

Kamil Ossendorf, Richard Podzemný, Antonín Tenzer.
Competition project for a collective building for the Včela
cooperative. 1931.

Architecture and the Great Depression

František M. Černý-Kamil Ossendorf, houses with small
apartments, Holešovice, U staré plynárny 2–10, 1937.

Josef Chochol, Richard Podzemný. Municipal building with
small apartments. Libeň, U školičky 31, 33. 1938–1940.

Architecture and the Great Depression

unit buildings designed by František Černý and Kamil Ossendorf in U městských domů, 1937–1939, was based on the rhythmical pattern of vertical color stripes and horizontal balcony floors. Another project for a municipal development comprising small units on U školičky Street, designed by Richard Podzemný and Josef Chochol and built in 1938 to 1940, impresses with its calculated contrast of white and brown and its precisely modeled boxlike shape. And finally, there was the outstanding complex of eight small-unit buildings on Mládeže and Nad Kajetánkou Streets, 1937–1939, designed by Václav Hilský, Rudolf Jasenský, Karel Koželka, and František Jech, with their precisely carved forms, meticulously balanced proportions, and effectively composed fenestration consisting of groups of three and four differently shaped windows. The total effect of this complex was enhanced by its dynamic urbanistic layout designed by Ladislav Machoň.

But the economical apartment, designed with respect to beautiful form, was not the only item on the agenda of the young generation active within *Mánes*. Its members also occasionally designed family houses, as was the case of Hilský's and Jasenský's villa on Jílovská Street, 1940–1941. The most successful undertaking of Prague's emotional functionalism was the luxury apartment buildings of Zemská Bank in Freedom Square, 1936–1937, designed by Richard Podzemný. The building, which was soon named the Glass Palace, impresses with the supple curves of its rounded corners, the gleaming white ceramic tiles, glass panes, and chrome plated details, and the harmony of its vertical and horizontal lines created by means of ribbon windows and projecting balconies. Its author paid great attention to the layout of the apartments and communal recreational spaces in the courtyard and on rooftop terraces, which were decorated with pergolas and plants after the example of Le Corbusier's purist villas.

The youngest generation of *Mánes* architects tested its outstanding talents also on tasks encompassing both architecture and town planning. In 1935, a team consisting of František Černý, Bohumil Holý, Kamil Ossendorf, and Richard Podzemný won the competition for a large indoor market that was to be situated on the Maniny Plain in Holešovice with a project that best combined the various trading activities of the hall in a unified whole. The following year a

*Richard Podzemný. Apartment building, the so-called Glass
Palace. Bubeneč, náměstí Svobody 1. 1936–1937.*

Architecture and the Great Depression

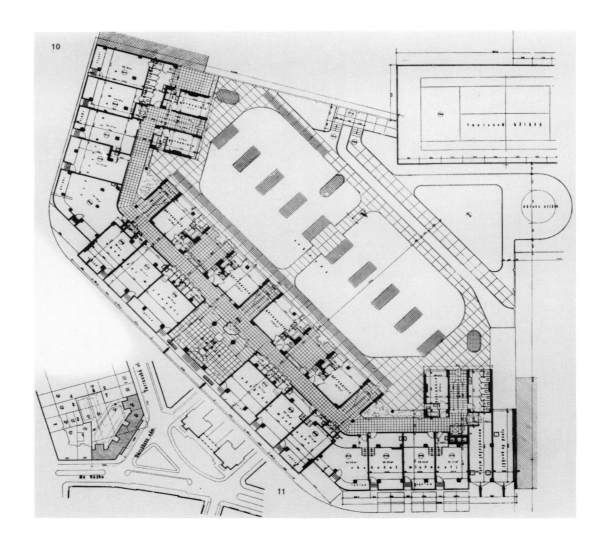

382

Richard Podzemný. Apartment building, the so-called Glass Palace, plan. Bubeneč, náměstí Svobody 1. 1936–1937.

František M. Černý, Bohumil Holý, Richard Podzemný, Kamil Ossendorf. Competition project for the indoor market in Maniny. 1935.

František M. Černý, Kamil Ossendorf, Stivo Vacek. Competition project for the teaching hospital in Motol. 1936.

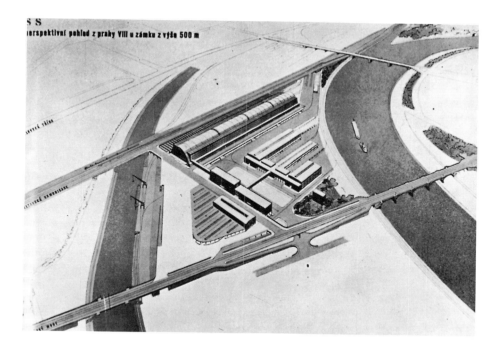

S S

perspektivní pohled z prahy VIII u zámku z výše 500 m

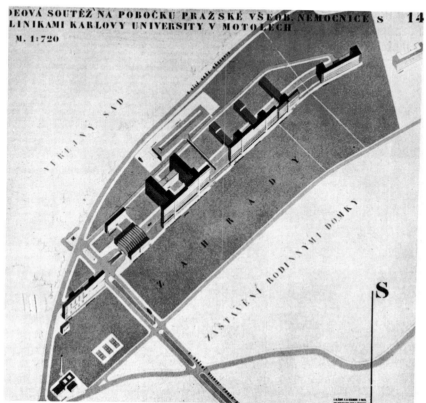

DEOVÁ SOUTĚŽ NA POBOČKU PRAŽSKÉ VŠEOB. NEMOCNICE S 14
LINIKAMI KARLOVY UNIVERSITY V MOTOLECH

M. 1:720

383

project entered for the competition for a teaching hospital in Motol by the team Černý, Ossendorf, and Vacek gained wide acclaim in architectural circles. The authors of the winning project, František Čermák and Gustav Paul, both associated with *Stavba*, based their design on the principles of orthodox functionalism, according to which each of the individual functions of the hospital was given a separate building. The former team, however, which came second in the competition, had already adopted the newer system of the so-called mono-block, which was designed to shorten the distances between the individual functional units of the hospital and to concentrate them, if possible, in one building. The team did not go that far, but they did line up the main buildings of the hospital in one row, separating them by relatively small gaps. Adolf Benš revealed the classicist subtext of this solution when he compared it to the "simple directness of earlier military engineers and architects who conquered situations by means a of frontal attack."[42]

Richard Podzemný, Antonín Tenzer, Kamil Ossendorf, Karel Koželka, and other graduates of the School of Applied Arts owed much of what they so successfully put into practice to their teacher Pavel Janák. Janák introduced his students to the best examples of European functionalism of the time in situ, assigned them various projects in the area of modern town planning, and cultivated in them a keen interest in the social aspects of architecture. The scope of Gočár's school at the Academy of Fine Arts was much narrower and concentrated on architecture as a fine art discipline. Gočár taught his students how to combine the modern appearance of a building with the required monumentality, how to fit the building compositionally into the existing street front, how to resolve its urban elements — in particular street corners, which in the new buildings of Gočár's school designed in the thirties received a variety of treatments. Among the most representative buildings of Gočár's school during this period were the monumental Savings Bank building on Sokolovská Avenue, 1939–1942, designed by František Stalmach and Jan Svoboda; the complex of apartment blocks with cinema *Oko* in Františka Křížka Street, 1938–1939, designed by Josef Šolc; and apartment buildings and family houses by Emanuel Hruška, Josef Mach, and Martin Reiner.

384

František Stalmach, Jan Svoboda. Savings bank, office, and
apartment building. Karlín, Sokolovská 1. 1939–1942.

Architecture and the Great Depression

Yet, in the thirties only Evžen Rosenberg's (1907–1991) apartment buildings could compete with the architectural qualities of Podzemný's Glass Palace. Rosenberg worked in Le Corbusier's office in Paris at the beginning of the decade and became acquainted with the changes in Le Corbusier's style much more intimately than other Prague followers of the great Paris architect, while being also the most perceptive — perhaps with the exception of Josef Havlíček — in understanding the transitions of Le Corbusier's work. But even Rosenberg in the end only managed to evoke Le Corbusier's post-1930 syntax by repeating Corbusier-like forms of the previous decade. Between 1935 and 1938, before he emigrated to Great Britain where he formed a successful architectural team with Yorke and Mardall, Rosenberg built in Prague six large apartment and commercial buildings. The symmetrical facades of the apartment blocks in Letohradská, 1935–1936, and Antonínská, 1936–1937, are dominated by the suspended *avant-corps* articulated by band windows and flanked by balcony railings made of perforated metal. The flatter facade of the building on Štěpánská Street, 1937–1938, is ultimately nothing but a collection of sensitively proportioned bands of grey plaster, reflective glass, and silver window trimmings.

Rosenberg's buildings represented a somewhat abstract position within the framework of emotional functionalism, based on the art of combining simple geometrical volumes into a balanced composition, selecting the optimal shape of windows, balconies, and doors, establishing the correct planar proportions for the walls and window openings, and paying special attention to detail. Next to Rosenberg, true masters of this approach in emotional functionalist architecture were Elly and Oskar Oehler, a husband-and-wife team who designed the beautiful villas in Na bateriích, 1931–1932, and V Nových Bohnicích, 1935. However, in the thirties, many Prague exponents of emotional functionalism found this strictly abstract architectural language insufficient. Functionalist architecture appeared to have lost its confidence and began to search for new means by which to evoke an emotional response in its users. Architects again became interested in color schemes, and next to the spatial qualities of buildings they emphasized their plastic qualities, trying to break the strict orthogonality of functionalist architecture by the use of richer and more varied forms.

Evžen Rosenberg. Apartment building. Holešovice, U průhonu 16. 1936.

387

Preceding pages:

Evžen Rosenberg. Apartment buildings. Holešovice, Antonínská 4, 6. 1936–1937.

Evžen Rosenberg. Commercial and apartment building. Nové Město, Štěpánská 36. 1937–1938.

CHAPTER 4

Elly Oehlerová, Oskar Oehler. Villa Marek, view from the garden. Střešovice, Na bateriích 13. 1931–1932.

Elly Oehlerová, Oskar Oehler. Villa Marek, view from the street. Střešovice, Na bateriích 13. 1931–1932.

GARÁŽ

KUCHYŇ

HALA

ŠATNA

PŘÍPRAVNA JÍDEL

POKOJ

JÍDELNA

ZIMNÍ ZAHRADA

Elly Oehlerová, Oskar Oehler. Villa Marek, floor plan.
Střešovice, Na bateriích 13. 1931–1932.

Some of these stylistic changes were apparent after 1930 in the work of two other architects who respected Le Corbusier's authority: Josef Havlíček and Karel Honzík. The most significant of their Prague projects was the administrative building of the General Pensions Institute in Winston Churchill Square, which was designed in 1932 and completed by 1934. The State Planning Commission at first wanted to have the building designed as a polygon with an enclosed courtyard in the center. Havlíček and Honzík, however, still guided by the functionalist notion of open space, gave the building an open layout in the shape of a cross placed between two additional parallel shoulders. The renewed taste for plasticity and physical materiality contributed to the building being seen as an "object in space," rather than allowing for the interpretation of "space in an object." This approach probably originated with Havlíček, who had started his artistic career as a sculptor and whose own works since 1936 when he ceased to work with Honzík bear witness to his sense for the plastic qualities of architecture. All Havlíček's projects and realized buildings from the late thirties made use of color, and in his 1937 competition project for the department store Brouk a Babka he enriched his vocabulary with a nontraditional use of typographical signs. The most beautiful of his works from this period was his apartment building in Letohradská Street, 1938–1939, another example of the way in which Prague's architects continued to respond to Le Corbusier's influence. Here Havlíček achieved an outstanding effect with the subtle combination of yellow and green ceramic tiles and warm brown timber shutters.

In the twenties, Czech purism and functionalism reflected Loos's vision of "cities white as Sion." White color distinguished purist-functionalist new architecture from the loud colors of Janák's and Gočár's rondocubism, it was associated with cleanliness and hygiene, and its popularity was unwittingly enhanced by the black and white photographs in architectural magazines in which even buildings using color appeared to be snow white. After 1930, more colors were added to the palette of Prague functionalist architecture. This development was aided by a new tiling material, glazed ceramic tiles, which were initially used mainly in white, as on the facade of the buildings of the Power Company, 1927–

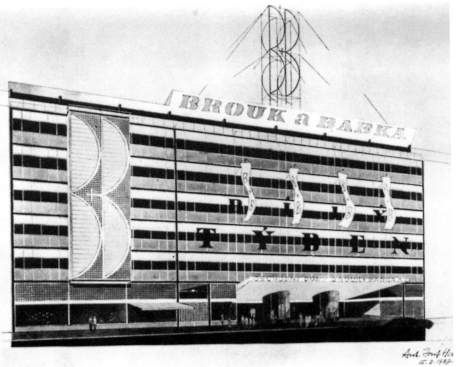

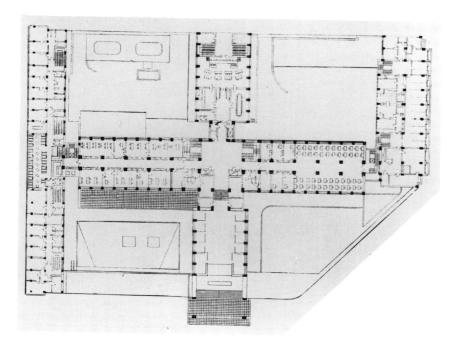

1935, and of the General Pensions Institute, 1932–1934, but were easy to manufacture in red, brown, black, yellow, or green. In addition to Josef Havlíček, there were other architects who designed impressive buildings with colored ceramic facades: Karel Dudych, J. K. Tesař, František Louda, and, above all, Karel Kotas.

   The enriched color range of Prague's functionalist buildings corresponded to the style's increasingly varied repertoire of formal composition that now included curves and oblique facets. Sometimes the front of the building would curve out or in, inspired by the uneven line of the street; at other times the architects simply wanted to achieve a contrast between straight lines and curves, the same kind of contrast Le Corbusier employed so impressively in his Villa Savoye

Josef Havlíček, Karel Honzík. General Pensions Institute Building. Žižkov, náměstí Winstona Churchilla 2. 1932–1934.

Josef Havlíček. Competition project for the department store Brouk a Babka. 1937.

Josef Havlíček, Karel Honzík. General Pensions Institute Building, plan. Žižkov, náměstí Winstona Churchilla 2. 1932–1934.

395

Architecture and the Great Depression

Josef Havlíček. Apartment building. Holešovice, Letohradská
60. 1938–1939.

Emanuel Hruška. Villa. Dejvice, Pod Bořislavkou 40. 1936–
1937.

or on the rear facade of the Swiss College. It was with this intention in mind that Gočár's pupil Emanuel Hruška (1906–1990) designed the wave-shaped recessed story of his villa in Pod Bořislavkou, 1936–1937. The interest of emotional functionalism in the psychological and emotional impact and subjective qualities of architecture created problems similar to those pyramidal cubism had been faced with from 1911. Yet again, architecture came to be viewed subjectively: its rectangular geometry became distorted and began collapsing under the weight of single-viewpoint motion perspective.[43]

The convex facade of the commercial building on the narrow Perlová Street, 1938–1940, was designed by Karel Kotas to offer a frontal view to the pedestrians approaching the building along the street. Other buildings were probably inspired by the shape of the upper floor of Le Corbusier's Salvation Army Building, like the zigzag-shaped facades of the apartment block in Jičínská Street, 1935–1936, designed by another of Gočár's pupils, Jaroslav Vančura, or of the isolation block of the dermato-venereological pavilion at Bulovka Hospital, 1935–1936, designed by a former member of *Devětsil* Jan Rosůlek (1900–   ). This shape can nevertheless also be interpreted as the outcome of a new approach to the old cubist principle of combining the direct frontal and oblique side view. Theoreticians of emotional functionalism did not examine these issues in the same depth as the cubists Pavel Janák and Jiří Kroha. Yet, their various comments suggest that they were concerned with the implications of optics and perspective in architecture. Karel Honzík, for instance, spoke about the "optical-motional" and "optical-tactile relationships,"[44] and Jan Mannsbarth arrived at the conclusion that "the aesthetic object is given to us primarily as data of our sensual experience" and therefore "the assumed general aesthetic norm would have to be based on . . . the logical nature of seeing."[45]

František Marek (1899–1971), a pupil of Gočár's and a member of *Mánes*, was also probably concerned with these problems, being an architect with a rather unorthodox approach to functionalist rules. This is obvious, for instance, in his family house on Pivoňková Street, 1936–1938, with its high pitched roof and symmetrically designed garden facade. But it was the interior of his most

Jan Rosůlek. Dermato-venereological pavilion of the Bulovka Hospital. Libeň, Bulovka. 1935–1936.

significant work, the second building of the Czechoslovak Legiobank in Na poříčí, 1937–1939, that best illustrates Marek's inclination toward free form, which must have been difficult to justify from a functional point of view. All the principal spaces of his building abound with curves, from the arcade with its unusual roof constructed of two cylindrical sectors of different radius, through the restaurant and bistro halls, to the foyer and concert hall in the basement. In the interior of the concert hall, the motifs of the segment and the S-shape were applied in the ground plan profile of the walls, in the outlines of the decorative panels, and especially in the billowing Bohemian vaults of the ceiling, pitched between supporting arches. The baroque character of this interior echoed the general interest in authentic baroque architecture that culminated in the 1938 exhibition of Prague baroque.

In spite of all its formally innovative nature, Marek's baroque curves did not interfere with the orthogonal frame of his work to which the curves served only as an accessory, not as an element determining its architectural structure. In Prague of the thirties, there were, however, architects who made an attempt at reversing the ratio between the curve and the straight line. Such attempts had a certain tradition in modern Prague architecture, dating back to Kotěra's improvisational sketches *Musical Impressions* from the years after 1900 and to several cubist studies by Vlastislav Hofman. In the theoretical field, of some interest in this respect is Teige's article "Naše základna a naše cesta" (Our Base and Our Path) from 1924. "In the modern metropolis, there are straight avenues," wrote Teige who would not have allowed other than straight lines in modern architecture; but it was "admissible, almost necessary, for the footpaths in parks to meander in odd and magical ways, protecting the meditation of a loner or the conversation of two lovers."[46]

It seems that in architecture built according to Teige's scientific notions, meditations or lovers' conversations were not permitted. That was why an "emotionalist" opposition formed against Teige within *Devětsil*. One of its spokesmen, the architect, poet, typographer, and stage designer Vít Obrtel, arrived after 1930 at a conception of architecture that could well be seen as the embodiment of

401

Jan Rosůlek. Dermato-venereological pavilion of the Bulovka Hospital. Libeň, Bulovka. 1935–1936.

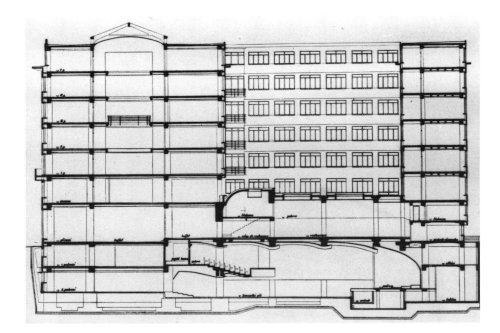

Teige's "paths meandering in odd and magical ways."[47] The salient characteristics of Obrtel's projects — curved, S-shaped floor plans in which the right angle appeared to be an exception rather than the norm, coalescing and colliding rounded sections of walls, dome-shaped and segment vaults — could hardly be related to the curves of emotional functionalism. Obrtel's style, which he himself called neo-constructivism, or later empirical functionalism, was probably closer to the theories of "organic creation of the natural" formulated by Frank Lloyd Wright or the German architects Hugo Häring (1882–1958) and Hans Scharoun (1893–1972), who all tried to emulate in their architectural systems various natural formations, from the growth of trees, leaves, and flowers, meanderings of rivers and country footpaths, to the structure of crystals and tectonics of the human body. In his own review *Kvart* (Quarto), Obrtel spoke in 1931 about the "straight line or curve in the created section of space," about "the shapeless shape, the line of lost points, the line of mists and stones."[48] Roughly at the same time he tried to express these vi-

František Marek. The second building of the Czechoslovak Legiobank, section. Nové Město, Na poříčí 26. 1937–1939.

František Marek. Concert hall in the second building of the Czechoslovak Legiobank. Nové Město, Na poříčí 26. 1937–1939.

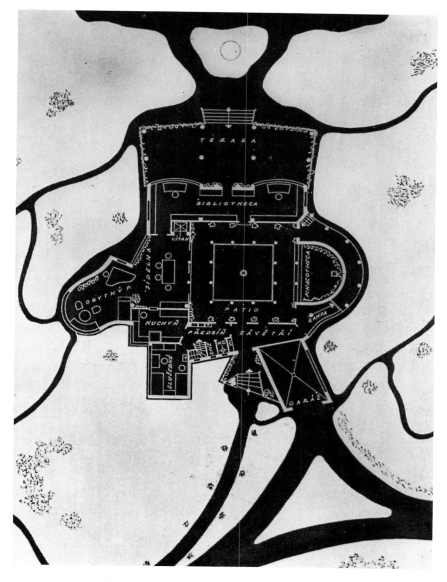

Vít Obrtel. Model for the Villa on a Classical Theme.
Between 1931 and 1935.

Vít Obrtel. Study for the interior of the Villa on a Classical
Theme. *Between 1931 and 1935.*

Vít Obrtel. Villa on a Classical Theme, *plan. Between 1931–
1935.*

sions in his unrealized projects of the *Functional Villa* and the *Villa on a Classical Theme*, where the classical theme was a glass-domed atrium with a pool.

Not many buildings in Prague were designed in the spirit of organic architecture. Traces of the organic style can be seen in Obrtel's only project realized in the thirties in Prague, the apartment block on Žitná Street, 1937–1939, whose corners flow into the striking elastic arch of the side facade. The curves of organic architecture probably provided inspiration for Augusta Müllerová and Ladislav Machoň when they designed the open pavilion adjacent to the garden wall of the Prague Museum of Applied Arts on Široká Street, 1940, which then became a venue for lectures and performances as part of the large exhibition *Za novou architekturu* (In Support of New Architecture). The most successful representative of organic architecture in Prague eventually became Vladimír Grégr (1902–1943), a prominent architect who designed seven luxury villas for film producers near the Barrandov film studios.

The look of some of Grégr's organic buildings — especially the villa on Skalní Street from 1932–1933 — can be characterized as "curvilinear international style." They were probably inspired by Scharoun's pension building at the exhibition *Wohnung und Werkraum* (Living and Working Space) held in Wroclaw in 1929.[49] Other villas designed by Grégr in Barrandovská and Filmařská Streets, built mainly between 1932 and 1941, sometimes also have the undulating organic ground plan, but their total form has little to do with contemporary architecture. The elongated volumes of the villas with their polygonal, timber-clad projections are topped with high pitched or hipped roofs with tall chimneys, reminiscent of the "cottages" of Kotěra's prewar modern style. The windows are protected by handmade grills, and the entrances are illuminated with metal lanterns. In his work, Grégr followed the principle that the architect must be "a psychologist with versatile education and orientation" and that spatial problems of modern living must be resolved "primarily with feeling." This principle would hardly be disputed by any of the emotional functionalists, but Grégr's view as to whose feelings should be heeded — the client's or the architect's — was in its time quite exceptional. "Because the dwelling will be occupied not by the architect but

Vít Obrtel, Zdeněk Hölzel. Apartment building with shops.
Nové Město, Žitná 23. 1937–1939.

Vít Obrtel, Zdeněk Hölzel. Apartment building, foyer. Nové Město, Žitná 23. 1937–1939.

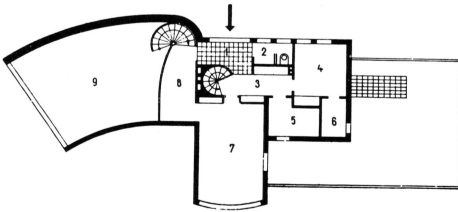

409

Vladimír Grégr. Villa Čelakovský. Hlubočepy, Skalní 10.
1932–1933.

Vladimír Grégr. Villa Čelakovský, floor plan. Hlubočepy,
Skalní 10. 1932–1933.

by the client, it is more than natural that the wishes and requirements of the owner should be taken into consideration, always and consistently, even if it is only within the framework of given possibilities."[50]

The wishes and requirements of the owners led Grégr to design villas that looked like a cross between a weekend cottage and a Spanish-style California hacienda—both of which evoked romantic visions of return to nature and of exotic escapes. Grégr's villas were, however, also reminiscent of early 1900s English cottages or of gabled farmhouses, evoking an atmosphere of homely coziness and security. The reactions of Prague's functionalists to Grégr's experiments varied. Some condemned him because of his affluent clientele: in their eyes, he could never be a "true" architect; others—for instance Emanuel Hruška in 1939—saw his buildings as the product of unsated romanticism, a new formalism: "simply bad architecture."[51] At the same time, Grégr also had his followers among Prague's functionalist architects: remarkable romantic buildings in a similar vein were designed for example by Kotěra's pupils Arnošt Mühlstein and Antonín Gabriel, or by the graduates from Gočár's school Jan Sokol and the brothers Jaroslav and Karel Fišer. Other works could be placed in the context of this stylistic direction: Wiesner's villa in U Mrázovky as well as Roškot's house on Vlašská Street, 1939–1940, whose neobaroque forms were designed to fit into the historical locale of Malá Strana.

Those who held Grégr's flirtation with the bad taste of his clients against him were probably right. But behind their rejection of his romantic style there may have been bad conscience. The functionalist credo was to serve life, society, and the needs of individuals. However, functionalists liked to confuse the concrete knowledge of human needs with mere assumptions or with speculation about such needs that masqueraded as science. This was not Grégr's approach; his pioneering contribution consisted of his attempt to find out what these needs really were.

The developmental tendencies of Prague architecture between 1935 and 1939 were discussed in Karel Honzík's book *Tvorba životního slohu* (Creating a Style of Living), published in 1946. He detected in this period an in-

411

Vladimír Grégr. Villa Pelc. Hlubočepy, Filmařská 4. 1934–1935.

clination to return to the modern style of 1900 and interpreted this tendency in terms of nostalgic escapism to which his generation resorted under the pressures of the economic depression and the imminent threat of war. Apart from this, Honzík saw in Prague architecture of the thirties a conspicuous shift from purely functionalist technicism to a kind of naturalism characterized by an interest in natural spaces and landscape. According to Honzík, the conflict between these two directions had "far deeper" causes, it stemmed from the inner struggle "between the love for the technical civilization on the one hand, and the love for nature on the other," which his generation experienced.[52] Honzík's words about naturalism, possibly inspired by Le Corbusier's ideas from the thirties, could refer to Grégr, who in designing his romantic houses chose styles, colors, and materials that suggested a harmony with their natural environment. But it is more likely that Honzík had in mind the activities of Ladislav Žák (1900–1973), an architect who fought the battle between technicism and naturalism within himself, without conforming to the conservative taste of his rich clients.

Žák studied under Gočár at the Academy of Fine Arts between 1924 and 1927. Later he designed residential interiors in which he tried to achieve the ideal of a free, almost empty space. This intention also governed the subtle shapes of his tubular furniture. After 1930, Žák joined ASLEF and the Association of Socialist Architects, and for many years he was concerned with issues of communal living and with the design of inexpensive interiors for the poor. His ideal of empty space, expressed in 1929 in the slogan "to build nothing," turned in the thirties into an approach that would be described today as "ecological." Žák began to dream about returning landscape to the city and transferring automated industrial production underground to make space for parks and forests in place of industrial suburbs. He thought about the ideal type of Bohemian landscape and presented proposals for its recultivation and protection in the daily press. For informed clients—mostly building contractors of his family villas—Žák projected his "living gardens," a kind of intimate grove that would extend the residential space of the house into its closest environment and would be designed with functionalist simplicity. The results of his inquiry into this subject were collected in his book

412

Obytná krajïna (The Residential Landscape), which he wrote in 1940–1941, and which was published in 1947 with an excellent introduction by Karel Teige.

Žák tried to achieve harmony between the building and the landscape in his architectural work as well. He did not sympathize with Grégr's notion of complete fusion between architecture and landscape: he considered buildings of this type to be far too conspicuous precisely because of their rather anxious desire to blend in with the environment. Žák could not see any reason why the "white prism of a purist building" could not harmoniously coexist with the beauty of nature as he wrote in 1947. Between 1932 and 1937, Žák built six family villas in Prague whose style, beside general references to Le Corbusier's purism, shows the influence of Krejcar's sanatorium Machnáč in the Slovak spa town Trenčianské Teplice, a building Žák respected as a "proto-image of socialist living."[53] Žák's Prague villas were intended to be similar models, "islands of the future." They had cabinlike bedrooms that fulfilled the function of individual cells in the collective house, while the communal life of the inhabitants of the villa was served by a large living hall. Terraces, which extended the space of the halls, were intentionally designed like naval decks. The "nautical symbolism," which was most pronounced in the villa he designed for the actress Lída Baarová on Neherovská Street, 1937, included round windows and cylindrical chimneys, and was reflected in the increasingly aerodynamic appearance of Žák's projects. To give an example, the position of the terrace in the villa built for the aircraft designer Miroslav Hajn in Na vysočanských vinicích, and the flexible way in which it was attached to the main body of the building, was certainly meant to evoke the image of an aircraft. It seems that Ladislav Žák was the one architect who in the thirties consistently developed the former program of *Devětsil* based on the beauty of technology, its emotive power, and romantic associations, and who did so at a level of quality matched only by Jaromír Krejcar's Czechoslovak pavilion at the International Exhibition of Art and Technology held in Paris in 1937. More precisely, Žák's program consisted in achieving harmony between the beauty of technology and the beauty of nature.

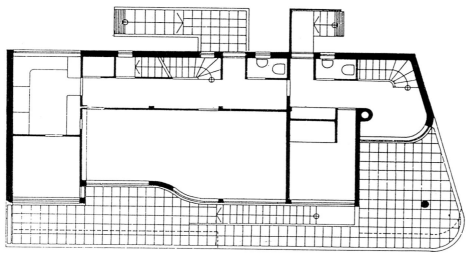

Ladislav Žák. Lída Baarová's villa, view from the street.
Dejvice, Neherovská 8. 1937.

Ladislav Žák. Lída Baarová's villa, view from the garden.
Dejvice, Neherovská 8. 1937.

Ladislav Žák. Lída Baarová's villa, floor plan. Dejvice, Neherovská 8. 1937.

Architecture and the Great Depression

Ladislav Žák. Villa Hajn, view from the street. Vysočany, Na vysočanských vinicích 31. 1932–1933.

Ladislav Žák. Villa Hajn, view from the garden. Vysočany, Na vysočanských vinicích 31. 1932–1933.

CHAPTER 4

In thinking about the realization of his program of residential landscape, Žák reached the conclusion that this program would not be possible without a radical policy of restraint, a radical reduction of people's needs, and he referred to the example of Diogenes in his barrel. Diogenes was not the only Ancient Greek philosopher whom the functionalists elevated to their imaginary Pantheon alongside engineers, sea captains, pilots, and other icons of modern civilization. The pioneers of purist-functionalist new architecture also admired Plato, who revealed the beauty of the simplest geometrical forms, and Protagoras, whose axiom that "man is the measure of all things" was used by Teige as early as the twenties. References to the authority of Greek philosophers were most characteristic of the writing of Vít Obrtel who—in a somewhat naive manner—tried to develop Plato's idea of "absolute beauty," which was immeasurably more perfect then the things of this world including architecture. Elsewhere, he highlighted the relationships of numbers as the ideal tool of creation: "Pythagoras's number," "the number as corrective agent and as form, the essence of connections between all things."[54]

In part, Obrtel reacted to Le Corbusier and his principle of *tracés régulateurs* (regulatory lines); in part, he expressed his own conception of architecture. But he also signaled the first appearance of neoclassicist tendencies in Prague's functionalist architecture.

For a long time he remained isolated, as other theoreticians became aware of the presence of neoclassicist characteristics in Prague's functionalist architecture only after 1935, when in the context of competitions for the Motol Hospital, 1936, for President Masaryk's memorial, 1937, and for the completion of the Old Town City Hall architects began discussing such qualities as proportion, regularity, balance, symmetry, and closed space. For many Prague architects and theorists, the manifestations of neoclassicist tendencies merged with the newly established monumentality for which the classicist vocabulary offered many tried and tested means of expression. More popular in the thirties was the new conception of monumentality, based on the emotional impact of purified architectural form. In 1944, for instance, Karel Hannauer characterized monumentality as something that "aims at the regular grouping of aesthetically perfect bodies," which means "aesthetic specificity, material durability, formal self-evidence, and independence of short-lived artistic directions."[55] The theorist and art historian Oldřich Stefan equated monumentality with neoclassicism: according to him both concepts meant "striving for rationally constructed but also sensitively balanced form."[56]

The key figure of Prague neoclassicism of the thirties was probably the former member of *Devětsil* Jaroslav Fragner, who in 1937 became the president of *Mánes*. Fragner's work from about 1930 can be seen as an apotheosis of the geometric order. Fragner—possibly influenced by reading Le Corbusier's *Urbanisme*, 1925—saw in geometry something specifically human, and he expressed his belief in the humanity of geometry in such magnificent buildings as the ESSO power plant in the Central Bohemian town of Kolín, 1929–1932.[57] After 1930, the emphasis in Fragner's sense for geometry shifted to latent neoclassical characteristics. In 1934–1935, Fragner's Merkur Building was erected on Revoluční Street. Its boxlike shape, suspended frontal *avant-corps*, wide oblong windows, and glazed ground floor still pointed to Fragner's association with functionalism. But the building's heavy stone cladding, with a hint of Corbusier-like pseudo-Renaissance pointing, prevented it from "floating in the air," as the functionalist aesthetic would have it. The neoclassicist character of the Merkur Building was reinforced by its coldly precise proportions and the projecting aedicule of the entrance with its slender marble columns.

Despite these clearly neoclassicist elements, Fragner expressed his vision of the new style primarily by means that were still functionalist. But there were other architects, mainly members of *Mánes*, whose work after 1930 tended toward a similar marriage between functionalist formal vocabulary and neoclassicist sensibility, evident mainly in the composition of their buildings and in their full, robust volumes. They were, for example, František M. Černý, one of the few Prague architects who in the thirties used Le Corbusier's system of *tracés régulateurs*, or Kamil Roškot, whose duplex porters' lodge at the Ruzyně Airport, 1934–1935, was a concrete example of Stefan's definition of classicism. In the circle around the magazine *Architekt SIA*, it was Milan Babuška, the author of the

419

Jaroslav Fragner. Building of the Merkur Insurance Company, detail of the entrance. Staré Město, Revoluční 25. 1934–1935.

Jaroslav Fragner. Building of the Merkur Insurance Company. Staré Město, Revoluční 25. 1934–1935.

Architecture and the Great Depression

Jaroslav Fragner. Apartment building, foyer. Bubeneč,
Terronská 62. 1936.

Kamil Roškot. Porters' lodge duplex at the so-called Old
Airport. Ruzyně, K letišti 533. 1934–1935.

Architecture and the Great Depression

*František M. Černý. Mölzer's family house. Dejvice, Na
Kodymce 14. 1938.*

425

Milan Babuška. Museum of Agriculture and Technology.
Holešovice, Kostelní 42, 44. 1935–1940.

Architecture and the Great Depression

*Milan Babuška. Exhibition hall in the Museum of Agriculture
and Technology. Holešovice, Kostelní 42, 44. 1935–1940.*

Agricultural and Technical Museum on Kostelní Street, 1935–1941, who followed a similar direction.

However, some exponents of this neoclassical revival had the courage to express their stylistic inclination in more explicit ways. An example is the work of Josef Gočár who preceded Fragner as chairman of *Mánes*. Gočár's most significant work of the interwar era was meant to be his prize-winning State Gallery project, which he was commissioned to design in 1924, and which in the end remained unrealized. At first, the gallery was supposed to be situated in the gardens on the Kampa island in Malá Strana, where Gočár located his most functionalist version of this project in 1929. Subsequently, the government decided to situate the gallery in Letná, in the vicinity of the planned governmental buildings. Gočár based his first designs for this site—all of them already consistently symmetrical—on the classicist horseshoe-shaped *court d'honneur*; but the details and overall articulation of the walls still conformed with the usual purist-functionalist look of the international style. In the subsequent versions of the project from 1938 to 1940, the *court d'honneur* was replaced by a portico entrance hall inserted into the white volume of the frontal section. The so-called third version from this stage of Gočár's project, which had completely dispensed with functionalist vocabulary, featured a long figurative frieze that adorned the inner wall of the entrance hall. Stylistically similar was the unrealized competition project for the City Gallery in Klárov by Gočár's colleague from *Mánes*, Adolf Benš.

These neoclassicist projects of the late thirties demonstrate the new attitude of Prague's architects of the "emotionalist" persuasion toward collaboration with painters, and sculptors. The traditional unity of architecture, painting, and sculpture, challenged already before World War I by some modernist and cubist architects, had been entirely rejected by the purist-functionalist avant-garde of the twenties. In 1924, Karel Teige described the basic break between architecture on the one hand and painting and sculpture on the other as the inevitable characteristic of the new style and even expressed the iconoclastic view that "a picture on the wall would fly in the face of architectural purity of the modern interior."[58] The quest for a new direction by means of which post-1930 functionalist

427

Josef Gočár. The third project for the State Gallery on Letná
Plain. 1939–1940.

Adolf Benš. Competition project for the City Gallery in
Klárov. 1937.

Vít Obrtel. Competition project for the second building of
the National Museum at the exhibition grounds in Bubeneč.
1939.

architecture sought to address its users and, in the words of Vít Obrtel, offer them a new "comfort of facts and impressions" brought it into conflict with the avant-garde doctrine. Architects of emotional functionalism, and, above all, those who tried to experiment with neoclassicist vocabulary, returned to the practice of decorating their buildings with paintings and sculpture.

The natural focus of the new program of synthesis, inspired to some extent by the developments in contemporary French art, became yet again the association *Mánes*, which since the end of the nineteenth century brought together artists working in all disciplines, presenting an ideal forum for professional contact. In the late thirties, *Mánes*-based theoreticians and art critics began dis-

Václav Hilský, Rudolf Jasenský, Karel Koželka. Competition project for the completion of the Old Town City Hall. 1938.

430

CHAPTER 4

cussing the problem of monumentality, mainly because this was the theme central to the work of many outstanding Czech painters and sculptors. Josef Chochol, for instance, spoke in 1939 about the desire of modern architecture to become again the "kindly carrier" of paintings and sculpture.[59] Finally, in 1941, *Mánes*'s *Volné směry* tried to explain this turnabout: "The space in which man lives, or at least spends some time, is also the refuge of the spirit and therefore paintings and sculptures should and ought to have their place in it."[60]

The developments in Prague architecture of the period between 1918 and 1929 were dominated by the battle of purist-functionalist architecture against older and more conservative styles. And it was only because architects of the older generation did not immediately retreat that Prague architecture of the twenties boasts such a great variety of styles and artistic views. After 1929, the victory of functionalism became certain, although Prague maintained its stylistic diversity even during this period, because — as we can clearly see in retrospect — there were new battles to be fought, mainly around the issue of the social role of modern architecture and of the appropriate design methods.

This ideological turmoil crystallized into four discernible positions. One was that of scientific functionalism of the strict variety promoted after 1929 by Karel Teige, Jan Gillar, and the PAS group. In opposition to it stood Obrtel's and Grégr's version of organic architecture. The third was Ladislav Žák's technological romanticism of buildings and the naturalist romanticism of his theories; and finally, there was Fragner's and Gočár's neoclassicism. These positions varied in obvious ways, but they all shared a certain lack of realism, a touch of the utopian, or at least of escapism. The aim of scientific functionalism was, according to Teige, to prepare for the imminent victory of socialist revolution in Czechoslovakia; Obrtel's organic architecture was also an architecture of the "coming order". While Ladislav Žák declared his family houses to be "islands of the future," Vladimír Grégr's luxury villas offered nostalgic returns and escapes into the world of the early 1900s' modern style, or the world of rural cottages, Californian haciendas, and weekend cabins in the picturesque valleys of Bohemian rivers. The interpretation of Fragner's and Gočár's neoclassicism would probably not be that simple

431

and clear-cut, but even here there is a return to the past, to certainties tested by a thousand-year tradition.

These four positions should be probably seen as four different answers to the questions posed by the climate of economic and political crisis of the thirties.

<table>
<tr><td>

THE END OF THE AVANT-GARDE

</td><td>

The search for radical solutions to these questions was delayed for several years by Hitler's annexation of Czechoslovakia between 1939 and 1945. After World War II, Czechoslovakia became part of the Soviet bloc and started adopting Soviet political and cultural standards from 1948. The question why this happened almost without resistance is partly answered in this book. The majority of left-wing politicians, intellectuals, artists, and, of course, architects, saw the Soviet Union as the "country where tomorrow means yesterday"—a slogan coined for Stalin's empire by the Czech journalist Julius Fučík—as a "laboratory of history," which, according to Jiří Kroha, tested the utopia of a better future dreamt up by the Western European Left.[61] Some of them, however, soon became aware that the Soviet reality was far removed from the utopian visions of the avant-garde: Vít Obrtel ridiculed Hannes Meyer's propagandist lectures about the USSR already in 1931,[62] and in 1933 Karel Teige described the advance of Stalinist classicism in architecture as a "symptom of some worse and so far hidden evil,"[63] Jaromír Krejcar, who experienced the manifestations of this evil first hand in Moscow in 1934–1935, subsequently condemned the Soviet political trials.[64] Their warnings were not taken seriously, and after 1945 their voices were drowned in the universal euphoria that followed the Soviet liberation of Czechoslovakia.

In 1948, Prague's left-wing architects finally saw the long-awaited arrival of socialism and could begin realizing their vision of perfectly functional architecture. Yet, it soon became clear that what the new society, for which they had been enthusiastically designing their "proto-images," expected of them was not functionalism, scientific or emotional, but Stalinist classicism to which they had to conform between 1949 and 1956. Only a few—including Jar-

</td></tr>
</table>

oslav Fragner who was the most resourceful in this respect—managed to apply their experience of classicizing functionalism of the thirties to the imported Soviet style. Fortunately, Prague at that time suffered from a severe lack of investment, and the new style therefore did not cause too much damage to its appearance.

Following Khrushchev's notorious "critique of superfluous elements in architecture," 1954–1955, Czechoslovak architecture became totally subjected to the method of assembling residential buildings from standardized prefabricated panels. In the course of the following thirty-five years, Prague was surrounded by a ring of prefabricated "new cities" providing housing for hundreds of thousands of inhabitants who were deprived of their dignity and identity by living in this monotonous, uncivilized wasteland. In these gigantic housing complexes, the old dreams of scientific functionalism about maximum economy of construction and standardization were turned into caricatures. Construction using prefabricated elements was not even economical because its ultimate purpose became the utilization of the excessive production of building materials, nor was it functional, in the sense of Sullivan's motto "form follows function," as the form had been determined a priori by the dimensions of the panels, as well as by the directives issued by planners in centralized government offices. Various attempts made by architects trying to humanize this bureaucratic conception of housing at least by the use of new and unusual forms, inspired most often by Western architectural developments, came into conflict with the deep-rooted functionalist slogans and stereotypes that condemned all unusual forms as uneconomical, superfluous, dysfunctional.

Fortunately, this did not lead to an overall rejection of functionalism on the part of young architects, and in the seventies some of them began to look back to its legacy. Rather than in the survival of functionalist ideological programs, they were interested in a revival of functionalist forms, which among other things evoked the "golden age" of Masaryk's first republic. Thus the functionalist utopia was replaced by a neofunctionalist nostalgia that retained little of its old, left-wing, avant-garde substance. I believe that this is unfortunate, although many of my fellow citizens, colleagues, and architects do not share this view. **433**

PREFACE

1. O. Schürer, *Prag*, Prague, 1930; Z. Wirth, *Praha v obraze pěti století* (Prague in the Pictures of Five Centuries), Prague, 1932; J. Janáček, ed., *Dějiny Prahy* (The History of Prague), Prague, 1964; V. Mencl, *Praha* (Prague), Prague, 1969; C. Norberg-Schulz, *Genius loci*, London, 1980; J. Kohout, J. Vančura, *Praha 19. a 20. století: Technické proměny* (Prague of the 19th and 20th Century: The Technological Changes), Prague, 1986; J. Hrůza, *Město Praha* (The City of Prague), Prague, 1989.

CHAPTER 1

1. V. Lorenc, *Nové Město Pražské* (Prague's New Town), Prague, 1973.

2. K., "Soutěž na plány na regulaci Malé Strany" (The Competition for Projects for the Redevelopment of Malá Strana), *Zprávy Spolku architektův a inženýrův v Království českém*, 34, 1900, pp. 94–96.

3. For easier orientation, only today's names of streets and squares are used in this book.

4. K., "Návrh regulace náměstí Havlíčkova" (The Project for the Redevelopment of Havlíčkovo Square), *Architektonický obzor*, 4 (39), 1905, pp. 1–2.

5. A. Čenský, "Návrh na úpravu letenské pláně dle prof. J. Kouly" (Prof. J. Koula's Project for the Development of the Letná Plain), *Architektonický obzor*, 6 (41), 1907, pp. 30, 37, 41.

6. J. Fanta, "Stavby pražské a snahy umělecké" (Prague's Buildings and Artistic Efforts), *Volné směry*, 3, 1899, pp. 239–243.

7. See K. Frampton, *Modern Architecture: A Critical History*, London, 1985, pp. 64–73.

8. Fanta's most significant work in the modern style is the *Mohyla míru* (Peace Monument), memorial of the Battle of Austerlitz, situated near Brno, 1907–1911.

9. A. Engel, "Veřejné budovy pražské" (Prague's Public Buildings), *Styl*, 4, 1910–1911, pp. 30–37.

10. See article "Jakých zásad nutno šetřiti při zamýšlené úpravě Prahy, zvláště Starého města" (What Principles Should Be Heeded in the Intended Rebuilding of Prague, and in Particular of the Old Town), *Zprávy Spolku architektův a inženýrův v Království českém*, 29, 1895, pp. 13–21.

11. J. Koula, "Všeobecná záložna v Praze" (The General Credit Bank in Prague), *Zprávy Spolku architektův a inženýrův v Království českém*, 34, 1900, pp. 74–75.

12. A. Bráf, "O některých nezdravých úkazech kolem nás" (On Some Unhealthy Phe-

nomena around Us), *Architektonický obzor*, 1 (36), 1902, pp. 47–52.

13. Ibid.

14. O. A. Graf, *Die vergessene Wagnerschule*, Vienna, 1969.

15. O. Schürer, "Kotěrova výstava v Obecním domě" (Kotěra's Exhibition in the Municipal House), *Tribuna*, 8, 22 Jan. 1926.

16. "Z dopisů Jana Kotěry svému příteli R. G. ve Vídni" (From Jan Kotěra's Letters to His Friend R. G. in Vienna), *Stavitel*, 5, 1924, pp. 61–65; Richard Gombrich was the uncle of the well-known British art historian Sir Ernst Gombrich. Between 1913 and 1915, Jan Kotěra designed a large villa at Grinzinger Allee 50 in Vienna for R. Gombrich and his father-in-law, Paul Lemberger.

17. J. Kotěra, "O novém umění" (On New Art), *Volné směry*, 4, 1900, pp. 189–195.

18. J. Kotěra, *Dělnické kolonie* (Workers' Housing Colonies), Prague, 1921, p. 1.

19. F. X. Harlas, *"Moderna v pražských ulicích"* (The Modern Style in the Streets of Prague), *Architektonický obzor*, 3 (38), 1904, pp. 33–37.

20. Bráf, pp. 51–52.

21. P. Wittlich, *Česká secese* (Czech Secession), Prague, 1982, p. 315.

22. K. B. Mádl, "Příchozí umění" (The Forthcoming Art), *Volné směry*, 3, 1899, pp. 117–142.

23. K. V. Mašek, "Studium ornamentiky" (The Study of Ornamental Decoration), *Dílo*, 1, 1902, pp. 121–127.

24. K., "Pustevně na Radhošti" (The Hermitages of Radhošt), *Zprávy Spolku architektův a inženýrův v Království českém*, 34, 1900, pp. 64–65.

25. J. Kotěra, "Luhačovice," *Volné směry*, 8, 1904, pp. 59–60.

26. P. Wittlich, *České sochařství ve XX. století* (Czech Sculpture in the 20th Century), Prague, 1978, pp. 63–64.

27. Engel, p. 34.

28. P. Janák, "Otto Wagner," *Styl*, 1, 1908–1909, pp. 41–48.

29. A. Engel, "Dům nájemný" (The Tenement Building), *Styl*, 3, 1911, pp. 189–196.

30. O. Novotný, "Architektura symbolická, pomník a Žižkův pomník" (Symbolic Architecture, the Memorial and Žižka's Memorial), *Volné směry*, 18, 1915, pp. 85–87.

31. *Styl*, 4, 1911–1912, p. 42.

32. *Socialistické listy*, 2, 19 Jan. 1919.

33. R. Švácha, "Poznámky ke Kotěrovu muzeu" (Notes on Kotěra's Museum), *Umění*, 34, 1986, pp. 171–179.

34. J. Kotěra, "Interiér C.K. Uměleckoprůmyslové školy v Praze pro světovou výstavu v St. Louis 1904" (The Interior of the School of Applied Arts in Prague for St. Louis World Exposition 1904), *Volné směry*, 8, 1904, pp. 119–120.

35. O. Novotný, "Shody a rozpory" (Harmonies and Dissonances), *Volné směry*, 18, 1915, pp. 27–40.

36. *Styl*, 2, 1909–1910, p. 39.

37. V. Šlapeta, "Jože Plečnik et Prague," in *Jože Plečnik Architecte 1872–1957*, exhibition catalog, ed. F. Buckhardt, C. Eveno, B. Podrecca, Paris, 1986, pp. 83–96.

38. O. Novotný, J. Benda, Zprávy 1, No. 4, *Volné směry*, 38, 1915, after p. 260.

39. J. Chochol, "Velkoměsto" (Metropolis), *Umělecký měsíčník*, 1, 1911–1912, p. 54.

40. Zs, "Die Grosstadt," *Technický přehled samosprávný*, 1, 1912, pp. 39–42.

41. F. "Sny o Letné" (Dreams about Letná), *Architektonický obzor*, 14, 1915, pp. 21–22.

42. R. Stockar z Bernkopfů, "Město budoucnosti" (The City of the Future), *Styl*, 4, 1912, pp. 43–67.

43. G., "Moderní dům v Praze" (The Modern House in Prague), *Volné směry*, 12, 1908, p. 159.

44. Janák, p. 46.

45. Reference to functionalism in the context of modern architecture before World War I was made, for instance, by the German historian of architecture Karin Wilhelm in the catalog *Wem gehört die Welt. Kunst und Gesellschaft der Weimarer Republik*, Berlin, 1977; or by the British theoretician of architecture Charles Jencks in his book *Le Corbusier and the Tragic View of Architecture*, London, 1973.

46. K. Passuth, "Sborník Život II" (The Anthology Life II), *Umění*, 35, 1987, pp. 9–15.

CHAPTER 2

1. P. Janák, "Od moderní architektury — k architektuře" (From Modern Architecture — to Architecture), *Styl* 2, 1909–1910, pp. 105–109.

2. See Z. Lukeš, "První kubistický projekt" (The First Cubist project), *Umění a řemesla*, 3, 1988, pp. 11–12.

3. See *Jože Plečnik Architecte 1872–1957*, project for the Viennese factory Stollwerk, 1910, p. 48, and crypt of the Viennese Church of the Sacred Spirit, 1910–1913, p. 119.

4. Today, Kramář's collection is exhibited in the National Gallery of Prague, French Modern Art section, Šternberk palace. Picasso's paintings from this collection are re-

produced in E. Petrová, *Picasso v Československu* (Picasso in Czechoslovakia), Prague, 1981. As for Kramář's personality, see the collection of his texts, V. Kramář, *O obrazech a galeriích* (On Paintings and Galleries), Prague, 1983.

5. V. Hofman, "Poznámky k nábytku" (Notes on Furniture), *Umělecký měsíčník*, 1, 1911–1912, p. 58.

6. P. Janák, "Hranol a pyramida" (The Prism and the Pyramid), *Umělecký měsíčník*, 1, 1911–1912, pp. 162–170.

7. Ibid.

8. P. Janák, "O nábytku a jiném" (On Furniture and Other Matters), *Umělecký měsíčník*, 2, 1912–1913, pp. 21–29.

9. P. Janák, "Obnova průčelí" (Renewal of the Facade), *Umělecký měsíčník*, 2, 1912–1913, pp. 85–93.

10. V. Hofman, "Duch moderní tvorby v architektuře" (The Modern Spirit in Architecture), *Umělecký měsíčník*, 1, 1911–1912, pp. 127–135.

11. V. Hofman, "Výstava skupiny výtvarných umělců" (The Exhibition of the Group of Visual Artists), *Přehled*, 12, 1913–1914, pp. 565–568.

12. J. Mareš, "Situace lázní v Bohdanči" (The Situation of the Spa in Bohdaneč), *Osvěta lidu*, 17, 3 Feb. 1912.

13. See T. Petrasová, "Paralely českého kubismu a gotiky" (Parallels between Czech Cubism and Gothic), *Umění*, 37, 1988, pp. 366–369.

14. Janák, "Obnova průčelí."

15. Janák, "Hranol a pyramida."

16. Hofman, "Duch moderní tvorby v architektuře."

17. J. Chochol, "K funkci architektonického článku" (On the Function of the Architectural Component), *Styl*, 5, 1913, pp. 93–94.

18. V. Wallerstein, "Anfänge einer neuen Architektur und Raumkunst in Prag," *Kunstgewerbeblatt*, 24, Neue Folge, 1912–1913, pp. 221–229. See also W. Pehnt, *Die Architektur des Expressionismus*, Stuttgart, 1973, p. 62.

19. Janák, "O nábytku a jiném."

20. V. Hofman, "K podstatě architektury" (On the Essence of Architecture), *Volné směry*, 17, 1913, pp. 11–14. In this essay Hofman criticizes the well-known cubist facade designed by Raymond Duchamp-Villon, 1912, which is discussed in relation to Czech cubist architecture by François Burkhardt in F. Burkhardt, M. Lamarová, *Cubismo cecoslovacco*, Milan, 1982, p. 53.

21. V. Hofman, "Individualizující forma v architektuře" (The Individualizing Form in Architecture), *Volné směry*, 18, 1915, pp. 241–251.

22. Janák, "Obnova průčelí."

23. V. Kramář, "Španělsko a kubismus" (Spain and Cubism), in Kramář, *O obrazech a galeriích*, pp. 152–172.

24. Janák, "O nábytku a jiném."

25. Chochol, "K funkci architektonického článku."

26. The most comprehensive critique of cubist architecture can be found in the essay by R. V., "Jak vypadají dobré případy" (What Good Examples Look Like), *Dílo*, 12, 1914, pp. 17–20.

27. On Králíček's authorship of the lamppost see Z. Lukeš and J. Svoboda, "Architekt E. Králíček — zapomenutý zjev české secese a kubismu" (Architect E. Králíček — the Forgotten Figure of Czech Secession and Cubism), *Umění*, 31, 1984, pp. 441–449.

28. Cf. V. V. Štech, *Tschechische Bestrebungen um ein modernes Interieur*, Prague, 1915.

29. V. V. Štech, "O uměleckém průmyslu" (On the Decorative Art Industry), *Venkov*, 11, 23 July 1916.

30. P. Janák, "Barvu průčelím!" (Color to the Facades!"), *Venkov*, 11, 3 Dec. 1916.

31. V. Hofman, "Nový princip v architektuře" (The New Principle in Architecture), *Styl*, 5, 1913, pp. 13–24.

32. Cf. R. Švácha, "Hofmanův Vyšehrad" (Hofman's Vyšehrad), *Výtvarná kultura*, 8, No. 6, 1984, pp. 30–33.

33. Hofman, "Individualizující forma v architektuře."

34. V. Hofman, "O dalším vývoji naší moderní architektury" (On Future Development of Our Architecture), *Volné směry*, 19, 1918, pp. 193–206.

35. Chochol, "K funkci architektonického článku." See also J. Chochol, "Z posledních desítiletí české architektury" (From the Last Decades of Czech Architecture), *Přehled*, 12, 1913–1914, pp. 237–239.

36. Cf. R. Švácha, "Josef Chochol 1880–1980," *Umění*, 28, 1980, pp. 545–552.

CHAPTER 3

1. Cf. A. Potůčková, "Dvacátá léta: Výtvarná umění a společnost" (The 1920s: Visual Arts and Society), *Umění a řemesla*, No. 3, 1988, pp. 17–24.

2. "Státní regulační komise pro hlavní město Prahu a okolí" (The Planning Commission

for Prague and Environs), *Časopis československých inženýrů a architektů Architektonický obzor*, 29, 1920, p. 10.

3. J. Krejcar, "Mrakodrapy v Praze" (Skyscrapers in Prague), *Československé noviny*, 2, 11 Feb. 1923.

4. J. Krejcar, "Cesta k moderní architektuře" (The Path to Modern Architecture), *Disk*, 2, 1925, pp. 26–30.

5. A. Engel, "Poznámky k výsledku soutěže na dostavbu škol technických v Praze" (Notes on the Outcome of the Competition for the Completion of Technical School Buildings in Prague), *Architektura ČSR*, 17, 1958, p. 233.

6. "O státní regulační komisi" (On the State Planning Commission), *Stavba*, 1, 1922, p. 82.

7. B. Hypšman (Hübschmann), "Regulace okolí Emaus" (Redevelopment of the Surroundings of Emmaus), *Styl*, 3 (8), 1922–1923, pp. 9–15.

8. A. Kubíček, *Bohumil Hypšman*, Prague, 1961, p. 9.

9. J. E. Koula, "Pražská revue II" (Prague Review II), *Stavba*, 5, 1926–1927, p. 93.

10. P. Janák, "K situaci ve stavebnictví" (On the State of the Building Industry), in *Nové snahy o rodinný dům* (New Efforts in the Development of the Family House), Prague, 1920, p. 1.

11. B. Sláma, "Ideální velká Praha" (The Ideal Greater Prague) *Časopis československých inženýrův a architektův Architektonický obzor*, 18, 1919, p. 36.

12. T., "Vlad. Zákrejs, Praha budoucí" (V. Zákrejs's Prague of the Future), *Stavba*, 1, 1922, p. 138.

13. "Klub za novou Prahu" (The Club in Support of New Prague), *Stavba*, 3, 1924–1925, p. 43.

14. Krejcar, "Cesta k moderní architektuře" (The Path to Modern Architecture).

15. Excerpts from the following articles: "K otázkám regulace Prahy" (On the Question of Redevelopment of Prague," editorial, *Stavba*, 4, 1925–1926, p. 97; J. K. Říha, "Stará Praha v regulačním plánu" (Old Prague in the Redevelopment Project), *Stavitel*, 10, 1929, pp. 144–149; Krejcar, "Cesta k moderní architektuře."

16. J. K. Říha, "Stará Praha v regulačním plánu."

17. 'Kotázkám regulace Prahy."

18. Krejcar, "Cesta k moderní architektuře."

19. Published in Krejcar's and Teige's anthology *Život*, 2, 1922.

20. Cf. R. Švácha, "Pavel Janák a český funkcionalismus" (Pavel Janák and Czech Functionalism), *Umění*, 30, 1982, pp. 516–524.

21. J. Krejcar, "Průvodní zpráva hesla Velká avenue" (Report Accompanying the Project of the Great Avenue), *Stavitel*, 10, 1929, pp. 21–23.

22. A. Brzotický, "K otázce zastavění pláně letenské budovami veřejnými" (On the Letná Plain Public Buildings Project), *Architekt SIA*, 28, 1929, pp. 82–85.

23. L. Žák, "K letenské soutěži" (On the Letná Development Competition), *Volné směry*, 27, 1929–1930, pp. 33–34.

24. Two of Kotěra's projets for redesigning the presidential residence at the Prague Castle from 1921 were published in the journal *Architektura ČSR*, 7, 1948, p. 12.

25. P. Janák, "Josef Plečnik v Praze" (Josef Plečnik in Prague), *Volné směry*, 26, 1928–1929, pp. 97–108.

26. Masaryk's letter to Plečnik dated Sept. 4, 1924 was kept in the now-defunct Museum of Klement Gottwald in Prague, P I II 148. It was kindly brought to my attention by Damjan Prelovšek.

27. A. Engel, "Problém monumentality v architektuře" (The Problem of Monumentality in Architecture), *Architekt SIA*, 42, 1944, p. 170.

28. A. Matějček-Z. Wirth, *Česká architektura 1800–1920* (Czech Architekture 1800–1920), Prague, 1922, p. 86.

29. P Janák, "Ve třetině cesty" (At One Third of the Journey), *Volné směry*, 19, 1918, pp. 218–226.

30. K. Teige, *MSA 2. Moderní architektura v Československu* (Modern Architecture in Czechoslovakia), Prague, 1930, p. 140.

31. J. Kroha, "Poznámky o monumentalitě a řadě tvarové" (Notes on Monumentality and Form Sequence), *Stavba* I, 1922, p. 77–81.

32. *Styl*, 1 (6), 1920–1921, p. 55.

33. J. Kroha, "O prostoru architektonickém a jeho mezích" (On Architectural Space and Its Delimitations), *Veraikon*, 6, 1920, p. 33.

34. Several of Fragner's and Linhart's cubist projects were included by P. Haiko and M. Reissberg in the catalog *Zauber der Medusa*, ed. W. Hoffmann, Vienna, 1987.

35. P. Janák, "Architektura — hmota či duch?" (Architecture — Matter or Spirit), *Styl*, 5 (10), 1924–1925, pp. 170–174.

36. Teige, *MSA 2*, p. 103.

37. K. Honzík, *Ze života avantgardy* (From the Life of the Avant-garde), Prague, 1963, p. 27.

38. J. Krejcar, "LXIII. výstava SVU Mánes" (63d Exhibition of SVU Mánes), *Československé noviny*, 2, 16 Jan. 1923.

39. J. E. Koula, "Pražská revue" (The Prague Review), *Stavba*, 5, 1926–1927, p. 79.

40. Cf. R. Švácha, "Architekti Devětsilu" (Devětsil's Architects), in *Devětsil: Česká výtvarná avantgarda dvacátých let* (Devětsil: Czech Art Avant-garde of the 1920s), catalog, ed. F. Šmejkal, Prague, 1986.

41. K. Teige, "Kubismus, orfismus, purismus a neokubismus v dnešní Paříži" (Cubism, Orphism, Purism and Neocubism in Today's Paris), *Veraikon*, 8, No. 192, pp. 98–112.

42. Cf. C. Leclanche-Boulé, "Šíření purismu ve střední a východní Evropě" (The Spreading of Purism in Central and Eastern Europe), *Umění*, 35, 1987, pp. 16–29.

43. Student records of the Prague Academy of Fine Arts, J. Kotěra's School of Architecture, 1910–1923.

44. Honzík, *Ze života avantgardy*, p. 31.

45. K. Teige, "Nové umění proletářské" (The New Proletarian Art), in *Revoluční sborník Devětsil*, Prague, 1922, pp. 5–18.

46. V. Obrtel, "Renesance" (Renaissance), *Tam-tam*, No. 6, 1926, pp. 3–4.

47. Víšek's model was Perret's theater set painting studio in Paris from 1922; cf. collection *Fronta. Mezinárodní sborník soudobé aktivity* (The Front: International Anthology of Contemporary Activities), Brno, 1927, pictures 103 and 124.

48. The meaning of this adjective is discussed by S. Waetzold in the catalog *Wem gehört die Welt*.

49. K. Teige, "Umění dnes a zítra" (Art Today and Tomorrow), in *Revoluční sborník Devětsil*, pp. 187–202.

50. J. Chochol, "Oč usiluji" (What I Strive For), *Musaion*, 2, 1921, p. 47.

51. J. E. Koula, *Obytný dům dneška* (The Residential Building of Today), Prague, 1931, p. 9.

52. "Zásady nové architektury" (The Principles of New Architecture), editorial, *Stavba*, 3, 1924–1925, pp. 153–158.

53. Teige, "Umění dnes a zítra."

54. J. Jíra, "U.S. Devětsil," *Veraikon*, 10, 1924, pp. 25–28.

55. To have one's head above the roof (rather than roof above one's head) paraphrases the Czech saying of having one's head in the clouds — that is, being dreamy, impractical. Obrtel's meaning is that it is more beautiful to be artistic and impractical than to be concerned with the practicalities of daily life such as shelter and so forth. *Trans.*

56. Teige, "Umění dnes a zítra."

57. K. Honzík, "Estetika v žaláři" (Aesthetics in Servitude), *Stavba*, 5, 1926–1927, pp. 166–172.

58. Ibid.

59. J. Krejcar, "Architektura průmyslových budov" (Architecture of Industrial Buildings), *Stavitel*, 4, 1922–1923, pp. 65–71.

60. J. Krejcar, "Vila dra. V. Vančury na Zbraslavi" (Vančura's villa in Zbraslav), *Stavba*, 2, 1923–1924, pp. 46–48.

61. L. Žák, "Stavební výstava — osada Baba" (The Architectural Exhibition of the Baba Estate), *Žijeme II*, 1932–1933, pp. 155–156.

62. This first drawing, which had been preserved in the archive of the architect Bohumil Steigenhöfer, Krejcar's collaborator from 1925 to 1927, was exhibited in the traveling exhibition of *Devětsil* in Budapest, Lodz, and Zagreb in 1989.

63. K. Teige, *Práce Jaromíra Krejcara* (The Work of Jaromír Krejcar), Prague, 1933, p. 36.

64. Cf. M. Buber-Neumann, *Kafkas Freundin Milena*, Munich, 1963.

65. G. Fučíková, *Život s Juliem Fučíkem* (Life with Julius Fučík), Prague, 1971, p. 283.

66. K. Teige, "K teorii konstruktivismu" (On the Theory of Constructivism), in Teige, *MSA 2*, p. 243.

67. K. Teige, "Konstruktivismus a likvidace 'umění'" (Constructivism and the Liquidation of 'Art'), *Disk*, 2, 1925, pp. 4–8.

68. *kt*, "Le Corbusier: Une Maison — un Palais," *ReD*, 2, 1928–1929, pp. 169.

69. G. Baird, "A Critical Introduction to Karel Teige's Mundaneum and Le Corbusier's *In Defence of Architecture*," *Oppositions* 4, Oct. 1974, pp. 80–81; Frampton, *Modern Architecture*, p. 160; J.-L. Cohen, "Teige" in *Le Corbusier. Un encyclopédie*, ed. J. Lucan, Paris, 1987, pp. 401–402.

70. K. Teige, "Mundaneum," *Stavba*, 7, 1928–1929, pp. 145–155.

71. H. Sedlmayr, *Verlust der Mitte*, Salzburg, 1948, p. 60; See also S. von Moos, *Le Corbusier — Elements of a Synthesis*, Cambridge, Mass., 1982, p. 51.

72. J. E. Koula, "Nová architektura funkcí nového života" (New Architecture of the Functions of New Life), *Stavba*, 5, 1926–1927, pp. 163–164.

73. "Zásady nové architektury."

74. V. Obrtel, "O architektuře a prostoru" (On Architecture and Space), *Kvart*, 1, 1930, pp. 23–26.

75. Teige, *MSA 2*, p. 127.

76. K. Teige, "Le Corbusier v Praze" (Le Corbusier in Prague), *Rozpravy Aventina*, 4, 1928–1929, pp. 31–32.

77. Archive of the planning department of the District National Council for Prague 1, Staré Město, reg. no. 355.

78. J. Krejcar, "Architektura průmyslových budov."

79. R. Venturi, *Complexity and Contradiction in Architecture*, New York, 1966, p. 20.

80. Z. Lukeš, "Nad dopisy Bedřicha Feuersteina Josefu Havlíčkovi" (Over the Letters of B. Feuerstein to J. Havlíček), *Umění*, 35, 1987, pp. 104–128.

81. Obrtel, "O architektuře a prostoru"; V. Obrtel, "Bloudění architektury" (The Wanderings of Architecture), *Kvart*, 2, autumn 1933, pp. 24–28.

82. V. Obrtel, "Úvod k neokonstruktivismu" (Introduction to Neoconstructivism), *Plán*, 1, 1929–1930, pp. 25–28.

83. Honzík, "Estetika v žaláři."

84. Obrtel, "Harmonie," in *Fronta*, pp. 137–139.

85. An account of Linhart's trip to Paris was given to me by the architect Jan Rosůlek in 1982.

86. Honzík, *Ze života avantgardy*, p. 91.

87. F. Šmejkal, "Český konstruktivismus" (Czech Constructivism), *Umění*, 30, 1982, pp. 214–243.

88. See R. Švácha, "Dva domy" (Two Houses), *Domov*, 28, 1988, no. 1, pp. 7–11.

89. Koula, *Obytný dům dneška*, p. 17.

90. V. Vančura, *Pole orná a válečná* (Ploughfields and Battlefields), Prague, 1925, p. 7.

91. Cf. R. Švácha, "Jiří Kroha," *Domov* 26, 3, 1986, pp. 3–6.

92. J. Krejcar, "Architektura — umění nebo věda?" (Architecture — Art or Science?), *Rozpravy Aventina*, 3, 1927–1928, p. 10.

CHAPTER 4

1. S, "Konference BAPSU pořádaná v Praze 7, 8. a 18. června 1934" (BAPS Conference Held in Prague 7, on 8 and 18 June 1934), *Architekt SIA*, 33, 1934, p. 103.

2. Cf. *Český funkcionalismus 1920–1940* (Czech Funtionalism 1920–1940), catalog, ed. A. Vondrová, Prague-Brno, 1978, heading "Zákony o stavebním ruchu" (Regulations on Construction Activities).

3. "Soutěž pražské obce na domy s nejmenšími byty" (The Prague Municipality Competition for Minimum Dwelling Housing), *Stavba*, 9, 1930–1931, pp. 20–27.

4. "Návrh kolektivizovaného obytného okrsku v Praze" (Proposal for a Communal Residential Suburb in Prague), *Stavba*, 9, 1930–1931, pp. 117–119.

5. K. Teige, "Minimální byt a kolektivní dům" (The Minimum Dwelling and the Communal House), *Stavba*, 9, 1930–1931, pp. 28–29, 47–50, 65–68.

6. J. Krejcar, in "Anketa Tvorby o bytové otázce" (Tvorba's Poll on the Housing Question), *Tvorba*, 5, 1930, p. 480.

7. K. Teige, "K soutěži na nájemné domy s malými byty pro dělnický spolek Včela v Praze" (On the Small-flat Competition of the Workers' Cooperative *Včela* in Prague), *Stavitel*, 12, 1931, p. 76.

8. J. Havlíček-K. Honzík, "Průvodní zpráva soutěžného návrhu nájemných domů pro dělnický spolek *Včela* v Praze" (Notes Accompanying the Competition Project for Workers' Housing of the Cooperative *Včela* in Prague), *Stavitel*, 12, 1931, pp. 85–87.

9. "Soutěž pražské obce na domy s nejmenšími byty."

10. J. Lisková, *Nájemný dům v současné výstavbě Velké Prahy* (The Tenement Building in Contemporary Development of Greater Prague), Prague, 1935, p. 12.

11. K. Teige, "K sociologii architektury" (On the Sociology of Architecture), *ReD*, 3, 1929–1931, pp. 163–223.

12. R. Švácha, "Osada Baba" (The Baba Estate), *Umění*, 28, 1980, pp. 368–379.

13. O. Starý, "Individuální a typový rodinný dům" (Individual and Standardized Family House), *Stavba*, 11, 1930–1931, pp. 121–123.

14. Obrtel, "O architektuře a prostoru."

15. A. Mikuškovic, "Regionální plán" (The Regional Plan), *Stavba*, 9, 1930–1931, pp. 10–13.

16. Teige, Práce Jaromíra Krejcara, p. 143.

17. "Staré město pražské a ochrana památek" (Prague's Old Town and Preservation of Historical Buildings), *Architect SIA*, 35, 1936, p. 7.

18. J. Mannsbarth, "Ruzyňské letiště a petřínská komunikace" (Ruzyně Airport and the Petřín Communication), *Architektura ČSR*, 1, 1939, p. 80.

19. K. Lynch, *What Time Is This Place?*, Cambridge, Mass., 1972; Ch. Norberg-Schulz, *Genius loci*, London, 1980.

20. Z. Rossmann, "Deset let tzv. československé moderní architektury" (Ten Years of the So-Called Czechoslovak Architecture), *Stavitel*, 11, 1930, pp. 2–5.

21. Teige, *Práce Jaromíra Krejcara*, p. 11.

22. J. Chochol, "Dva domy" (Two Houses), *Věstník Inženýrské komory*, 8, 1929, pp. 341–342; J. Krejcar, "Hygiena bytu" (The Sanitary Conditions of a Dwelling," *Žijeme*, 2, 1932–1933, p. 132.

23. K. Janů, "K výstavě sovětské architektury v Praze" (On the Exhibition of Soviet Architecture in Prague), *Stavba*, 9, 1932–1933, pp. 33–35.

24. Honzík, *Ze života avantgardy*, p. 205.

25. J. Krejcar, "Soudobá architektura a společnost," in *Za socialistickou architekturu* (In Support of Socialist Architecture), Praha, 1932, pp. 15–16.

26. Obrtel, "O architektuře a prostoru."

27. Cf. R. Švácha, "Sovětský konstruktivismus a česká architektura" (Soviet Constructivism and Czech Architecture), *Umění*, 36, 1988, pp. 54–70.

28. K. Janů and J. Štursa, J. Voženílek, "Je možná vědecká syntéza v architektuře?" (Is Scientific Synthesis Possible in Architecture?), *Magazín družstevní práce*, 4, 1936–1937, p. 176–182.

29. Cf. K. Teige, J. Kroha, eds., *Avantgardní architektura* (Avant-garde Architecture), Praha, 1969, p. 40.

30. O. Starý et al., *Československá architektura od nejstarší doby po současnost* (Czech Architecture from Early Beginnings to Contemporary Time), Praha, 1965, p. 232.

31. Cf. Švácha, "Pavel Janák a český funkcionalismus."

32. Kudělka, *Brněnská architektura 1919–1928*, p. 68.

33. O. Stefan, "Architektura, teorie, život" (Architecture, Theory, Life), *Život*, 17, 1942, pp. 50–58.

34. Venturi, *Complexity and Contradiction in Architecture*, pp. 22, 25.

35. Stefan, in "Problém monumentality v architektuře." p. 166.

36. K. Honzík, "Fyzioplastika" (Physioplastics), *Stavba*, 14, 1937–1938, pp. 77–86.

37. J. Chochol, "Nová architektura" (New Architecture), *Architektura ČSR*, 1, 1939, pp. 8–9.

38. See chapter 3, note 69.

39. Černošice near Prague, Poštovní Street, no. 215; cf. Švácha, "Dva domy."

40. Statement made by architect Václav Hilský in 1989.

41. K. Koželka, "Snahy v českém obytném stavebnictví" (Endeavours in the Czech Residential Building Industry), *Architektura*, 2, 1940, pp. 193–202.

42. A. Benš, "Motolská nemocnice a urbanistická forma" (The Motol Hospital and Urbanist Form), *Volné směry*, 33, 1937, pp. 40–43.

43. The effects of motion perspective in visual arts is discussed by the Russian cubist painter L. F. Zhegin in his interesting book *Jazyk zhivopisnogo proizvedeniya*, Moscow, 1970.

44. K. Honzík, "Ke studiu psychologického účinku v architektuře" (On the Study of the Psychological Effect of Architecture), *Život*, 18, 1942, pp. 58–60.

45. J. Mannsbarth, "Z poetiky architektury" (From the Poetics of Architecture), *Život*, 19, 1943–1944, pp. 174–176.

46. Cf. K. Teige, *Stavba a báseň* (The Building and the Poem), Prague, 1927, p. 183.

47. Cf. V. Obrtel, *Vlaštovka, která má geometrické hnízdo. Projekty a texty* (The Swallow with a Geometrical Nest. Projects and Texts), ed. R. Švácha and R. Matys, Prague, 1985.

48. V. Obrtel, "K pracovní metodě" (On Working Method), *Kvart*, 1, 1930–1931, pp. 291–292.

49. V. Šlapeta, "K počátkům organické architektury" (On the Beginnings of Organic Architecture), *Umění a řemesla*, 15, No. 3, 1978, pp. 38–45.

50. Quoted from Grégr's manuscript, which was kindly lent to me by his collaborator from the 1930s, the architect J. Vančura.

51. E. Hruška, "Nový formalismus" (New Formalism), *Architektura ČSR*, 1, 1939, pp. 171–172.

52. K. Honzík, *Tvorba životního slohu* (Creating a Style of Living), 2d edition, Prague 1947, pp. 75, 361.

53. L. Žák, "Předobraz nového bydlení" (Proto-image of New Living), *Magazín Družstevní práce*, 1, 1933–1934, pp. 147–150.

54. Obrtel, "K pracovní metodě."

55. Hannauer, "Úvodní přednáška" (Introductory Lecture) in *Problém monumentality v architektuře*, p. 162.

56. Stefan, in *Problém monumentality v architektuře*.

57. R. Švácha, "Fragnerovy názory na architekturu" (Fragner's Views on Architecture), *Umění*, 35, 1987, pp. 129–138.

58. Teige, *Stavba a báseň*, p. 177.

59. Chochol, "Nová architektura."

60. m, "Přestavba budovy Zemské banky" (Rebuilding of the Zemská Bank), *Volné směry*, 37, 1941–1942, p. 55.

61. Cf. Švácha, "Sovětský konstruktivismus a česká architektura." pp. 54–70.

62. V. Obrtel, "Políři" (Building Foremen), *Rok. Kulturní leták*, Oct. 1931, p. 2.

63. Cf. Effenberger, *Realita a poezie* (Reality and Poetry), Prague, 1969, p. 204.

64. J. Krejcar, "Neohrožená žena nesmí zemřít" (The Brave Woman Must Not Die), *Přítomnost*, 15, 1938, p. 84.

The bibliography includes works in major languages and Czech works, most of which are richly illustrated and have foreign language summaries. It is is arranged according to the periods covered in the main chapters of this book, with two sections given to general works.

GENERAL WORKS I (1895–1939)

Books

Benešová, M., *Česká architektura v proměnách dvou století* (The Metamorphoses of Czech Architecture through Two Centuries), Prague, 1984.

Brožová, M., A. Hebler, and C. Scaler, *Prague: Passages et Galeries*, Paris, 1993.

Dostál, O., J. Pechar, and V. Procházka, *Moderní architektura v Československu* (Modern Architecture in Czechoslovakia), Prague, 1970.

Hrůza, J., *Město Praha* (The City of Prague), Prague, 1989.

Hypšman, B., P. Janák, and Z. Wirth, *Jak rostla Praha* (How Prague Developed), Prague, 1939.

Janáček, J., *Malé dějiny Prahy* (A Short History of Prague), Prague, 1977.

Janák, P., *Sto let obytného domu nájemného v Praze* (A Hundred Years of the Tenement Building in Prague), Prague, 1933.

Koula, J. E., *Nová česká architektura a její vývoj ve XX. století* (New Czech Architecture and Its Development in the 20th Century), Prague, 1940.

Kroutvor, J., *Praha, město ostrých hran* (Prague, City of Sharp Edges), Prague, 1992.

Lukeš, Z., *Pražské vily* (Prague Villas), Prague, 1993.

Lukeš, Z., and J. Svoboda, *Praha 7—100 let moderní architektury 1885–1985* (Prague 7—A Hundred Years of Modern Architecture), Prague, 1986.

Margolius, I., *Prague. A Guide to Twentieth-Century Architecture*, Zurich, Munich, London, 1994.

Morávanszky, Á., *Die Erneuerung der Baukunst*, Salzburg and Vienna, 1988.

Nový, O., *Architekti Praze* (Architects' Gifts to Prague), Prague, 1971.

Pechar, J., and P. Urlich, *Programy české architektury* (The Programs of Czech Architecture), Prague, 1981.

Poche, E., et al., *Praha našeho věku* (The Prague of Our Age), Prague, 1978.

———, *Prahou krok za krokem* (Walks through Prague), Prague, 1985.

Starý, O., et al., *Československá architektura od nejstarší doby po současnost* (Czechoslovak Architecture from Earliest Years to Present Time), Prague, 1962.

Širc, O., "Pražské mosty" (Prague Bridges), in *Praha na evropských vodních cestách* (Prague in European River Journeys), Prague, 1947.

Šlapeta, V., *Praha 1900–1978. Průvodce po moderní architektuře* (Prague 1900–1978: Guide to Modern Architecture), Prague, 1978.

Catalogues

Šlapeta, V., *Adolf Loos a česká architektura* (Adolf Loos and Czech Architecture), Louny, 1984.

Stanislavski, R., and C. Brockhaus, *Europa, Europa. Das Jahrhundert der Avantgarde in Mittel- und Osteuropa*, Bonn, 1994.

Articles

Švácha, R., "Adolf Loos a česká architektura" (Adolf Loos and Czech Architecture), *Umění*, 31, 1983, pp. 490–513.

————, "Josef Chochol. Pokus o intimnější portrét" (Josef Chochol. An Attempt at a More Intimate Portrait). *Umění*, 41, No. 1, 1994, pp. 21–49.

1. THE MODERN STYLE IN THE STREETS OF PRAGUE (1895–1911)

Books

Fuchs, B., *In margine uměleckého odkazu Jana Kotěry* (Notes on the Artistic Legacy of Jan Kotěra), Brno, 1972.

Kubiček, A., *Bohumil Hypšman*, Prague, 1961.

Mádl, K. B., *Jan Kotěra*, Prague, 1922.

Moravánszky, Á., *Die Architektur der Donaumonarchie*, Budapest-Berlin, 1988.

Novotný, O., *Jan Kotěra a jeho doba* (Jan Kotěra and His Times), Prague, 1958.

Pečírka, J., *Otakar Novotný*, Genf, 1931.

Šetlík, J. ed., *Otakar Novotný*, Prague, 1984.

Vlček T., *Praha 1900*, Prague, 1986.

Witlich P., *Česká secese* (Czech Secession), Prague, 1982, 1985.

————, *Prague. Fin de Siécle*, Paris, 1992, (French and English editions).

Žákavec, F., *Dílo Dušana Jurkoviče* (The Work of Dušan Jurkovič), Prague, 1929.

Catalogues

Kotalík, J., *Tschechische Kunst 1878–1914*, Darmstadt, 1985.

Kotalík, J., J. Mašín, and E. Poche, *Česká secese—umění 1900* (Czech Secession—Art 1900), Hluboká nad Vltavou, 1966.

Šlapeta, V., *Otakar Novotný*, Prague—Olomouc, 1980.

Articles

Klein, D., Z. Lukeš, and J. Svoboda., "Der Architekt Josef Zasche (1971–1957)", *Oesterreichische Ostehefte*, 34, 1992, pp. 396–409.

Lukeš, Z., and J. Svoboda, "Hradčanské bašty" (The Hradčany Fortifications), *Umění a řemesla*, 1, 1986, pp. 37–44.

Svoboda, J. E., "Vojtěšká a zderazská asanace na pražském Novém Městě" (The Re-

449

development of the Vojěšská and Zderazská Quarters in the New Town), *Zprávy památkové péče*, 53, 1993, pp. 273–278.

2. THE PRISM AND THE PYRAMID (1911–1918)

Books

Benešová, M., *Josef Gočár*, Prague, 1958.

Benešová, M., *Pavel Janák*, Prague, 1959.

Burkhardt, F., and M. Lamarová, *Cubismo cecoslovacco*, Milan, 1982.

Lamač, M., *Osma a Skupina výtvarných umělců* (The Eight and the Group of Visual Artists), Prague, 1988.

Margolius, I., *Cubism in Architecture and the Applied Arts*, London, 1979.

Matějček, A., and Z. Wirth, *L'art tchéque contemporain*, Prague, 1921.

Šetlík, J., and O. Herbenová, eds., *Pavel Janák*, Prague, 1985.

Štech, V. V., *Tschechische Bestrebungen um ein modernes Interieur*, Prague, 1915.

———, *Včera* (Yesterday), Prague, 1921.

Wirth, Z., *Josef Gočár*, Genf, 1930.

Catalogues

Burkhardt, F., *Vlastislav Hofman. Architektur des böhmischen Kubismus*, Berlin, 1982.

Herbenová, O., and V. Šlapeta, *Pavel Janák 1882–1956. Architektur und Kunstgewerbe*, Vienna, 1984.

Švestka, J. and T. Vlček, eds., *Kubismus in Prag. 1909–1925*, Stuttgart, 1991.

Vegesack, A. von, ed., *Tschechischer Kubismus 1910–1925*, Weil am Rhein, 1992. English edition *Czech Cubism. Architecture, Furniture and Decorative Arts 1910–1925*, London, 1992.

Articles

Benešová, M., "O kubismu v české architektuře" (On Cubism in Czech Architecture), *Architektura ČSSR*, 28, 1966, pp. 171–184.

Burkhardt, F., "Notes on Cubism in Czech Architecture," *Lotus International*, 20, September 1978, pp. 44–53.

Lamarová, M., "Cubism and Expressionism in Architecture and Design," ibid., pp. 54–62.

Pistorius, M., "Kubistická architektura v Praze," *Staletá Praha*, 4, 1969, pp. 139–153.

Švácha, R., "Hofmanův Vyšehrad," *Výtvarná kultura*, 6, No. 6, 1984, pp. 30–33.

———, "Josef Chochol," *Zlatý řez/Golden Section*, 1, 1992, pp. 6–11.

Vokoun, J., "Český architektonický kubismus 1911–1914" (Czech Architectural Cubism), *Domov*, 7, No. 3, 1966, pp. 24–30.

———, "Bohemian Cubism," *Architectural Review*, 139, 1966, pp. 229–233.

450

GENERAL WORKS II (1918–1939)

Books

Adlerová, A., *České užité umění 1918–1938* (Czech Decorative Arts 1918–1938), Prague, 1983.

Burkhardt, F., C. Eveno, and B. Podrecca, *Jože Plečnik Architecte 1972–1957*, Paris, 1986.

Císařovský, J., *Jiří Kroha a meziválečná avantgarda* (Jiří Kroha and the Interwar Avant-Garde), Prague, 1967.

Doesburg, T. Van, *Uber Europaische Architektur*, Basel, 1990.

Havlíček, J., *Návrhy a stavby* (Designs and Buildings), Prague, 1964.

Honzík, K., *Ze života avantgardy* (from the Life of the Avant-Garde), Prague, 1963.

Obrtel, V., *Vlaštovka, která má geometrické hnízdo* (The Swallow with a Geometrical Nest), Praha, 1985.

Prelovšek, D., *Josef Plečnik*, Salzburg-Vienna, 1992.

Teige, K., *Modern Architecture in Czechoslovakia*, Prague, 1947.

Teige, K., *Nejmenší byt* (The Minimum Dwelling), Prague, 1932.

Šlapeta, V., *Czech Functionalism 1918–1938*, London, 1987.

Catalogues

Alborch, C., and J. Anděl, *The Art of the Avant-Garde in Czechoslovakia, 1918–1938*, Valencia, 1993.

Adlerová, A., J. Rous, and A. Vondrová, *Český funkcionalismus 1920–1940* (Czech Functionalism 1920–1940), Prague-Brno, 1978.

Anděl, J., ed., *Umění pro všechny smysly* (Art for All the Senses), Prague, 1993.

Kotalík, J., et al., *Tschechische Kunst der 20er und 30er Jahre*, Darmstadt, 1989.

Máčel, O., K. Sierman, and H. Císařová, *Teige animator*, Amsterdam, 1994.

Šlapeta, V., *Kamil Roškot 1886–1945*, Olomouc-Vlašim, 1978.

Srp, K., ed., *Karel Teige 1900–1951*, Prague, 1994.

Švácha, R., and H. Rousová, eds., *Vít Obrtel (1901–1988). Architektura, typografie, nábytek* (Architecture, Typography, Furniture), Prague, 1992.

Articles and Journals

Lukeš, Z., and R. Švácha, "Moravští architekti v meziválečné Praze" (Moravian Architects in Prague of the Interwar Period), *Vlastivědný věstník moravský* 36, No. 1, 1984, pp. 20–32.

Máčel, O., "Karel Teige und die tschechische Avantgarde," *Archithese* 10, No. 6, 1980, pp. 20–32.

Šlapeta, V., "Bauhaus a česká avantgarda" (Bauhaus and the Czech Avant-Garde), *Umění a řemesla*, 3, 1977, pp. 29–35.

———, "Česká meziválečná architektura z hlediska mezinárodních vztahů" (Czech Interwar Architecture in International Context), *Umění*, 29, 1981, pp. 309–319.

451

———, "Le Corbusier a česká architektonická avantgarda" (Le Corbusier and the Czech Architectural Avant-Garde) in *Ars. Revolučné myšlienky vo výtvarnom umení* (Ars. Revolutionary Ideas in Visual Arts), Bratislava, 1989, pp. 85–106.

Švácha, R., "Sovětský konstruktivismus a česká architektura," (Soviet Constructivism and Czech Architecture), *Umění*, 36, 1988, pp. 54–70.

Castagnara Codeluppi, M., and H. Císařová, eds., *Karel Teige. Architecture and Poetry*, *Rassegna*, 15, No. 53/1, March 1993.

3. TOWARD A NEW PRAGUE (1918–1929)

Books

Bedřich Feuerstein, Prague, 1936.

Krejcar, J., *L'architecture contemporaine en Tchécoslovaquie*, Prague, 1928.

Koula, J. E., *Obytný dům dneška* (The Residential Building of Today), Prague, 1931.

Novosti Pražského hradu a Lán (New Developments at the Prague Castle and in Lány), Prague, 1928.

Svrček, J. B., *Jiří Kroha*, Genf, 1930.

Regulační plán Velké Prahy s okolím (The Redevelopment Program for Greater Prague and Environs), Prague, 1931.

Teige, K., ed., *MSA 1: Mezinárodní soudobá architektura* (Contemporary International Architecture), Prague, 1929.

———, *MSA 2: Moderní architektura v Československu* (Modern Architecture in Czechoslovakia), Prague, 1930.

———, *MSA 3. Josef Havlíček & Karel Honzík. Stavby a plány* (Buildings and Drawings), Prague, 1931.

———, *Práce Jaromíra Krejcara*, (The Works of Jaromír Krejcar), Prague, 1933.

Catalogues

Horneková, J., ed., *České art deco* (Czech Art Deco), Prague, 1993.

Krise, J., and O. Stefan, *Dílo architekta Antonína Engla* (The Work of the Architect Antonín Engel), Prague, 1956.

Rous, J., F. Šmejkal, and R. Švácha, eds., *Devětsil. Česká výtvarná avantgarda dvacátých let* (Devětsil. Czech Art Avant-Garde of the 1920s), Prague, 1986.

Srp, K., *Tvrdošíjní a hosté. 2. část* (The Stubborn Ones and Guests, Part II), Prague, 1987.

Švácha, R., ed., *Devětsil. Czech Avant-Garde Art, Architecture and Design of the 1920s and 1930s*, Oxford-London, 1990.

Articles and Journals

Benešová, "Česká architektura dvacátých let" (Czech Architecture of the 1920s), *Umění*, 21, 1973, pp. 440–452.

———, "Rondokubismus" (Rondocubism), *Architektura ČSSR*, 28, 1969, pp. 303–317.

Flegl, J., and M. Flegl, "Ořechovka—nejstarší z moderních vilových čtvrtí Prahy" (Ořechovka—the Oldest of Prague's Garden Suburbs), *Domov*, 4, No. 4, 1981, pp. 40–42.

Janák, P., "L'Architecture Tchécoslovaque sous la République," in *La République Tchécoslovaque au XXéme Siècle*, ed. M. Hipmanová, Prague, 1931, pp. 115–125.

"L'Architecture moderne en Tchécoslovaquie," series of articles in *L'Architecture d'Aujourd'hui*, 5, June 1933, pp. 3–54.

Pechar, J., "Purismus v české architektuře" (Purism in Czech Architecture), *Architektura ČSSR* 29, 1970, pp. 178–191.

4. ARCHITECTURE AND THE GREAT DEPRESSION (1929-1939)

Books

Czumalo, V., *Česká teorie architektury v letech okupace* (Czech Architectural Theory in the Period of Occupation), Prague, 1990.

Hruška, E., *Urbanistická forma* (Urbanistic Form), Prague, 1947.

Nový, O. and J. Šetlík, *Cubr-Hrubý-Pokorný*, Prague, 1962.

Za socialistickou architekturu (Toward a Socialist Architecture), Prague, 1932.

Catalogues

Janák, P., ed., *Výstava bydlení—stavba osady Baba* (Housing Exhibition - Building the Baba Estate), Praha, 1932.

Kroutvor, J., Z. Lukeš, and A. Pařík, *František Zelenka*, Prague 1991.

Palkovský, J., and V. Šlapeta, *Skleněný obytný dům v Praze-Dejvicích. Richard F. Podzemný 1936–1938.* (The Glass Residential Building in Prague-Dejvice), Louny-Prague, 1985.

Pechar, J., *Václav Hilský. Architektonické dílo* (Václav Hilský. Architectural Work), Prague, 1981.

Articles

Šlapeta, V., "Architektonické dílo Ladislava Žáka" (The Architectural Work of Ladislav Žák), *Sborník Národního technického muzea*, 14, 1975, pp. 189–225.

Švácha, R., "Osada Baba" (The Baba Estate), *Umění*, 28, 1980, pp. 368–379.

453

ADOLF BENŠ
18 May 1894, Pardubice–8 March 1982, Prague

Architect, town planner, editor of magazine *Stavitel*. Studied under Jan Kotěra and Josef Gočár at the Prague Academy of Fine Arts, 1921–1924, professor at the Prague School of Applied Arts, 1945–1965. Works in Prague include apartment building on Sudoměřská Street, 1926–1931; Power Company Building on Bubenské Embankment in collaboration with Josef Kříž, 1927–1935; family houses on Trójská Street, 1928–1930, and Nad Paťankou, 1937–1938; departures building of the old airport on the street K letišti, 1932–1934; landscaping of the gardens below the Prague Castle, 1965–1967. Outside Prague he designed school buildings in Mladá Boleslav, 1926–1927, and in Ružomberok, 1938–1940; family houses in Bratislava, 1929–1930, Skalsko, after 1930, and Zlín with František Jech, 1935; Czechoslovak Pavilion at the Industrial Exposition in Liège, 1930. His work represents the artistically oriented line of Prague functionalism and is distinguished by elegance and subtle monumentality.

FRANTIŠEK MARIA ČERNÝ
13 August 1903, Prague–9 November 1978, Prague

Architect. Studied under Pavel Janák at the Prague School of Applied Arts, 1921–1923, and under Josef Gočár at the Academy of Fine Arts, 1924–1926. Member of *Devětsil*. Realized works in Prague include apartment buildings on Chrudimská Street, 1928–1929, and U staré plynárny in collaboration with Kamil Ossendorf, 1937; family house on Na Kodymce Street, 1938; tramway depot on Plzeňská Street, circa 1939; new church steeples of the Emmaus Monastery, 1964–1965. Outside Prague he designed the hospital and doctors' accommodation building in Kolín, 1949–1952. Černý's limited work belongs to the emotional branch of functionalism. His designs from the twenties, in particular the unrealized competition project for the Workers' Accident Insurance Building from 1924, show the influence of De Stijl. Later Černý followed Le Corbusier's example and became interested in the problem of modern expression of monumentality.

JOSEF CHOCHOL
13 November 1880, Písek–6 June 1956, Karlovy Vary

Architect, town planner, furniture designer, theoretician of architecture. Studied under Otto Wagner at the Vienna Academy of Fine Arts, 1907–1909. Member of the Cubist Group of Visual Artists, 1911–1912, and *Devětsil*, 1923–1930. Prague works include Brožík Hall in the Old Town City Hall, 1909–1911; triplex at Rašín Embankment, 1912–1913; villa on Libušina Street, 1912–1913; apartment buildings on Neklanova Street, 1913, 1913–1914; office buildings on Jindřišská Street, 1920–1921, and Dittrichova Street, 1923–1925; the bridge connecting the suburb of Holešovice with Trója (later demolished, 1924–1928); villa on Neherovská Street, 1931; apartment buildings on the streets U vody, 1927–1929, U elektrárny, 1938–1939, U školičky in collaboration with Richard Podzemný, 1938–1940, and Dělnická, 1939–1940. His realizations outside Prague include the District Council building in Ledeč nad Sázavou, 1928–1935, and the hotel in Nové Město nad Metují, 1948–1950. Until 1911, Chochol worked in the Wagnerian modern style, but from 1912, he pioneered architectural cubism, in which he emphasized innovative elements: the rationalist inner framework, the dynamic and nonornamental architectural form. His purist projects, designed from 1914, demonstrate his remarkable ability to depart from tradition and from the prevailing architectural currents of the time. After 1926, he created several impressive projects in the style of Soviet constructivism, including his project for the Liberated Theater, 1926–1927, all of which, however, remained unrealized.

ANTONÍN ENGEL
4 May 1879, Poděbrady–12 October 1958, Prague

Architect, town planner, theoretician of architecture. He studied under Otto Wagner at the Vienna Academy of Fine Arts, 1905–1908. Professor of architecture at the Czech Polytechnic in Prague, 1922–1945. His Prague works include apartment buildings on the street U starého hřbitova, 1910–1911; family houses on the streets Břehová, 1913–1915, and Na Karlovce, 1927; Masaryk student dormitories on Thákurova Street, 1923–1925; water filtration station on Podolská Street, 1923–1928, 1953–1956; school buildings of the Czech Polytechnic on Technická Street in collaboration with Theodor Petřík and Severin Ondřej, 1925–1937; Ministry of Railways on Ludvík Svoboda Embankment, 1927–1931; Army

455

Headquarters in Vítězné Square, circa 1935–1938. His main project was the development plan for the new Prague suburb of Dejvice around Vítězné Square, 1922–1924. His works outside Prague include hospital pavilions, 1910, and water lock, 1913–1915, in the spa town of Poděbrady. As architect and town planner, Engel promoted Wagner's monumentalist town-planning conception set out in the book *Die Großstadt*, as early as 1909. At first, he saw architecture as an austere "tectonic organism," but after 1918 he adopted the neoplatonic conception of neoclassicism as the reflection of an eternal metaphysical order.

JAROSLAV FRAGNER
25 December 1898, Prague–3 January 1967, Prague

Architect, furniture designer, painter. Studied at the Czech Polytechnic in Prague, 1917–1922, but left without graduating owing to conflict with his professors. Between 1934 and 1935 he studied under Josef Gočár at the Prague Academy of Fine Arts. Member of *Devětsil* and of the Czech chapter of CIAM, chairman of the Artists' Association *Mánes* in the forties, professor at the Prague Academy of Fine Arts, 1945–1967. His realized works in Prague include apartment buildings on Pod Kavalírkou Street, 1927; family house on Glinkova Street, 1932; Merkur Insurance Company Building on Revoluční Avenue, 1934–1935; reconstruction of the university building Karolinum, 1946–1966, and of the Bethlehem Chapel, 1949–1965; and the Planetarium in Stromovka Park, 1954–1959. Among his numerous realizations outside Prague are the children's pavilion of the sanatorium in Mukačevo, Ukraine, 1924–1928; pharmaceutical plant in Dolní Měcholupy, 1929–1931; villa, 1928–1929; ESSO power plant, 1929–1932; Auto-Tatra showroom, 1932; and ESSO administrative building, 1940–1944, all in Kolín; villa, 1931–1932, and power distribution plant, 1934–1937, in Kostelec nad Černými lesy; set of four summer houses in Nespeky, 1932–1940; house of culture in Ostrava, 1955–1962. Around 1924, following his interesting cubist and purist experiments, Fragner arrived at international functionalism, whose abstract, boxlike syntax he interpreted as the expression of a new humanism based on geometry. His family houses designed after 1931 were surrounded with intimate residential gardens, an arcadian environment where he increasingly applied his organic vocabulary influenced by Wright and Aalto. In designing his public buildings after 1934, he was concerned with the modern expression of monumentality. From the forties, his main projects were reconstructions of historical buildings and sites.

JAN GILLAR

24 June 1904, Příbor–7 May 1967, Prague

Architect, town planner, furniture designer. Studied under Josef Gočár at the Prague
Academy of Fine Arts, 1925–1928, worked in Jaromír Krejcar's architectural studio, 1928–
1931. Member of *Devětsil* and of the Czech chapter of CIAM. Works in Prague include
French schools on Božkova Street, 1932–1934; apartment buildings on the streets Vinohradská, 1932, Veletržní, 1934, Vinařská, 1936–1938, Družstevní ochoz, 1936–1937, and
Za Hládkovem, 1939–1940; villas on the streets Na Babě, 1934, and Nad Bertramkou,
1939; Karel Teige's house on U Šalamounky Street, 1937–1938; interiors of the White Swan
department store (Bílá labut') on Na poříčí Street, 1937–1939. Outside Prague his realized
works include houses for persons in the care of the District Department of Social Work in
Kostelec nad Černými lesy, 1939–1942, and in Zbraslav, 1941–1946; and school buildings in
Plzeň, 1949–1952. In the thirtiès, supported by Teige, Gillar took over from Jaromír Krejcar as the leading architect of the left-wing avant-garde. He adopted Teige's program of
scientific functionalism and concentrated on designing "collective houses" and "minimum
dwellings."

JOSEF GOČÁR

13 March 1880, Semín–10 September 1945, Jičín

Architect, town planner, furniture designer. Studied under Jan Kotěra at the Prague School
of Applied Arts, 1903–1905, professor at the Prague Academy of Fine Arts, 1924–1945.
Member of the Cubist Group of Visual Artists, 1911–1914, chairman of Artist's Association
Mánes in the thirties, picture editor of *Styl*. Works in Prague include The Black Madonna
Building in Ovocný trh, 1912; duplex on Tychonova Street, 1912–1913; Czechoslovak
Legiobank on Na poříčí Street, 1921–1923; bank buildings on Jindřišská, 1922–1923, and
Hybernská streets, 1923–1926; Rural Education Building on Slezská Street, 1924–1926;
facade of the Fénix Building in Wenceslas Square, 1927–1929; Church of Saint Wenceslas
in Svatopluk Čech Square, 1928–1930; villas on the streets Na Marně, 1925–1926, Nad
Paťankou, 1932, Jarní, 1934, Pod Bořislavkou, 1934, and Na Babě, 1935–1936; and apartment
building on Bubenská Street, 1935–1936. Outside Prague, Gočár designed a villa in Kru-
cemburk, 1907–1908; staircase of the Church of Virgin Mary in Hradec Králové, 1910;

457

Wenke department store in Jaroměř, 1910–1911; steam mill in Pardubice, 1910–1911; sanatorium in Bohdaneč, 1912–1913; villa in Libodřice, 1912–1914; factory in Třebíč, 1919–1921; villa in Červený Kostelec, 1921–1922; bank buildings in Hradec Králové, 1922–1926, Ostrava, 1923–1924, and Pardubice, 1925; complex of three schools, 1923–1927; evangelical meeting house Ambrožův sbor, 1926–1929; directorate of the State Railways, 1928–1933; and District Council Building, 1931–1936; in Hradec Králové, Czechoslovak pavilion for the Paris International Exposition, 1925; hotel in Pardubice, 1930; post office in Užhorod in the Ukraine, 1930; and many other buildings. One of the most important Czech architects of the twentieth century, Gočár remained faithful to the classical and neoclassical tradition, which he combined with the geometrical modern style, cubism, rondocubism, purism, and functionalism in interesting syntheses. He used the newly developed metal and reinforced concrete skeleton constructions as early as 1910–1913.

VLADIMÍR GRÉGR
3 August 1902, Prague–22 February 1943, Berlin-Plötzensee

Architect, interior and industrial designer. Studied at the Czech Polytechnic in Prague, 1922–1927. Until 1930 he worked with the developer Václav Havel (father of the president), with whom he collaborated on the "Czech Hollywood" project of the Barrandov film studios and surrounding villas. His Prague works include floating sports club building situated on the Vltava below Barrandov, 1930 (the present whereabouts of the structure are not known); and villas on the streets Barrandovská, 1930–1932, 1931–1932, 1932, 1936, 1939–1941, Skalní, 1932–1933, Filmařská, 1934–1935, Na Hubálce, 1936, and Nad výšinkou, 1938–1940. Outside Prague he designed the savings bank in Sedlec, 1932; family houses in Jevany, 1932, and Luhačovice, 1938–1939, 1940; and an apartment building in Kolín, 1934. He designed the locomotive and carriage bodies for the express train the Slovak Arrow, which provided the service between Prague and Bratislava, 1932. Grégr was the leading representative of the romantic current in architecture of the thirties. In his early works he was inclined toward aerodynamic functionalism and organic architecture. After 1932 he developed his own style, which combined elements of the English arts and crafts style, Czech vernacular architecture, and the so-called neo-Hispanic style created in the twenties for the affluent suburbs of Hollywood.

458

Josef Havlíček

5 May 1899, Prague–30 December 1961, Prague

Architect, painter, sculptor, furniture designer, town planner. Studied under Josef Gočár at the Prague Academy of Fine Arts, 1923–1926. Member of *Devětsil* and the Czech chapter of CIAM. Works in Prague include apartment buildings on the streets Kafkova, 1925–1926, Pátého května ín collaboration with Karel Honzík, 1931–1932, Milady Horákové, 1937–1938, and Letohradská, 1938–1939; department stores Chicago on Národní Street, 1927–1929, and Habich on Štěpánská Street, 1927–1928, both in collaboration with Jaroslav Polívka; family house on U dívčích hradů Street with Karel Honzík, 1929; General Pensions Institute in Winston Churchill Square with Karel Honzík, 1932–1934. Outside Prague, Havlíček designed the residential house at the Brno Trade Fair grounds with Jaroslav Polívka, 1927–1928; school buildings in Lipenec near Žatec with Karel Honzík, 1935–1936; sanatorium in Poděbrady, 1936–1940; housing estate Labská Kotlina in Hradec Králové with František Bartoš, 1947–1950; dried milk factory in Zábřeh in Moravia and in Strakonice, 1947–1953, with Josef Hrubý and František Kerhart; high-rise apartment buildings in Kladno-Rozdělov with Karel Filsak and Karel Bubeníček, 1951–1959. In 1947 he participated in the project for the OSN Building in New York. During his studies with Gočár, Havlíček worked his way to purism and emotively based functionalism, in which he translated Le Corbusier's syntax into a monumental or even gigantic scale. Among his unrealized, visionary projects, the most significant were the competition project for the Nusle Bridge, 1927, and the project for the redevelopment of Prague's central business district, 1943.

Václav Hilský

Born 6 September 1909, Valašské Meziříčí

Architect, town planner. He studied under Otakar Novotný at the Prague School of Applied Arts, 1929–1935. Member of Artists' Association *Mánes*. His Prague works include small-apartment buildings on Mládeže and Nad Kajetánkou Streets in collaboration with Rudolf Jasenský, František Jech, Karel Koželka, 1937–1939; apartment buildings on the streets Patočkova, with Rudolf Jasenský, 1938, Baranova, 1954, Černokostelecká, 1955; villas on the streets Jílovská with Rudolf Jasenský, 1940–1941, and Pod Palatou, 1981–1990; Centrotex office building with Otakar Jurenka, 1970–1978; and the Metro ventilation duct in Hrdinů Square, 1972–1973. Outside Prague he designed buildings with small apartments in

Brno with Rudolf Jasenský, František Jech, Karel Koželka, 1937–1939; department store in Rousínov with Rudolf Jasenský, 1939; communal house *Koldům* in Litvínov with Evžen Linhart, 1946–1957; standardized duplexes in Lidice, 1946; housing estates in Kladno-Rozdělov, 1947–1950, Ostrava-Poruba, 1952–1954, Příbram-Březové Hory, 1957–1960, and in Kladno-Sítná, 1962–1987, the last two with Jiří Náhlík and Otakar Jurenka; theater in Příbram, 1956–1959; and a memorial to the last battles of World War II in Slivice near Příbram, 1967–1970. Hilský represents the second generation of the functionalist avant-garde, whose vision of buildings designed for communal living he tried to realize after 1945. After 1957, he adopted the international style, and by the end of the sixties his work bordered on brutalism, a direction not common for his generation.

Bohumil Hypšman (Hübschmann)
10 January 1878, Prague–3 November 1961, Prague

Architect, town planner, theoretician of architecture. Studied with Otto Wagner at the Vienna Academy of Fine Arts, 1900–1904. Member of the circle of architects around the magazine *Styl*. In Prague, he collaborated with Quido Bělský, Bedřich Bendelmayer, and Jan Letzel on Hotel Evropa on Wenceslas Square, 1903–1905; his other projects include the steam mills on the streets U Uranie, circa 1905, and U továren, 1919–1922; family houses on the streets Pod kaštany, 1908–1909, Půlkruhová, 1909, V nových domcích, 1921–1925, Holečkova, 1924–1927, V tišině, 1925–1928, and U laboratoře, 1926–1927; apartment buildings on the streets Široká, 1910–1911, Jirečkova, 1911, Národní, 1911–1912, Kaprova, 1919–1921, Dolnoměcholupská, 1920–1923, Vratislavova, 1924, and U starého hřbitova, 1928–1929; ministerial buildings in Palacký Square, 1923–1931; health insurance company building on Klimentská Street in collaboration with František Roith, 1924–1926; extension to the Agricultural Produce Exchange in Maxim Gorky Square, 1928–1929; and gymnasium in Vršovické Square with Alois Dryák, 1932–1933. Outside Prague, Hypšman designed family houses in Klánovice, 1905, and Mělník, 1906; apartment building in Rakovník, 1923; nitrogen factory in Ostrava, 1927–1930; school in Litoměřice, 1928; and other buildings. Hypšman's early work followed the progress of Wagnerian modern style from the ornamental to the geometrical. After 1920, Hypšman's works tended to be austere, monumental palatial buildings in the style of modern classicism. True to his reputation as connoisseur of historical buildings, he designed his works with utmost sensitivity to the diverse and picturesque environment of old Prague.

PAVEL JANÁK

12 March 1882, Prague–1 August 1956, Prague

Architect, town planner, furniture designer, theoretician of architecture. Studied under Otto Wagner at the Vienna Academy of Fine Arts, 1906–1908. Worked in Jan Kotěra's architectural studio, 1907–1909. Professor at the Prague School of Applied Arts, 1921–1941. Member of the Cubist Group of Visual Artists, 1911–1914, and Artists' Association *Mánes*. In Prague, Janák designed the Hlávka Bridge, 1909–1912; standardized houses in Bylanská Street in collaboration with Josef Gočár, 1919–1921; villas on the streets Na lysinách, 1921–1922, Lomená, Cukrovarnická, and Na Ořechovce, 1923–1924; Adria Building with Josef Zasche, 1922–1925; and Škoda Building, both on Jungmannova Street, 1923–1926; Libeň Bridge, 1924–1928; Autoclub Building in Opletalova Street, 1925–1928; apartment buildings in Rooseveltova Street, 1927–1929; reconstruction and completion of Černín Palace for the Ministry of Foreign Affairs, 1927–1937; Hotel Juliš in Wenceslas Square, 1931–1933; evangelical meeting house Husův sbor on Dykova Street, 1931–1933; layout of the Baba estate, 1929–1931; villas on the streets Na Babě, Nad Paťankou, Na ostrohu, and U páté baterie, 1932–1934; reconstruction of the riding school and ballroom at the Prague Castle, 1948–1950; reconstruction of the Hvězda pavilion, 1948–1952. Outside Prague, Janák designed the water lock in Obříství, 1909–1911, and in Předměřice nad Labem, 1913–1915 (demolished 1929); family houses in Jičín, 1911–1912, Pelhřimov, 1912–1913 and 1913–1914, in Ljubljana, Slovenia, 1914, and in Jaroměřice, 1920–1921; crematorium in Pardubice, 1922–1923; savings bank and villa Petrův dvůr in Náchod, 1927–1929; airport building in Mariánské Lázně, 1928–1930, and many other buildings. Janák was the ideological leader of Czech architectural cubism, and he interpreted the cubist method in an expressionist manner as the struggle of spirit with dead matter. After 1919, together with Gočár, he developed a national style called rondocubism that was characterized by its pseudofolkloric, colorful ornaments. During the twenties, Janák severely limited his formal range and proceeded to create elegant functionalist buildings.

Jan Kotěra

18 December 1871, Brno–17 April 1923, Prague

Architect, town planner, furniture designer, theoretician of architecture. Studied under Otto Wagner at the Vienna Academy of Fine Arts, 1894–1897. Professor at the Prague School of Applied Arts, 1898–1910, and at the Academy of Fine Arts, 1911–1923. Long-time chairman of the Artists' Association *Mánes*. Author of books *Práce mé a mých žáků* (My Work and That of My Students), 1902, and *Dělnické kolonie* (Workers' Housing Colonies), 1921. His Prague works include facade of the Peterka Building in Wenceslas Square in collaboration with Vilém Tierhier, 1899–1900; *Mánes* exhibition pavilion in Kinský Gardens, 1902 (demolished 1917); villas on the streets Vilová, 1902–1903, Slavíčkova, 1905–1907, and Hradešínská, 1908–1909, and in Sibiřské Square, 1907; waterworks and pumping station on the streets Baarova and Modřanská, 1906–1907; buildings for the publishers Laichter and Urbánek (the so-called Mozarteum) on the streets Chopinova, 1908–1909, and Jungmannova, 1912–1913; Villa Bianca on Na seníku Street, 1910–1911 (rebuilt after 1920); family houses on Mickiewiczova Street, 1910–1911; office building of the General Pensions Institute on Rašínovo Embankment in collaboration with Josef Zasche, 1912–1914; School of Architecture of the Academy of Fine Arts on U akademie Street, 1919–1924, completed by Josef Gočár; office building of the Vítkovické Ironworks on Olivová Street, 1921–1924; and Charles University Law School building in Curieových Square, 1921–1931, completed by Ladislav Machoň. In the Bohemian and Moravian countryside, Kotěra designed family houses in Černošice, 1902–1903, 1908–1910, Bechyně, 1902–1903, Holoubkov, 1907–1909, Chrustenice, 1908, Vysoké Mýto, 1909–1910, Zlín, 1911, Solnice, 1916, Dobruška, 1917–1918, Všenory, 1921–1922; District Council Building, 1901–1904, Municipal Museum, 1909–1913, Hotel Grand, 1910–1911, and bridge, 1910–1912, in Hradec Králové; National House, 1905–1907, and memorial to the couple named Vojáček, 1910, in Prostějov; *chateau* in Radboř, 1911–1913; garden city for railway employees in Louny, 1909–1919; workers' housing colonies in Zlín, 1918, and in Králův Dvůr, 1920, and many other buildings. Outside Czechoslovakia, he designed the Czechoslovak pavilion for the 1904 St. Louis Exposition; Villa Tonder in St. Gilgen, 1905–1906; bank building Slavia in Sarajevo, 1911–1912; and Lamberger-Gombrich Palace in Vienna, 1913–1915. Kotěra is considered the founder of Czech modern architecture. The lyricism and subtle floral decorativeness of his early works suggested connections with the late nineteenth century "aesthetic of impression." Under the

462

influence of the circle around the poet J. S. Machar and philosopher T. G. Masaryk, Kotěra, however, sought the means to express the moralistic "aesthetic of truth," professed by the more advanced modern directions. He found it in 1907–1908 in the work of Berlage, Wright, and Hoffmann with their unconcealed constructions, asymmetrical ground plans, and unrendered brick masonry. In his key works from the period between 1908 and 1912, such as the Museum of Hradec Králové or the buildings designed for Laichter and Urbánek, Kotěra suppressed the latent decorative aspect of this austere syntax, characteristic of Hoffmann's works, and at the same time strove to emphasize its pathos.

JAROMÍR KREJCAR
25 July 1895, Hundsheim, Austria–5 October 1949, London

Architect, furniture designer, town planner, theoretician of architecture, typographer, editor of the anthology *Život II* (Life) and broadsheet *Disk*. Studied under Jan Kotěra at the Prague Academy of Fine Arts, 1917–1921. Worked with Josef Gočár in 1921–1923, and with Moise Ginzburg in the GIPROGOR town-planning institute in Moscow, 1934–1935. Professor at the Brno Polytechnic, 1947–1948, lecturer at the Architectural Association School in London, 1948–1949. Member of *Devětsil* and the Czech chapter of CIAM. Married to journalist Milena Jesenská, one-time friend and correspondent of Franz Kafka. Krejcar's Prague works include apartment building on Domažlická Street in collaboration with Kamil Roškot, 1923–1924; Olympic commercial building on Spálená Street, 1925–1928; villas on the streets Nad olšinami, 1926–1927, and Charlese de Gaulla, 1927–1929; extension to Karel Teige's house on Černá Street, 1927–1928; association building of the Association of Private Clerical Employees on Francouzská Street, 1930–1931; villa on Nad koupadly Street, 1939. Outside Prague he designed two villas in Zbraslav, 1926–1929, 1927; spa building Machnáč in Trenčianské Teplice, 1930–1932; and the Czechoslovak pavilion for the Paris International Exposition, 1936–1937. Krejcar was the most important architect among Czech functionalists of the twenties, whose best buildings strove to express the beauty of modern industrial technology through their aerodynamic and "nautical" shapes. He extolled the beauty of steamships and factories in *Devětsil*'s publications, and in 1925 he entered into a polemic with the scientific functionalist conception of his closest friend, Karel Teige. In retrospect, Krejcar's Paris pavilion, constructed of steel and glass, 1936–1937, appears to be one of the most impressive forerunners of high tech architecture.

463

Hana Kučerová-Záveská
21 March 1904, Prague–7 November 1944, Stockholm

Furniture designer, architect. Studied under Pavel Janák at the Prague School of Applied Arts, 1922–1927. Edited the anthology *Byt* (Dwelling), 1934. Designed villas in Na Babě, 1931–1932, and Na ostrohu, 1932, on the Baba estate in Prague. She was mainly known as a designer of functionalist interiors and furniture. Her folding garden furniture for the restaurant Terasy in Prague-Barrandov gained wide acclaim, and variations of it are still manufactured today.

Ludvík Kysela
25 April 1883, Kouřim–10 February 1960, Prague

Architect, town planner. Studied under Josef Schulz and Antonín Balšánek at the Czech Polytechnic in Prague, 1901–1909, then employed by the Prague Municipal Construction Authority. Member of the Club of Architects, which published the magazine *Stavba*. All of Kysela's realized works are situated in Prague and include apartment buildings on the streets Karmelitská, 1912–1913, and Kostelní, 1922–1924; factory in Nitranská Street, circa 1920; building of the Praha Insurance Company on Na příkopě Street, 1925–1929; commercial buildings Lindt, 1925–1927, and Alfa, 1927–1929, in Wenceslas Square; family house on Čimická Street, 1928; Patria Insurance Company on Štěpánská Street, 1928–1929; commercial building on Revoluční Avenue, 1929–1931. In his role as consultant he also had some influence on the Bat'a Building in Wenceslas Square, designed by the architectural office of the Bat'a Company. Following his cubist beginnings, Kysela turned into an enthusiastic functionalist in the twenties, and his commercial buildings designed for the central business district of Prague were distinguished by their bold skeleton structures and abundance of glass.

František Albert Libra
8 April 1891, Český Herálec–30 June 1958, Prague

Architect, town planner. Studied at the Czech Polytechnic in Prague, circa 1914–1920. Member of the Club of Architects and of the circle around the magazine *Stavba*. His Prague works include villas on the streets Hradešínská, 1921–1922, Pod altánem, 1923–1924, Na dračkách, 1931, and Barrandovská, 1937; apartment buildings on Podolské Embankment, 1924–1927, on the streets Průběžná, 1923–1924, Bulharská, 1925–1926, Jankovská, and U nových domů I in collaboration with Jiří Kan, 1932–1933, Obětí 8. května with Jiří Kan, 1935–1937, Osadní, Humpolecká with Jiří Kan, 1936–1938; Edison power station on Jeruzalémská Street, 1926–1930; office building for the Central Social Insurance Company on Křížová Street with Jiří Kan, 1935–1937; factories Aga and Hydroxygen on Kolbenova, 1936–1938, and Hlubočepská Streets, 1937–1939; commercial building on Londýnská Street, 1936; and office building on Gorazdova Street, 1953. Outside Prague he designed the miners' housing estate in Most, 1923, and Úpice, 1948; apartment buildings in Ledeč nad Sázavou, 1925–1926, and Rakovník, 1927–1931, 1939; business school, 1927; warehouse of the workers cooperative shop, 1929–1930; municipal savings bank, 1932–1934, and financial institution office building, 1938, in Rakovník; municipal savings banks in Louny, 1928–1931, Chrudim, after 1929, Kutná Hora, 1937–1939, and many other buildings. Following his cubist beginnings, Libra proceeded to develop the purist and functionalist program of *Stavba*. From 1930 he worked in partnership with the Latvian architect Jiří Kan (1895–1944), who had been a student of Hans Poelzig. Together they also designed and built the tuberculosis sanatorium in Vyšné Hágy in Slovakia, 1932–1938, a hypermodern complex whose central accommodation building was the largest functionalist structure in Czechoslovakia.

Evžen (Eugen) Linhart
20 March 1898, Kouřim–29 December 1949, Prague

Architect, furniture designer. Studied under Antonín Engel at the Czech Polytechnic in Prague, 1918–1924, then worked for the Prague Municipal Construction Authority, and after 1945 for the Ministry of Culture and Information. Member of *Devětsil* from 1923. In Prague he designed small-unit apartment buildings on the streets Pod Plískavou, 1925–

1927, Radhošťská, 1925–1928, Pivovarnická, 1927–1931, and Jičínská, 1929–1932; villas on the streets Na viničních horách, 1927–1929, Tylišovská in collaboration with V. F. Hofman, 1927–1929, Na ostrohu with Antonín Heythum, 1931–1932, and Na pískách, 1932–1933; and a secondary school building on Evropská Street, 1937–1938. In the Czech countryside he designed a villa in Tábor, circa 1940; communal house in Litvínov with Václav Hilský, 1946–1957; experimental houses in Záluží u Mostu with Václav Hilský, 1947–1948. Linhart's cubist and purist projects from 1920–1925 may be seen as the architectural counterpart of Henri Rousseau's magical realism—compare, for instance, the Pneu Pirelli project, 1923. Even his functionalist projects from the time after 1927—influenced by Le Corbusier, whose work Linhart had studied in Paris and Stuttgart—were imbued with his subtle and magical sense of form. After the mid-thirties, Linhart focused on the celebratory and monumental aspects of functionalism, which he expressed in his postwar communal building *Koldům* in Litvínov.

Otakar Novotný
11 January 1880, Benešov–4 April 1959, Prague

Architect, furniture designer. Studied under Jan Kotěra at the Prague School of Applied Arts, 1900–1903. Professor at the same school, 1929–1953. His Prague works include villas on the streets Pětidomí, 1905, Vnislavova, 1912–1913, Trójská, 1923, Nad Rokoskou, 1928, Na Zátorce, 1929, and Na dračkách, 1931–1932; the building for the publisher Jan Štenc on Salvátorská Street, 1909–1911; apartment buildings on the streets Elišky Krásnohorské, 1919–1921, Kamenická, 1923–1924, and U pošty, 1928; hostel for resettled persons on Pod Balkánem Street, 1928; and the building of the *Mánes* Association of Artists on Masaryk Embankment, 1928–1930. Outside Prague, he built villas in Újezd nad Lesy, 1904, Jindřichův Hradec, 1904, Senohraby, 1906, Čimelice, 1907, Rakovník, 1908, Zbraslav, 1909, Lštění, 1911, Holice, 1911–1912, Benešov, 1912, Žichlice, 1921, Česká Skalice, 1924, Třemošnice, 1930; gymnasiums in Holice, 1910–1911 and Rakovník, 1912; apartment buildings in Znojmo, 1920–1921, water tower at Kbely Airport, 1924; workers' hostel in Černožice nad Labem, 1926–1927; savings bank in Benešov, 1926–1929; the palatial residence of the industrialist Steinský in Hradec Králové, 1926–1927; and post office in Louny, 1928. Abroad, he designed Villa Reimer in St. Gilgen, 1906, and the Czechoslovak pavilion for the Venice Biennale, 1924–1925. Novotný was the most faithful of Kotěra's disciples,

466

and he offered an appraisal of his teacher's work and legacy in his book *Jan Kotěra a jeho doba* (Jan Kotěra and His Time), 1958. Novotný shared Kotěra's passion for austere buildings of unrendered bricks, a common denominator of many of his works whether designed in the style of the geometrical modern, purism, or functionalism. He also created interesting cubist and rondocubist projects several years after his contemporaries Janák and Gočár.

VÍT OBRTEL
22 March 1901, Olomouc–12 June 1988, Prague

Architect, poet, theoretician of architecture, typographer, theater set designer, editor of the magazine *Kvart*. Studied under Rudolf Kříženecký and Antonín Engel at the Czech Polytechnic in Prague, 1918–1925. Member of *Devětsil* and *Mánes*. His Prague works include office building in Peace Square (náměsti Miru, 1927–1930; apartment building on Žitná Street, with Zdeněk Hölzel, 1937–1938, and family house in Za Pekařkou, 1941–1942. Outside Prague, his realized projects were apartment building with bakery, 1927–1928, and hospital boiler room, 1948–1950, in Jičín; family house in Rožnov pod Radhoštěm, 1937–1928; old people's home in Plzeň, 1958–1960; and hospital in Česká Lípa, 1976–1982. As architect, Obrtel first made a mark with his early purist designs in 1921, and later with his projects for villas in the style of organic architecture, 1931–1935, which he conceived as the ideal dwelling for a philosopher or poet. Together with Karel Honzík, he was the most determined critic of Teige's concept of scientific functionalism within *Devětsil*, demanding that architecture should provide a synthesis of purposefulness and emotiveness, "the comfort of facts and feelings." In the thirties, Obrtel's thinking focused on surrealist and neoplatonic visions, and his theoretical work gradually turned into poetic creation.

RICHARD FERDINAND PODZEMNÝ
16 March 1907, Křivé near Valašské Meziříčí–17 January 1987, Prague

Architect, town planner. Studied under Pavel Janák at the Prague School of Applied Arts, 1926–1931. Member of Artists' Association *Mánes*. Prague buildings include the so-called Glass Palace; apartment building in Freedom Square (náměstí Svobody), 1936–1937; apartment buildings on the streets U školičky, in collaboration with Josef Chochol, 1938–1940; and Mánesova, 1954–1955; family house on Čimická Street, 1941; swimming stadium

467

at Podolské Embankment, 1959–1963; polyclinic on Pod Marjánkou Street, 1959–1963; teaching hospital on the street V úvalu, 1959–1972, both projects in collaboration with Antonín Tenzer. Outside Prague he built villas in Louňovice near Jevany, 1931, in České Budějovice, with Kamil Ossendorf, 1933, in Čisovice, 1938; apartment building in Kutná Hora, 1939; standardized houses and school buildings in Lidice, 1946–1956. Podzemný was one of the leading architects among the second generation of Prague functionalists. Following Le Corbusier's example, he placed emphasis on the aesthetic components of a work of architecture.

EVŽEN (EUGEN) ROSENBERG
24 February 1907, Topolčany, Slovakia–21 November 1990, London

Architect, town planner. Studied under Josef Gočár at the Prague Academy of Fine Arts, 1929–1932. Worked in Le Corbusier's studio around 1929 and in the office of Josef Havlíček and Karel Honzík in 1932. In 1938 Rosenberg emigrated to Great Britain where he became partner in the architectural firm Yorke-Mardall-Rosenberg, which specialized in designing airports, large factories, school buildings, and hospitals. His Prague works include apartment buildings on the streets Letohradská, 1935–1936, U průhonu, 1936, Antonínská, 1936–1937, and Schnirchova, 1937, and in Orten Square, 1936; commercial building in Milady Horákové, 1937; and commercial and office building with an arcade situated between Štěpánská and Ve Smečkách Streets, 1937–1938. In Slovakia, Rosenberg designed a family house in his native Topolčany, 1933–1934; and in the countryside near Prague the Foresta restaurant in Slapy, 1935 (later destroyed). Rosenberg made his mark as the author of large commercial, office, and residential buildings for the central business district of Prague, and his elegant functionalist forms, reflective glass, shiny metal materials and meticulously designed details expressed the beauty of metropolitan life in the language of the thirties.

468

KAMIL ROŠKOT

29 April 1886, Vlašim–12 July 1945, Paris

Architect, town planner. Studied under Jan Kotěra at the Prague Academy of Fine Arts, 1919–1922. Member of Artists' Association *Mánes*. In Prague he designed apartment buildings on the streets Domažlická, with Jaromír Krejcar, 1923–1924, Čechova, 1923–1924, and Evropská, 1924; villas in Chorvatská, 1924, and Milady Horákové, 1926; houses for the airport manager and porters on K letišti Street, 1934–1935; tombs of the Bohemian kings for the Cathedral of Saint Vitus, 1934–1935; building of the Ministry of Home Affairs on Milady Horákové Street, with Josef Kalous and Jan Zázvorka, 1935–1939; and a family house on Vlašská Street, 1939. Outside Prague Roškot built family houses in Zbraslav, 1924–1925, and Jílové, 1939–1940; a gymnasium in Vlašim, 1928; water locks in Vrané nad Vltavou, 1931–1939, and Brandýs nad Labem, 1931–1934; theater building in Ústí nad Orlicí, 1934–1935, and the Czechoslovak pavilions for the International Exposition in Milan, 1926–1927, Chicago, 1933, and New York, with Antonín Heythum, 1938–1939. Roškot was a visionary who tried to shape extensive urban areas into ideal geometrical formations that appeared to be cut out of solid material, as in his town-planning projects for the Prague quarter of Těšnov, 1927–1929, and Letná Plain, 1928–1929. Stylistically, Roškot based his work on a classicizing modern style, which he developed through the dual process of abstraction and monumentalization from the early twenties onward.

OLDŘICH TYL

12 April 1884, Ejpovice–4 April 1939, Prague

Architect. Studied under Josef Schulz at the Czech Polytechnic in Prague, 1902–1909, and worked in Matěj Blecha's architectural office until 1914. In 1922 he established his own architectural and building firm Tekta. Member of the Club of Architects and of the editorial board of *Stavba*. In Prague, he designed the administrative pavilion of the general hospital in Charles Square, in collaboration with Miloš Tereba, 1921–1926; apartment buildings on the streets Nezamyslova, 1922–1923, Žerotínova, 1923, Domažlická, 1923–1924, Benediktská, 1928–1929, Skořepka, 1928–1930, Masná, 1928–1930, Rooseveltova, 1929–1930, and Vršovická, 1930, and in Charles Square, 1933–1934; hostels in Kubelíkova, 1923–1926 and Žitná Street, 1926–1929; Trade Fair Palace in Dukelských hrdinů, with Josef Fuchs, 1924–

469

1928; Academic House on Spálená Street, 1928–1930; family house on the street Na čihadle, 1929; the Black Rose commercial building and arcade (Černá růže) on Panská Street, 1929–1933; multistory garages on Trojická Street, 1929–1933; and Police Headquarters on Přípotoční Street, 1932–1938, later rebuilt. Outside Prague he designed the synagogue in Milevsko, 1914–1919; hospital pavilions in Rakovník, 1921–1925, and Nová Paka, 1926–1927; apartment buildings in Rakovník, 1922–1923, and Olomouc, 1931–1932; savings bank in Uhříněves, 1926–1927; family house in Hořovice, 1934–1935. Tyl began as a cubist, and after 1922 he became one of the most significant representatives of Prague purism and functionalism. His buildings, the most prominent of which are the grandiose Trade Fair Palace and the elegant interior of the Black Rose arcade, combined an inclination toward utmost austerity and objectivity in the spirit of *Die Neue Sachlichkeit* with a taste for classical composition.

JOSEF ZASCHE
9 November 1871, Jablonec nad Nisou–11 November 1957, Schackensleben, Germany

Architect. Studied under Karl von Hasenauer at the Vienna Academy of Fine Arts, 1889–1892. His Prague works include villas on the streets Na Špejcharu, 1904–1905, Pod kaštany, 1922–1923, and Na Zátorce, 1927–1928; bank building of the Wiener Bankverein on Na Příkopě Street, with Alexander Neumann, 1906–1908; casino, 1906–1908; and office building, 1913–1915, in Maxim Gorky Square; office buildings in Opletalova Street, 1906–1907, on Rašín Embankment, with Jan Kotěra, 1912–1914, on Jungmannova Street, with Pavel Janák, 1922–1925; school building on Šimáčkova Street, 1929–1931; and apartment building with cinema on Klimentská Street, 1932–1933. Outside Prague he worked mainly in the German-speaking borderland, where he built two churches in Jablonec nad Nisou, 1903, 1930–1935; savings bank in Aš, 1904; school building in Počáply, 1905; family houses in Králův Dvůr, 1906, Jablonec nad Nisou, 1906, Teplice, 1912, Graz, Austria, 1930; library building in Ústí nad Labem, 1909; and bank building in Dvůr Králové, 1929. Zasche was the most significant architect of the Prague German minority after 1900. In his early work he followed the ornamental modern style, but from 1906 he returned to the tradition of austere classicism of the early nineteenth century, a style apparent in his major work, the bank building on Na příkopě Street. He often collaborated with Czech architects including Kotěra and Janák, as well as the functionalists Havlíček and Honzík, to whose project of the General Pensions Institute in Winston Churchill Square he allegedly contributed as consultant.

LADISLAV ŽÁK
25 June 1900, Prague–26 May 1973, Prague

Architect, furniture designer, theoretician of architecture, painter. Studied under Josef Gočár at the Prague Academy of Fine Arts, 1924–1927, where he was appointed associate professor of garden architecture and landscape planning. Member of Artists' Association *Mánes* and of the Czech chapter of CIAM. His Prague works include villas on the streets Na Babě and Na ostrohu, 1931–1932, Na vysočanských vinicích, 1932–1933, Na lysinách, 1935, and Neherovská, 1937. Between 1932 and 1936 Žák rebuilt his own apartment building on Korunovační Street into a "popular pension." Outside Prague, Žák designed and partially realized a memorial to the victims of Nazism in Ležáky, 1946–1951. Žák was a leading architect of the so-called aerodynamic and nautical functionalism in Prague architecture of the thirties. His villas for Prague artists and intellectuals, designed under Teige's influence, were conceived as prototypes of the socialist communal house, the *koldom*. His interest in residential gardens and landscapes resulted in the book *Obytná krajina* (The Residential Landscape), 1947. His concept of "pannaturalist socialism," however, clashed with the Stalinist dogma, and Žák retired in 1948.

471

COMPILED BY ROSTISLAV
ŠVÁCHA AND ZDENĚK LUKEŠ

The directory follows the Czech alphabetical order, placing accented consonants after unaccented ones and the letter "ch" after "h."

Abbreviations used:

(6 Bub, 200) = (Praha 6-Bubeneč, second house number 200)

(P 1923) = (project 1923)

Where this information is omitted, the year of design and construction is the same.

Boh = Bohnice	Koš = Košíře	StM = Staré Město
Bra = Braník	Krč = Krč	Str = Strašnice
Bře = Břevnov	Lib = Libeň	Stř = Střešovice
Dej = Dejvice	MaS = Malá Strana	Tró = Trója
DoL = Dolní Liboc	Mich = Michle	Vel = Veleslavín
Hod = Hodkovičky	Mot = Motol	Vin = Vinohrady
Hlu = Hlubočepy	NoM = Nové Město	Vok = Vokovice
Hol = Holešovice	Nus = Nusle	Vrš = Vršovice
Hos = Hostivař	Pod = Podolí	Vys = Vysočany
Hra = Hradčany	Ruz = Ruzyně	Záb = Záběhlice
Jos = Josefov	Smí = Smíchov	Žiž = Žižkov
Kar = Karlín		

STREETS

Albertov 4 (2 NoM, 2048 II), Alois Špalek, Purkyně Institute of Physiology, 1924–1925 (P 1923)

Americká 3 (2 Vin, 703), František Čermák, upper extension to apartment building, 1934–1935

Americká 12 (2 Vin, 316), Jaroslav Baťa, apartment building, 1939–1940

Americká 22 (2 Vin, 508), Václav Hudec, apartment building, 1937–1938

Andrštova 3, 5 (8 Lib, 1079, 1080), Julius Liebstein, apartment buildings, 1920–1921

Anenská 5 (1 StM, 186), František Kavalír, Methodist chapel, 1929–1931

Anglická 16 (2 Vin, 242), Ladislav Bartl, Antonín Knotek, apartment building with shops, 1934–1935

Anglická 17 (2 Vin, 391), Jan Majer-Josef Veselý, apartment building, 1911; portico designed by Pavel Albert Kopetzky, before 1930

Anglická 19 (2 Vin, 390), Bedřich Bendelmayer, apartment building with shops and offices, 1911

Anglická 25 (2 Vin, 384), Bohumír Kozák, apartment building, 1937–1938

Anny Letenské 7 (2 Vin, 34), Josef Kovařovic, apartment building, 1915–1916

Antonínská 4, 6 (7 Hol, 422, 423), Evžen Rosenberg, apartment buildings, 1936–1937

Apolinářská 3 (2 NoM, 436 II), Jan Jarolím, family house, 1932

Apolinářská 6 (2 NoM, 445), Josef Kalous, pension, 1932–1933

Baarova 5 (4 Mich, 1121), Jan Kotěra, waterworks, 1906–1907

Badeniho 1 (6 Hra, 290), Tomáš Amena, apartment building, 1913–1916

Badeniho 2 (7 Hol, 491), Miroslav Stöhr, family house, 1902; rebuilt by Vojtěch Tuka, 1915–1916

Badeniho 3 (6 Hra, 291), Vladislav Martínek, apartment building, 1913

Baranova 4 (3 Žiž, 1901), Rudolf Wels, Guido Lagus, apartment building, 1937–1938

Baranova 10 (3 Žiž, 1878), Václav Ložek, apartment building, 1935–1939

Baranova 22–28 (3 Žiž, 1517, 1518, 1587, 1588), Alois Dryák, apartment buildings, 1924–1926

Baranova 23, 25 (3 Žiž, 1803, 1904), Čeněk Nečásek, Jaroslav Lorenc, apartment building, 1932

Barrandovská 1 (5 Hlu, 165), Max Urban, restaurant, 1929; modified by Vladimír Grégr, 1929; swimming pool by Václav Kolátor, 1929–1923

Barrandovská 11 (5 Hlu), Otakar Štěpánek, family house, circa 1932

Barrandovská 13 (5 Hlu, 160), Alois Houba, family house, 1928–1930

Barrandovská 14 (5 Hlu), 158, Antonín Hloušek, František Niklas, family house, 1929–1930

Barrandovská 15 (5 Hlu, 155), Vojtěch Krch, family house, 1929–1930

Barrandovská 16 (5 Hlu, 177), Vladimír Grégr, family house, 1931–1932 (P 1930)

Barrandovská 17 (5 Hlu, 444), Vladimír Grégr, family house, 1939–1941

Barrandovská 20 (5 Hlu), 190), Vladimír Grégr, family house, 1932

Barrandovská 22 (5 Hlu, 268), Ladislav Syrový, Jaroslav Fragner(?), family house, 1937

Barrandovská 24 (5 Hlu, 186), Bruno Rücker, family house, 1932, 1940–1941

Barrandovská 25 (5 Hlu, 307), Vladimír Grégr, family house, 1936

Barrandovská 29 (5 Hlu, 385), František Albert Libra, family house, 1937

Barrandovská 46, (5 Hlu, 180), Vladimír Grégr, family house, 1931–1932

Barrandovská 60 (5 Hlu, 335), Heřman Abeles, Leo Mayer, family house, 1933–1934

Bartolomějská 1 (1 StM, 304), Hilar Pacanovský, apartment building, 1936

Bartolomějská 3 (1 StM, 305), Václav Kopecký, apartment building, 1937–1938

Bartolomějská 7 (1 StM, 307), Bohumír Kozák, office building, 1936–1940

Bartolomějská 10, 12 (1 StM, 310), Karel Roštík, office building, 1936

Bělehradská 96 (2 Vin, 644), Arnošt Mühlstein, Victor Fürth, apartment building with shops, 1934–1936

Bělehradská 120 (2 Vin, 234), Václav Kopecký, apartment building with shops, 1929–1930

Bělehradská 130 (2 Vin, 269), Jan Matoušek, apartment building, 1932–1933

Bělohorská 36 (6 Bře, 1937), Vladimír Maršal, apartment building with shops, 1937

Bělohorská 156 (6 Bře, 1228), Josef Kříž, power station with a dwelling, circa 1930

Bělohorská 177–189 (6 Bře, 454, 455, 513–516), František Havlena, family duplexes, 1923–1924

Benátská (2 NoM, 499), Ferdinand Balcárek, Karel Kopp, hospital boiler house, 1937

Benediktská 2 (1 StM, 685), Ervín Katona, K. Fischl, office building, 1928–1929

Benediktská 6 (1 StM, 688), Karel Frisch, apartment building with shops, 1928–1929

Benediktská 8 (1 StM, 689), Oldřich Tyl, apartment building with shops, 1928–1929

Benediktská 11 (1 StM, 722), Ladislav Šimek, Josef Šimůnek, apartment building, 1939–1940

Benešovská 5–33 (10 Vin, 1858–1890), Tomáš Pražák, Pavel Moravec, family houses, 1923–1924

Benešovská 42 (10 Vin, 2398), Josef Rein, apartment building, 1939–1940

Benešovská 114 (10 Vrš, 818) Vlastimil Brožek, Jan Mentberger, Karel Polívka, family house, 1930–1931

Besední 3 (1 MaS, 487), František Janda, Čeněk Vořech, cultural venue and residential dwelling of the cultural organisation *Umělecká beseda*, 1924–1925 (P 1923–1924)

Bílá 5 (6 Dej, 1615), Jan Zázvorka, apartment buildings, 1930

Bílkova 6 (1 Jos, 122), Josef Kovařovic, apartment building, 1912

Bílkova 8 (1 Jos, 6) František Novotný, apartment building, 1912–1913

Bílkova 13, 15 (1 StM, 884) František Velich, apartment building, 1905

Biskupský dvůr 7 (1 NoM, 1146) Arnošt Mühlstein, Victor Fürth, office building, 1929

Blanická 15 (2 Vin, 2028), Arnošt Mühlstein, Victor Fürth, commercial and apartment building, 1926–1928

Blanická 22 (2 Vin, 1787) Miloš Vaněček, Richard Klenka, apartment building with shops, 1922–1923

Boční 32 (4 Záb, 650), Vlastimil Brožek, Karel Polívka, family house with doctor's surgery, 1927

Boleslavova 9 (4 Nus, 45) Karel Hannauer Sr., apartment building, 1913

Boleslavská 4, 6 (3 Vin, 1776, 1777), Václav Zákostelna, apartment buildings, 1931–1932

Bozděchova 1 (5 Smí, 29), Stanislav Brázda, apartment building, 1936

Bozděchova 9 (5 Smí, 637) Ferdinand Fencl, apartment building, circa 1940

Božkova 3 (6 Dej, 1784), Jan Gillar, French Schools, 1932–1934 (P 1931–1932)

Božkova 13 (6 Dej, 1610), Miroslav Brych, apartment building, 1938–1939

Branická 94 (4 Bra, 447), Vojtěch Krch, Jaroslav Mašek, family house with studio, 1927–1928

Bratří Čapků 18 (10 Vin, 1848), Ladislav Machoň, family house, 1923–1924; extension by Bedřich Bendelmayer, 1929

Bratří Čapků 21, (10 Vin, 1842), Tomáš Pražák, Pavel Moravec, family house, 1923–1924

Bratří Čapků 25 (10 Vin, 1840), Ladislav Machoň, family house, 1923–1924

Bratří Čapků 28, 30 (10 Vin, 1853, 1854), Ladislav Machoň, family duplex of Josef and Karel Čapek, 1923–1924 (P 1922)

Bratří Čapků 32 (10 Vin, 1855), Bohumír Kozák, family house, 1923–1924

Břehová 3 (1 Jos, 43), Antonín Engel, family duplex, 1913–1915

Břehová 6 (1 Jos, 209), V. Pickl, Václav Vejrych, apartment building, 1908–1922

Břehová 7 (1 StM, 78) Josef Sakař, Ministry of Commerce and school building, 1920–1922

Březinova 11 (8 Kar, 495), Emil Králíček, Matěj Blecha, apartment building, 1908

Březinova 29 (8 Kar, 473), Ferdinand Brož, apartment building, 1905

Březinova 31 (8 Kar, 524), Václav Klatovský, apartment building, 1910

Bubenečská 25 (6 Bub, 347), Jaroslav Vondrák, apartment building, 1911

Bubenečská 27 (6 Bub, 388), Jaroslav Vondrák, apartment building, 1913

Bubenečská 28 (6 Bub, 810), František Vahala, family house, 1929

Bubenečská 51, 53 (6 Bub, 495, 496), Jaroslav Vondrák, apartment buildings, 1922

Bubenečská 57 (6 Bub, 606), Bedřich Bendelmayer, family house, 1923

Bubenská 1 (7 Hol, 1477), Adolf Benš, Josef Kříž, Prague Power Company building, 1927–1935

Bubenská 3 (7 Hol, 421), Josef Gočár, apartment building, 1935–1936

Budečská 33, 35 (2 Vin, 2165), Jan Jarolím, commercial and apartment building with dance hall and cinema, 1927–1929

Budějovická 72 (4 Krč, 559), Nikola Dobrovič, commercial and residential building, 1927–1930

Budínova 2 (8 Lib, 67), František Velich, (1909–1913), Karel Roštík (1927–1928), Jan Rosůlek (pavilion above Bulovka Street, 1935–1936), Vladislav Martínek, Mečislav Petrů, Vratislav Lhota and others, Bulovka Hospital buildings

Bulharská 29–41 (10 Vrš, 714–720, 705–711), František Albert Libra, apartment buildings, 1925–1926

Buštěhradská 17–25 (6 Stř, 952–956), Miloš Vaněček, Bohumil Švarc, family houses, 1926–1928

Buzulucká 8, 10 (6 Dej, 570) Karel Polívka, apartment buildings, 1926–1927

Bylanská 7, 9 (10 Str, 326), Karel Koníček, family duplex, 1920

Bylanská 17–27 (10 Str, 314–319), Josef Gočár, Pavel Janák, Josef Zavadil, family houses, 1919–1921

Celetná 15 (1 StM, 596), Josef Gočár, Baťa architectural studio, commercial and apartment building, 1934 (P 1933)

Celetná 30 (1 StM, 567), Friedrich Ohmann, commercial and apartment building At the Bohemian Eagle, 1896–1897

Cukrovarnická 1 (6 Stř, 563), Maxmilian Duchoslav, family house, 1926–1927

Cukrovarnická 10 (6 Stř, 112), Josef Záruba-Pfeffermann, Antonín Mendl(?), school building, 1923

Cukrovarnická 11 (6 Stř, 495), Ladislav Machoň, family house, 1923–1924

Cukrovarnická 22 (6 Stř, 491), Ladislav Machoň, family house, 1923–1924

Cukrovarnická 24 (6 Stř, 492), Pavel Janák, family house of painter Vincenc Beneš, 1923–1924

Cukrovarnická 25, 27, (6 Stř, 359, 360), Jaroslav Vondrák, family duplex, 1922

Cukrovarnická 39 (6 Stř, 649), Josef Kalous, family house, 1931

Cukrovarnická 51 (6 Stř, 778), František Fiala(?), Josef Kadlec, family house of sculptor Břetislav Benda, 1932

Cukrovarnická 53 (6 Stř, 777), Jaroslav Kučera, family house, 1932

Čáslavská 1 (3 Vin, 1791), František Roith, apartment building, 1922

Čáslavská 15 (3 Vin, 1793), František Matějíček, apartment building, 1922–1923

Čechova 7 (7 Bub, 217), Josef Havlíček, facade, 1927

Čechova 9 (7 Bub, 239), Antonín Balšánek, apartment building, 1904

Čechova 11, 13 (7 Bub, 514, 515), Bohumír Kozák, apartment buildings, 1921–1923

Čechova 16 (7 Bub, 282), Ferdinand Šamonil, apartment building, 1908

Čechova 17 (7 Bub, 236), Rudolf Stockar, reconstruction and extension to apartment building, 1932

Čechova 20, 22 (7 Bub, 294, 295), Václav Řezníček, apartment buildings, 1909

Čechova 29 (7 Bub, 587), Kamil Roškot, family house, 1924 (P 1923), modified by Ladislav Machoň, 1936

Černá 9 (1 NoM, 646), František Xaver Čtrnáctý, Antonín Parkman, school building, 1927–1928

Černá 14 (1 NoM, 1610), Jaromír Krejcar, Jindřich Pollert, rebuilding of Karel Teige's apartment building, 1928 (P 1927)

Černokostelecká 9 (10 Str, 178), Václav Ittner, rebuilding of family house, 1936

Černokostelecká 88 (10 Str, 1504, 1168), František Souček, family house, 1932

České družiny 3 (6 Dej, 1647), Miloslav Kopřiva, family house, 1932

České družiny 7, 9 (6 Dej, 1672, 1671), Magda Jansová, family houses, 1932

České družiny 19 (6 dej, 1947), Antonín Mendl, family house, 1936

Českomalínská 11, 13 (6 Bub, 527, 528), Jaroslav Vondrák, apartment buildings, 1922–1923

Českomalínská 15 (6 Bub, 592), Čeněk Vořech, František Janda, apartment building, 1923–1924

Českomalínská 16 (6 Bub, 767), Eduard Žáček, apartment building, 1927

Českomalínská 23 (6 Bub, 777), Václav Ort, apartment building, 1928

Českomalínská 41 (6 Bub, 519), Arnošt Mühlstein, Victor Fürth, family house, 1923

Českomoravská 25 (9 Vys, ?), Matěj Blecha, apartment building, 1913–1914, demolished 1987

Československá armády 4, 6 (6 Bub, 346, 345), Jaroslav Vondrák, apartment buildings, 1911

Československá armády 7 (6 Bub, 369), Jan Petrák, apartment building, 1912

Československá armády 17, 19 (6 Bub, 927, 926), Arnošt Mühlstein, Victor Fürth, apartment buildings, 1932–1933

Československá armády 27 (6 Bub, 471), J. Fiedler(?), office building, no later than 1924

Čimická 72 (8 Kob, 776), Ludvík Kysela, family house, 1928

Čimická 76 (8 Kob, 772), Richard Ferdinand Podzemný, family house, 1941

Čínská 12 (6 Bub, 884), Jan Žák, family house, 1931

Dačického 8 (4 Nus, 1225), Karel Hannauer, apartment building, 1936–1937

Dejvická 3 (6 Dej, 209), Jindřich Řehoř, apartment building, 1937–1938

Dejvická 36 (6 Bub, 555), Jaroslav Vondrák, apartment building, 1923

Děkanská vinice I 16 (4 Nus, 819), Karel Hannauer, apartment building, 1937–1938

Dělnická 3 (7 Hol, 217), Čeněk Nečásek, bakery extension, 1924

Dělnická 21 (7 Hol, 417), Josef Chochol, apartment building, 1939–1940

Dělnická 55 (7 Hol, 1150, 1151, 1248, 1249), Karel Roštík, Bohumír Kozák, apartment buildings, 1920–1921 (P 1919)

Dělnická 65–71 (7 Hol, 1067, 1481, 1484, 1485), Josef Martínek, apartment buildings, 1936–1937

Dělostřelecká 17 (6 Stř, 553), Josef Kalous, family house, 1928–1929 (P 1926)

Dělostřelecká 33–34 (6 Stř, 233–238), František Vahala, family houses, 1920

Dittrichova 9 (2 NoM, 337), Josef Mařík, apartment building, 1929–1930

Dittrichova 11, 13 (2 NoM, 338, 349), František Kavalír, Bohumil Steigenhöfer, apartment buildings, 1930–1931

Dittrichova 15, 17 (2 NoM, 329, 330), Matěj Blecha, apartment buildings, 1920–1922

Dittrichova 19 (2 NoM, 328), Josef Chochol, Chamber of Engineers association building and apartment building, 1923–1925

Dobrovského 15 (7 Hol, 375), Rudolf Wels, Guido Lagus, apartment building, 1935

Dobrovského 38, 40 (7 Hol, 1074, 1075), Rudolf Stockar, apartment buildings, 1911

Dobrušská (4 Bra, 879), Felix Paukert, family house, 1939–1940

Dobrušská 13 (4 Bra, 538), František Míšek, family house, 1931

Dolnoměcholupská 15 (10 Hos, 253), Bohumil Hypšman, apartment building, 1920–1923

Domažlická 2, 4 (3 Žiž, 1505, 1506), Rudolf Hrabě, apartment buildings, 1924–1926

Domažlická 8 (3 Žiž, 1488), Oldřich Tyl, apartment building, 1923–1924

Domažlická 10 (3 Žiž, 1479), Jaromír Krejcar, Kamil Roškot, apartment building, 1924 (P 1923)

Dr. Zikmunda Wintra 23 (6 Bub, 796), Jan Zázvorka, apartment building, 1930

Drtinova 1 (5 Smí, 1861), Jaroslav Rössler, high school building, 1926–1928

Družstevní ochoz 22–30 (4 Nus, 1303–1307), Jan Gillar, apartment building, 1936–1937

Dřevná 2 (2 NoM, 382), František Roith, apartment building, 1911–1912

Dřevná 4 (2 NoM, 381), Rudolf Stockar, apartment building, 1911–1912

Dukelských hrdinů 7 (7 Hol, 1500), Oldřich Tyl, Josef Fuchs, former Trade Fair Palace, 1924–1928

Dukelských hrdinů 17 (7 Hol, 848), František Velich, municipal baths, 1904

Dukelských hrdinů 21, 23 (7 Hol, 359, 406), František Voráček, apartment buildings with garages, 1930–1940

Dušní 11 (1 Jos, 8), Josef Limax, apartment building, 1913–1914

Dušní 17 (1 StM, 900), Emil Králíček, school building, 1922

Dvacátého osmého pluku 21 (Vrš, 575), Karel Vítězslav Mašek, apartment building, 1910

Dvacátého osmého října 11 (1 St M, 376), Friedrich Ohmann, apartment building with shops, 1894–1895

Dvacátého osmého října 13 (1 StM, 377), Matěj Blecha, Celda Klouček, Prague Credit Bank, 1900–1902

Dykova 1 (10 Vin, 51), Pavel Janák, Husův sbor (evangelical meeting house) and apartment building, 1932–1933 (P 1931); Jiří Jakub, renovation of columbarium, 1937

Dykova 4 (10 Vin, 960), Ladislav Machoň, rebuilding of family house, 1926–1928

Dykova 6 (10 Vin, 1039), Alois Dryák, family house, 1898–1899

Dykova 16 (10 Vin, 999), František Marek, family house, 1938

Dykova 20 (10 Vin, 50), Milada Pavlíková-Petříková, Theodor Petřík, almshouse for women, 1923, 1928

Ďáblická (8 Ďáblice), Vlastislav Hofman, cemetery wall and gate with twin kiosks, 1912–1914

Eliášova 5 (6 Dej, 273), Ladislav Skřivánek, Josef Paroulek, apartment house, 1911

Eliášova 12 (6 Dej, 327), Karel Herman, apartment building, 1912

Eliášova 19, 21 (6 Bub, 921, 922), Bohumil Kněžek, Josef Václavík, apartment buildings, 1939–1940

Eliášova 50 (6 Bub, 763), Josef Havlíček, apartment building, circa 1935–1938 (P 1927)

Elišky Krásnohorské 7 (1 Jos, 135), Bohuslav Homoláč, apartment building, 1910–1911

Elišky Krásnohorské 10–14 (1 StM, 123, 1021, 1037), Otakar Novotný, apartment buildings, 1919–1921

Elišky Krásnohorské 11 (1 Jos, 133), Vendelín Hron, apartment building, 1910–1911

Elišky Krásnohorské (1 Jos, 123), Vratislav Lhota, tradesmen's house, 1913–1919

Erbenova 3 (5 Koš, 228), Ferdinand Šamonil, apartment building, 1905

Evropská 6–10 (6 Dej, 515–517), Kamil Roškot, apartment buildings, 1924

Evropská 18, 20 (6 Dej, 694, 695) Alex Hanuš, apartment buildings, 1926–1929

Evropská 24 (6 Dej, 529), Václav Ort, Igor Landa, apartment building, 1927–1928

Evropská 33 (6 Dej, 330), Evžen Linhart, high school building, 1937–1938

Evropská 36 (6 Dej, 214), Karel Janů, Jiří Štursa, apartment building, 1937–1938

Evropská 155–167 (6 Vel, 261–267), Josef Kříž(?), apartment buildings, 1932–1933

Farní 13–17 (6 Stř, 727–729), František Kavalír, apartment buildings, 1928–1931

Farní 21, 23 (6 St, 879), J. and F. Kotrba, apartment buildings, 1936–1937

Farského 3 (7 Hol, 1386), Franta Kubelka, apartment building with evangelical meeting hall (Husův sbor), 1935–1937.

Farského 4 (7 Hol, 425), Julius Landsmann, Martin Reiner, apartment building, 1936

Fetrovská 12 (6 Dej, 910), Antonín Mendl, family house, 1932

Fialková 12–26 (10 Záb, 1264–1271), Alex Hanuš, Zdeněk Kruliš, Vladimír Vlček, family houses, 1928–1929

Fialova 3 (6 Dej, 1633), Vojtěch Krch, own family house, 1931–1932

Fibichova 19, 21 (3 Žiž, 1500), Bohumír Kozák, telegraph and telephone exchange, 1922–1926(?)

Filmařská 3 (5 Hlu, 336), Jaroslav Fröhlich, family house, 1934

Filmařská 4 (5 Hlu, 337), Vladimír Grégr, family house, 1934–1935

Filmařská 9 (5 Hlu, 404), Vilém Lorenc, Jan Čermák, family house, 1938–1939

Filmařská 10 (5 Hlu, 384), Václav Girsa, family house, 1936–1937

Finkovská 1 (6 Dej, 1663), Karel Lhota, family house, 1936–1937

Foersterova 9 (10 Str, 1051), František and Václav Beneš, family house of composer J. B. Foerster, 1938

Francouzská 4 (2 Vin, 75), Jaromír Krejcar, club, offices and apartment building of the Association of Private Clerical Employees, 1930–1931 (P 1927–1930)

Francouzská 14 (2 Vin, 175), Josef Mach, apartment building with shops, 1938–1939

Francouzská 22 (2 Vin, 145), Antonín J. Novotný, apartment building, circa 1930

Františka Křížka 1 (7 Hol, 362), Antonín Hrubý, factory, 1907–1908

Františka Křížka 10 (7 Hol, 1173), Bohuslav Homoláč, apartment building, 1912–1914

Františka Křížka 11–15 (7 Hol, 460, 461), Josef Šolc, apartment buildings with cinema, 1938–1939

Františka Křížka 14, 16 (7 Hol, 402, 403), František Magnusek, apartment buildings, 1936

Františka Křížka 18 (7 Hol, 515) Otto Zucker, apartment building, 1933–1935

Františka Křížka 22 (7 Hol, 683), Antonín Vítek, Baťa design studio and shop, 1935

Františka Křížka 32, 34 (7 Hol, 1163, 1164), Karel Beran, apartment buildings, 1919–1923

Gabčíkova 3 (8 Lib, 1385), Alois Houba, František Kavalír, family house, 1930–1931

Glinkova 14 (6 Dej, 1659), Jaroslav Fragner, family house, 1932

Gogolova 1 (1 Hra, 212), Friedrich Ohmann, family house, 1908–1911

Gogolova 2 (1 Hra, 225), Alois Čenský, family house, 1911

Gogolova 8 (1 Hra, 228), František Schlaffer, family house, 1911

Gorazdova 11 (1 NoM, 1995), Jan Petrák, family house, 1907

Grafická 40 (5 Smí, 1296), Jaroslav Mayer, Alois Zázvorka, apartment building, 1213

Gymnaziální 1 (6 Dej, 510), Rudolf Hrabě, school and laundry, 1922–1925

Hálkova 11 (2 NoM, 1629), J. R. Moschner, apartment building, 1937–1938

Haškova 1, 3 (7 Hol, 393), Jaroslav Gruber(?), František Troníček, apartment buildings, 1936–1937

Haškova 2, 4 (7 Hol, 1157, 1175), Bohumír Kozák, Otto Máca, apartment buildings, 1915–1917

Haštalská 4, 6 (1 StM, 749, 1072), Osvald Polívka, Václav Vítězslav Chytrý, Václav Havel, apartment buildings, 1901–1902

Haštalská 20 (1 StM, 731), Rudolf Winternitz, office building, 1928–1929(?)

Havanská 4 (7 Bub, 450), Adolf Liebscher, apartment building, 1920–1921

Havanská 14 (7 Bub, 131), Václav Pospíšil, apartment building, 1938–1939

Havelská 6 (1 StM, 522), Friedrich Ohmann, apartment building At the Golden Cross, 1890

Havelská 29 (1 StM, 469), Rudolf Eisler, apartment building, 1938–1939

Hellichova 13 (1 MaS, 300), Karel Popp, kindergarten building, 1936–1937 (P 1935)

Hermelínská 6 (6 Dej, 1203), Karel Caivas, Vladimír Weiss, apartment building, 1934

Heřmanova 8, 10 (7 Hol, 1087, 1088), Leopold Neugebauer, apartment buildings, 1912–1913

Heřmanova 9 (7 Hol, 1119), Josef Gočár(?), apartment building, 1922–1924

Heřmanova 12 (7 Hol, 408), Emanuel Hruška, apartment building, 1936

Heřmanova 24 (7 Hol, 1168), Václav Zákostelna, apartment building, 1914–1915

Heřmanova 26 (7 Hol, 1167), V. Nekvasil architects & building contractors, apartment building, 1922

Heřmanova 33 (7 hol, 742), A. Ackermann, apartment building, 1936

Heřmanova 46 (7 Hol, 836), Jan Zázvorka, apartment building, 1926–1927

Hládkov 6 (6 Stř, 703), Vlastimil Lada, Josef Hlaváček, apartment building, 1931–1933

Hlavní 6 (4 Záb, 1152), Vlastimil Brožek, Karel Polívka, apartment building, 1930

Hlavní 92–102 (4 Záb, 1590–1595), Vlastimil Brožek, Karel Polívka, apartment buildings, 1928

Hlubočepská 31 (5 Hlu, 409), Kurt Spielmann, apartment building, 1937–1938

Hlubočepská 70 (5 Hlu, attached to No. 94), František Albert Libra, factory, circa 1937–1939

Holandská 52 (10 Vrš, 1052), Josef Gočár, apartment building facade, 1930–1932

Holečkova 6 (5 Smí, 105), Bohumil Hypšman, family house, 1924–1927

Holečkova 66 (5 Smí, 1785), Berthold Schwarz, family house, 1926–1927

Holečkova 72–78 (5 Smí, 2464, 2477, 2282, 2284), Eduard Bíba, apartment buildings, 1937–1940

Holubova 1 (5 Smí, 2527), Josef Beneš, family house, 1931–1932

Holubova 3–9 (5 Smí, 2526), Josef Domek, family houses, 1925–1926

Hornokrčská 23 (4 Krč, 698), Jan Rejchl, apartment building, 1934

Hošťálkova 68, 70 (6 Bře, 689, 690), Emil Šulc, family duplex, 1927–1928

Hošťálkova 99 (6 Bře, 1138), Jiří Palička, family house, 1936

Hradební 7 (1 StM, 940), Emil Králíček, Matěj Blecha, pension, 1907–1908

Hradecká 18 (3 Vin, 92), Antonín Moudrý, apartment building, 1937–1939

Hradeckých 5 (4 Nus, 882), Jan Zázvorka, apartment building, 1930–1931

Hradešínská 6 (10 Vin, 1542), Jan Kotěra, own family house, 1908–1909

Hradešínská 9 (10 Vin, 1429), Vojtěch Sedláček, family house, 1905

Hradešínská 26 (10 Vin, 1770), František Albert Libra, Josef Rein, family house, 1921–1922

Hradešínská 27 (10 Vin, 2373), Viktor Lampl, Otto Fuchs, apartment building, 1937–1938

Hradešínská 29 (10 Vin, 2362), František Řehák, apartment building, 1936–1937

Hradešínská 33 (10 Vin, 2374), Josef Douda, apartment building, 1937

Hradešínská 37 (10 Vin, 2334), Josef Douda, Vladimír Holeček, apartment building, 1935–1936

Hradešínská 39–41 (10 Vin, 2319, 2320), Václav Šourek, apartment building, 1934–1935

Hradešínská 53–59 (10 Vin, 2408–2410), Vladimír Holeček, apartment buildings, 1939–1940

Humpolecká 6–16 (4 Krč, 521), Jarmila Lisková, Ivan Šula, apartment buildings, 1937

Humpolecká 22–26 (4 Krč, 556), František Albert Libra, Jiří Kan, apartment buildings, 1936–1938

Husitská 32 (3 Žiž, 753), Bohuslav Homoláč, apartment building, 1913–1914

Husitská 44, 46 (3 Žiž, 790, 791), Theodor Petřík, K. Manday, apartment building, 1918

Hybernská 5 (1 NoM, 1034), Josef Gočár, rebuilding of the Anglo-Czechoslovak Bank, 1923–1926

Hybernská 7 (1 NoM, 1033 — courtyard), Jaroslav Lorenc, Čeněk Nečásek, cinema, 1934–1935

Hybernská 10 (1 NoM, 1001), Friedrich Ohmann, Bedřich Bendelmayer, Alois Dryák, Hotel Central, 1899–1901; theater building redesigned by Petr Kropáček, 1929

Hybešova 5 (8 Kar, 519), Emil Králíček, Matěj Blecha, apartment building, circa 1910

Hybešova 9, 11 (8 Kar, 550, 551), Karel Špera, Jan Soukup, apartment buildings, 1920

Hybešova 10 (8 Kar, 14), Josef Sakař, Karlín Municipal House, 1911

Charlese de Gaulla 11, 13 (6 Bub, 540, 541), Josef Karel Říha, apartment buildings, 1923–1925

Charlese de Gaulla 16 (6 Bub, 832), Egon Votický, family house, 1937–1938

Charlese de Gaulla 22 (6 Bub, 816), Jaromír Krejcar, Richard Gibian's family house, 1927–1929

Charlese de Gaulla 25 (6 Bub, 914), Stanislav Tobek, family house, 1939–1940

Charlese de Gaulla 27 (6 Bub, 915), Bedřich Ehrmann, family house, 1929–1930

Charvátova 10 (1 NoM, 39), František Zelenka, Oldřich Starý, office building, 1938

Chittussiho 14 (6 Bub, 45), Arnošt Mühlstein, Victor Fürth, family house, 1934

Chodská 2 (2 Vin, 1705), Emil Králíček, Josef Veselý, apartment building, 1913–1914

Chopinova 4 (2 Vin, 1543), Jan Kotěra, Jan Laichter's family house, 1908–1909

Chopinova 6 (2 Vin, 1556), Bohumil Waigant, apartment building, 1909–1910

Chopinova 8 (2 Vin, 1564), Bohumil Waigant(?), apartment building, 1909

Chorvatská 7 (10 Vin, 1969), Kamil Roškot, family house, 1924–1925

Chorvatská 12 (10 Vin, 2316), Antonín Nesnídal, apartment building, 1935

Chorvatská 14 (10 Vin, 2268), Stanislav Brázda, apartment building, 1931–1932

Chrudimská 4 (3 Vin, 2364), Jaroslav and Karel Fišer, apartment building, 1936

Chrudimská 5–7 (3 Vin, 2158), František Maria Černý, apartment buildings, 1928–1929

Jáchymova 3 (1 Jos, 63), Rudolf Schlosser, association building, 1907–1908

Jana Masaryka 18, 20 (2 Vin, 1993, 1994), Alois Dryák, apartment buildings, 1926–1927

Jana Masaryka 46 (2 Vin, 312), Hilar Pacanovský, apartment building, 1939–1940

Jana Želivského 2 (3 Žiž, 2200), Karel Caivas, Vladimír Weiss, goods station, 1934-before 1937

Jankovcova 37 (7 Hol, 778, 785, 1057–1059), František Sander, docks buildings, 1905

Jankovská 6 (4 Krč, 526), František Albert Libra, Jiří Kan, apartment building, 1932–1933

Janovského 17 (7 Hol, 986), František Novotný, apartment building with post office, 1914

Janovského 27 (7 Hol, 447), Josef Martínek, apartment building, 1935

Janovského 28 (7 Hol, 195), Arnošt Mühlstein, Victor Fürth, apartment building, 1934–1935

Jarní 3 (6 Dej, 1798), Josef Gočár, family house, 1933–1934

Jaromírova 2 (2 Nus, 789), František Matějíček, apartment building, 1929

Jaromírova 13 (2 Nus, 759), Karel Hannauer, apartment building, 1928; modified by Jaroslav Fragner, 1939

Jaromírova 38 (2 Nus, 1036), Vladimír Šeda, apartment building, 1931

Jaselská 11 (6 Dej, 291), Josef, Jaroslav and Vratislav Mayer, apartment building, 1910

Jasná 10 (4 Bra, 742), Jindřich Homoláč, family house, 1939

Jateční 25, 27 (7 Hol, 1224, 1225), Oldřich Tyl, apartment building, 1926

Jaurisova 11 (4 Nus, 1484), Alfred Schwarz, apartment building, 1925(?)

Ječná 2 (2 NoM, 550), Karel Roštík, Theodor Petřík, apartment building with shops, 1911–1912

Ječná 29 (2 NoM, 529), Karel Kotas, apartment building with shops, 1936–1937

Jenštejnská 1 (2 NoM, 1966), Josef Fanta, student dormitory halls, 1903–1904 (P 1902)

Jeruzalémská 2 (1 NoM, 1321), František Albert Libra, power transformation station, 1926–1930

Jeruzalémská 3 (1 NoM, 962), František Krásný, extension to the bank building, 1933–1935

Jeseniova 87 (3 Žiž, 1924), Stanislav Kohout, apartment building, 1938–1939

Jeseniova 121 (3 Žiž, 1596), Emil Jech, apartment building, 1926–1928

Jeseniova 123 (3 Žiž, 1726), Otto Grams, apartment building, 1929–1932

Jičínská (3 Vin, 2285), Rudolf Stockar, apartment building, 1932

Jičínská 10 (3 Vin, 2348), Jaroslav Vančura, apartment building, 1935–1936

Jičínská 35–39 (3 Žiž, 1797), Emil Jech, apartment buildings, 1931–1932

Jičínská 43 (3 Žiž, 1775), Evžen Linhart(?), apartment building, 1929–1932

Jihozápadní V 28 (4 Záb, 998), Vlastimil Brožek, Karel Polívka, family house, 1929

Jílovská 3 (4 Lho, 349), Jiří Jakub, family house, 1940

Jílovská 9 (4 Lho, 351), Václav Hilský, Rudolf Jasenský, family house, 1940–1941

Jilská 4 (1 StM, 353), Josef Fanta, rebuilding of house and restaurant, 1908–1911

Jindřišská 15 (1 NoM, 1308), Josef Gočár, rebuilding of bank building, 1922–1923
(P 1921)

Jindřišská 17 (1 NoM, 889), Antonín Pfeiffer, bank building, 1923–1926

Jindřišská 27 (1 NoM, 873), Josef Chochol, rebuilding of office and commercial building, 1920–1921; modified by Leo Lauermann, 1931–1932

Jirečkova 4 (7 Hol, 1073), Bohumil Hypšman, apartment building, 1911

Jižní IV 10 (4 Záb, 1750), Vlastimil Brožek, Karel Polívka, school building, 1929–1931, 1933–1934

Jižní VII 13, 15 (4 Záb, 1070, 1071), Vlastimil Brožek, Karel Polívka, family duplex, 1928

José Martího (6 Vel, 258, 259), Josef Kříž, administrative building and porters' lodge of the depot, 1932–before 1938

Juárezova 12 (6 Bub, 428), Arnošt Mühlstein, Victor Fürth, family house, 1922

Jugoslávská 1 (2 Vin, 934), Tomáš Pražák, Pavel Moravec, extension to school building, 1926–1928

Jungmannova 5 (1 NoM, 18), Václav Ložek, department store, 1932

Jungmannova 7 (1 NoM, 19, 20), František Roith, office and apartment building, 1934–1935

Jungmannova 9 (1 NoM, 22), Bohumír Kozák, Hus's House, 1923

Jungmannova 15 (1 NoM, 26), Osvald Polívka, publishing house offices and apartment building, 1908–1912

Jungmannova 16 (1 NoM, 737), František Jech, office and apartment building, 1937–1938

Jungmannova 21 (1 NoM, 30), Viktor Lampl, Otto Fuchs, rebuilding of office and commercial building, 1922–1923

Jungmannova 28 (1 NoM, 747), Arnošt Mühlstein, Victor Fürth, commercial and apartment building, 1933

Jungmannova 29 (1 NoM, 35, 41), Pavel Janák, Škoda office building, 1924–1926 (P 1923–1924)

Jungmannova 30 (1 NoM, 748), Jan Kotěra, Urbánek's commercial and apartment building with a concert hall, Mozarteum, 1912–1913

Jungmannova 31 (1 NoM, 36), Pavel Janák, Josef Zasche, Adrie office and commercial building with a theater, 1922–1925

Jungmannova 32 (1 NoM, 749), V. A. Beneš, apartment building with shops, 1925

Jungmannova 34 (1 NoM, 750), Fritz Lehmann, office and commercial building, 1929–1931

K Brusce 6 (6 Hra, 282), Václav Vacek, apartment building, 1914

K Brusce 6 (6 Hra, 124), Josef Gočár, apartment building, 1922–1923

K Habrovce 8 (4 Krč, 675), Lev Krča, Stanislav Tobek, Jaroslav Kincl, family house, 1934

K letišti 2 (6 Ruz, 550), Adolf Benš, control tower and main building of the airport, 1932–1934

K letišti (6 Ruz, 533), Kamil Roškot, porters' lodge of the airport, 1935 (P 1935)

K letišti (6 Ruz, 536–543), Vojtěch Kerhart, apartment buildings, 1936

K letišti, (6 Ruz, 544–546), Kamil Roškot, family duplex, 1935 (P 1934)

K letišti (6 Ruz, ?), Bohumil Sláma, Eduard Hnilička, Ferdinand Hruška, hangars, 1932–1937

K Moravině 5 (9 Lib, 1872), Bohumil Švarc, apartment building, 1938

K novému dvoru 24 (4 Lho, 222), Jan Chomutovský, family house estate, 1932

K Rybníčkům 17 (10 Str, 620), Emil Moravec, family house, 1923–1926

Kadeřávkovská 9 (6 Dej, 1074), Jaroslav Fröhlich, family house, before 1931

Kadeřávkovská 11 (6 Dej, 1073), Theodor Petřík, Milada Pavlíková-Petříková, family house, 1929

Kafkova 16 (6 Dej, 605), Jaroslav Vondrák, apartment building, 1926–1927

Kafkova 20 (6 Dej, 608), Zdeněk Husák, apartment building, 1928

Kafkova 22 (6 Dej, 1676), Josef Václavík, apartment building, 1931

Kafkova 23–29 (6 Dej, 544–547), Josef Havlíček, apartment buildings, 1925–1926(?)

Kafkova 32, 34 (6 Dej, 679, 680), Vladimír Wallenfels, apartment buildings, 1926–1927

Kamenická 1 (7 Hol, 365), Rudolf Hildebrand, apartment building, 1937–1939

Kamenická 5 (7 Hol, 673), Jaroslav Vondrák, apartment building, 1906

Kamenická 35 (7 Hol, 811), Otakar Novotný, apartment building, 1923–1924

Kaprova 5 (1 Jos, 19), Jiří Stibral, apartment building, 1904

Kaprova 6 (1 StM, 52), Bedřich Bendelmayer, apartment building with shops, 1906

Kaprova 10 (1 StM, 45), Bohumil Hypšman, apartment building, 1919–1921

Kaprova 11 (1 Jos, 69), František Pohl, Leopold Neugebauer, apartment building, 1906–1907

Kaprova 12 (1 StM, 40), Karel Janda, apartment building, 1913–1914

Kaprova 14 (1 StM, 42), Matěj Blecha, apartment building, 1914–1915

Karafiátová 52–64 (10 Záb, 1901–1907), building company Alois Vavrouš & Son, family houses, 1933–1936

Karafiátová 44–48 (10 Záb, 2310–2312), František Marek, apartment buildings with shops, 1940

Karlova 22, 24 (1 StM, 174, 178), Osvald Polívka, apartment buildings, 1905–1906

Karlova 26 (1 StM, 223), Josef Havlíček, renovation of building, 1928

Karmelitská 5, 7 (1 MaS, 529 — courtyard), Oldřich Tyl, extension to office building, 1922

Karmelitská 26 (1 MaS, 268), František Štorch, apartment building, 1913

Karmelitská 30 (1 MaS, 270), Ludvík Kysela, apartment building, 1912–1913

Kartouzská 4 (5 Smí, 200), Matěj Blecha Architects and Building Contractors, office building, 1922

Kartouzská (5 Smí, 20), Osvald Polívka, factory, 1901(?)

Ke Klíčovu 1 (9 Vys, 256), Hubert Gessner, mill and bakery, before 1913, after 1920–1921

Ke Klimentce 1 (5 Smí, 1852), Alois Mezera, family house, 1927–1928

Ke Klimentce 2–6 (5 Smí, 2436, 2431, 2446), Jiří Michálek, family houses, 1939

Ke Klimentce 9 (5 Smí, 1863), Josef Štěpánek, family house, 1927–1928

Ke Klimentce 49 (5 Smí, 1899), Ladislav Machoň, family house, 1928–1929

Ke Lhotce 29 (4 Lho, 43), Konstantin Ahne, family house, 1928

Kesnerka 1 (5 Smí, 2323), František Magnusek, family house, 1936–1937

Kladenská 2 (6 Dej, 1138), Josef Kříž, power station, circa 1930

Kladenská 61 (6 Vok, 278), Ludvík Hilgert, apartment building with workshop, 1931–1932

Klánova 3 (4 Hod, 89), J. F. Regenerml, family house, 1924

Klánova 46 (4 Hod, 57), Václav Velvarský, family house, circa 1938

Klidná 13–23 (6 Stř, 288–293), Jindřich Freiwald, Josef Paroulek, family house, 1920

Klimentská 4 (1 NoM, 1205), Josef Zasche, apartment building with cinema, 1932–1933

Klimentská 6 (1 NoM, 2062), Ervín Katona, apartment building, 1936–1937

Klimentská 11 (1 NoM, 1235), Bohumil Hypšman, František Roith, medical insurance company building, 1924–1926

Klimentská 12 (1 NoM, 1208), Jaroslav Nebeský, apartment building, 1938

Klimentská 17 (1 NoM, 2065), Fritz Lehmann, apartment buildings, 1936–1938

Klimentská 34 (1 NoM, 2067), Kurt Spielmann, apartment building, 1936

Klimentská 36 (1 NoM, 1652), František Berger, office and commercial building, 1928–1929

Klimentská 48 (1 NoM, 1172), Matěj Blecha, apartment building, 1913–1917

Kloboučnická 3 (4 Nus, 1424), Vladimír Nevšímal, apartment building, 1941

Kodaňská 7 (10 Vrš, 444), Osvald Polívka, apartment building, 1905–1906

Kodaňská 14 (10 Vrš, 989), Vladimír Frýda, kindergarten building, 1930–1932

Kodaňská 43, 45 (10 Vrš, 61), Antonín Belada, club and apartment building, 1911–1912

Kolbenova (9 Vys, 37), Jiří Krofta, apartment building, after 1935

Kolbenova 38 (9 Vys, 609), František Albert Libra, factory, 1936–1938

Kolínská 3 (3 Vin, 1962), Leopold Hron, apartment building, 1923–1925

Komunardů 40 (7 Hol, 1467), Jan Zázvorka, apartment building, 1930–1931

Konopišťská 16 (10 Vrš, 739), František Čermák, Ladislav Tříška, Jaroslav Bezecný, family house, 1931–1932

Konviktská 5 (1 StM, 263), Viktor Kafka, commercial and apartment building, 1927–1928

Konviktská 14 (1 StM, 296), Antonín Fric, home for persons in social care with workshops, 1931

Koperníkova 7 (2 Vin, 1071), Edvard Sochor, parsonage, 1899–1901

Korunní 2 (2 Vin, 586), Tomáš Šašek, high school building, 1937–1938

Korunní 30 (1 Vin, 926), Stivo Vacek, rebuilding of apartment building with theater, 1926–1927

Korunní 68 (2 Vin, 2160), Mečislav Petrů, library, 1928–1929

Korunní 89 (3 Vin, 483), Josef Martínek, Václav Šafránek, apartment building, 1939

Korunní 106, 108 (10 Vin, 986), Otakar Novotný, office building and factory warehouse, 1925

Korunní 109 (3 Vin, 1961), Jan Vodňaruk, apartment building, 1923–1925

Korunní 111, 113 (3 Vin, 1901, 1902), Ladislav Machoň, apartment buildings, 1923–1924

Korunní 115 (3 Vin, 1779), Leopold Hron, apartment building, 1922–1923

Korunní 129 (3 Vin, 1740), Josef Čácha, Josef Rokos, apartment building, 1921

Korunovační 2 (7 Bub, 310), Josef Kovařovic(?), apartment building, 1910–1911; modified by Josef Havlíček, 1937

Korunovační 4 (7 Bub, 907, 917), Josef Kovařovic, apartment buildings, 1910–1911

Korunovační 24 (7 Bub, 50), František Šulc, apartment building, 1911

Korunovační 26 (7 Bub, 594), Ladislav Machoň, apartment building, 1923

Korunovační 28 (7 Bub, 127), Ladislav Žák, rebuilding of apartment building, 1931–1932, 1935–1936

Kosatcová 16–30 (10 Záb, 1317–1324), Alex Hanuš, Zdeněk Kruliš, Vladimír Vlček, family houses, 1928–1929

Kostelní 36 (7 Hol, 36), Bohumír Kozák, apartment building, 1940

Kostelní 38 (7 Hol, 1291), Ludvík Kysela, apartment building, 1922–1924

Kostelní 42, 44 (7 Hol, 1300, 1320), Milan Babuška, Technical (and former Agricultural) Museum, 1937–1940 (P 1935–1937)

Košická 11 (10 Vrš, 50), Josef Veselý, apartment building, 1913

Koulova 4 (6 Dej, 1593), Rudolf Stockar, apartment building, 1937

Kouřimská 4 (3 Vin, 2368), Jaroslav Vančura, apartment building, 1936–1937

Kouřimská 18 (3 Vin, 2367), Václav Vlk, apartment building, 1936–1937

Kouřimská 28 (3 Vin, 2388), Jiří Mašek, apartment building, 1939

Kouřimská 30 (3 Vin, 2293), František Stalmach, Jan Svoboda, apartment building, 1932–1933

Kováků 7 (5 Smí, 1192), František Kavalír, apartment building, 1909–1910

Kováků 12, 13 (5 Smí, 1498, 1499), V. Nekvasil Architects and Building Contractors, apartment building, 1922–1923

Kozí 9 (1 StM, 914), Antonín Makovec, apartment building, 1904–1905

Kozlovská 1 (6 Dej, 265), Richard Klenka, own family house, 1909

Kozlovská 5 (6 Dej, 1390), Alois Mezera, family house, 1930–1939

Kozlovská 7 (6 Dej, 1389), Jaroslav Rössler, family house of painter Oldřich Blažíček, 1927–1928

Krakovská 12 (1 NoM, 1363), František Voráček, apartment building, 1938

Krakovská 22 (1 NoM, 1307), Ervín Katona, facade, 1938(?)

Králodvorská 4 (1 StM, 652), František Malýpetr, hotel, 1925–1927

Krátká 6 (10 Vin, 2408), František Marek, apartment building, 1940

Krocínova 3 (1 StM, 333), Ladislav Suk, apartment building, 1937–1938

Krocínovská 8 (6 Dej, 822), Vladimír František Hofman, family house, 1928

Křesomyslova (4 Nus, 626), Josef Dneboský, Alois Zima, theatre, 1921

Křesomyslova 2 (4 Nus, 724), Municipal Construction Authority, rebuilding and new school building, 1924–1925

Křišťanova 4,6 (3 Žiž, 1543, 1544), Rudolf Hrabě, apartment buildings, 1925–1927

Křišťanova 15 (3 Žiž, 1698), Ervín Katona, apartment building, 1929–1930

Křišťanova 20 (3 Žiž, 1678), Jan Rosůlek(?), apartment building, 1929–1930

Křižíkova 2 (8 Kar, 552), Vojtěch Krch(?), Kulhavý, office building, 1920–1921

Křižíkova 10 (8 Kar, 283), Friedrich Ohmann, rebuilding of theatre, 1896–1898

Křižíkova 9 (8 Karlín, 267), František Xaver Čtrnáctý, apartment building, 1907–1938

Křižíkova 48 (8 Kar, 23, 52, 290, 556), Jaroslav Stránský, Josef Šlégl, apartment buildings, 1931–1939

Křižíkova 49 (8 Kar, 212), Jindřich Freiwald, Jaroslav Böhm, rebuilding of office and apartment building, 1930–1931

Křižíkova 64 (8 Kar, 452), Bohumil Štěrba, apartment building, 1905

Křižíkova 65 (8 Kar, 55), František Troníček, apartment building, 1938–1940

Křížová 23 (5 Smí, 2143), František Čermák, Gustav Paul, office and apartment building, 1934–1935

Křížová 25 (5 Smí, 1292), Adolf Foehr, office building, circa 1925

Křížová 27 (5 Smí, 2383), František Albert Libra, Jiří Kan, office building, 1935–1937

Křižovnická 8 (1 StM, 97), František Sander, apartment building, 1897

Kubelíkova 16 (3 Žiž, 1250), Oldřich Tyl, pension, 1923–1926

Kubelíkova 18 (3 Žiž, 1494), František Janda, Čeněk Vořech, apartment building, 1923–1924

Kyjevská 9, 11 (6 Bub, 778, 779), Ferdinand Hruška, apartment buildings, 1926

Laubova 8 (3 Vin, 1729), František Havlena, office and apartment building, 1927–1928

Laubova 10 (3 Vin, 2128), František and Vojtěch Kerhart, apartment building, 1927–1928

Lazarská 7 (1 NoM, 15), Josef Karel Říha, Mining and Metallurgy Company office building with shops and cinema, 1928–1930

Lesnická 8 (5 Smí, 1155), Karel Vítězslav Mašek, apartment building, 1907

Letenská 15 (1 MaS, 525), František Roith, Karel Pecánek, Ministry of Finance, 1929–1934

Letohradská 2 (7 Hol, 479), Josef Herink, hotel, 1922–1923

Letohradská 52 (7 Hol, 756), Evžen Rosenberg, apartment building, 1935–1936

Letohradská 60 (7 Hol, 760), Josef Havlíček, apartment building, 1938–1939

Levá 10 (5 Pod, 586), Ladislav Panchártek, family house, 1939–1940

Libocká 33 (6 DoL, 274), Bohumil Hypšman, family house, 1906

Libušina 3 (2 Vyš, 49), Josef Chochol, family house, 1912–1913

Libušina (2 Vyš, 65), František Roith, gymnasium, 1931–1933

Lihovarská 14 (9 Lib, 1847), Adolf Erben, apartment building with shops, 1936–1937

Lipanská 9 (3 Žiž, 405), Otakar Burian, modification of apartment building, 1929

Lípová 15 (2 NoM, 511), Gustav Paul, club and apartment building, 1936–1937

Lodecká 3 (1 NoM, 1184), František Zelenka, Leopold Ehrmann, apartment building, 1938

Lomená 10, 12 (6 Stř, 493, 494), Pavel Janák, family duplex of painter Emil Filla and philosopher František Krejčí, 1923–1924

Lomená 15–36 (6 Stř, 305–315, 322–330), Jaroslav Vondrák, family houses, 1920

Lomená 41 (6 Stř, 810), Václav Vlk, family house, 1931–1932

Londýnská 28 (2 Vin, 596), Václav Kopecký, pension, 1938–1939

Londýnská 31 (2 Vin, 218), Rudolf Pokorný, apartment building, 1940–1941

Londýnská 35 (2 Vin, 216), Josef Jaroslav Hukal, V. Němec, apartment building, 1937–1938

Londýnská 41 (2 Vin, 506), Berthold Schwarz, renovation and extension to sanatorium, 1931

Londýnská 47 (2 Vin, 613) Václav Pospíšil, apartment building, 1934–1936

Londýnská 48 (2 Vin, 575), Jaroslav Pelc, apartment building, 1913(?)

Londýnská 54 (2 Vin, 136), Václav Vejrych, Jaroslav Kabeš, savings bank and apartment building, 1930–1933; Osvald Polívka, old hall of the savings bank, 1912

Londýnská 61 (2 Vin, 375), Rudolf Hrabě, Hilar Pacanovský, apartment building, 1935

Londýnská 62 (2 Vin, 565), Jiří Mašek, commercial and apartment building, 1937

Londýnská 81 (2 Vin, 309), František Albert Libra, commercial and apartment building, 1936

Londýnská 83 (2 Vin, 334), Josef Kittrich, Josef Hrubý, commercial and apartment building, 1938–1939

Lopatecká 7 (4 Pod, 204), Eduard Hnilička, family house of violinist Karel Hoffmann, 1923–1926; modifications by Pavel Smetana, 1935

Lopatecká 11 (4 Pod, 225), Antonín Mendl, Václav Šantrůček, family house, 1923–1924

Lopatecká 24 (4 Pod, 340), Miloš Laml, family house, 1929–1930

Lucemburská 14 (3 Vin, 1733), Stanislav Svoboda, V. Křesadlo, apartment building, 1937

Lucemburská 27–31 (3 Žiž, 1599), Karel Caivas, Vladimír Weiss, apartment buildings, 1927–1928

Lukášova 4 (3 Žiž, 1820), Jaroslav Jelínek, commercial and apartment building, 1932

Lumièrů 25 (5 Hlu, 189), K. Rudl, family house, 1930–1931; rebuilt by Zdeněk Lakomý, 1939–1940

Lumièrů 41 (5 Hlu, 181), Max Urban, family house, 1932

Mahenova 4 (5 Koš, 294), Karel Šidlík, apartment building, 1919–1921

Maiselova 15 (1 Jos, 38), Josef Vajshajtl, apartment building, 1910–1912

Maiselova 17 (1 Jos, 39), František Troníček, Josef Čácha, apartment building, 1910–1912

Maiselova 21 (1 Jos, 41), František Weyr, Richard Klenka, apartment building, 1910–1911

Malá Štěpánská 4 (2 NoM, 554), Vojtěch Kerhart, polyclinic, 1937–1953

Malá Štěpánská 12 (2 NoM, 546), Matěj Blecha Architects and Building Contractors, prayer hall, 1925–1926

Malířská 9 (7 Bub, 327), Václav Vacek, apartment building, 1910

Markova 3 (5 Jin, 442), Antonín Nesnídal, family house with workshop, 1931–1932

Martinská 8 (1 StM), Kamil Hilbert, renovation of Saint Martin's Church, 1905–1906(?)

Maříkova 11 (6 Dej, 303), Josef Kovařovic, apartment building, 1911

Masná 7 (1 StM, 703), Oldřich Tyl, apartment building, 1929–1930

Masná 21 (1 StM, 696), Ervín Katona, apartment building, 1936

Matějská 3 (6 Dej, 1953), A. and L. Těrechov, family house, 1939–1941

Matějská 7 (6 Dej, 1988), Josef Grus, family house, 1939–1940

Matějská 9 (6 Dej, 1986), Antonín Černý, own family house, 1939–1940

Matějská 11 (6 Dej, 1877), Antonín Kučera, Štěpán Zelenka, family house, 1939–1940

Matějská 13 (6 Dej, 1987), Josef Grus, 1939–1940

Matějská 17 (6 Dej, 1177), Josef Grus, family house, 1938–1940

Matějská 19 (6 Dej, 1985), František Kerhart, family house, 1939

Matějská 28 (6 Dej, 1983), Camil Zupanc, family house, 1936–1937

492

Matoušova 8–16 (5 Smí, 1354–1357), Municipal Construction Authority, housing estate, 1919–1923

Melantrichova 5 (1 StM, 504), František Kavalír, Bohumil Steigenhöfer, renovation and extension to bank building, 1928–1929

Melantrichova 12 (1 StM, 472), Bohumil Hypšman, facade, 1913

Mendíků (4 Mich, 1000), Municipal Construction Authority, city architect Mečislav Petrů, kindergarten, 1929; school building, 1929, 1933–1934

Mickiewiczova 1 (6 Hra, 233), František Bílek, own family house, 1910–1911

Mickiewiczova 3 (6 Hra, 234), František Bílek(?), Antonín Hulán, family house, 1910–1911

Mickiewiczova 7 (6 Hra, 258), František Roith, Josef Vaňha, family house, 1911

Mickiewiczova 13, 15 (6 Hra, 239, 240), Jan Kotěra, family houses, 1910–1911

Michalovicova 1 (6 Bře, 1154), Max Gerstl, family house, 1936

Michalská 9 (1 StM, 441), František Dittrich, apartment building, 1933

Michalská 17 (1 StM, 437), Rudolf Novotný, apartment building with shops, 1939–1941

Mikovcova 3 (2 Vin, 574), Mikuláš Gottdiener, apartment building, 1938

Milkulandská 6 (1 NoM, 151), Václav Kopecký, extension to apartment building, 1922

Milady Horákové 19 (7 Hol, 479), Jan Chládek, hotel, 1935

Milady Horákové 56 (7 Hol, 387), Evžen Rosenberg, commercial and apartment building, 1937

Milady Horákové 62 (7 Hol, 499), Jan Gillar, interior design of commercial building, 1938

Milady Horákové 63 (7 Hol, 386), Karel Janů, apartment building with shops, 1938–1939

Milady Horákové 71 (7 Hol, 1071), Alois Masák, apartment building with shops, 1911

Milady Horákové 72–96 (7 Bub, 845–862), Josef Havlíček, project for group of apartment buildings, individual buildings designed by Otto and Karel Kohn, Arnošt Mühlstein and Victor Fürth, Leo Lauermann, František Votava, Josef Havlíček, 1937–1938

Milady Horákové 79 (7 Hol, 383), Ladislav Machoň, telephone exchange, 1929–1931 (P 1928?)

Milady Horákové 85 (7 Hol, 1498), Kamil Roškot, Josef Kalous, Jan Zázvorka, Ministry of Interior Affairs, 1935–1939

Milady Horákové 102 (6 Bub, 179), Kamil Roškot, rebuilding of own family house, 1926

Milady Horákové 107 (6 Hra, 115), Hilar Pacanovský, commercial and apartment building, 1939–1940

Milady Horákové 133 (6 Hra, 5), Josef Weingärtner, archives, 1931–1932

Milady Horákové 139 (6 Hra, 223), Josef Rosipal, orphanage, 1912–1913

Mládeže 1 (6 Bře, 1024), Karel Hannauer, apartment building, 1939–1941

Mládeže 2–10 (6 Bře, 1436–1440), Václav Hilský, Rudolf Jasenský, František Jech, Karel Koželka, apartment buildings, 1937–1939

Mládeže 3 (6 Bře, 1479), Jiří Mašek, apartment building, 1940–1941

Mládeže 5 (6 Bře, 1237), Josef Donát, apartment building, 1939

Mládeže 7 (6 Bře, 1375), Jan Luň, apartment building, 1939–1940

Mládeže 9 (6 Bře, 1443), Josef Kubín, Jindřich Lášek, apartment building, 1939

Mlékárenská 3 (9 Vys, 292), Bohumír Kozák, Karel Roštík, home for persons in social care, circa 1921–1922

Modřanská (4 Bra, 229), Jan Kotěra, pumping station, 1905–1906

Modřanská (4 Bra, 238), Josef Kovařovic, ice-making plant, 1911–1913

Moravská 19 (2 Vin, 1502), Felix Kveting, Antonín Kotek, apartment building, 1908–1909

Moskevská 24, 26 (10 Vrš, 53, 151), Stivo Vacek, apartment building with shops, 1938–1939

Moskevská 66 (10 Vrš, 771), Josef Štěpánek, apartment building, 1926–1927

Moskevská 70, 72 (10 Vrš, 696, 697), Rudolf Hrabě, apartment building, 1924–1925

Moskevská 74 (10 Vrš, 981), Ladislav Bartl, apartment building, 1931–1932

Moskevská 78 (10 Vrš, 861), Municipal Construction Authority, architect identified by inititials J. K., apartment building, 1930–1932

Mostecká 18 (1 MaS, 46), Josef Paroulek, Jindřich Freiwald, rebuilding of apartment building, 1920

Mrštíkova 4, 6 (10 Str, 492, 493), František Havlena, apartment buildings, 1922–1924

Myslíkova 7 (1 NoM, 208), Matěj Blecha, polyclinic, 1906–1907

Myslíkova 23 (1 NoM, 174), V. Nekvasil Architects and Building Contractors, apartment building, 1936–1937

Myslíkova 32 (2 NoM, 284), Osvald Polívka, František Buldra, apartment building, 1905–1906

Na Babě 1 (6 Dej, 1783), Josef Gočár, family house, 1935–1936 (P 1933?)

Na Babě 3 (6 Dej, 1782), Ladislav Žák, family house, 1932 (P 1928?–1932)

Na Babě 4 (6 Dej, 1799), František Kerhart, family house, 1933

Na Babě 5 (6 Dej, 1781), Hana Kučerová-Záveská, family house, 1932 (P 1931)

Na Babě 6 (6 Dej, 1800), Pavel Janák, family house, 1933–1934

Na Babě 7 (6 Dej, 1780), Oldřich Starý, family house, 1932 (P 1931)

Na Babě 9 (6 Dejvice 1779), Mart Stam, Jiří Palička, family house, 1932 (P 1929–1931)

Na Babě 11 (6 Dej, 1777), Ladislav Machoň, family house, 1932–1933

Na Babě 12 (6 Dej, 1803), Jan E. Koula, family house, 1932

Na Babě 13 (6 Dej, 1778), František Kavalír, family house, 1932; modifed by Ladislav Žák, 1936

Na Babě 17 (6 Dej, 1813), Jaroslav Rössler, family house, 1934

Na Babě 20 (6 Dej, 1826), Jan Gillar, family house, 1934

Na Babě 29 (6 Dej, 1807), Ladislav Machoň, family house, 1938

Na baště sv. Jiří 3 (6 Hra, 256), Theodor Petřík, Karel Roštík, family house, 1912–1913

Na baště sv. Jiří 15 (6 Hra 262), Antonín Ausobský, family house, 1912

Na baště sv Ludmily 11 (6 Hra, 248), A. Neumann, B. Hollmann, family house, 1912–1913

Na baště sv. Ludmily 13 (6 Hra, 247), Emil Králíček, family house, 1913

Na baště sv. Tomáše 3 (1 Hra, 232), Alois Čenský, family house, 1911; modified by Kamil Hilbert, 1924

Na baště sv. Tomáše 5 (1 Hra, 231), Rudolf Stockar, family house, 1910–1911

Na bateriích 13 (6 Stř, 820), Oskar and Elly Oehler, family house, 1931–1932

Na Beránce 16 (6 Dej, 1684), Vladimír Maršal, family house, 1933

Na Beránce 18 (6 Dej, 1685), Josef Václavík, family house, 1933

Na bitevní pláni 17, 19 (4 Nus, 1217, 1218), Karel Hannauer, apartment buildings, 1936

Na bitevní pláni 46, 48 (4 Nus, 1155, 1156), Karel Hannauer, apartment buildings, 1934

Na břehu 13, 15 (9 Vys, 496, 497), Rudolf Hrabě, apartment buildings, 1924–1925

Na březince 3, 5 (5 Smí, 1367, 1368), Karel Herman, apartment buildings, 1920–1922

Na Bučance 7 (4 Nus, 1065), Václav Burda, family house, 1931–1932

Na Cihlářce 5 (5 Smí, 1570), Jaro Král, family house, 1925–1926

Na Cihlářce 10 (5 Smí, 2092), Adolf Loos, Karel Lhota, family house, 1932 (P 1931)

Na Cihlářce 14 (5 Smí, 2267), František Zelenka, family house, 1936

Na Černém vrchu 1 (5 Smí, 2296), Jaroslav Mašek, family house, 1936

Na Černém vrchu 1 (5 Smí, 2296), Jaroslav Mašek, family house, 1936

Na čihadle 14 (6 Dej, 868), Oldřich Tyl, family house, 1929

Na Dionysce 12 (6 Dej, 1757), Hilar Pacanovský, apartment building, 1937–1938

Na dolinách 1 (4 Pod, 86), Rudolf Ehrmann-Steuer, apartment building, 1936

Na dolinách 15 (4 Pod, 23), Ladislav Machoň, apartment building, 1927

Na dračkách 5 (6 Stř, 755), Otakar Novotný, family house of painter Václav Špála, 1931–1932

Na dračkách 7 (6 Stř, 754), František Albert Libra, family house of painter Alfred Justitz, 1931

Na dračkách 10 (6 Stř, 773, 994), Antonín Mendl, family house, 1934

Na dračkách 12 (6 Stř, 774), Alois Mikuškovic, family house, 1933

Na dračkách 25 (6 Stř, 847), Pavel Simonov, family house of graphic artist Václav Fiala, 1934

Na Doubkové 6 (5 Smí, 2033), Ferdinand Fencl, family house, circa 1933

Na Fišerce 4 (6 Dej, 1045), Antonín Mendl, family house, 1932

Na Florenci 3 (1 NoM, 1420), Josef Karel Říha, commercial and office building, 1927–1928 (P 1926?)

Na Florenci 5 (1 NoM, 1496), Josef Gočár(?), Josef Stoklasa, apartment building, 1923–1925

Na Františku 8 (1 StM, 847), Vilém Kvasnička, J. Mayer, hospital, 1923–1927

Na Františku 32 (1 StM, 1039), Josef Fanta, Ministry of Commerce, 1926–1933 (P 1925)

Na Hanspaulce 6 (6 Dej, 1664), Stanislav Brázda, family house, 1932–1933

Na Hanspaulce 9 (6 Dej, 1377), Alois Dryák, family house, 1928–1929

Na Hanspaulce 15 (6 Dej, 1840), Josef Karel Říha, family house, 1934

Na Hanspaulce 29 (6 Dej, 1000), Alois Dryák, school building, 1931

Na hrobci 1 (2 NoM, 410), Alois Dryák, Tomáš Amena, apartment building, 1912–1913

Na hrobci 5 (2 NoM, 294), V. Nekvasil Architects and Building Contractors, 1921–1922

Na Hřebenkách 12 (5 Smí, 1882), Jan E. Koula, family house, 1928, modified by František Zelenka, 1937

Na Hřebenkách 18 (5 Smí, 1755), B. Vávra, family house, 1926–1927

Na Hřebenkách 41 (5 Smí, 2365), Jacques Groag, family house, 1938

Na Hřebenkách 44 (5 Smí, 1304), František Kavalír, family house, 1912–1914

Na Hřebenkách 45 (5 Smí, 142), Karel Kotas, family house, between 1932–1935

Na Hubálce 1 (6 Stř, 922), Vladimír Grégr, family house, 1936

Na Hubálce 5 (6 Stř, 924), František Fuchs, apartment building, 1938

Na Hubálce 18 (6 Stř, 567), Josef Kalous, family house, 1926–1927

Na hutách 10, 12 (6 Bub, 755, 756), Ferdinand Hruška, apartment building, 1926

Na hutích 13 (6 Bub, 693), Antonín Hamann, apartment building, 1926–1927

Na hutích 14 (6 Bub, 757), Josef Kříž, apartment building, 1926

Na Jezerce 1–7 (4 Nus, 1196–1199), Josef Kučera, Miroslav Tryzna, Karel Hannauer, apartment buildings, 1935

Na Karlovce 6 (6 Dej, 1387), Antonín Engel, own family house, 1927

Na Kodymce 14 (6 Dej, 25), František Maria Černý, family house, 1938

Na Kodymce 21 (6 Dej, 1442), Antonín Moudrý, family house, 1932

Na kopečku 3 (8 Lib, 1281), Aleš Hübschmann, apartment building, 1938

Na Kotlářce 2 (6 Dej, 1079), Karel Caivas, Vladimír Weiss, family house, 1927

Na květnici 5 (4 Nus, 1118), Antonín Fric, family house, 1932

Na květnici 20 (4 Nus, 850), Berthold Schwarz, family house, 1929–1930

Na květnici 29 (4 Nus, 642), František Krásný, family house, 1923

Na lysinách 2 (4 Hod, 48), Pavel Janák, family house, 1921–1922

Na lysinách 9 (4 Hod, 208), Ladislav Žák, family house of film director Martin Frič, 1935

Na lysinách 33 (4 Hod, 62), Josef Mlíka, family house, 1940

Na lysině 13 (4 Pod, 269), Antonín Řehák, family house, 1926–1927

Na Maninách 14 (7 Hol, 1040), Bedřich Adámek, garages, 1927

Na Markvartce 13 (6 Dej, 1103), Bedřich Adámek, family house, 1929–1930

Na Marně 5 (6 Bub, 608), Josef Gočár, family house, 1926–1927 (P 1925)

Na Míčánce 27 (6 Dej, 1918), Antonín Mendl, family house, 1934–1935

Na Míčánce 39 (6 Dej, 1044), Karel Štipl, family house, 1933

Na Míčánce 421 (6 Dej, 1043), Čeněk Vořech, family house, circa 1934

Na Míčánce 49, 51 (6 Dej, 1038, 1039), Karel Štipl, family house, 1929

Na Míčánkách 6 (10 Vrš, 901), Jaroslav Vančura, apartment building, 1937

Na Opyši (1 Hra, 192), Otto Rothmayer, renovation of family house, 1933

Na Ořechovce 32, 34 (6 Stř, 251, 252), Jaroslav Vašta, family duplex, 1920

Na Ořechovce 35 (6 Stř, 487), Ladislav Machoň, family house of sculptor Otakar Španiel, 1923–1924

Na Ořechovce 37 (6 Stř, 486), František Vahala, family house, 1923–1924

Na Ořechovce 39 (6 Stř, 485), Jaroslav Vondrák(?), family house of graphic artist Jaroslav Benda, 1923–1924

Na Ořechovce 41 (6 Stř, 484), Pavel Janák, family house of sculptor Bohumil Kafka, 1923–1924

Na Ořechovce 59 (6 Stř, 477), Jaroslav Vondrák, family house, 1922; rebuilt by Vladimír Grégr, 1932

Na ostrohu 41 (6 Dej, 1791), František Kerhart, family house, 1933–1934

Na ostrohu 43 (6 Dej, 1797), Pavel Janák, family house, 1932

Na ostrohu 45 (6 Dej, 1796), František Kerhart, family house, 1933–1933

Na ostrohu 46 (6 Dej, 1712), Oldřich Starý, family house of graphic artist Cyril Bouda, 1932

Na ostrohu 47 (6 Dej, 1795), František Kavalír, family house, 1932

Na ostrohu 48 (6 Dej, 1711), Jaroslav and Karel Fišer, family house, 1932

Na ostrohu 49 (6 Dej, 1794), Hana Kučerová-Záveská, family house, 1932

Na ostrohu 50 (6 Dej, 1710), Antonín Heythum, Evžen Linhart, family house, 1932 (P 1931)

Na ostrohu 51 (6 Dej, 1793), Ladislav Žák, family house, 1932 (P 1931)

Na ostrohu 52 (6 Dej, 1709), Oldřich Starý, family house, 1932 (P 1931)

Na ostrohu 53 (6 Dej, 1792), František Zelenka, family house, 1934

Na ostrohu 54 (6 Dej, 1708), Ladislav Žák, family house, 1932 (P 1931)

Na ostrohu 56 (6 Dej, 1707), Vojtěch Kerhart, family house, 1932

Na ostrohu 57 (6 Dej, 1827), Emil Král, family house, 1934

Na ostrohu 58 (6 Dej, 1706), František Kerhart, family house, 1933

Na ovčinách 2 (7 Hol, 440), Pavel Kopetzky, apartment building, 1935

Na ovčinách 4 (7 Hol, 970), Jan Šebánek, apartment building with shops, 1928–1929

Na Pahoubce 10 (6 Dej, 1509), Josef Fuchs, family house, 1930

Na Pahoubce (6 Dej, 1510), Antonín Mendl, family house, 1933

Na Pankráci 67 (4 Nus, 1252), Vojtěch Kerhart, apartment building, 1936

Na Pankráci 109 (4 Nus, 1337), Karel Dudych, apartment building, 1939–1940

Na Perštýně 11 (1 StM, 347), Alois Dryák, office building, 1920–1922

Na Petřinách 7 (6 Bře, 1482), Pavel Simonov(?), family house, 1939–1940

Na pískách 32 (6 Dej, 1835), Evžen Linhart, family house, 1932–1933

Na pískách 36 (6 Dej, 1667), Františk Nejdl, family house, 1931

Na pískách 85–95 (6 Dej, 1411–1416), František Kotrba, family houses, 1927–1929

Na podkovce 12 (4 Pod, 282), Karel Stráník, family house, 1935–1936

Na Popelce 7 (5 Koš, 38), Josef Štěpánek, renovation of existing house and new garage, 1939

Na poříčí 12 (1 NoM, 1041), Eduard Hnilička, pension, 1925–1928

Na poříčí 15 (1 NoM, 1072), Jaroslav Benedikt, hotel, 1913–1914

Na poříčí 23 (1 NoM, 1068), Josef Kittrich, Josef Hrubý, Bílá labuť (White Swan) department store, 1937–1939; interiors by Jan Gillar

Na poříčí 24 (1 NoM, 1046), Josef Gočár, Czechoslovak Legiobank, 1922–1923 (P 1921)

Na poříčí 26 (1 NoM, 1047), František Marek, bank building with restaurant and concert hall, 1937–1939

Na poříčí 30 (1 NoM, 1048), Josef Blecha of Matěj Blecha Architects and Building Contractors, office building, 1926–1928

Na poříčí 30 (1 NoM, 1024 — courtyard), Bohumil Steigenhöfer, printing plant, 1938–1946

Na poříčí 36, 38 (1 NoM, 1933, 1934), Josef Fanta, commercial building, 1900–1902

Na poříčí 40 (1 NoM, 1051), Václav Pilc, hotel with bath house, 1930–1932

Na poříčí 42 (1 NoM, 1052), Jindřich Freiwald, hotel and commercial building, 1938–1939

Na poříčí 46 (1 NoM, 1894), Julius Landsmann, Martin Reiner, Otto Zucker, apartment building, 1937–1938

Na poříčském právu 1 (12 NoM, 376), Bohumil Hypšman, Ministry of Public Health, 1923–1931

Na přesypu 7 (8 Tró, 246), Karl Simon, family house, 1931–1932

Na příkopě 1 (1 StM, 390), Josef Zasche, Alex Neumann, bank building, 1906–1908

Na příkopě 6 (1 NoM, 848), Ladislav Machoň, facade of bank building, 1921–1923

Na příkopě 7 (1 StM, 391), Jiří Justich, Matěj Blecha, commercial and apartment building, 1904–1906; modified by Josef Mayer, 1939

Na příkopě 14 (1 NoM, 854), Bedřich Bendelmayer, bank building, 1927–1933

Na příkopě 15 (1 StM, 583), Ludvík Kysela, commercial building, 1927–1929 (P 1925–1927)

Na příkopě 18 (1 NoM, 857), Osvald Polívka, bank building, 1908–1910; modified by Karel Stráník, 1937, 1939–1941

Na příkopě 20 (1 NoM, 858), Osvald Polívka, bank building, 1894–1896

Na příkopě 22 (1 NoM, 859 — courtyard), Fritz Lehmann, club building, 1934

Na příkopě 31 (1 StM, 998), Antonín Černý, Bohumír Kozák, commercial and apartment building with arcade and cinema, 1936–1938

Na příkopě 33, 35 (1 StM, 969), Josef Sakař(?), Karl Jaray, bank building, 1930(?)–1932

Na Rokytce 8 (8 Lib, 1081), Karel Šidlík, apartment building, 1921–1922

Na Rybníčku 14 (2 NoM, 1350), Karel Dudych, apartment building, 1937–1939

Na seníku (6 Bub, 48), Jan Kotěra, rebuilding of the Villa Bianca, 1910–1911, further rebuilt by Max Spielmann, circa 1920

Na Smetance 16 (2 Vin, 504), Jaroslav Vančura, apartment building, 1937–1938

Na struze 6 (1 NoM, 230), Osvald Polívka, apartment building, 1903–1904

Na Šafránce 7 (10 Vin, 1759), Josef Rokos, František Albert Libra, family house, 1921–1922

Na Šmukýřce 18 (5 Koš, 728), Bedřich Bernard, family house, 1932–1933

Na Švihance 3 (2 Vin, 1475), Ladislav Čapek, apartment building, 1907–1908

Na špejcharu 7 (7 Hol, 291), Alois Potůček, family house, 1904

Na Truhlářce 4 (8 Lib, 100), František Xaver Nevole, radiotherapy institute, 1934–1936

Na Truhlářce 5 (8 Lib, 1459), Václav Velvarský, family house, 1932

Na Truhlářce 7 (8 Lib, 1458), Otto and Karel Kohn, family house, 1933

Na Truhlářce 23 (8 Lib, 1580), Gustav Paul, family house, 1930–1931

Na Třebešíně 38 (10 Str, 487), J. F. Regenerml, family house, 1923

Na úbočí 3, 7 (8 Lib, 1397, 1395), Josef Fuchs, family houses, 1928–1929

Na usedlosti 11 (4 Bra, 656), Franz Hruška, family house, 1933

Na Václavce 1 (5 Smí, 117), V. Nekvasil Architects and Building Contractors, evangelical meeting house (Husův sbor), 1933

Na Václavce 22 (5 Smí, 1789), František Stalmach, apartment building, 1927–1928

Na Václavce 30 (5 Smí, 1078), Alois Korda, family house, 1903

Na valech 24–28 (6 Hra, 272–276, 292, 295), František Velich, Jan Žák, apartment buildings, 1912–1914

Na valech 32–34 (6 Hra, 45, 46), Václav Velvarský, apartment building, 1929

Na Veselí 3 (4 Nus, 825), Bohuslav Kněžek, Josef Václavík, apartment building, 1937

Na viničních horách 44 (6 Dej, 773), Jan Rosůlek, own family house, 1927–1929; rebuilt by Vladimír Grégr, 1939

Na viničních horách 46 (6 Dej, 774), Evžen Linhart, own family house, 1927–1929

Na vinobraní 10 (10 Záb, 1640), Josef Kosek, family house, 1934

Na výsluní 10, 12 (10 Str, 742, 788), Viktor Lampl, Otto Fuchs, family duplex, 1927–1928

Na výspě 8 (4 Hod, 198), Václav Stach, family house, 1935

Na vysočanských vinicích 31 (9 Vys, 404), Ladislav Žák, family house of aircraft engineer Miroslav Hajn, 1932–1933

Na výšinách 6 (7 Bub, 901), Josef Schindler, apartment building, 1906

Na výšinách 10, 12 (7 Bub, 899, 890), Jan Pacl, apartment buildings, 1909–1910

Na Zatlance 11 (5 Smí, 1330), Viktorin Šulc, high school building, 1915–1917

Na Zatlance 15 (5 Smí, 22), Antonín Cechner, Václav Libánský, bath house, 1906–1909

Na Zátorce 3 (6 Bub, 289), Matěj Blecha, Emil Králíček, family house, circa 1910

Na Zátorce 5 (6 Bub, 350), Antonín Pfeiffer, family house, 1911–1912

Na Zátorce 11 (6 Bub, 807), Josef Zasche, family house, 1927–1928

Na Zátorce 17 (6 Bub, 783), Rudolf Stockar, family house, 1926–1928

Na Zátorce 18 (6 Bub, 469), Otakar Novotný, family house, 1929; modified by Adolf Loos(?), 1930–1931

Na Zavadilce 4 (6 Dej, 1434), Vladimír Bolech, family house, 1935

Na zbořenci 7 (2 NoM, 264), Ferdinand Fencl, student dormitories, 1935–1936

Na zbořenci 8 (2 NoM, 274), Hilar Pacanovský, Rudolf Hraba, apartment building, 1936–1937

Na zbořenci 16 (2 NoM, 277), Antonín Stanzer, Antonín Nesnídal, apartment building, 1937

Na Zlatnici 3 (4 Pod, 265), Rudolf Stockar, family house, 1929

Na Zlatnici 28 (4 Pod, 85), Jan Závorka, apartment building, 1927

Nad Bertramkou 1 (5 Smí, 2416), Jan Gillar, family house, 1939

Nad Bertramkou 4 (5 Smí, 2158), Ladislav Syrový, Jan Gillar(?), family house, 1934

Nad Bertramkou 16 (5 Smí, 2094), Miloš Vaněček, family house, 1932–1933(?)

Nad cementárnou 23 (4 Pod, 331), Karel Honzík, family house of writer František Langer, 1929–1930

Nad hradním vodojemem 4, 6 (6 Stř, 367, 369), Jaroslav Vondrák, family house, 1922

Nad hradním vodojemem 14 (6 Stř, 642), Adolf Loos, Karel Lhota, family house of František Müller, 1928–1930

Nad Kajetánkou 1–8 (6 Bře, 1401, 1402, 1410–1415), Antonín Černý, apartment buildings, 1938–1947

Nad Kajetánkou 18 (6 Bře, 1423), Jiří Štursa, apartment building, 1939–1940

Nad Kajetánkou 20–24 (6 Bře, 1433–1435), Václav Hilský, Rudolf Jasenský, František Jech, Karel Koželka, apartment buildings, 1937–1939

Nad Kajetánkou 23 (6 Bře, 1480), Václav Klouček, apartment building, 1940–1941

Nad Kazankou 19 (7 Tró, 185), Záboj Merz, family house, 1920, porter's lodge, 1919

Nad Kazankou (8 Tró, 222), Arnošt Mühlstein, Victor Fürth, family house, 1928–1930

Nad královskou oborou 3 (7 Bub, 101), Martin Reiner, Julius Landsmann, apartment building, 1936

Nad královskou oborou 29 (7 Bub, 242), Václav Vítězslav Chytrý, apartment building, 1905

Nad královskou oborou 53 (7 Bub, 320), Jaroslav Rössler, apartment building, 1929

Nad Krocínkou 66 (9 Vys, 647), Ludvík Hilgert, family house, 1933–1934

Nad lesem 16 (4 Hod, 206), Václav Stach, family house, 1935

Nad lesem 26 (4 Hod, 189), Jan Salák, family house, 1933

Nad lesíkem 3 (6 Dej, 1816), Jindřich Freiwald, Jaroslav Böhm, family house, 1939

Nad lomem 14, 16 (4 Bra, 745, 746), Pavel Bareš, family duplex, 1939–1940

Nad lomem 21 (4 Bra, 747), Emanuel Losenický, family house, 1934

Nad lomem 23 (4 Bra, 775), Oldřich Starý, family house, 1935

Nad octárnou 1–23 (6 Stř, 401–412), V. Nekvasil Architects and Building Contractors, 1922–1923

Nad olšinami 4 (10 Str, 672), Jaromír Krejcar, family house, 1926–1927

Nad olšinami 5 (10 Str, 448), Jan Kloub, apartment building, 1922–1924

Nad ohradou (3 Žiž, 1700), Municipal Construction Authority, city architects Mečislav Petrů and Vlastislav Martínek, school building, 1928–1929, 1938

Nad Panenskou 1–5 (6 Stř, 522–524), Miloš Vaněček, apartment buildings, 1923–1926

Nad Paťankou 16 (6 Dej, 1785), Pavel Janák, own family house, 1932 (P 1931)

Nad Paťankou 18 (6 Dej, 1786), Josef Gočár, family house, 1932 (P 1931)

Nad Paťankou 20 (6 Dej, 1788), Josef Gočár, family house, 1932–1933

Nad Paťankou 24 (6 Dej, 1789), František Kerhart, family house, 1935–1936

Nad Paťankou 42 (6 Dej, 1808), Adolf Benš, own family house, 1937–1938

Nad pomníkem 5 (5 Hlu, 398), Jiří Gočár, family house, 1938–1939

Nad Primaskou 2 (10 Str, 143), Antonín Mazáč, family house, 1906

Nad Primaskou 4 (10 Str, 293), Václav Romováček, family house, 1920

Nad Rokoskou 6 (8 Lib, 1900), Josef Fuchs, family house, 1938–1939

Nad Rokoskou 8 (8 Lib, 909), Rudolf Stockar, family house, 1912

Nad Rokoskou 15 (8 Lib, 829), Jan Zázvorka, family house, 1936–1937)

Nad Rokoskou 29 (8 Lib, 1321), Otakar Novotný, family house, 1928

Nad Rokoskou 36 (8 Lib, 1227), Josef Jelínek, family house, 1938–1939

Nad Rokoskou 38 (8 Lib, 1228), Rudolf Stockar, family house, 1926

Nad Santoškou 1 (5 Smí, 1911), Josef Karel Říha, own family house, 1929–1930

Nas Santoškou 12 (5 Smí, 1397), František Kavalír, family duplex, 1922

Nad studánkou 7 (4 Nus, 847), Karel Janů, apartment building, 1937

Nad Šárkou 9 (6 Dej, 1718), Jindřich Freiwald, Jaroslav Böhm, family house, 1934

Nad Šárkou 12 (6 Dej, 1763), Josef Čapek, Pastyřík, apartment building, 1939

Nad štolou 6 (7 Hol, 1277), Josef Záruba-Pfeffermann, office and apartment building, 1921–1923

Na štolou 12 (7 Hol, 950)), Antonín Zámek, apartment building, 1906

Nad údolím 36 (4 Hod, 166), Rudolf Miňovský, family house, 1933

Nad vodovodem 3 (3 Žiž, 23), Leopold Ehrmann, columbarium, before 1934

Nad výšinkou 13 (5 Smí, 2469), Vladimír Grégr, family house, 1938–1940

Nad výšinkou 15 (5 Smí, 1258), Viktor Beneš, family house, 1909–1910

Nad Zámečnicí 15 (5 Smí, 2073), Václav Zralý, Václav Dvořák, Stanislav Kohout, family house with workshop, 1932

Nad Zátiším 26 (4 Lho, 326), Jaromír Krejcar, family house, 1939

Nádražní 16 (5 Smí, 274), Zdeněk Pštross, office building, 1938–1939

Náplavní 5 (2 NoM, 2011), Josef Hercík, apartment building, 1907

Národní 7 (StM, 1011), Osvald Polívka, commercial, office and apartment building, 1905(?)–1908

Národní 9 (1 StM, 1010), Osvald Polívka, František Topič publishing house — commercial and office building, 1905–1908

Národní 15 (1 StM, 984), Berthold Schwarz, commercial and office building, 1927–1928

Národní 18 (1 NoM, 117), Matěj Blecha Architects and Building Contractors, commercial and office building, 1926–1927

Národní 19 (1 StM, 949), Bohumil Hypšman, commercial and office building, 1910–1912

Národní 27 (1 StM, 1022), Artur Payr, commercial and apartment building, 1929–1930

Národní 28 (1 NoM, 60), Matěj Blecha, commercial and office building, 1924–1926

Národní 30 (1 NoM, 59), František Zelenka, reconstruction of a commercial building, 1938

Národní 32 (1 NoM, 58), Josef Havlíček, Jaroslav Polívka, commercial and office building, 1927–1928

Národní 34 (1 NoM, 40), J. L. Plešinger, commercial and office building, 1935–1936

Národní 36 (1 NoM, 38), Oldřich Starý, commercial and apartment building with exhibition space, 1936–1938 (P 1934)

Národní obrany 4 (6 Bub, 457), Jan Petrák, apartment building, 1914

Národní obrany 6 (6 Bub, 455), František Xaver Čtrnáctý, apartment building, 1921–1922

Národní obrany 8 (6 Bub, 595), František Xaver Čtrnáctý, apartment building, 1923–1924

Národní obrany 14 (6 Bub, 714), Rudolf Stockar, apartment building, circa 1930

Národní obrany 15 (6 Bub, 936), Ferdinand Hruška, apartment building, 1926–1927

Národní obrany 22, 24 (6 Bub, 718, 719), Rudolf Bettelheim, apartment buildings, 1931, 1934

Národní obrany 45 (6 Bub, 909), František Fischl, apartment building, 1935

Neherovská 8 (6 Dej, 677), Ladislav Žák, family house of actress Lída Baarová, 1937

Neherovská 10 (6 Dej, 1522), Josef Chochol, family house, 1931

Neherovská 20 (6 Dej, 1920), J. Štrobl, family house, 1934–1936

Neherovská 22 (6 Dej, 1921), Josef Fuchs, family house, 1938

Nekázanka 19 (1 NoM, 876), Viktor Lampl, Otto Fuchs, commercial and apartment building, 1928–1929

Neklanova 2 (2 Vyš, 56), Josef Chochol(?), Antonín Belada, apartment building, 1913

Neklanova 12 (2 Vyš, 127), Oktáv Koutský, apartment building, 1926–1928

Neklanova 30 (2 Vyš, 98), Josef Chochol, apartment building, 1913–1914

Nepomucká 11 (5 Koš, 659), Jaroslav Kincl, Lev Krča, Stanislav Tobek, family duplex, 1937–1938

Nepomucká (5 Koš), Jaroslav Čermák, Church of St Jan Nepomuk, from 1938

Nerudova 9 (1 MaS, 254), Otokar Homoláč, apartment building, 1936–1939

Nezamyslova 14, 16 (2 Nus, 638, 639), Oldřich Tyl, apartment buildings, 1922–1923

Nikoly Tesly 1–11 (6 Dej, 1420, 1424), Bohumír Kozák, apartment buildings, 1928–1929

Nikoly Tesly 6, 8 (6 Dej, 1093, 1904), Vladimír Weiss, apartment buildings, 1931

Nitranská (10 Vin, 2226), Ludvík Kysela, factory of the inventor František Křižík, circa 1920

Novákových 2, 4 (8 Lib, 59), Stivo Vacek, apartment building, 1932–1933

Novovysočanská 1 (9 Vys, 501), Bohumír Kozák, refuge for the homeless, 1924

Novovysočanská 10–14 (9 Vys, 502–504), Rudolf Hrabě, apartment building, 1924–1925

Nuselská (4 Mich, 319), Josef Kříž, Jiří Palička, renovation of house, 1913

Nuselská 76 (4 Mich, 513), Otakar Burian, apartment building, 1925–1928

Obětí 8. května 2–6 (4 Krč, 553–555), František Albert Libra, Jiří Kan, apartment buildings, 1935–1937

Oblouková (10 Vrš, 951), Miloslav Kopřiva, apartment building, 1930

Odborů 6 (2 NoM, 278), Oktáv Koutský, association club, 1934–1935

Olivova 1, 3 (1 NoM, 1419), Jan Kotěra, office building, 1922–1924 (P 1921)

Ondříčkova 8 (3 Vin, 2296), Ladislav Suk, apartment building, 1933

Ondříčkova 9 (3 Žiž, 1304), Čeněk Nečásek, František Kándl, apartment building, 1921–1922

Ondříčkova 10 (3 Vin, 1975), Tomáš Pražák, Pavel Moravec, apartment building, 1924–1925

Ondříčkova 20 (3 Vin, 2284), Oldřich Liska, apartment building, 1932

Ondříčkova 26 (3 Vin, 2395), A. Ackermann, apartment building, 1938–1939

Ondříčkova 30 (3 Vin, 2379), Jindřich Řehoř, apartment building, 1937–1938

Opatovická 18 (1 NoM, 160), Bohumil Belada, Jaroslav Vorlíček(?), publishing house, 1927–1928

Opatovická 26 (1 NoM, 154), Alois Dryák, Jan Mayer, printing plant and apartment building, 1932–1939

Opletalova 4 (1 NoM, 1535), Bohuslav and Stanislav Kratochvíl, commercial and apartment building, 1939–1940; modifications by Jaroslav Kincl, 1940–1941

Opletalova 5 (1 NoM, 9191), Václav Velvarský, Czechoslovak Press Agency building, 1928–1930

Opletalova 9 (1 NoM, 917), Ferdinand Fencl, apartment building with shops and garages, 1936–1939

Opletalova 29 (1 NoM, 1337), Pavel Janák, Autoclub building, 1925–1928

Opletalova 55 (1 NoM, 1015), Josef Zasche, office building, 1906–1907

Opletalova 59 (1 NoM, 1013), Ladislav Kuřák, commercial and apartment building, 1938–1939

Orelská 11 (10 Vrš, 741), Josef Prskavec, apartment building, 1926–1927

Orlická 2 (3 Vin, 2020), Alois Krofta, hotel with cinema, 1926–1934

Osadní 10 (7 Hol, 313), Rudolf Stockar, commercial and office building, 1920

Osadní 39–45 (7 Hol, 46, 1476), František Albert Libra, Jiří Kan, apartment buildings, 1936

Osamocená 20 (6 Vok, 441), František Louda, apartment building, 1939

Osmého listopadu 2–28 (6 Bře, 560–571), František Roith, apartment buildings, 1921

Ostrovní 5 (1 NoM, 2064), Rudolf Wels, Guido Lagus, apartment building, 1938)

Ostrovní 9 (1 NoM, 2070), Vladimír Nevšímal, Ivan Vaníček, school building, 1937–1938

Ostrovní 21 (1 NoM, 124), Rudolf Kestřánek, apartment building, 1911

Ostrovní 22 (1 NoM, 128), A. Hartman, Bohuslav Dašek, apartment building, 1938–1939

Ostrovského 3 (5 Smí, 253), Vlastimil Lada, Josef Hlaváček, women's refuge for the homeless, 1935–1936

Ovenecká 23, 35 (7 Bub, 953, 79), Jaroslav Gruber, František Troníček, apartment buildings, 1933–1935

Ovenecká 43 (7 Bub, 98), Jan Gillar, Jan Karhan, apartment building, 1935

Pacovská 1 (4 Krč, 527), Antonín Černý, laundry, 1932–1933

Pacovská 4 (4 Krč, 350), Municipal Construction Authority, city architect Mečislav Petrů, school building, 1935

Palackého 9 (1 NoM, 718), František Zelenka, commercial and apartment building, 1937

Palmovka 7 (8 Lib, 522), Ladislav Kuřák, apartment building, 1911–1912

Pampelišková 2–24 (10 Záb, 2005–2016), Václav Rajdl, family houses, 1938

Panská 4 (1 NoM, 894), Oldřich Tyl, Black Rose (Černá růže) commercial and apartment building with arcade and restaurant, 1930–1931 (P 1929)

Panská 12 (1 NoM, 897), Jiří Justich, František Buldra, hotel, 1907–1909

Papírenská 30 (6 Dej, 219), František Bartoš, institute of hydrology, 1925–1929

Paprsková 12 (4 Krč, 442), Václav Kopecký, family house, 1933–1934

Parléřova 2 (6 Hra, 118), Municipal Construction Authority, city architects Mečislav Petrů and Karel Beneš, school building, 1930–1932

Parléřova 6 (6 Stř, 682), Nikola Dobrovič, association club and student dormitories, 1931–1933

Parléřova 8 (6 Stř, 681), Bohumil Sláma, post office, 1940–1942 (P 1937?)

Partyzánská 1 (7 Hol, 3), Josef Mlíka, power transformation station, 1937

Partyzánská 7a (7 Hol, 188), František Buriánek, office building, 1937

Pařížská 1 (1 StM, 1073), Jan Koula, apartment building, 1901–1902

Pařížská 9 (1 Jos, 68), Jan Vejrych, apartment building, 1903–1904

Pařížská 13 (1 Jos, 66), Jan Vejrych, apartment building, 1902–1903

Pařížská 16 (1 Jos, 125), Jiří Justich(?), Matěj Blecha, apartment building, 1905–1906

Pařížská 17 (1 Jos, 98), Richard Klenka, František Weyr, apartment building with restaurant, 1906–1907

Pařížská 23 (1 Jos, 205), Jiří Justich, apartment building, 1906

Pařížská 28 (1 Jos, 131), Karel Vítězslav Mašek, apartment building, 1906–1908

Pátého května 37–41 (4 Nus, 1120, 1035), Josef Havlíček, Karel Honzík, apartment buildings, 1931–1932

Pátého května 51 (4 Nus, 200), Ferdinand Fencl, high school building, 1937–1941

Patočkova 5 (6 Stř, 711), Jiří Kodl, family house, 1929–1931

Patočkova 6 (6 Stř, 4), Václav Hilský, Rudolf Jasenský, Václav Linhart, apartment building, 1938

Patočkova 8–14 (6 Stř, 5, 9, 673, 689), Bohumil Kněžek, Josef Václavík, apartment buildings, 1938–1939

Pechlátova 16 (5 Smí, 2503), Rudolf Hrabě, apartment building, 1924–1925

Perlová 1 (1 StM, 412), Karel Kotas, commercial and apartment building, 1938–1940

Perlová 3 (1 NoM, 378), František Havlena, commercial building, circa 1930

Perlová 5 (1 StM, 371), František Řehák, commercial building, 1927–1931

Pernerova 44, 4a (8 Kar, 558, 559), Antonín Černý, Karel Beran, apartment buildings, 1940–1941

Pernerova 59–63 (8 Kar, 533, 536), Ludvík Kander, apartment buildings, 1929

Perucká 18 (2 Vin, 2274), Karel Stráník, family house, 1931

Petra Rezka 3 (4 Nus, 1090), Václav Ložek, apartment building, 1932–1933

Petra Rezka 16 (4 Nus, 810), Karel Hannauer, apartment building, 1938

Petrohradská 29 (10 Vrš, 278), Jan Gillar, apartment building, circa 1932

Petrská 1 (1 NoM, 1426), Victor Fürth, apartment building, 1937

Pětidomí 2 (6 Bub, 238), Alois Dryák, family house, circa 1900–1901

Pětidomí 5 (6 Bub, 247), Otakar Novotný, family house, 1905; rebuilt by Jan Jarolím, 1923

Pevnostní 1 (6 Stř, 581), Jaroslav Fröhlich, family house, 1927

Pevnostní 7 (6 Stř, 588), Arnošt Mühlstein, Victor Fürth, family house, 1928

Písecká 17 (3 Vin, 1672), Jaroslav and Karel Fišer, apartment building, 1939–1940

Píseckého 1–19 (5 Koš, 326–333), František Kavalír, apartment buildings, 1910–1922

Pivoňková 59 (10 Záb, 1950), František Marek, family house, 1936–1938

Pivovarnická 2 (8 Lib, 1814), Jan Nedbal, apartment building, 1939

Pivovarnická 9 (8 Lib, 1435), Cyril Seifert, apartment building, 1927–1929

Pivovarnická 10, 12 (8 Lib, 1618, 1619), Evžen Linhart, apartment buildings, 1927–1931

Platnéřská 4 (1 StM, 191), Josef Sakař, completion of monastery, 1909–1913 (P 1907–1908)

Plavecká 3 (2 NoM, 1291), Alois Dryák, apartment building, 1912

Plavecká 8, 10 (2 NoM, 402, 202), Bohumír Kozák, apartment building, 1937–1938

Plzeňská 2, 4 (5 Smí, 23, 232), Ferdinand Fencl(?), Gustav Fantl, apartment buildings with shops, 1936

Plzeňská 55–59 (5 Koš, 246, 247), Miroslav Stöhr, apartment buildings, 1906–1907

Plzeňská 174 (5 Smí, 2076), Josef Kalous, pension, 1932–1934

Plzeňská 207 (5 Koš, 441), Jan Rosůlek(?), apartment building, 1927–1928

Plzeňská 217, 219 (5 Mot, 101, 102), František Maria Černý, depot administration building, up to 1939

Počernická 5 (10 Str, 723), Eduard Hnilička, family house, 1927–1928

Počernická 9 (10 Str, 1106), Jaroslav, Jan and Josef Mayer, family house, 1932

Počernická 19 (10 Str, 1353), Karel Kupka, family house, 1937–1938

Počernická 23 (10 Str, 1477), J. L. Plešinger, family house, 1940–1941

Pod altánem 37–47 (10 Str, 535–540), František Albert Libra, family houses, 1923–1924

Pod Andělkou 15 (6 Stř, 915), Jan Gillar, family house, 1937

Pod Balkánem (9 Vys, 599), Otakar Novotný, hostel for resettled persons, 1928

Pod bání 15 (8 Lib, 1929), Karel Míšek, family house, 1940–1941

Pod Bořislavkou 26 (8 Dej, 1730), Josef Gočár, family house, 1940–1941

Pod Bořislavkou 40 (6 Dej, 1722) Emanuel Hruška, family house, 1936–1937

Pod Děvínem 10 (5 Smí, 2449), Eduard Rouček, family house, 1939–1940

Pod Habrovou 3 (5 Hlu, 445), Jiří Štursa and Vlasta Štursová, family house, 1939–1940

Pod Habrovou 11 (5 Hlu, 371), Otto and Karel Kohn, family house, 1936–1937

Pod Habrovou 12 (5 Hlu, 159), Alois Houba, family house, 1929–1930

Pod Habrovou 14 (5 Hlu, 153), Alois Houba(?), family house, 1929

Pod Habrovou 15 (5 Hlu, 184), Rudolf Bettelheim, family house, 1932–1933

Pod Habrovou 16 (5 Hlu, 350), Karel Caivas, Vladimír Weiss, family house, 1934–1935

Pod Habrovou 18 (5 Hlu, 389), Otto Glas, family house, 1937–1938

Pod hájem 7, 9 (5 Smí, 1541, 1542), Václav Kopecký, family houses, 1923–1924

Pod hradbami 4 (6 Stř, 656), Bohumír Kozák, Franz Hruška(?), family house, 1927–1928

Pod hradbami 13 (6 Stř, 660), Ladislav Machoň, family house, 1927–1928

Pod hradbami 17 (6 Stř, 658), Bruno Paul, family house, 1928–1929

Pod kaštany 18 (6 Bub, 286), Bohumil Hypšman, family house, 1908–1909

Pod kaštany 22 (6 Bub, 526), Kamil Hilbert, family house, circa 1925

Pod kaštany 24 (6 Bub, 545), Josef Zasche, family house, 1922–1923

Pod Kavalírkou 30, 32 (5 Koš, 448, 486), Jaroslav Fragner, apartment building, 1927

Pod Kesnerkou 3 (5 Smí, 2325), Jindřich Žáček, family house, 1937

Pod Klikovkou 15 (5 Smí, 2279), Otto Grams, family house, circa 1932

Pod Klaudiánkou 13 (4 Pod, 300), Josef Jelínek, family house, 1934

Pod Klaudiánkou 15 (4 Pod, 299), František Votava, family house, 1937

Pod kostelem 3 (6 Stř, 109), Antonín Fric, family house, 1939

Pod Kotlářkou 28 (5 Smí, 2424), Bohumil Kněžek, Josef Václavík, family house, 1939

Pod krčským lesem 24 (4 Krč, 763), J. Černý, family house, 1939

Pod lipkami 16–30 (5 Smí, 1407–1414), Jindřich Freiwald, Jaroslav Böhm, family duplexes, 1921–1922

Pod pekárnami 9 (9 Vys, 300), Hubert Gessner(?), Viktor Kafka, apartment building, 1921–1922

Pod Plískavou 4 (10 Hos, 371), Evžen Linhart, apartment building. 1926–1927 (P 1925)

Pod Slovany 13 (2 NoM, 1913), Rudolf Hraba, Hilar Pacanovský, apartment building, 1937

Pod Stárkou 4 (4 Mich, 36), Josef Kučera, gymnasium, 1937–1938

Pod strašnickou vinicí 35 (10 Str, 1010), Jan Žák, family house, 1935–1936

Pod vilami 12 (4 Nus, 696), Otakar Burian, family house, 1926–1929

Pod vilami 13 (4 Nus, 1038), Antonín Fric, apartment building, 1931–1932

Pod vilami 26 (4 Nus, 1772), Ludvík Hilgert, family house, 1926–1931

Pod vyhlídkou 14–24 (6 Stř, 331–336), Eduard Hnilička, family houses, 1920

Pod Zvonařkou 7 (2 Vin, 1746), Maxmilian Duchoslav, family house, 1921–1922

Pod Žvahovem 22 (5 Hlu, 191), František Stalmach, Jan Svoboda, family house, 1932

Podbabská 7 (6 Dej, 1895), construction department of the Prague Power Company, architect A. Janda, bus garages, 1931

Podbělohorská 1 (5 Smí, 2185), Jaroslav Brada, kindergarten, 1933–1934

Podbělohorská 4–28 (5 Smí, 1446–1453), Eduard Hnilička, family houses, 1922–1923

Podléšková 81–95 (10 Záb, 2375–2382), Václav Rajdl, František Weigner, family houses, 1939–1940

Podolská 1–4 (4 Pod, 367–369), V. Nekvasil Architects and Building Contractors, apartment buildings, 1932

509

Podolská 5 (4 Pod, 90), Jaroslav Stejskal, Bohumil Skalický, gymnasium, 1933

Podolská 17 (4 Pod, 15), Antonín Engel, water treatment station, 1923–1928

Podolská 31 (4 Pod, 208), Josef Prskavec, apartment building, 1923–1924

Podolská 116 (4 Pod, 245), František Svoboda, apartment building, 1926–1927

Podolská 118–120 (4 Pod, 606, 607), František Louda, apartment buildings, 1940–1941

Podskalská 7 (2 NoM, 392), Kamil Hilbert, apartment building, 1921–1922

Podskalská 10 (2 NoM, 365), Prague Municipal Construction Authority, city architect Mečislav Petrů, Jiří Kodl(?), school building, 1927–1930

Podskalská 17, 19 (2 NoM, 1290), Ladislav Skřivánek, office building, 1920–1922

Podskalská 18 (2 NoM, 1908), Ladislav Čapek, apartment building, 1914–1915

Podskalská 31, 33 (2 NoM, 370, 378), Max Spielmann, Matěj Blecha, apartment building, 1921

Polední 6 (4 Bra, 871), Antonín Šimek, František Urban, family house, 1923–1924

Polední 18 (4 Bra, 675), Max Brüll, family house, 1938

Polská 1 (2 Vin, 2400), František Marek, Zbyněk Jirsák, Václav Vejrych, gymnasium, 1938–1946

Polská 56, 58 (2 Vin, 1751), Viktor Lampl, Otto Fuchs, apartment building, 1921–1922

Pomněnková 22–38 (10 Záb, 1369–1377), Alex Hanuš, Zdeněk Kruliš, Vladimír Vlček, family houses, 1928–1929

Pomněnková 46, 48 (10 Záb, 2222, 2223), Václav Rajdl, František Weigner, family duplex, 1939

Pplk. Sochora 34 (7 Hol, 740, 765), Emanuel Hruška, apartment buildings, 1937–1938

Prachnerova 8 (5 Koš, 674), Julius Landsmann, Martin Reiner, apartment building, 1938

Pravá 18 (4 Pod, 287), Jaroslav Herink, apartment building, 1932–1933

Pravoúhlá 28 (5 Smí, 1901), Emil Šulc, family house, 1929

Preslova 17 (5 Smí, 1269), Stanislav Vávra, apartment buildings, up to 1911

Primátorská 20 (8 Lib, 325), Kamil Zupanc, apartment building with restaurant, up to 1936

Provaznická 9 (1 StM, 400), Fritz Lehmann, apartment building, 1938

Provaznická 12 (1 StM, 397), Adolf Foehr, commercial building, 1930–1932

Průběžná 24, 26 (10 Str, 573), Fratišek Albert Libra, apartment buildings, 1923–1924

Průhledová 2 (6 Dej, 1790), Oldřich Starý, family house of graphic artist Ladislav Sutnar, 1932

Průhledová 6 (6 Dej, 1804), Zdeněk Blažek, family house, 1932 (P 1931)

Průhledová 10 (6 Dej, 1705), Josef Fuchs, family house, 1932

Prvního pluku 18 (8 Kar, 539), Matěj Blecha, apartment building with savings bank and café, 1912–1913

Před Cibulkami 6, 8 (5 Koš, 316, 317), Josef Dlouhý, apartment building, 1919–1922; modified by Václav Suk, 1933–1934

Předvoje 21 (6 Vel, 279), Jaroslav Bezecný, family house, 1938

Přemyslovská 17–21 (3 Vin, 1912–1914), Hanuš Hladík, apartment building, 1923–1924

Příčná 1 (1 NoM, 668), Karel Kotas, commercial and apartment building, 1934–1935

Přístavní 28 (7 Hol, 1273), Eduard Skřivan, apartment building, 1941–1942

Přístavní 55 (7 Hol, 1190), Milada Pavlíková-Petříková, Theodor Petřík, apartment building, 1922

Psohlavců 30 (4 Bra, 680), Václav Stach, apartment building, 1939

Pštrossova 11 (1 NoM, 204), Vratislav Lhota, kindergarten, 1909

Půlkruhová 42 (6 Vok, 99), Bohumil Hypšman, family house, 1909

Purkyňova 2 (1 NoM, 74), Adolf Foehr, office building, 1927–1928; modified by Bedřich Feuerstein, 1931

Purkyňova 9, 11 (1 NoM, 2050, 2053), František Troníček, apartment building, 1940

Radhošťská 18–22 (3 Žiž, 1623), Evžen Linhart, apartment buildings, 1926–1928 (P 1925)

Radimova 38 (6 Bře, 622), Antonín Jednorožec, family house, 1925

Radlická 38 (5 Smí, 2000), Vlastimil Lada, Josef Hlaváček, single women's hostel, 1932

Radlická 103 (5 Smí, 2485), Jan Rosůlek, apartment building, 1926–1928 (P 1925)

Rejskova 13 (2 Vin, 2330), Josef Filip, apartment building, 1935

Revoluční 1 (1 StM, 655, 1003), Jan Žák, commercial and apartment building, 1928–1929

Revoluční 3 (1 StM, 1033), Max Spielmann, Rudolf Weiser, office building, 1928–1929

Revoluční 5 (1 ŠtM, 1006), Fritz Lehmann, commercial and apartment building, 1936–1937

Revoluční 17 (1 StM, 764), František Berger, commercial and apartment building, 1927–1930

Revoluční 23 (1 StM, 1044), Ludvík Kysela, commercial building, 1929–1931

Revoluční 24 (1 NoM, 1546), Václav Ložek, renovation and extension to building, 1926

Revoluční 25 (1 StM, 767), Jaroslav Fragner, commercial, office and apartment building with café, 1934–1935

Romaina Rollanda 6 (6 Bub, 522), Arnošt Mühlstein, Victor Fürth(?), family house, up to 1921

Rooseveltova 7 (6 Bub, 497), Tomáš Pražák, Pavel Moravec, family house, 1922

Rooseveltova 14 (6 Bub, 831), Arnošt Mühlstein, Victor Fürth, family house, 1928

Rooseveltova 23 (6 Bub, 620), Bedřich Feuerstein, Institute of Geography, 1921(?)–1925

Rooseveltova 24–42 (6 Bub, 611–619), Rudolf Hrabě, apartment buildings, 1923–1925

Rooseveltova 31 (6 Bub, 764), Jaroslav Vondrák, apartment building, 1927–1928

Rooseveltova 47 (6 Bub, 893), Oldřich Tyl, apartment building, 1929–1930

Rooseveltova 49 (6 Bub, 892), Pavel Janák, apartment buildings, 1928–1929 (P 1927)

Ruská 6–12 (10 Vrš, 451, 452, 470, 473), Osvald Polívka, apartment buildings, 1904–1906

Ruská 38 (10 Vrš, 604), Josef Mayer, Alois Zázvorka, apartment building, 1911

Ruská 58 (10 Vrš, 804), Jan Mentberger, Tomáš Pražák, apartment building, 1927–1928

Ruská 62 (10 Vrš, 828), Adolf Kuthan, apartment building, circa 1940

Ruská 66 (10 Vrš, 764), Václav Klouček, apartment building, 1938

Ruská 84 (10 Vrš, 1039), František Svatoš, Josef Martínek, Ladislav Svatoš, apartment building, 1931–1933

Ruská 106 (10 Vrš, 788), Jaroslav Vančura, family house, 1940

Ruská 152 (10 Vrš, 777), Jan Gillar, apartment building, 1939(?)

Růžová 6 (1 NoM, 943) Josef Sakař, printing plant, 1923–1926

Růžová 8 (1 NoM, 947), Bohumír Kozák, apartment building, 1922–1923

Rybná 8 (1 StM, 677), Rudolf Weiser, hotel, 1928–1930

Rybná 9 (1 StM, 678), Otto and Karel Kohn, commercial building, circa 1930

Rybná 25, 27 (1 StM, 732, 1091), Jaroslav Vančura, apartment buildings, 1936–1938

Rytířská 3 (1 StM, 529), Ludvík Hilgert, shop portal, before 1925

Řásnovka 8 (1 StM, 770), František Marek, office building, 1941–1950

Řeznická 17 (1 NoM, 662), Antonín Žižka, pension, 1936–1937

Řeznická 19 (1 NoM, 661), Rudolf Wels, Guido Lagus(?), apartment building, circa 1937

Řeznická 20 (1 NoM, 649), Josef Oldřich Schüller, V. J. Prokop, commercial and apartment building, 1935

Římská 20 (2 Vin, 526), B. Hollmann, commercial building, 1929–1930

Římská 42 (2 Vin, 1389), Vilém Hofman, apartment building, 1938

Římská 44 (2 Vin, 2312), Václav Kopecký, apartment building, 1933–1934

Římská 45 (2 Vin, 2135), Pavel Moravec, apartment building with club and theater, 1926–1928

Řipská 15 (3 Vin, 767), Josef Čeleda, apartment building, 1937–1938

S. K. Neumanna 22 (8 Lib, 1135), Antonín Makovec, family house, 1925–1926

Salmovská 10 (2 NoM, 1539), Hilar Pacanovský, apartment building, 1937–1938

Salvátorská 8, 10 (1 StM, 931, 1092), Otakar Novotný, apartment building, printing plant and Jan Štenc publishing house, 1909–1911

Sámova 5, 7 (10 Vrš, 29), Antonín Černý, apartment buildings, 1936–1938

Sámova 8 (10 Vrš, 664), Jindřich Pollert, factory, 1927

Sarajevská 5 (2 Vin, 1278), Mikuláš Gottdiener, apartment building, 1937–1939

Sauerova 2 (3 Žiž, 1836), Ervín Katona, children's home, 1933

Sázavská 19 (2 Vin, 1971), František Kavalír, school building, 1924–1925

Sbíhavá II 2 (6 DoL, 360), Karel Beneš, Mečislav Petrů, kindergarten, 1933–1934

Sdružení 19–27 (4 Nus, 1293–1297), Karel Hannauer, apartment buildings, 1937

Sedlčanská 17 (4 Mich, 1102), Hilar Pacanovský, apartment building, 1941

Sedlčanská 20 (4 Mich, 1059), Jiří Štursa, Vlasta Štursová, apartment building, 1939–1940

Sekaninova 22, 24 (2 Nus, 710, 711), Vladimír František, Hofman, Rudolf Hrabě, apartment building, 1926–1927

Sekaninova 28–32 (2 Nus, 1087), Alois Vavrouš & Son Architects and Building Contractors, apartment buildings, 1931–1932

Sekaninova 36 (2 Nus, 1204), Václav Urban, apartment building, 1953–1936

Severovýchodní I 2–6 (4 Záb, 1422, 1224), Vlastimil Brožek, Karel Polívka, apartment buildings with shops, 1927–1928

Severovýchodní I 52–64 (4 Záb, 1460–1466), Vlastimil Brožek, Karel Polívka, family houses, 1926

Severovýchodní VI 33–39 (4 Záb, 1527–1530), Vlastimil Brožek, Karel Polívka, family houses, 1925–1926

Sezimova 15 (4 Nus, 481), Karel Hannauer Sr., apartment building, 1908

Schnirchova 11 (7 Hol, 199), Arnošt Mühlstein, Victor Fürth, apartment building, 1934–1935

Schnirchova 29 (7 Hol, 1084), Evžen Rosenberg, apartment building, 1937

Skalecká 15 (7 Hol, 356), Fritz Lehmann, rebuilding of own house, 1936

Skalní 10 (5 Hlu, 327), Vladimír Grégr, family house, 1932–1933

Skalní 17 (5 Hlu, 172), Rudolf Stockar, family house, 1931

Skalní 20 (5 Hlu, 446), Antonín Gabriel, family house, 1931

Skořepka, 2 (1 StM, 355), Oldřich Tyl, apartment building, 1929–1930 (P 1928?)

513

Sládkova 4 (7 Bub, 631), Bohuslav Homoláč, apartment building, 1919–1921 (P 1914)

Slavíčkova 6 (6 Bub, 248), Jan Kotěra, family house of sculptor Stanislav Sucharda, 1906–1907 (P 1905)

Slavíčkova 7 (6 Bub, 196), Karel Vítězslav Mašek, own family house, 1901

Slavíčkova 9 (6 Bub, 173), Gustav Papež, family house, 1899

Slavíčkova 17 (6 Bub, 153), Jan Koula, own family house, 1895–1896; modified by Jan E. Koula, 1928

Slavíkova 1 (2 Vin, 1657), Bohuslav Homoláč, apartment building, 1912–1913

Slavíkova 22 (3 Žiž, 1499), Jan Chládek, student dormitories, 1924–1925

Slávy Horníka 13 (5 Koš, 82), Josef Oldřich Schüller, apartment building, 1936–1938

Slezská 7 (2 Vin, 100), Josef Gočár, office and association building, 1924–1926

Slezská 9 (2 Vin, 2000), Alois Dryák, office building, 1923–1928

Slezská 13 (2 Vin, 2127), Alois Dryák, printing plant, 1927–1928

Slezská 99–105 (3 Vin, 1736–1739), Bohumil Sláma, Jaroslav Pelc, Václav Vejrych, apartment buildings, 1920–1921

Slezská 107 (3 Vin, 2130), Václav Zákostelna, apartment building, 1928

Slezská 114 (3 Vin, 2140), Ladislav Machoň, apartment building, 1928

Slezská 122 (3 Vin, 2271), Vladimír Frýda, kindergarten, 1929–1932

Slezská 125 (3 Vin, 482), Karel Květoň, apartment building, 1938

Slovenská 23, 25 (2 Vin, 1694, 1697), Emil Králíček(?), Josef Veselý, apartment buildings, 1913–1914

Slovinská 18, 20, 27–31 (10 Vrš, 991–997), Vladislav Všetička, apartment buildings, 1931–1932

Slunná 1 (6 Stř, 543), Miloš Vaněček, own family house, 1929

Smolenská 29 (10 Vrš, 42), Vlastimil Brožek, Jan Mentberger, Karel Polívka, apartment building, 1934–1935

Sněmovní 8 (1 Mas, 164), Josef Fanta, renovation of building, 1903

Soběslavská 6–16 (3 Vin, 2043–2048), Tomáš Pražák, Pavel Moravec, family houses, 1926–1928

Soběslavská 15 (3 Vin, 2314), František Stalmach, Jan Svoboda, apartment building, 1934

Sochařská 16 (7 Bub, 343), Jaromír Uhlíř, apartment building, 1911

Sokolovská 1 (8 Kar, 371), František Stalmach, Jan Svoboda, savings bank, office and apartment building, 1939–1942

Sokolovská 57, 59 (8 Kar, 30, 40), Bohumír Kozák, František Svatoš, apartment buildings, 1938–1939

Sokolovská 81 (8 Kar, 79), Josef Blecha, office building, 1934–1935

Sokolovská 96 (8 Kar, 98), Arnošt Mühlstein, Victor Fürth, commercial and apartment building with garages, 1928–1930

Sokolovská 99 (8 Kar, 101), Alois Mezera, apartment building, 1937–1938

Sokolovská 125 (8 Lib, 890), Emil Králíček, Matěj Blecha, commercial and apartment building, 1910–1911

Sokolská 20 (2 NoM, 1868), František Louda, apartment building, 1938–1939

Sokolská 27, 29 (2 NoM, 464), Karel Kotas, apartment building, 1936–1937

Sokolská 31 (2 NoM, 490), František Vahala, club and apartment building, 1928–1930

Sokolská 33 (2 NoM, 486), Vojtěch Kerhart, Jan Zázvorka, association and apartment building, 1929–1930

Sokolská 68 (2 NoM, 1578), Ladislav Machoň, extension to office building, 1927–1928

Soukenická 11 (1 NoM, 1196), Ervín Katona, apartment building, 1935–1936

Soukenická 27, 29 (1 NoM, 1187, 2060), Arnošt Mühlstein, Victor Fürth, apartment building with shops, 1935–1937

Spálená 4 (1 NoM, 82), Matěj Blecha, commercial and apartment building, 1912–1913

Spálená 12 (1 NoM, 78), Oldřich Tyl, commercial and apartment building, 1928–1930

Spálená 14 (1 NoM, 76), Osvald Polívka, office and apartment building, 1907–1909

Spálená 16 (1 NoM, 75), Jaromír Krejcar, Olympic commercial and apartment building with cinema, 1923–1926 (left courtyard wing), 1925–1928 (street wing)

Spálená 33 (1 NoM, 99), Tomáš Pražák, Pavel Moravec, commercial and office building, 1922

Spálená 51 (1 NoM, 108), Bedřich Bendelmayer, office building, 1927–1929

Spálená 55 (1 NoM, 112), Osvald Polívka, apartment building, 1902–1903

Spálená 57 (1 NoM, 113), Bohumír Kozák, commercial and apartment building, 1931–1932

Spálená 59 (1 NoM, 114), Ferdinand Fencl, commercial building, 1931–1932

Sportovní 22 (10 Vrš, 864), Bohumil Sláma, post office, 1929–1933

Srbská 2 (6 Dej, 347), Karel Herman, apartment building, 1914–1915

Starokošířská 5 (5 Koš, 449), Karel Honzík, Josef Domek, apartment building, 1926–1928 (P 1925)

Strakonická 14 (5 Smí, 1123), Josef Podhajský, apartment building, 1904–1905

Strojnická 6 (7 Hol, 852), František Hodek, sports hall, 1904–1906

Stroupežnického 32 (5 Smí, 290), Leopold Ehrmann, rebuilding of synagogue, 1930

Střemchová 2 (10 Záb, 2100), unknown architect, family house, 1939

Střešovická 15 (6 Stř, 566), Josef Kalous, family house, 1926

Střešovická 31 (6 Stř, 722), Václav Burda, family house, 1928–1930

Střešovická 44 (6 Stř, 746), Otakar Chodounský, family house, 1932

Střešovická 64 (6 Stř, 858), Karel Stráník, Pavel Smetana(?), family house, 1936

Střešovická 66 (6 Stř, 906), František Vokál, family house, 1938

Střížkovská 84 (8 Střížkov, 50), František Marek, residential building and factory, 1931–1932

Studentská 3–5 (6 Dej, 541), Václav Ort, Igor Landa, apartment buildings, 1929

Studentská 8, 10 (6 Dej, 700), Bohumír Kozák, student dormitories, 1930–1931

Studničkova 2, 4 (2 NoM, 2039 II), Alois Špalek, Hlava Institute of Pathology, 1913–1921

Sudoměřská 1 (3 Žiž, 1897), Julius Landsmann, Martin Reiner, apartment building, 1936–1937

Sudoměřská 11, 13 (3 Žiž, 1895), Stanislav Vondráček, apartment building, 1936–1937

Sudoměřská 29 (3 Žiž, 1649), Petr Kropáček, apartment building, 1925–1929

Sudoměřská 31, 33 (3 Žiž, 1650, 1651), Petr Kropáček, apartment building, 1926–1927

Sudoměřská 35 (3 Žiž, 1636), Adolf Benš, apartment building, 1926–1931

Suchardova 4 (6 Bub, 284), Dušan Jurkovič, family house, 1907–1908

Sulická 57 (4 Krč, 120), Bohuslav Černý, sanatorium, 1909

Sušická 25 (6 Dej, 1829), Jan E. Koula, family house, 1932

Sušická 7 (6 Dej, 1847), Jindřich Freiwald, Jaroslav Böhm, family house, 1934

Svátkova 1–7 (5 Smí, 2195–2205), Vilém Beer, family houses, 1934–1935

Svatovítská 3 (6 Dej, 518), Antonín Pfeiffer, apartment building, 1924–1925

Svornosti 15 (5 Smí, 1250), Ladislav Bartl, rebuilding of brewery, up to 1942

Šafaříkova 10 (2 Vin, 253), Oldřich Stibor, apartment building, 1938–1939

Šaldova 4, 8 (8 Kar, 543, 545), Prague Municipal Construction Authority, apartment buildings, from 1919

Šaldova 12, 14 (8 Kar, 425), Jindřich Freiwald, Jaroslav Böhm, Josef Blecha, warehouse and repair workshop, 1933–1934

Šaldova 34 (8 Kar, 492), Alois Čenský, apartment buildings, 1902

Šárecká 13 (6 Dej, 1029), Karel Roštík, family house, 1927

Šárecká 17, 19 (6 Dej, 1026, 1027), Jaroslav Mašek, family houses, 1928

Šárecká 27 (6 Dej, 1022), František Strnad, Alois Mezera, family house, 1931–1932

Šárecká 43, 45 (6 Dej, 929, 928), Arnošt Mühlstein, Victor Fürth, apartment duplex, 1932–1933

Šeříková 10 (1 MaS, 566), Hilar Pacanovský, Rudolf Hraba, apartment building, 1936

Šestidomí 2–6 (6 Bub, 986–988), František Louda, apartment buildings, 1940–1941

Ševce Matouše 14 (4 Krč, 111), Čeněk Vořech, rebuilding of family house, 1930

Ševčíkova 5 (3 Žiž, 1493), Hroch and Hilse architects and building contractors, apartment building, 1924–1925

Šimáčkova 9 (7 Hol, 1450), Jan Zázvorka, apartment building, 1930–1931

Šimáčkova 14, 16 (7 Hol, 1452), Josef Zasche, club building, 1929–1931

Široká (1 Jos, garden of the Museum of Applied Arts), Augusta Müllerová, Ladislav Machoň, exhibition pavilion, 1940

Široká 4, 6 (1 Jos, 24, 25), Richard Klenka, Antonín Makovec, apartment buildings, 1912–1913

Široká 5, 7 (1 Jos, 36, 37), Bohumil Hypšman, apartment building, 1910–1911

Široká 9 (1 Jos, 96), Karel Vítězslav Mašek, apartment building, 1908

Školní 5 (4 Bra, 700), Prague Munipal Construction Authority, city architect Mečislav Petrů, school building, 1936

Školská 7 (1 NoM, 1335), Václav and František Beneš, apartment building, 1937

Šlejnická 13 (6 Dej, 1547), Jan Zázvorka, family house, 1913

Šmeralova 10 (7 Bub, 143), Jindřich Freiwald, Jaroslav Böhm, apartment building, 1933–1934

Šmeralova 15 (7 Bub, 390), Václav Hortlík, apartment building, 1913–1914

Šmeralova 17 (7 Bub, 359), Václav Klatovský, Antonín Mašita, apartment building, 1911

Šmeralova 28, 30 (7 Bub, 378, 360), Václav Vacek, apartment buildings, 1911–1912

Šolínova 1, 3 (6 dej, 344, 513), Milada Pavlíková-Petříková, apartment buildings, 1923–1924

Špitálská (9 Vys, 700, 789), Vladimír Frýda, school buildings, 1927–1929, 1936–1937

Špitálská 3–7 (9 Vys, 759, 775, 795), Ludvík Kander, apartment building, 1932

Špitálská 6–10 (9 Vys, 657, 669, 670), Rudolf Kraus, apartment buildings, 1933–1934

Šrobárova 12 (10 Vin, 1868), Tomáš Pražák, Pavel Moravec, family house, 1923–1924

Šrobárova 23 (3 Vin, 2391), Jaroslav Šťastný, apartment building, 1938–1940

Šrobárova 30–36 (10 Vin, 1835–1838), Ladislav Machoň, family duplexes, 1923–1924

Šrobárova 38 (10 Vin, 1839), Josef Kalous, family house, 1925–1926 (P 1923)

Šrobárova 48 (10 Vin, 49), Rudolf Kvěch, medical institute, 1923–1930

Štefánikova 5 (5 Smí, 229), František Svatoš, apartment building, 1937–1938

Štefánikova 17 (5 Smí, 247), Leo Lauermann, apartment building and savings bank, 1935–1936

Štefánikova 27 (5 Smí, 17a), Jiří Stibral, apartment building, 1904

Štefánikova 28 (5 Smí, 249), Adolf Foehr, apartment building with shops, 1937

Štefánikova 51 (5 Smí, 259), Bohumír Kozák, apartment building, 1934–1935

Štefánikova 57 (5 Smí, 7), Ladislav Machoň, rebuilding of theatre, 1918–1920

Štěpánská 4 (2 NoM, 534), Julius Landsmann, Martin Reiner, apartment building, 1938 (P 1936)

Štěpánská 15 (2 NoM, 567), Bohumír Kozák, apartment building, 1939–1949

Štěpánská 18 (1 NoM, 613), Ludvík Kysela, insurance company building, 1928–1929

Štěpánská 23 (1 NoM, 650), Jaroslav Vančura, apartment building, 1937–1938

Štěpánská 28 (1 NoM, 619), Stivo Vacek, office building, 1939

Štěpánská 33 (1 NoM, 645) Josef Havlíček, Jaroslav Polívka, Habich department store and office building, 1927–1928

Štěpánská 35 (1 NoM, 644), Hugo Vraný, association building, 1930

Štěpánská 36 (1 NoM, 622), Evžen Rosenberg, commercial and apartment building, 1937–1938

Štěpánská 37 (1 NoM, 2071), Rudolf Novotný, apartment building, 1938–1939

Štěpánská 40 (1 NoM, 624), Alois Krofta, hotel, 1929–1930

Švédská 17, 19 (5 Smí, 1036, 1037), Miroslav Stöhr, apartment buildings, 1902

Švédská 35–43 (5 Smí, 107, 1716, 1844, 1845), František Kavalír, apartment buildings with shops, planning of estate, 1924–1926(?)

Táborská 27, 29 (4 Nus, 63, 65), Josef Kratochvíl, Otto Panuš, apartment buildings, 1937–1938

Talafúsova 1 (4 Bra, 292), Theodor Petřík, family house, 1922

Technická 3 (6 Dej, 1903), Antonín Engel, Theodor Petřík, School of Agriculture and Forestry, 1926–1937 (P 1926)

Technická 5 (6 Dej, 1905), Antonín Engel, Severin Ondřej, School of Chemistry and Technology, 1926–1933 (P 1925)

Terronská 20 (6 Bub, 200), Prague Municipal Construction Authority, city architect Mečislav Petrů, kindergarten, 1933–1934

Terronská 24, 26 (6 Bub, 838, 839), Alexander Rott, family duplex, 1928–1929

Terronská 39–43 (6 Bub, 657–659), Vojtěch Krch, apartment buildings, 1926–1927

Terronská 62 (6 Bub, 879), Maxmilian Duchoslav, apartment building, 1928–1929; modified by Jaroslav Fragner, 1936

Terronská 72, 74 (6 Bub, 871), Josef Karel Říha, apartment buildings, 1929–1930

Těšnov 5 (1 NoM, 1163), Adolf Foehr, office building, 1927–1928

Těšnov 17 (1 NoM, 65), František Roith, Ministry of Agriculture building, 1928–1932 (P 1925–1927)

Thákurova 1 (6 Dej, 550), Antonín Engel, Josef Záruba-Pfefferman, student dormitory, 1923–1925

Thákurova 3 (6 Dej, 676), Jaroslav Rössler(?), František Havlena, Archiepiscopal seminary, from 1925–1926

Thámova 20 (8 Kar, 181), Vlastimil Brožek, Jan Mentberger, Karel Polívka, apartment building, 1939–1940

Thámova 21 (8 Kar, 191), Hilar Pacanovský, apartment building, 1936–1937

Thámova 24 (8 Kar, 133), Vladimír Ježek, Oktáv Koutský, apartment building, 1930–1932

Tichá 3 (5 Smí, 1224), Josef Fanta, family house, 1910

Tomanova 44 (6 Bře, 1351), Jan Sokol, family house, 1937–1938

Tomanova 72 (6 Bře, 1149), Vojtěch Krch, family house, 1933

Tovární 6–10 (7 Hol, 1262, 1269), Rudolf Hrabě, apartment buildings, circa 1922

Trojanova 7 (2 NoM, 336), Petr Kropáček, apartment building, 1928–1929

Trojická 4 (2 NoM, 1449), Ladislav Čapek, apartment building, 1912

Trojická 20 (2 NoM, 437), Oldřich Tyl, double-story garages, 1929–1933

Trójská 110 (7 Tró, 211) Prague Municipal Construction Authority, city architect Mečislav Petrů, school building, 1927–1928

Trójská 118 (7 Tró, 193), Otakar Novotný, family house, 1923

Trójská 134 (7 Tró, 224), Adolf Benš, family house, 1928–1930

Truhlářská 12 (1 NoM, 1115), Vilém Hofmann, apartment building, circa 1937

Tržiště 9 (1 MaS, 368), Karel Pacánek, office and apartment building, 1930

Tusarova 35 (7 Hol, 429), František Magnusek, Rudolf Winternitz, apartment building, 1934

Tychonova 4, 6 (6 Hra, 268, 269), Josef Gočár, family duplex, 1912–1913

Tylišovská 1 (6 Dej, 772), Evžen Linhart(?), Vladimír František Hofman, family house, 1927–1929

U akademie 2 (7 Bub, 172) Jan Kotěra, Josef Gočár, School of Architecture, 1919–1924

U akademie 4 (7 Bub, 172), Václav Roštlapil, Academy of Fine Arts, 1898–1902

U branek (10 Hos, 674), Ladislav Machoň, gymnasium with cinema, 1931–1933

U čtyř domů 1 (4 Nus, 1089), Čeněk Vořech, apartment building, 1931–1932

U dělnického cvičiště 1 (6 Bře, 1100), Prague Municipal Construction Authority, city architect Mečislav Petrů, Vít Obrtel(?), school building, circa 1933

U dívčích hradů 18 (5 Smí, 1971), Zikmund Kerekes, Viktor Ehrenhaft, family building, 1930–1931

U dívčích hradů 20 (5 Smí, 1905), Josef Havlíček, Karel Honzík, family house, 1929

U Dobřanských (1 StM, 270), Osvald Polívka, completion of museum building, 1899

U dubu 26 (4 Bra, 470), Ludvík Hilgert, own family house, 1929

U elektrárny 8, 10 (7 Hol, 9, 205), Josef Chochol, apartment buildings, 1938–1939

U garáží 2 (7 Hol, 1434), Josef Hlaváček, Vlastimil Lada, apartment building, 1932

U Hadovky 7, 9 (6 Dej, 1493, 1496), Jan Zázvorka, family duplex of sculptor Ladislav Kofránek, 1928–1929

U Havlíčkových sadů 1 (2 Vin, 422), František Stárek, apartment building, 1911–1912

U Havlíčkových sadů 7 (2 Vin, 1526), Eduard Paroubek, apartment building, 1909

U Kavalírky 1 (5 Koš, 500), Karel Hannauer, pension, 1931

U Kavalírky 2 (5 Koš, 463), Václav Ložek, apartment building, 1927–1929

U Klikovky 19 (5 Smí, 2067), Otto and Karel Kohn, family house, 1932

U kněžské louky 22–30 (3 Žiž, 2142–2146), Arnošt Mühlstein, Victor Fürth, apartment building, 1930–1931

U krbu 4 (10 Str, 1101), Otto Klein, family house, 1931

U krčské vodárny 18 (4 Krč, 375), Karel Štipl, family house, 1929

U Kublova 1 (4 Pod, 537), Jaroslav Nebeský, apartment building, 1937

U laboratoře 4 (6 Stř, 565), Bohumil Hypšman, own family house, 1926–1927

U laboratoře 9, 11 (6 Stř, 436, 437), Maxmilian Duchoslav, family houses, 1922–1923

U laboratoře 18 (6 Stř, 552), Jaroslav Rössler, own family house, 1926–1927

U laboratoře 19 (6 Stř, 559), Maxmilian Duchoslav, family house, 1925–1926

U Ladronky 31 (6 Bře, 1334), Pavel Smetana, family house, 1938–1939

U Ladronky 40 (6 Bře, 1006), Josef Obalil, family house, 1940–1942

U letenského sadu 5 (7 Hol, 374), Julius Landsmann, Martin Reiner, apartment building, circa 1938

U libeňského pivovaru 14–18 (8 Lib, 1613–1615), Arnošt Mühlstein, Victor Fürth, apartment buildings, 1930–1932

U Malvazinky 9 (5 Smí, 2189), Otakar Chodounský, family house, 1934–1935

U Malvazinky 13 (5 Smí, 2162), Otakar Chodounský, family house, 1933–1934

U Malvazinky 20 (5 Smí, 2112), František Zelenka, family house, 1932–1933

U městských domů 5–13 (7 Hol, 181), František Maria Černý, Kamil Ossendorf, apartment buildings, 1937–1939

U Mrázovky 7 (5 Smí, 2071), Arnošt Wiesner, family house, 1930–1931; modified by Evžen Rosenberg, 1938

U Mrázovky 13 (5 Smí, 2344), Arnošt Mühlstein, Victor Fürth, family house, 1937

U Mrázovky 15 (5 Smí, 1970), Josef Falout, family house, 1930–1931

U Mrázovky 24 (5 Smí, 1827), Vilém Kvasnička, family house, 1927–1928

U Nesypky 2 (5 Smí, 108), František Petráš, family house, 1921–1923

U Nikolajky 12 (5 Smí, 1264), Antonín Šimek, apartment building, 1911–1912

U nových domů I 1–4 (4 Krč, 524), František Albert Libra, Jiří Kan, apartment buildings, 1932–1933

U nových domů III 1–11 (4 Krč, 533–538), Antonín Černý, apartment building, 1932–1937

U Obecního domu 1 (1 StM, 1080), Jan Vejrych, hotel, 1904–1905

U památníku (3 Žiž, 1600), Jan Zázvorka, Jan Gillar, museum, 1927–1930 (P 1926)

U páté baterie 24 (6 Bře, 946), Bedřich Bernard, family house, 1931–1932

U páté baterie 38 (6 Bře, 939), Bedřich Adámek, family house, 1928–1929

U páté baterie 40 (6 Bře, 938), Pavel Janák, family house of sculptor Josef Mařatka, 1933

U páté baterie 50 (6 Bře, 896), Otto Rothmayer, own family house, 1928–1929

U Pergamenky 8 (7 Hol, 1445), Jindřich Linek, apartment building, 1940

U Pergamenky 8 (7 Hol, 1471), Construction department of the Mining and Metallurgy Company, Miroslav Koněrza, apartment building, 1938–1939

U Pergamenky 9 (7 Hol, 454), Josef Blecha(?), apartment building, 1936–1937

521

U Pergamenky 11 (7 Hol, 1455), Josef Kříž, warehouse, 1928–1929

U Pernikářky 10 (5 Smí, 1507, 1508), Alois Mezera, family duplex, 1922–1923

U plátenice 3 (5 Smí, 2042), Otto Máca, family house, 1932

U plynárny 44 (4 Mich, 500), Josef Kalous, offices and gasworks buildings, porter's lodge, 1925–1932

U plynárny 46–56 (4 Mich, 501–505, 254), Josef Kalous, family houses, 1925–1927

U podchodu 3 (6 Stř, 827), Václav Girsa, family house, 1932

U podolského hřbitova 8 (Pod, 668), Karel Hannauer, family house, 1935

U podolského sanatoria (4 Pod, 4, 5, 157), Rudolf Kříženecký, sanatorium, 1911–1913(?)

U pošty 1 (8 Lib, 1474), Otakar Novotný, apartment building, 1928–1929

U pošty 8 (8 Lib, 1098), Bohumír Kozák, Unity of Brethren meeting house, 1922–1923

U Prašné brány 1, 3 (1 StM, 1078, 1079), Bedřich Bendelmayer, E. Weichert, apartment building, 1903–1904

U průhonu 9 (7 Hol, 1156), Leo Lauermann, apartment building, 1931

U průhonu 10 (7 Hol, 700), Emil Králíček, factory office building, 1905

U průhonu 16 (7 Hol, 477), Evžen Rosenberg, apartment building, 1936

U průhonu 23 (7 Hol, 1201), František Kavalír, apartment building, 1914

U průhonu 40 (7 Hol, 1079), Antonín Engel, factory, 1910–1911

U průhonu 44–52 (7 Hol, 1236–1246), Rudolf Hrabě, apartment buildings, 1919–1922

U půjčovny 6 (1 NoM, 954), Alois Houba, apartment building, 1937–1938

U radnice 3 (1 StM, 16), Oktáv Koutský, Vladimír Ježek, office building of the City Hall, 1926–1928

U rajské zahrady 3 (3 Žiž, 1912), Václav Šantrůček, club and office building, 1937–1938

U silnice 22 (6 DoL, 469), Pavel Bareš, apartment building, 1939

U smaltovny 15 (7 Hol, 259), Hilar Pacanovský, Rudolf Hraba, apartment building, 1934–1935

U smaltovny 16 (7 Hol, 245), Ervín Katona, apartment building, 1938–1939

U smaltovny 20–22 (7 Hol, 1334, 1335), Franz Hruška, Adolf Foehr, apartment buildings, 1937–1939

U smíchovského hřbitova 20 (5 Smí, 2450), Josef Kučera, Miroslav Tryzna, family house, 1939

U Sovových mlýnů 9 (1 MaS, 543), Ferdinand Rudolf, home for the blind, 1931–1932

U Sparty 10–16 (7 Bub, 513, 551, 552), Vladislav Martínek, apartment buildings, 1922–1924

U staré plynárny 2–10 (7 Hol, 47), František Maria Černý, Kamil Ossendorf, apartment buildings, 1937

U starého hřbitova 3 (1 Jos, 248), Bohumil Hypšman, apartment building, 1928–1929

U starého hřbitova 4–8 (1 Jos, 40), Antonín Engel, apartment building, 1910–1911

U studánky 1 (7 Hol, 276), Ervín Katona, apartment building, 1936–1938

U sv. Ducha 3 (1 Jos, 9), Václav Zákostelna, apartment building, 1914–1915

U svobodárny 2–6 (9 Lib, 1063–1065), Rudolf Hrabě, apartment buildings, 1923–1924

U Šalamounky 5 (5 Smí, 2369), Jan Gillar, Karel Teige's family house, 1937–1938

U školičky 27, 29 (9 Lib, 1912a, b), František Míšek, apartment buildings, 1937–1940

U školičky 31, 33 (9 Lib, 1913a, b), Josef Chochol, Richard Ferdinand Podzemný, apartment buildings, 1938–1940

U tenisu 3, 5 (5 Koš, 476, 477), Ludvík Hilgert, family duplex, 1929

U topíren 4 (7 Hol, 861), Emil Králíček(?), Matěj Blecha, office building, 1911–1912

U továren 27 (10 Hos, 261), Bohumil Hypšman, bakery, silo and mill, 1919–1922

U trati 1–33, 6–24 (10 Str, 397–475), Václav Gail, family houses, 1922

U trati 42 (10 Str, 1226), František Magnusek, Rudolf Winternitz, factory, 1932–1934

U trójského zámku 3 (7 Tró, 120), K. Mužík, L. Nitsch, Prague Zoo administrative buildings, 1931–1937

U tržnice 4 (2 Vin, 1162), František Xaver Jiřík(?), Josef Vyskočil, apartment building, 1902–1903

U Uranie 14 (7 Hol, 1037 — building off Jankovcova Street), Bohumil Hypšman, steam mill, after 1905

U vinohradské nemocnice 9, 11 (3 Vin, 2381, 2992), Eduard Bíba, apartment building, 1939

U vodárny 16 (3 Vin, 878), František Marek, apartment buildings with shops, 1934–1935

U vody 1–9 (7 Hol, 1399, 1406), Josef Chochol, apartment buildings, 1928–1929

U Vorlíků 3 (6 Bub, 367), Josef Vaňha, family house, 1912

U Vorlíků 17 (6 Bub, 353), Jaro Hlaváček, family house, 1911

U vršovického nádraží (10 Vrš, 950), Municipal Construction Authority, city architect Mečislav Petrů, school building, 1928–1930

U vršovického nádraží 2–8 (10 Vrš, 870–873), Emil Jech, apartment buildings, 1929–1930

U Zámečnice 2 (5 Smí, 2024), Vojtěch Šašek, apartment building with workshops, 1930–1932

U zeměpisného ústavu 6 (6 Bub, 399), Vojtěch Šašek, apartment building, 1920–1921

U zdravotního ústavu 1 (10 Vin, 1857), Tomáš Pražák, Pavel Moravec, family house, 1923–1924

Újezd 3 (1 MaS, 609), Karel Hugo Kepka, Alois Čenský, gymnasium, 1896–1897

Újezd 11, 13 (5 MaS, 414, 415), Jaroslav Šťastný, apartment buildings with shops, 1937–1939

Újezd 26 (1 MaS, 426), František Janda, Ladislav Čapek, apartment building with restaurant, 1932–1933

Újezd 40 (1 MaS, 450), František Krásný, rebuilding of the Michna Palace for the Center for Physical Education, 1922–1926

Újezd 44 (1 MaS, 452), Václav Krásný, J. Balabán, apartment building with shops, 1938–1939

Újezd 46 (1 MaS, 454), Bohumír Kozák, Otto Máca, apartment building, 1936

Ukrajinská 9–13 (10 Vrš, 899, 909), Václav Kopecký of Karel Skorovský Architects, apartment buildings, 1937–1940

Umělecká 3, 5 (7 Hol, 1004, 1005), Bohumír Kozák, Otto Máca, apartment buildings, 1923

Urxova 1 (8 Kar, 470), Jiří Justich, apartment building, 1904

Urxova 5 (8 Kar, 483), Osvald Polívka, apartment building, 1902

Úřednická II 10–24, 9–23 (6 Dej, 390–397, 406–413), Rudolf Hrabě, family houses, between 1922 and 1925

Ústavní (8 Boh, 91–93, 130, 191), Václav Roštlapil, V. Heller, buildings of mental hospital, 1904–1914

Úvoz 5 (1 MaS, 228), Rudolf Stockar, family house, 1938

Úvoz 13 (1 Hra, 156), Tomáš Šašek, Bohumil Hypšman(?), family house, 1927–1929

V bezpečí 12 (3 Žiž, 1350), Ladislav Machoň, family house, 1922

V Cibulkách 47 (5 Koš, 515), Vojtěch Kerhart, family house, 1933–1934

V háji 18 (7 Hol, 1185), Václav Pilc, apartment building, 1928–1929

V háji 30 (7 Hol, 1069), Bedřich Bendelmayer, apartment building, 1910

V Hodkovičkách 25 (4 Hod, 131), Miroslav Kroupa, family house, 1910

V Holešovičkách (8 Lib, 1879), Eduard Hnilička, power station, 1937–1939

V kolkovně 6 (1 StM, 909), Karel Vítěžslav Mašek, apartment building, 1904–1905

V lučinách 3 (4 Hod, 269), Josef Jíra, family house, 1939

V mezihoří 17 (8 Lib, 1212), Vlastimil Brožek, Jan Mentberger, Karel Polívka, apartment building, 1932–1933

V Nových Bohnicích 34 (8 Boh, 280), Oskar and Elly Oehler, family house, 1935

V nových domcích 36 (10 Str, 1031), Bohumil Hypšman, family house, 1921–1925

V olšinách 6, 16 (10 Str, 1668, 1411), Josef K. Tesař, apartment buildings, 1939–1940

V olšinách 15 (10 Vrš, 1069), Hilar Pacanovský, apartment building, 1939–1940

V olšinách 18 (10 Str, 1452), Václav Müller, apartment building, 1940–1941

V olšinách 36 (10 Str, 1031), František Stalmach, Jan Svoboda, apartment building, 1931

V olšinách 50–62 (10 Str, 1122–1128), Karel Beran, apartment buildings, 1931–1932

V olšinách (10 Str, 200), Prague Municipal Construction Authority, city architect Mečislav Petrů, extension to school building, 1927

V pevnosti 4 (2 Vyš, 13), Matěj Blecha, extension to medical institute, 1912–1913

V podvrší 1 (8 Lib, 1352), Václav Velvarský, family house, 1930

V předpolí 13–19 (10 Str, 289, 1456, 1464, 1480), Josef K. Tesař, apartment buildings, 1940–1941

V tišině 3 (6 Bub, 781), Antonín Pfeiffer, family house, 1921–1922

V tišině 4 (6 Bub, 781), Bohumil Hypšman, family house of painter Alfons Mucha, 1926–1928

V tišině 10 (6 Bub, 483), František Kavlír, family house of painter T. F. Šimon, 1922–1923

V tůních 2 (2 NoM, 584), Ladislav Machoň, extension to building, 1922–1923

V tůních 13 (2 NoM, 1356), V. Nekvasil Architects and Building Contractors, apartment building, 1932–1934

V úvalu 14 (5 Mot, 71), Josef Prouza, family house of painter Vlasta Vostřebalová, 1930

V úvalu 84 (5 Mot), František Čermák, Gustav Paul, provisional hospital pavilions, 1938–1942; Rudolf Kvěch, tuberculosis clinic, 1936

V Zahradním městě 41 (10 Záb, 1938), František Marek, family house, 1937

V zahrádkách 48 (3 Žiž, 1966), Prague Municipal Construction Authority, city architect Rezner, school building, 1926–1928

Václavkova 2 (6 Dej, 176), Jaroslav Vondrák, apartment building, 1931

Václavkova 18 (6 Dej, 335), Oldřich Starý, apartment building, 1923–1924, 1928

Václavkova 20 (6 Dej, 343), Josef Stoklasa, apartment building, 1923–1924

Václavkova 22, 24 (6 Dej, 364, 365), Bohumír Kozák, apartment building, up to 1922

Václavkova 28, 30 (6 Dej, 505, 508)), Miroslav Kroupa, apartment buildings, 1921–1922

Václavská 12 (2 NoM, 316), Ferdinand Rudolf, office and apartment building, 1927–1929

Václavská 18 (1 NoM, 2069), František Jech, apartment building with garages, 1937–1938

525

Valčíkova 1 (8 Lib, 1453), Josef Fuchs, family house, 1934–1935

Valčíkova 2 (8 Lib, 1587), Oldřich Starý, family house, 1936

Valčíkova 8 (8 Lib, 1146), Josef Fuchs, family house, 1936

Valčíkova 11 (8 Lib, 1371), Vilém Kvasnička, Ladislav Suk, family house, 1927–1928

Valčíkova 11 (8 Lib, 1371), Vilém Kvasnička, Ladislav Suk, family house, 1927–1928

Valčíkova 16 (8 Lib, 1150), Václav Starec, family house, 1929–1930

Valdštejnská 6 (1 MaS, 152), Josef Velflík, family house, 1915

Valentinská 9 (1 StM, 57), Josef Vajshajtl, apartment building, 1906–1907

Valentinská 10, 12 (1 Jos, 20, 22), Bedřich Bendelmayer, apartment buildings, 1906–1907

Vaníčkova (6 Stř), Ferdinand Balcárek, Karel Kopp, sports stadium, 1932–1938

Vápencová 13 (4 Pod, 569), Jaroslav and Karel Fischer, family house, 1939

Ve Smečkách 2 (1 NoM, 585), Miloš Vaněček, apartment building with shops, 1928–1929

Ve Smečkách 15 (1 NoM, 602), Josef Blecha, Rudolf Winternitz, commercial and apartment building, 1937–1938

Ve Smečkách 26 (1 NoM, 594), Milada Pavíková-Petříková, club building, 1931–1933

Ve Smečkách 27 (1 NoM, 1920), Evžen Rosenberg, commercial and apartment building with arcade, 1937–1938

Ve Smečkách 31 (1 NoM, 598), Bedřich Bendelmayer, Jaroslav Pelc, apartment building, 1912–1913

Velehradská 7 (3 Vin, 2340), Jindřich Řehoř, apartment building, 1936

Veletržní 9 (7 Hol, 209), Jan Gillar, apartment building, 1936

Veletržní 13 (7 Hol, 198), Emanuel Hruška, apartment building, 1934

Veletržní 17 (7 Hol, 196), Jindřich Řehoř, apartment building, 1934

Veletržní 19 (7 Hol, 528), Arnošt Mühlstein, Victor Fürth, apartment building, 1934; modified by Karel Janů, 1944

Veletržní 29 (7 Hol, 484), Ervín Katona, apartment building, 1936–1937

Veletržní 59 (7 Hol, 828), Václav Novotný(?), apartment building, 1904

Velvarská 1 (6 Dej, 1654), Arnošt Mühlstein, Victor Fürth, family house, 1937

Velvarská 3 (6 Dej, 1951), Jaroslav Čermák, family house, 1937–1938

Velvarská 7 (6 Dej, 1652), Antonín Mendl, apartment building, 1933

Verdunská 15 (6 Bub, 707), Jaroslav Vondrák, apartment building, 1927–1928

Verdunská 17 (6 Bub, 801), František Strnad, apartment building, 1932–1933

Verdunská 20–26 (6 Bub, 487–490), Vladislav Martínek, apartment buildings, 1919–1923

Veverkova 1 (7 Hol, 1101), Otto and Karel Kohn, apartment building, 1932–1933

Veverkova 3 (7 Hol, 459), Jan Urbach, apartment building, 1933–1934

Veverkova 9 (7 Hol, 1229), Adolf Foehr, apartment building, 1932

Veverkova 25 (7 Hol, 741), Rudolf Wels, Guido Lagus, apartment building, 1938

Veverkova 31, 33 (7 Hol, 1171, 1172), Karel Beran, Josef Čácha(?), apartment buildings, 1922–1923

Vězeňská 1 (1 Jos, 141), Karel Pecánek, completion of synagogue, 1935

Vězeňská 6 (1 StM, 912), Alois Stárek, apartment building, 1906

Vídeňská 5, 7 (4 Krč, 800, 818), Bohumír Kozák, Ladislav Kozák, municipal homes for people in social care, 1926–1940

Vídeňská 188 (4 Krč, 756), Vladimír Wallenfels, home for the blind, 1930–1933

Vilová 11 (10 Str, 91), Jan Kotěra, family house, 1903 (P 1902)

Vilová 20 (10 Str, 252), František Sedláček, family house, 1911

Vilová 26 (10 Str, 512), Rudolf Sandholz, prayer house, 1923–1924

Vinařská 3 (7 Hol, 1136), Jan Gillar, apartment building, 1937–1938

Vinařská 6 (7 Hol, 1136), Jan Gillar, apartment building, 1936–1937

Vinařská 7 (7 Hol, 1134), Jan Gillar, apartment building, 1937

Vinohradská 1 (1 NoM, 52), Jaroslav Rössler, stock exchange building, 1936–1937

Vinohradská 6 (2 Vin, 343), Vlastimil Brožek, Jan Mentberger, Karel Polívka, Ladislav Tříška, apartment building with shops, 1937–1939

Vinohradská 12 (2 Vin, 1409), Bohumil Sláma, radio building, 1927-circa 1930

Vinohradská 40, 42 (2 Vin, 1789, 1790), Alois Dryák, commercial and club building with cinema and restaurant, 1922–1924

Vinohradská 46 (2 Vin, 1896), Alois Dryák, office building, 1925

Vinohradská 83 (2 Vin, 1485), Josef Pospíšil, apartment building, 1907

Vinohradská 153 (3 Žiž, 1835), Prague Municipal Construction Authority, city architect Mečislav Petrů, cemetery building, 1931–1934

Vinohradská 176 (3 Vin, 1513), Jan Gillar, apartment building, 1932

Vinohradská 214–218 (10 Vin, 2263, 2264, 2254), Alois Mezera, crematorium, 1929–1931 (P 1926–1927)

Vladislavova 4 (1 NoM, 1494), Josef Karel Říha, Emil Kovařík, office building, 1939–1941

Vladislavova 5, 7 (1 NoM, 47, 48), Václav Kolátor, rebuilding of school building, 1933–1934 (P 1930)

Vladislavova 13 (1 NoM, 51), Leo Lauermann, office and apartment building, 1937–1938

Vlašimská 10 (10 Vin, 1865), Tomáš Pražák, Pavel Moravec, family house, 1923–1924

Vlašská 13 (1 MaS), 591), František Troníček, apartment building, 1938–1939

Vlašská 23 (1 MaS, 345), Kamil Roškot, family house, 1939–1940

Vlnitá 19 (4 Bra, 552), Franz Hruška, family house, 1931–1933

Vnislavova 4 (2 Vyš, 48), Otakar Novotný, family house, 1912–1913

Voděradská 2 (10 Str, 900), Prague Municipal Construction Authority, city architect Mečislav Petrů, school building, 1932–1934

Vodičkova 6 (1 NoM, 674), Bohumil Sláma, commercial and apartment building with cinema and restaurant, 1927–1928

Vodičkova 18 (1 NoM, 681), Adolf Foehr, office building, 1928–1930

Vodičkova 28 (1 NoM, 699), Osvald Polívka, commercial building with theater and restaurant, 1927–1930

Vodičkova 30 (1 NoM, 699), Osvald Polívka, commercial and apartment building, 1901–1904

Vodičkova 31 (1 NoM, 710), Josef Čapek, rebuilding of office and commercial building, 1922

Vodičkova 32 (1 NoM, 701), V. Nekvasil Architects and Building Contractors, office and commercial building, 1928–1929

Vodičkova 36 (1 NoM, 704), Václav Havel, Lucerna commercial and office building with arcade, restaurants and cinema, 1907–1910 (Vodičkova Street wing), 1913–1921 (Štěpánská Street wing)

Vodičkova 37 (1 NoM, 707), Alois Dryák, rebuilding of commercial and apartment building, 1905

Vojtěšská 13 (1 NoM, 216), František Velich, school building, 1904–1906

Vojtěšská 15, 17 (1 NoM, 231, 232), Osvald Polívka, apartment buildings, 1903–1904

Voršilská 3 (1 NoM, 139), Jaroslav Rössler, rebuilding of house with exhibition gallery, 1933

Voršilská 6 (1 NoM, 142), E. Králíček, Rudolf Šolc, apartment building, 1939–1940

Voršilská 10 (1 NoM, 140), Friedrich Ohmann, Valtera Palace, 1890–1891

Voršilská 14 (1 NoM, 138), Adolf Foehr, commercial and office building, 1927–1930

Vostrovská 11 (6 Dej, 1264), Ferdinand Fencl, family house, 1936

Vostrovská 17, 19 (6 Dej, 1619, 1620), František Roith, family houses, 1931–1933

Vratislavova 22–28 (2 Vyš, 20), Bohumil Hypšman, apartment buildings, 1924

Vrázova 6 (5 Smí, 1163), František Kavalír, apartment building with gymnasium, 1908–1909

Vrchlického 1a (5 Koš, 520), Ferdinand Balcárek, Karel Kopp, apartment building, 1937

Vrchlického 45–51 (5 Koš, 479, 482–484), František Ptáček, apartment buildings, 1929

Vršovická 38 (10 Vrš, 823), Oldřich Tyl, apartment building, 1930

Vršovická 39, 41 (10 Vrš, 776), Josef Franců, apartment building, 1925–1932

Vykáňská 5, 7 (10 Str, 1482, 1483), Hilar Pacanovský, apartment building, 1940–1941

Vykáňská 6 (10 Str, 1443), František Voráček, apartment building, 1940

Washingtonova 19 (1 NoM, 1600), Fritz Lehmann, hotel, circa 1930

Wenzigova 20 (2 Vin, 1982), Bohumír Kozák, student dormitory, 1923–1925

Wilsonova (2 Vin, 300), Josef Fanta, train station, 1900–1909

Wolkerova 10 (6 Bub, 565), Severin Ondřej, family house, 1927

Wolkerova 12 (6 Bub, 566), Tomáš Pražák, Pavel Moravec, family house, 1923–1926

Wolkerova 15 (6 Bub, 965), Rudolf Bettelheim, apartment building, 1937

Wuchterlova 14 (6 Dej, 585), Oktáv Koutský, Vladimír Ježek, apartment building, 1929

Xaveriova 39 (5 Smí, 1894), Josef Prouza, family house, 1928–1930

Za Hanspaulkou 15 (6 Dej, 874), Oldřich Starý, family house, up to 1931

Za Hládkovem 10–20 (6 Stř, 676–680, 896), Jan Gillar, apartment buildings, 1939–1940

Za papírnou 5 (7 Hol, 116), Alois Špalek, facade, 1920

Za Pekařkou 20 (4 Pod, 620), Vít Obrtel, family house, 1941–1942

Za Poříčskou bránou 10 (9 Kar, 315), František Xaver Čtrnáctý, apartment building, 1937–1939

Za Strahovem 55 (6 Bře, 378), Karel Honzík, rebuilding of family house, 1925–1926

Za vokovickou vozovnou 4, 6 (6 Vel, 257), Josef Blecha, apartment building, 1933

Za vokovickou vozovnou 8, 10 (6 Vel, 256), Josef Kříž, apartment building, 1932–1933

Za vokovickou vozovnou 9, 11 (6 DoL, 366, 367) V. Nekvasil Architects and Building Contractors, apartment building, 1936–1937

Za Zelenou liškou 2–14 (4 Krč, 546–552), Bohumír Kozák and Ladislav Kozák, apartment buildings, 1932–1933

529

Zahradníčkova 18 (5 Mot, 32), Miloš Jirko, family house with a shop, 1922–1923

Záhřebská 18 (2 Vin, 989), Stivo Vacek, apartment building, 1937–1938

Záhřebská 39 (2 Vin, 246), Hilar Pacanovský, apartment building, 1938–1939

Zámecká 5 (1 MaS, 200), Tomáš Šašek, apartment building, 1935

Západní 19 (6 Stř, 489), Alois Dryák, own family house, 1923–1924

Západní 21 (6 Stř, 466), Jaroslav Vondrák, own family house, 1923–1924, 1930

Západní 27–39 (6 Stř, 253–259), Jaroslav Vondrák, family houses, 1920–1922(?)

Zapova 20 (5 Smí, 1496), František Kavalír, family house, 1922–1923

Závěrka, 11 (6 Bře, 768), Josef Skokan, apartment building, 1928–1929

Zborovská 13 (5 Smí, 1505), Adolf Liebscher, Ministry of Health, 1922–1924

Zelená 9 (6 Dej, 1087), Jaroslav Vondrák, apartment building, 1928–1929

Zelená 14a, b (6 Dej, 1570), Josef Karel Říha, apartment buildings, 1928–1930

Zenklova 3 (8 Lib, 2), Emil Králíček, Matěj Blecha, gymnasium, 1907–1910

Zenklova (8 Lib), Matěj Blecha, Church of Saint Vojtěch, 1904–1905

Zikova 1 (6 Dej, 514), Miroslav Purkyně, pension, 1924–1925

Zikova 3 (6 Dej, 522), Jan Rosůlek, apartment building, 1925–1927

Zikova 13 (6 Dej, 702), Pavel Bareš, hostel for single men, 1934–1935

Zlatnice 1 (6 Dej, 1511), Oldřich Starý, family house, 1929–1930

Zubatého 1 (5 Smí, 269), Arnošt Mühlstein, Victor Fürth, apartment building with shops, 1936–1937

Žatecká 2 (1 StM, 110), Ladislav Skřivánek, Stanislav Vávra, Josip Plečnik, apartment building, 1914–1915

Žatecká 5 (1 Jos, 18), Jiří Stibral, apartment building, circa 1900

Žatecká 10 (1 Jos, 53), Václav Vejrych, V. Pickl, apartment building, circa 1909–1910

Žateckých 4–8 (4 Nus, 761–763), Jan Rosůlek, apartment buildings, 1927

Žateckých 11 (4 Nus, 1169), Bohumír and Ladislav Kozák, evangelical meeting house (Husův sbor), 1934

Žateckých 14 (4 Nus, 1211), Karel Polívka, Vlastimil Brožek, Jan Mentberger, apartment building, 1935–1936

Žateckých 15, 17 (4 Nus, 1257, 1258), Karel Hannauer, apartment buildings, 1936

Žernovská 6, 8 (10 Str, 1316, 1317), Jiří Krofta, family duplex, 1936–1937

Žerotínova 41 (3 Žiž, 1489), Oldřich Tyl, apartment building, 1923

Žerotínova 45 (3 Žiž, 1272), Ludvík Hilgert, apartment building, 1926–1927

Žerotínova 47, 49 (3 Žiž, 1641, 1642), Petr Kropáček, apartment buildings, 1927

Žerotínova 48 (3 Žiž, 1902), Václav Kříž, apartment building, 1937–1938

Žitná 12 (2 NoM, 563), Oldřich Tyl, pension, 1926–1929; modified by Josef Mikyna and Miloš Tereba, 1929–1932

Žitná 23 (1 NoM, 610), Vít Obrtel, Zdeněk Hölzel, apartment building with shops, 1937–1939

Žitná 36, 38 (2 NoM, 2072, 573), V. Křesadlo, Stanislav Svoboda, apartment buildings, 1938

Žitomírská 46 (10 Vrš, 1058), Josef Martínek, apartment building, 1934–1935

SQUARES AND MARKETPLACES

Elznicovo náměstí 6 (8 Lib, 41), František Havlena, apartment building with restaurant and cinema, 1932–1934

Flemingovo náměstí 2 (6 Dej, 542), Josef Záruba-Pfeffermann, Jan Zázvorka(?), Chemical and Biological Institute, after 1925

Hollarovo náměstí 1–5 (3 Vin, 2255–2260), Jiří Kan, apartment buildings, 1931–1932

Jungmannovo náměstí 4 (1 NoM, 764), Rudolf Stockar, rebuilding of commercial and apartment building, 1922

Jungmannovo náměstí 17 (1 NoM, 754), Vlastimil Brožek, Jan Mentberger, Karel Polívka, commercial building, 1938–1939

Karlovo náměstí 1 (2 NoM, 1359), Václav Křepel, rebuilding and completion of polyclinic, 1925–1926

Karlovo náměstí 3 (2 NoM, 319), Josef Fejgl, rebuilding of apartment building, 1926–1927

Karlovo náměstí 4 (2 NoM, 318), Ervín Katona, apartment building with restaurant, 1937–1938

Karlovo náměstí 6 (2 NoM, 315), Karel Schmeisser, apartment building with arcade, 1937–1938

Karlovo náměstí 14, 15 (2 NoM, 292), Karel Kotas, commercial and apartment building with restaurant, 1932(?)–1934

Karlovo náměstí 19 (2 NoM, 285), Jan Matoušek, Oldřich Tyl(?), apartment building with shops, 1933–1934

Karlovo náměstí 32 (2 NoM, 552, 224), Ferdinand Fencl, Nursing School student dormitory, 1937–1950

Karlovo náměstí 34 (2 NoM, 551), Josef Martínek, Václav Šafránek, apartment building with restaurant, 1939–1940

Karlovo náměstí 37 (2 NoM, 500), Matěj Blecha, hospital pavilion, 1915–1920

Karlovo náměstí 38 (2 NoM, 501 — courtyard), Miloš Tereba, Oldřich Tyl, hospital administration building, 1921–1926

Kříženeckého náměstí 5 (5 Hlu, 322), Max Urban, film studios, 1931–1934

Křižovnické náměstí 4 (1 StM, 1040 — courtyard), Ladislav Machoň, rebuilding and completion of University Library, 1924–1929 (P 1923)

Loretánské náměstí 5 (1 Hra, 101), Pavel Janák, renovation of the Černín Palace for the Ministry of Foreign Affairs, 1927–1937, Keplerova Street wing, circa 1929–1937, Otakar Fierlinger, design and landscaping of the garden, 1933–1934

Lyčkovo náměstí 6 (8 Kar, 460), Josef Sakař, school building, 1903–1905

Lyčkovo náměstí 9, 10 (8 Kar, 411, 462), Bohumil Štěrba, apartment buildings, 1902–1903

Macharovo náměstí 30a, b (6 Stř, 250), Jaroslav Vondrák, covered market, restaurant and cinema, 1921

Malostranské náměstí 25 (1 MaS, 2 — courtyard), Alois Špalek, hall of the Treasury, 1922–1926

Mariánské náměstí 1 (1 StM, 98), František Roith, library, 1924–1928

Mariánské náměstí 2 (1 StM, 2), Osvald Polívka, City Hall, 1906–1911

náměstí Barikád (3 Žiž, 1520), František Kaliba, evangelical meeting house (Husův sbor), 1925

náměstí Curieových 7 (1 StM, 901), Jan Kotěra, Ladislav Machoň, Law School building, 1926–1931 (P 1921–1923)

náměstí 14. října 15 (5 Smí, 83), Alois Čenský, covered market, 1905–1908

náměstí 14. října 16 (5 Smí, 82), Alois Čenský, club building, 1906–1908

náměstí Hrdinů 11 (4 Nus, 1300), Bedřich Bendelmayer, courthouse, 1928–1930 (P 1926)

náměstí hrdinů 15 (4 Nus, 886), Jan Zázvorka, apartment building, 1930–1931

náměstí Jana Palacha 2 (1 Jos, 1), Josef Sakař, School of Philosophy, 1924–1930

náměstí Jiřího z Lobkovic 22 (3 Vin, 121), Bohumil Kněžek, Josef Václavík, school building, 1936–1937

náměstí Jiřího z Poděbrad (3 Vin), Josip Plečnik, Church of the Sacred Heart, 1928–1932 (P 1922–1928)

náměstí Maxima Gorkého 10 (1 NoM, 1984), Matěj Blecha, apartment building, 1903 náměstí Maxima Gorkého 11 (1 NoM, 1985), Josef Podhajský, apartment building, 1902

náměstí Maxima Gorkého 22 (1 NoM, 980), Rudolf Jonáš, apartment and association building, 1923–1924

náměstí Maxima Gorkého 23 (1 NoM, 978), František Krásný, renovation and extension to bank building, 1920–1921

náměstí Maxima Gorkého 24 (1 NoM, 977), Bohumír Kozák, office building, 1924–1926, Ervín Katona, ground floor design, 1930

náměstí Maxima Gorkého 25 (1 NoM, 872), Theodor Petřík, rebuilding of bank, 1921–1922

náměstí Maxima Gorkého 28 (1 NoM, 869), Josef Zasche, apartment and club building, 1906–1908; Helmuth Wagner, theatre, after 1910

náměstí Maxima Gorkého 29 (1 NoM, 866), Bohumil Hypšman, agricultural produce exchange, 1928–1929

náměstí Maxima Gorkého 30 (1 NoM, 866), Friedrich Ohmann, agricultural produce exchange, 1893–1894

náměstí Maxima Gorkého 33 (1 NoM, 978), Josef Zasche, club, 1912–1915

náměstí Mezi zahrádkami 1–12 (10 Záb, 1801–1812), Alois Vavrouš & Son, Architects and Building Contractors, family houses, 1931–1937

náměstí Mezi zahrádkami 14–23 (10 Záb, 1814–1824), Alois Vavrouš & Son, Architects and Building Contractors, family houses, 1932–1933

náměstí Míru (2 Vin, 1450), Alois Čenský, theater, 1905–1909 (P 1902–1904)

náměstí Míru 20 (2 Vin, 600), Vít Obrtel, rebuilding of office building, 1927–1930

náměstí Před bateriemi 1 (6 Stř, 916), Antonín Moudrý, family house, 1936

náměstí Před bateriemi 22 (6 Stř, 690), Tomáš Šašek, family house, 1928–1929

náměstí Před bateriemi (6 Stř, 950), Bohumír Kozák, Unity of Brethren meeting house, 1937–1939

náměstí Republiky 5 (1 StM, 1090), Antonín Balšánek, Osvald Polívka, Municipal House, 1905–1912 (P 1903–1904)

náměstí Republiky 6 (1 StM, 660), Antonín Turek, office building, 1904

náměstí Republiky 7 (1 StM, 1081), Karel Stieger, office building, 1904–1905

náměstí Republiky 28 (1 NoM, 864), František Roith, bank building with arcade, 1935–1938 (P 1928–1929)

náměstí Svatopluka Čecha (10 Vrš), Josef Gočár, Church of Saint Wenceslas, 1929–1930 (P 1927–1928) námĕstí Svatopluka Čecha 1 (10 Vrš, 262), Zdenĕk Pštross, museum and apartment building, circa 1919

námĕstí Svatopluka Čecha 3 (10 Vrš, 307), Václav Rais, apartment building, 1912–1913

námĕstí Svobody 1 (6 Bub, 728), Richard Ferdinand Podzemný, apartment building, 1936–1937

námĕstí Svobody 2 (6 Bub, 930), Jan Pacl, school building, 1928–1931

námĕstí Winstona Churchilla 2 (3 Žiž, 1800, 1839, 1840), Josef Havlíček, Karel Honzík, General Pensions Institute office building, 1932–1934 (P 1929–1931)

námĕstí Winstona Churchilla 4 (3 Žiž, 1938), Prague Municipal Construction Authority, city architect Mečislav Petrů, school building, 1936–1938

Nedvĕdovo námĕstí 1 (4 Pod, 100), Antonín Belada, hotel, 1912–1914

Ortenovo námĕstí 10 (7 Hol, 450), Evžen Rosenberg, apartment building, 1936

Ortenovo námĕstí 12 (7 Hol, 1487), Stanislav Brázda, apartment building, 1935–1937

Ortenovo námĕstí 33 (7 Hol, 1242), J. F. Regenerml, children's home, 1921

Ovocný trh 19 (1 StM, 569), Josef Gočár, Black Madonna commercial and office building, 1912 (P 1911–1912)

Palackého námĕstí 4 (2 NoM, 375), Bohumil Hypšman, Ministry of Social Welfare, 1924–1931 (P 1923)

Petrské námĕstí 1 (1 NoM, 1186), Otto Zucker, apartment building, 1938–1941

Petrské námĕstí 2 (1 NoM, 1185), Jan Urbach, apartment building, 1937

Puškinovo námĕstí 2, 3 (6 Bub, 681, 682), Stivo Vacek, apartment buildings, 1939

Puškinovo námĕstí 4 (6 Bub, 494), Bohumil Sláma, apartment building, 1922–1923

Puškinovo námĕstí 7 (6 Bub, 480), Jaroslav Rössler, apartment building, 1937 (P 1928)

Puškinovo námĕstí 8 (6 Bub, 518), Antonín Pfeiffer, apartment building, 1922–1923

Sibiřské námĕstí 5 (6 Bub, 280), Jan Kotĕra, family house, 1907

Staromĕstské námĕstí 3 (1 StM, 1), Josef Chochol, Brožík Hall in the Old Town City Hall, 1910–1911; Pavel Janák, design of the staircase and elevators, 1936, 1947

Staromĕstské námĕstí 5 (1 StM, 934), Rudolf Kříženecký, apartment building, 1895–1897

Staromĕstské námĕstí 6 (1 StM, 932), Osvald Polívka, insurance company building, 1899–1901

Staromĕstské námĕstí 10 (1 StM, 608), Richard Klenka, apartment building, 1904–1906

Staromĕstské námĕstí 16 (1 StM, 552), Friedrich Ohmann, Štorch commercial and apartment building, 1896–1897

Strossmayerovo náměstí 10 (7 Hol, 965), Richard Klenka, apartment building, 1906–1910

Strossmayerovo náměstí (7 Hol), František Mikš, Church of Saint Anthony, 1908–1914

Trhanovské náměstí 8 (10 Hos, 129), Prague Municipal Construction Authority, city architect Mečislav Petrů, kindergarten, 1927–1928, extension to school building, 1931–1932

Václavské náměstí 1, 3 (1 NoM, 846), Antonín Pfeiffer, commercial and office building with snack-bar and cinema, 1911–1914; modified by Ladislav Machoň, 1912–1914, 1931–1932

Václavské náměstí 4 (1 NoM, 773), Ludvík Kysela, Lindt department store, 1926–1927 (P 1925)

Václavské náměstí 5 (1 NoM, 840), František Weyr, Richard Klenka, hotel, 1912–1913, 1918–1919

Václavské náměstí 6 (1 NoM, 774), Baťa architectural office, Ludvík Kysela, department store, 1928–1929 (P 1927)

Václavské náměstí 7 (1 NoM, 839), Emil Králíček(?), Matěj Blecha, hotel, 1909–1912; modified by Ladislav Machoň, 1933

Václavské náměstí 8 (1 NoM, 775), Matěj Blecha, commercial and apartment building, 1911–1913; Emil Králíček(?), Matěj Blecha, lamppost behind the building in Jungmannovo Square, 1912

Václavské náměstí 9 (1 NoM, 838), Josef Sakař, office building, 1913–1914

Václavské náměstí 10 (1 NoM, 776), Alois Dlabač, office and apartment building, 1899–1900

Václavské náměstí 12 (1 NoM, 777), Jan Kotěra, Vilém Thierhier, Peterka commercial and apartment building, 1899–1900

Václavské náměstí 16 (1 NoM, 779), Jan Jarolím, Vilém Kvasnička, commercial and apartment building, 1922–1926

Václavské náměstí 17 (1 NoM, 834), Rudolf Stockar, rebuilding of the publishing house with arcade and cinema, 1927–1929

Václavské náměstí 19 (1 NoM, 832), Friedrich Ohmann, Osvald Polívka, insurance company building, 1895–1896

Václavské náměstí 22 (1 NoM, 782), Pavel Janák, Juliš Hotel and commercial building, 1925–1926 (Franciscan Garden wing), 1931–1933 (P 1928–1931) (Wenceslas Square wing)

Václavské náměstí 25 (1 NoM, 826) Quido Bělský, Bedřich Bendelmayer, Bohumil Hypšman, Jan Letzel, hotel, 1903–1905

Václavské náměstí 27 (1 NoM, 825), Ludvík Kysela, Jan Jarolím, Alfa commercial building with arcade, 1927–1929

Václavské náměstí 32 (1 NoM, 791), Josef Sakař, Osvald Polívka, bank building, 1914–1916

Václavské náměstí 36 (1 NoM, 793), Bedřich Bendelmayer, Josef Vaňha, publishing house, 1910–1914; Jan E. Koula, design for cinema, 1930

Václavské náměstí 38 (1 NoM, 794, 626), Matěj Blecha, apartment building with restaurant and shops, 1913–1916

Václavské náměstí 41 (1 NoM, 820), Bohumír Kozák, office building, with restaurant and cinema, 1924–1926

Václavské náměstí 42–46 (1 NoM, 796), František Roith, bank building, 1928–1931 (P 1924–1927)

Václavské náměstí 47 (1 NoM, 1601), Josef Zasche(?), Bohumír Kozák, rebuilding of office building, 1926

Václavské náměstí 56 (1 NoM, 802), Bedřich Ehrmann, Josef Gočár, Fénix commercial and office building, 1927–1929

Václavské náměstí 64 (1 NoM, 807), Bohumil Kněžek, Josef Václavík, commercial and office building, 1938–1939

Václavské náměstí 66 (1 NoM, 808), František Kavalír, Bohumil Steigenhöfer, commercial and apartment building, 1927–1930

Vítězné náměstí 5 (6 Dej, 1500), Antonín Engel, Army office building, circa 1934 (P 1926–1928)

Vršovické náměstí 2 (10 Vrš, 111), Alois Dryák, Bohumil Hypšman, gymnasium and commercial building, 1932–1933

Vršovické náměstí 8 (10 Vrš, 67), Antonín Balšánek, Josef Bertl, savings bank and apartment building, 1911–1912

Vršovické náměstí 32 (9 Vys, 500), František Vahala, school building, 1921–1922

Žižkovo náměstí 1 (3 Žiž, 1300), František Vahala, school building, 1924–1927

Bubenské nábřeží 9 (7 Hol, 861), Emil Králíček (?), Matěj Blecha, office building, 1911

Hořejší nábřeží 9 (5 Smí, 486), Antonín Belada, apartment building, 1913–1914

Janáčkovo nábřeží 5 (5 Smí, 85), František Weyr, Richard Klenka, apartment building, 1909–1910

Janáčkovo nábřeží 9 (5 Smí, 94), Emil Dufek, apartment building, 1909

Masarykovo nábřeží 1 (1 NoM, 250), Otakar Novotný, Artists' Association Mánes building, 1928–1930 (P 1927–1928)

Masarykovo nábřeží 10 (1 NoM, 2018), František Cuc, apartment building, 1908

Masarykovo nábřeží 16 (1 NoM, 248), Josef Fanta, Čeněk Gregor, František Schlaffer, *Hlahol* cultural association offices and apartment building, 1903–1906

Masarykovo nábřeží 26 (1 NoM, 234), Kamil Hilbert, apartment building, 1904–1905

Masarykovo nábřeží 28 (1 NoM, 235), Matěj Blecha, own apartment building, 1904–1906

Masarykovo nábřeží 32 (1 NoM, 224), Jiří Stibral, bank and apartment building, 1904–1905

Masarykovo nábřeží 34, 36 (1 NoM, 227, 1648), Gustav Papež, apartment buildings, 1906–1907

Masarykovo nábřeží 38 (1 NoM, 2058), Arnošt Mühlstein, Victor Fürth, apartment building with shops, 1937–1939

nábřeží kapitána Jaroše (7 Hol, 1000), Jaroslav Rössler, insurance company building, 1927–1929 (P 1926)

nábřeží Ludvíka Svobody 12 (1 NoM, 1222), Antonín Engel, Ministry of Railways, 1927–1931

Podolské nábřeží 12, 14 (4 Pod, 250, 251) František Albert Libra, apartment buildings, 1925–1927 (P 1924)

Podolské nábřeží 24, 25 (4 Pod, 9), Josef Donát, apartment building, 1938–1939

Rašínovo nábřeží 2 (2 Vyš, 44), František Velich, tunnel with the watchman's house, 1902–1905

Rašínovo nábřeží 6–10 (2 Vyš, 42, 47, 71), Josef Chochol, family triplex, 1912–1913

Rašínovo nábřeží 14 (2 Vyš, 70), František Hodek, family house, 1912–1913

Rašínovo nábřeží 42 (2 noM, 390), Jan Kotěra, Josef Zasche, office building, 1913–1914 (P 1912)

Rašínovo nábřeží 54 (2 NoM, 385), Čeněk Micka, apartment building, 1911–1912

Rašínovo nábřeží 70, 78 (2 NoM, 1980, 2000), Václav Havel, apartment buildings, 1904–1905

537

BRIDGES

Čechův most (1 StM), Jan Koula, Jiří Soukup, 1905–1908

Hlávkův most (7 Hol), Pavel Janák, František Mencl, 1909–1912

Jiráskův most (2 NoM), Vlastislav Hofman, František Mencl, 1926–1932

Libeňský most (7 Hol), Pavel Janák, František Mencl, 1924–1928

Mánesův most (1 Jos, MaS), Prague Municipal Construction Authority, city architect
Mečislav Petrů, František Mencl, 1910–1914

most Legií (1 NoM, MaS), Antonín Balšánek, Jiří Soukup, 1898–1901

PARKS AND GARDENS

Kinského zahrada (5 Smí, 97), Jan Víšek, extension to museum, 1923–1924

Petřínské sady (1 MaS), František Šrámek, cable car terminal, 1932

Riegrovy sady (2 Vin, 28), František Marek, restaurant, 1931–1933, concert pavilion, 1934

ISLANDS

ostrov Štvanice (7 Hol, 867), František Sander, waterlock watchman's house, 1911–1912

ostrov Štvanice (7 Hol, 1125), Josef Fuchs, Bohumil Steigenhöfer, café and winter stadium,
1930–1932, 1939

ostrov Štvanice (7 Hol, 1340), Alois Dlabač(?), power plant, 1912–1913

CASTLES

Prague Castle (1 Hra), Kamil Hilbert, completion of Saint Vitus Cathedral, 1899–1929;
Josip Plečnik, landscaping of the gardens Rajská, 1920–1925, Na valech, 1920–1925,
Na baště, 1927–1928, design of the presidential residence, from 1921, further works and
modifications, between 1920 and 1934; Otto Rothmayer, Teresian wing, 1931–1950

HILLS

hora Vítkov (Žižkov) (3 Žiž, 1900), Jan Zázvorka, Liberation Monument, 1928–1933
(P 1926–1927)

DOCKS

Holešovický přístav (7 Hol, 1366), František Bartoš, warehouse, 1926–1929

The number at the beginning of each description indicates the house number.

Important buildings in the commercial center of Prague. Drawing by Rostislav Švácha.

(1) 773, Ludvík Kysela, Lindt department store, 1925–1927.

(2) 774, Baťa architectural studio and Ludvík Kysela, department store, 1927–1929.

(3) 775, Emil Králíček(?), Matěj Blecha, commercial and apartment building, 1911–1913, lamppost, 1912–1913 (behind the building in Jungmannovo Square).

(4) 777, Jan Kotěra, Vilém Thierhier, Peterka commercial and apartment building, 1899–1900.

(5) 782, Pavel Janák, Juliš Hotel, 1931–1933.

(6) 785, Ludvík Kysela, Jan Jarolím, Alfa commercial building with arcade, 1927–1929.

(7) 794, 626, Matěj Blecha, apartment building with shops, 1913–1916.

(8) 796, František Roith, bank, 1924–1931.

(9) 704, Václav Havel, Lucerna commercial building with arcade, 1907–1921.

(10) 710, Josef Čapek, rebuilding of commercial building, 1922.

(11) 699, Osvald Polívka, Novák department store with arcade, 1901–1904.

(12) 718, František Zelenka, department store, 1937.

(13) 737, František Jech, office building, 1937–1938.

(14) 26, Osvald Polívka, Beaufort publishing house, 1908–1912.

(15) 15, Josef Říha, office building with shops and cinema of the Mining and Metallurgy Company, 1928–1930.

(16) 1494, Josef K. Říha, Emil Kovařík, office building, 1939–1941.

(17) 82, Matěj Blecha, Diamant commercial and apartment building, 1912–1913.

(18) 78, Oldřich Tyl, commercial and apartment building, 1928–1930.

(19) 76, Osvald Polívka, office building, 1907–1909.

(20) 75, Jaromír Krejcar, Olympic Building, 1925–1928.

(21) 74, Adolf Foehr, office building, 1927–1928. Ground and first floor were rebuilt by Bedřich Feuerstein, 1931.

(22) 151, Václav Kopecký, vertical extension to apartment building, 1922.

(23) 949, Bohumil Hypšman, commercial and apartment building, 1910–1912.

(24) 984, Berthold Schwarz, commercial and office building, 1927–1928.

(25) 305, Václav Kopecký, apartment building, 1937–1938.

(26) 307, Bohumír Kozák, office building, 1936–1941.

(27) 347, Alois Dryák, office building, 1920–1922.

(28) 355, Oldřich Tyl, apartment building, 1929–1930.

(29) Kamil Hilbert, renovation of Saint Martin's Church, 1905–1906.

(30) 412, Karel Kotas, commercial and apartment building, 1938–1940.

(31) 371, František Řehák, department store, 1927–1931.

(32) 36, Pavel Janák, Josef Zasche, Adrie commercial and office building with theatre, 1922–1925.

(33) 38, Oldřich Starý, commercial and office building with arcade and exhibition hall, 1934–1938.

(34) 59, František Zelenka, exhibition hall, 1938.

(35) 58, Chicago commercial and office building, 1927–1928.

(36) 114, Ferdinand Fencl, department store, 1931–1932.

(37) 113, Bohumír Kozák, department store, 1931–1932.

(38) 108, Bedřich Bendelmayer, office building, 1927–1929.

(39) 39, František Zelenka, Oldřich Starý, office building, 1938.

(40) 35, 41, Pavel Janák, Škoda office building, 1923–1926.

(41) 747, Arnošt Mühlstein, Victor Fürth, Teta department store, 1933.

(42) 748, Jan Kotěra, Urbánek's Mozarteum, commercial and apartment building with concert hall, 1912–1913.

(43) 750, Fritz Lehmann, commercial and office building, 1929–1931.

(44) 754, Vlastimil Brožek, Jan Mentberger, Karel Polívka, commercial building, 1938–1939.

(45) 764, Rudolf Stockar, rebuilding of department store, 1922.

(46) 376, Friedrich Ohmann, department store, 1894–1895.

(47) 377, Matěj Blecha, Celda Klouček, bank building, 1900–1902.

(48) 504, František Kavalír, Bohumil Steigenhofer, rebuilt bank, 1928–1929.

(49) 496, Rudolf Eisler, apartment Building, 1938–1939.

(50) 567, Friedrich Ohmann, Bohemian Eagle Building, 1896–1897.

(51) 569, Josef Gočár, Black Madonna Building, 1912.

(52) 596, Josef Gočár, Bat'a department store, 1933–1934.

(53) 1078, 1079, Bedřich Bendelmayer, apartment building, 1903–1904.

(54) 1080, Jan Vejrych, Hotel Paříž, 1904–1905.

(55) 1090, Antonín Balšánek, Osvald Polívka, Municipal House, 1905–1912.

(56) 864, František Roith, bank and arcade, 1928–1938.

(57) 969, Josef Sakař(?), Karel Jaray, bank, 1930–1932.

(58) 998, Bohumír Kozák, Antonín Černý, commercial and apartment buildings with arcade and cinema, 1936–1938.

(59) 858, Osvald Polívka, bank, 1894–1896.

(60) 857, Osvald Polívka, bank, 1908–1910.

(61) 854, Bedřich Bendelmayer, bank, 1927–1933.

(62) 894, Oldřich Tyl, Černá růže (Black Rose) commercial building with arcade, 1929–1933.

(63) 581, 583, Ludvík Kysela, commercial building, 1927–1929.

(64) 397, Adolf Foehr, commercial building, 1930–1932.

(65) 391, Jiří Justich, Matěj Blecha, commercial and apartment building, 1904–1906.

(66) 390, Josef Zasche, Alexander Neumann, Viennese Bank Union, 1906–1908.

(67) 846, Antonín Pfeiffer, Koruna commercial and office building with cinema, 1911–1914.

(68) 840, František Weyr, Richard Klenka, Hotel Ambassador, 1912–1913.

(69) 839, Emil Králíček(?), Matěj Blecha, Hotel Zlatá husa, 1909–1912.

(70) 832, Friedrich Ohmann, Osvald Polívka, insurance company building, 1895–1896.

(71) 826, Quido Bělský, Bedřich Bendelmayer, Bohumil Hypšman, Jan Letzel, Hotel Evropa, 1903–1905.

(72) 825, Quido Bělský, Alois Dryák, hotel, 1903–1905.

(73) 897, Jiří Justich, František Buldra, hotel, 1907–1909.

(74) 1308, Josef Gočár, rebuilt bank, 1922–1923.

(75) 1419, Jan Kotěra, office building, 1921–1924.

(76) 947, Bohumír Kozák, apartment building, 1922–1923.

(77) 943, Josef Sakař, printing plant, 1923–1926.

(78) 954, Alois Houba, apartment building, 1937–1938.

(79) 1321, František A. Libra, Edison power transformation station, 1926–1930.

(80) 978, František Krásný, rebuilt bank, 1920–1921.

(81) 976, Josef Zasche, club and office building, 1912–1915.

(82) 866, Friedrich Ohmann, agricultural produce exchange, 1893–1894.

(83) 866a, Bohumil Hypšman, extension to the agricultural produce exchange, 1928–1929.

(84) 869, Josef Zasche, casino, 1906–1908.

(85) 872, Theodor Petřík, rebuilt bank, 1921–1922.

(85) 873, Josef Chochol, rebuilt office building, 1921.

(87) 876, Viktor Lampl, Oto Fuchs, commercial and apartment building, 1928–1929.

(88) 889, Antonín Pfeiffer, bank, 1923–1926.

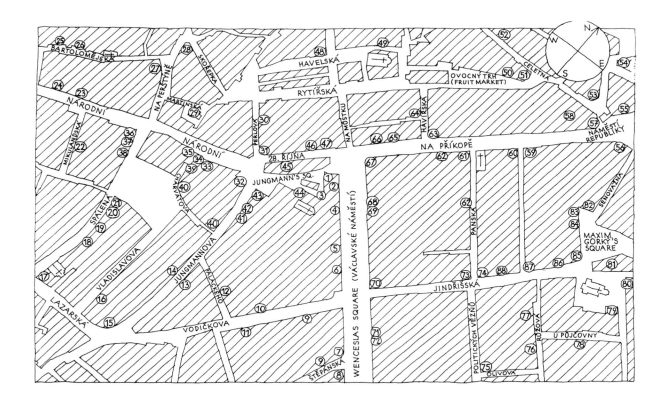

BARTOLOMĚJSKÁ
SKOŘEPKA
NA PERŠTÝNĚ
HAVELSKÁ
OVOCNÝ TRH
(FRUIT MARKET)
CELETNÁ
RYTÍŘSKÁ
NÁRODNÍ
MARTINSKÁ
NÁRODNÍ
MIKULANDSKÁ
NA MŮSTKU
HAVÍŘSKÁ
NÁMĚSTÍ
REPUBLIKY
PERLOVA
28. ŘÍJNA
NA PŘÍKOPĚ
CHARVÁTOVA
SPÁLENÁ
JUNGMANN'S SQ.
JUNGMANNOVA
WENCESLAS SQUARE (VÁCLAVSKÉ NÁMĚSTÍ)
PANSKÁ
SENOVÁŽNÁ
MAXIM
GORKÝ'S
SQUARE
VLADISLAVOVA
PALACKÉHO
LAZARSKÁ
JINDŘIŠSKÁ
VODIČKOVA
POLITICKÝCH VĚZŇŮ
RŮŽOVÁ
U PŮJČOVNY
ŠTĚPÁNSKÁ
OLIVOVA

541

Directory of Buildings

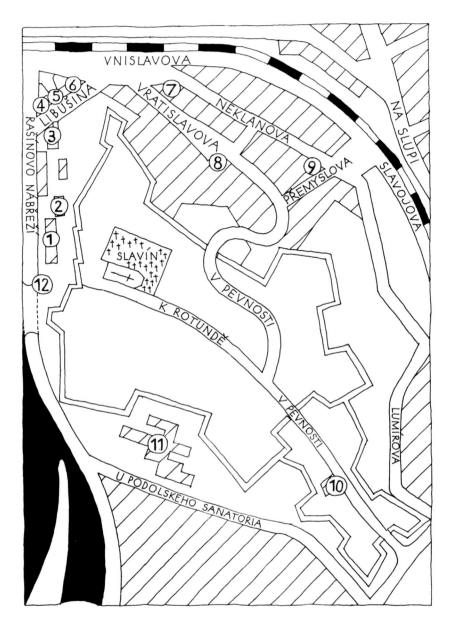

Important buildings below the Vyšehrad Citadel. Drawing
by Rostislav Švácha.

(1) 42, 47, 71, Josef Chochol, family triplex, 1912–1913.

(2) 70, František Hodek, family house, 1912–1913.

(3) 62, František Roith, gymnasium, 1931–1933.

(4) 50, Emil Králíček, family house, 1912–1913.

(5) 49, Josef Chochol, Kovařovič's family house, 1912–
1913.

(6) 48, Otakar Novotný, family house, 1912–1913.

(7) 56, Josef Chochol(?), Antonín Belada, apartment building, 1913.

(8) 20, Bohumil Hypšman, apartment buildings, 1924.

(9) 13, Matěj Blecha, extension to Jedlička Institute, 1912–
1913.

(11) 4, 5, 157, Rudolf Kříženecký, sanatorium, 1911–1913.

(12) 44, František Velich, tunnel with caretaker's house,
1903–1905.

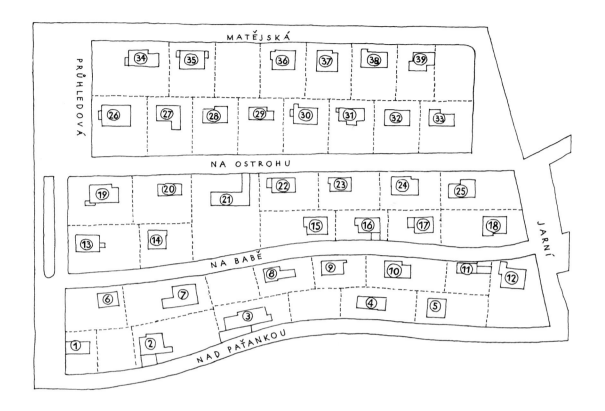

Family houses on the Baba estate and their authors. Drawing
by Rostislav Švácha.

(1) 1790, Oldřich Starý, 1932.

(2) 1789, František Kerhart, 1935–1936.

(3)˙1788, Josef Gočár, 1932–1933.

(4) 1786, Josef Gočár, 1932.

(5) 1785, Pavel Janák, 1932.

(6) 1778, František Kavalír, 1932.

(7) 1777, Ladislav Machoň, 1932–1933.

(8) 1779, Mart Stam, Jiří Palička, 1932.

(9) 1780, Oldřich Starý, 1932.

(10) 1781, Hana Kučerová-Záveská, 1932.

(11) 1782, Ladislav Žák, 1932.

(12) 1783, Josef Gočár, 1935–1936.

(13) 1804, Zdeněk Blažek, 1932.

(14) 1803, Jan E. Koula, 1932.

(15) 1801, Vojtěch Kerhart, 1933–1934.

(16) 1800, Pavel Janák, 1933–1934.

(17) 1799, František Kerhart, 1933.

(18) 1798, Josef Gočár, 1933–1934.

(19) 1792, František Zelenka, 1934.

(20) 1793, Ladislav Žák, 1932.

(21) 1794, Hana Kučerová-Záveská, 1932.

(22) 1795, František Kavalír, 1932.

(23) 1796, František Kerhart, 1932–1933.

(24) 1797, Pavel Janák, 1932.

(25) 1791, František Kerhart, 1933–1934.

(26) 1705, Josef Fuchs, 1932.

(27) 1706, František Kerhart, 1933.

(28) 1707, Vojtěch Kerhart, 1932.

(29) 1708, Ladislav Žák, 1932.

(30) 1709, Oldřich Starý, 1932.

(31) 1710, Antonín Heythum, Evžen Linhart, 1932.

(32) 1711, Jaroslav Fišer, Karel Fišer, 1932.

(33) 1712, Oldřich Starý, 1932.

(34) 1985, František Kerhart, 1939.

(35) 1177, Josef Grus, 1938–1940.

(36) 1987, Josef Grus, 1939–1940.

(37) 1877, Antonín Kučera, Štěpán Zelenka, 1939–1940.

(38) 1986, Antonín Černý, 1939–1940

(39) 1988, Josef Grus, 1939–1940.

Page numbers set in italic type refer to figures. In alphabetizing, letters with hačeks (ˇ) appear after the unaccented letters.

Roofs, flat, in geometrical modern style, 62–
        63
Rosenberg, Evžen, 466
        apartment buildings by, 314, *315*, 316
        buildings by, *386*, 387, *388–389*
        career of, 387
Rosipal, Josef, *86*
Rössler, Jaroslav, *185*
Rossmann, Zdeněk, on social content of
        architecture, 326–327
Rosůlek, Jan
        apartment buildings by, 223
        Bulovka Hospital dermato-venereal pavi-
                lion, 398, *399–400*
        villa by, 276–277
Roškot, Kamil, 419, 467
        apartment building by, *220*
        buildings by, 232
        competition designs for Letná Plain, *233*
        Ministry of Public Works project, *234*
        Old Airport, Porters' Lodge, *423*
Rothmayer, Otto, Prague Castle reconstruc-
                tions by, 177
Row housing
        functionalists and, 158, 311–312
        by Janák, 170
        public health complex by Kozák, 170, *171*
Royal Palace, rebuilding in late 15th century,
        14
Rudolf II, Hapsburg Emperor, court estab-
                lished in Prague, 14
Rural Education Building, by Gočár, 198,
        199

Říha, Josef K.
        buildings by, 296–297, *302*
        design for *Včela* cooperative, 310

Saint John Nepomuk, cubist canopy by
        Blecha, 130
Saint Martin, Church of, Hilbert's restora-
        tion of, 41
Saint Nicholas, Church of, construction of
        (1737–1751), 15
Saint Vitus, Cathedral of
        begun by Charles IV, 11
        restoration of, Hilbert's work on, 39–40
Saint Vitus, Church of, 4
Sakař, Josef, 22
Santini, Jan, 15, 125
Satellite towns, plans for, 24
Scharoun, Hans, 402, 406
School buildings
        by Fencl, 347
        Frýda's functionalist design, 270, *272*
        Gillar's French school project, 331, *335–
        336*
        by Linhart, 367, *369*
School of Applied Arts, Department of
        Architecture, 84. *See also* Janák,
        Pavel
Sculpture, architecture and, 427–428
Sdružení architektů (Association of Architects),
        213
Secese. See Modern style
Seifert, Jaroslav, "Nové emění proletářské"
        (The New Proletarian Art), 213

Stavitel and, 296

    Tyrš House competition, 236, *236*

Šupich Building, by Blecha, 86, *87*

Šverma Bridge, 24

Technology

    decorative use by Žák, 413

    Devětsil group's attitude toward, 215–217, 253

    functionalism and, 240

    purist vs. functionalist attitude to, 297

"Tectonic organisms," buildings as

    Engel's view, 62–63

    geometrical modern style and, 93

Teige, Karel

    apartment of, 311

    architectural theories of, 240, 256–258

        criticism of, 275

    on collective housing, 308–311

    criticism of the family house, 316

    on curve vs. straight line in architecture, 401

    on emotional functionalism, 276

    functionalist theories of, 167

    "K sociologii architektury" (On the Sociology of Architecture), 316

    Mezinárodní soudobá architektura (Contemporary International Architecture), 256

    "Naše základna a naše cesta" (Our Base and Our Path), 401

    on painting and sculpture vs. architecture, 427

    on proletarian art, 213

    purge of older architecture advocated by, 237

    on purism and social change, 239

    on rondocubists, 187

    on scientific functionalism and socialism, 329

    on social content of architecture, 326

    on Stalinist classicism, 432

    subconscious in architecture acknowledged by, 330

Tenement buildings. *See* Apartment buildings

Tenzer, Antonín, 304, 374, *376*

Theaters, Liberated Theater design by Chochol, 283, *284*

Thierhier, Vilém, 49, *50*

Tolerance, religious, Prague as center of, 14

Town planning. *See* Urban planning

Traffic, competition for solutions to, in 1930, 318, 322, 324

Traffic problems, State Planning Commission's decisions, 150

Transportation. *See also* Railways

    competition for Greater Prague plan (1930), 322, 324

    functionalist proposals for Prague, 166–167

    hindered by late-nineteenth-century administrative fragmentation, 19

    public, Krejcar and Špalek plan for (1930), 322, *323*, 324

    suggestions for redesign in interwar years, 150

571